CUSTER'S LAST CAMPAIGN

JOHN S. GRAY

Foreword by Robert M. Utley

USTER'S

UNIVERSITY *of* NEBRASKA PRESS

Lincoln and London

LAST CAMPAIGN

Mitch Boyer

and the

Little Bighorn

Reconstructed

✓

The paper in this book meets the minimum
requirements of American National Standard
for Information Sciences—Permanence of
Paper for Printed Library Materials, ANSI
Z39.48–1984.

Library of Congress Cataloging-in-Publication Data

Gray, John S. (John Stephens), 1910–

    Custer' last campaign : Mitch Boyer and the little bighorn
reconstructed / John S. Gray ; foreword by Robert M. Utley.

      p.   cm.

    Includes bibliographical references and index.

    ISBN 0-8032-2138-X (alk. paper)

    1. Boyer, Mitch.   2. Scouts and scouting—Montana—Biography.
3. Little Big Horn, Battle of the, 1876.   4. Soldiers—United
States—Biography.   5. Custer, George Armstrong, 1839–1876.
6. United States. Army. Cavalry, 7th.   7. Dakota Indians—Wars,
1876—Scouts and scouting.   I. Title.

E83.876.B79G73   1991

973.8'2—dc20   90-37673

                                          CIP

951784

CONTENTS

PART I   THE MITCH BOYER STORY

PART II   CUSTER'S LAST CAMPAIGN

Illustrations

Maps

Tables

Figures

FOREWORD

Robert M. Utley

I have called John S. Gray's *Centennial Campaign: The Sioux War of 1876*, published in 1976, the best single volume dealing with the Battle of the Little Bighorn and the Sioux War of 1876. For the campaign as a whole, it remains so. For the Battle of the Little Bighorn, it has now been superseded.

Custer's Last Campaign: Mitch Boyer and the Little Bighorn Reconstructed is the most important book ever written about the Battle of the Little Bighorn. It does no less than persuasively, authoritatively, and clearly reconstruct the entire sequence of events of the campaign of 1876 and the Battle of the Little Bighorn. Much of it is a refinement and elaboration of *Centennial Campaign*. But now Gray ventures boldly beyond Medicine Tail Coulee to the battlefield from which there were no white survivors. His analysis of what happened to the Custer battalion is brilliant, revolutionary, and all but unassailable. For this achievement alone the book is destined for top rank in the literature of the Little Bighorn.

Gray's historical method is impressive. He has mastered and achieved absolute control over the sprawling mass of firsthand material bearing on the Little Bighorn. A retired physiology professor and medical doctor, he brings a scientific mind to the handling of evidence. His original technique of time-motion study, plotted graphically, orders the evidence and brings it to bear at each pivotal point in the battle sequence. The time-motion charts, in tandem with uncommon powers of logic and deduction, make the scholarship both imposing and unique.

Gray's most important contribution is to shed light on what happened to the Custer battalion after the last courier dashed to the rear. These final stages of the battle have stoked great fires of debate and speculation. Gray once vowed to me that he would never be enticed into this inferno. His scientifically oriented intellect demanded more credible evidence than the progress of the Custer battalion from Medicine Tail Coulee to Custer Hill afforded. *Centennial Campaign,* so lucid and authoritative as far as Medicine Tail, the very threshold of the climax, reflects this attitude.

Two circumstances diluted Gray's resolve. First, he grew interested in Mitch Boyer, for years an important but unsung figure on the northern plains. Boyer went beyond Medicine Tail to die with Custer, and Gray had no choice but to follow. Second, Gray made sense of crucial evidence that had been ignored and even scorned for many years. This was the testimony of the Crow scout Curley, widely discounted by earlier students as imaginative invention.

Indian testimony is difficult to use. It is personal, episodic, and maddeningly detached from time and space, or sequence and topography. It also suffers from a language barrier often aggravated by incompetent interpreters, from the cultural gulf between questioner and respondent, and from assumptions of the interviewer not always in accord with reality.

Curley's testimony is a prime example of the blind interviewer leading the seeing witness, for in Gray's estimate Curley accurately saw, remembered, and reported. Guided by erroneous assumptions, however, interviewers quizzed Curley on Custer's movements toward the Sioux village, then bent the responses to fit those erroneous assumptions. The results, distorted by the interviewers rather than Curley, have baffled students ever since and earned Curley low marks as a witness. Gray penetrates the fog, makes sense of Curley's testimony, shows him to have been at Custer's side all the way to Calhoun Hill, where the final half-hour of the Last

Stand began, and validates his claim to have watched the end from a distance.

Curley's testimony is critical to tracing Custer's movements from Medicine Tail Coulee to Calhoun Hill, a phase of the battle that has perplexed students for more than a century. Critical also, in clarifying Curley's observations as well as other evidence, is the remarkable "surround" of the Custer battalion constructed in the time-motion study. Linking all the players in the drama with "interconnections"—written, visual, and auditory—lays out the entire battle sequence in time and space, eliminating what could not have happened and establishing what could have happened and probably did. Critics may quarrel with timing as exact as the half-minute, but to me the overall reconstruction is more persuasive than any that has gone before.

Gray's tracking of Custer from Medicine Tail Coulee to Calhoun Hill is not entirely original. It was prefigured by Jerome A. Greene in "Evidence and the Custer Enigma" (1973) and by Richard G. Hardorff in *Markers, Artifacts and Indian Testimony* (1985). But Gray refines and extends their theories and, in my judgment, establishes the sequence and motivation beyond serious dispute.

True to his scientific mindset, Gray is reluctant to venture beyond Calhoun Hill, for here is where Curley, his last witness, departed the scene. The Sioux and Cheyenne participants, of course, left reams of testimony, but no one has succeeded in structuring it in time and space as Gray has done for Curley. To deal with the final half-hour of fighting and the death of Mitch Boyer, Gray switches from documented reconstruction to hypothesis. His hypothesis is as good as any, and better than most, but skeptics who have been unable to demolish earlier chapters will find more latitude for dispute in this one.

John Gray has radically and enduringly transformed the historiography of the Battle of the Little Bighorn. His work is not for beginners. His reasoning and documentation cannot be followed unless one has a firm grasp of the literature and the topography. For the legion of students infected with the incurable virus of the Little Bighorn, however, here is rich fare—a story within a story. It is the story of the Little Bighorn, of course; but even more, it is the story of a master historical sleuth in action.

PREFACE

Many years ago, I chanced on a thoroughly mysterious character who made a fleeting appearance in history as the sole army scout to stick with Gen. George A. Custer to the last fatal minutes in the legendary Battle of the Little Bighorn. Though he was obviously competent, courageous, and faithful, the references divulged little more than that he was half Sioux and half white, and no two persons spelled his name the same way. Where had he come from? How had he mastered his demanding trade? And why was he fighting against his own tribesmen?

Haunted by this shadowy figure, I uncovered his story, bit by piece and over years. He was the son of a French trader and a Sioux mother, and his name proved to be Michel Boyer, but his friends called him Mitch. His thirty-nine years of adventures were interesting enough in themselves, but they also took place in the context of a fascinating movement not well delineated by history. That movement was the gradual encroachment of white civilization on the lands of the western division of the Sioux Nation, which roamed the plains west of the Missouri (the eastern division had experienced similar troubles, earlier and east of the river). Such encroachment provoked continual friction and several outright wars, for government "peace commissions" either precipitated immediate hostilities or set the stage for future outbreaks. This movement, as well as its culmination in the tragic Sioux War of 1876, was summarized briefly in my *Centennial Campaign* (1976, reprinted 1988), but Mitch's active participation in the entire chain of events provides further valuable insight.

Two concurrent themes are interwoven throughout the present book. One is the thread of Mitch's activities; the other is the fabric of their historical context. The title indicates the book's division into two parts, not by theme, but by date and the manner of presentation.

The first part (Chapters 1–14) covers, in narrative fashion, nearly the whole of Mitch's adventurous life, placed in historical context, as he moved from the Missouri to present Wyoming (1849) and then northward to the Yellowstone country (1864), where he was adopted into the Crow tribe (1870). Adapting readily to both Indian and white ways and fluent in English and native tongues, he served both races. His mentor was Jim Bridger, and his varied experiences trained him expertly for the profession of guide and scout. In Red Cloud's War (1866–68) he served the beleaguered army, and while with the Crow tribe he worked alternately for their Indian agents and for the army. By 1875 he was widely recognized as the best guide in the country. In the spring of 1876, when the major Sioux war had been programmed and was being launched, Gen. John Gibbon sought out Mitch as chief guide for his Montana column, as it marched down the Yellowstone to make connection with Gen. Terry's Dakota column. This service led to Mitch's transfer to Custer's 7th Cavalry, on June 10, which ends Part I.

The second part (Chapters 15–25), though longer, covers only two weeks, while Mitch served as a key guide and scout for Custer's last campaign to its fatal end on June 25. The Boyer theme turns thin and intermittent, for he can accompany only one party when the huge cast of troops and scouts separates into many parties. The manner of presentation also changes from narration to analysis of the military campaign. Readers will find that they must shift gears, too. Many features of this campaign have never been clarified, and the final action of Custer's own battalion, which Mitch served, has remained in limbo. There was simply no way to proceed without reconstructing the Custer battle in rigorous detail, step by step.

Two things encouraged such an undertaking: significant new evidence had surfaced in recent years, and more useful information, it seemed to me, might be extracted from the voluminous interviews with the ubiquitous Indian scouts. The obstacle was the dearth of objective methods for assessing the reliability of participant accounts from any source and for judging the validity of possible interpretations. Persistence paid off, however, for it gradually emerged that the systematic use of the best topographic maps helped marvelously to maintain geographic orientation, and the systematic use of time-motion analysis achieved the same for temporal orientation. A key to both reliability and validity was found in a simple principle: anything that actually happened had to be possible. An essential element of time-motion analysis is speed of motion, which provides a feasibility check that exposes impossibilities. When an account contains blatant contradictions, one version usually proves feasible and the other impossible.

The application of these methods to all primary sources yielded a harvest of feasible data. Each step of the way, I began by reconstructing itineraries for troop movements between identifiable landmarks at feasible speeds (cavalrymen often give the pace). In the light of this information, the interviews with Indian scouts suddenly blossomed into lucidity and contributed mightily. As I progressed, the time-motion pattern grew ever more complex, for there were frequent interconnections between the numerous parties, resulting from separations, meetings, and courier messages, as well as cross-sightings and hearings. In such a pattern no event can remain independent of others; all must be compatible with one another, and the more interconnections, the stronger the constraint they impose. They also provide validity checks on the growing pattern, for each interconnection must prove feasible as judged by speed. Every time the pattern failed a feasibility check, I had to start over again. Working this out proved a formidable exercise in historical detective work, challenging but exciting, and incredibly suspenseful, for each piece of the pattern had to remain tentative until the last piece locked them all together.

To present this analysis in the form of conclusions only is as ridiculous as to present a jury with a mere indictment. It is mandatory to quote the primary sources and then expose their analysis fully, so that readers may judge for themselves. This I have done. Next I assembled the data in itinerary tables and, what is most helpful, rendered the time-motion pattern visible at a glance in the form of graphs that show where everyone was at every moment. Such full disclosure is the only procedure that generates progress in any discipline, for it alone enables others to spot flaws, to perceive the significance of new evidence, and thus to continue building on a growing and increasingly firm foundation.

For these reasons Part II became much longer and more complex than Part I. I hope that readers will not be dismayed by such exposure of the working gears and that some will be fascinated by historical detective work and even discover that it is a venture within their grasp.

A NOTE ON DOCUMENTATION

This book is based almost entirely on primary sources, that is, accounts of various kinds from persons who participated in the events they describe. Since the standard method of historical documentation demands a great deal of unnecessary repetition, I have used a modified system that furnishes all the information needed, yet minimizes duplication.

Every reader, whether casual or professional, needs to know certain things about a quotation of evidence even before reading it: Who is the informant? Was he a participant? Was it recorded at the time or long afterward? Did he, or an interviewer, record it? I shall make a practice of including such information in the lead-in to a quotation *in the text*, rather than relegate it to a footnote. Footnotes and a bibliography, however, are also used, but their functions are separated in a fashion that reduces unnecessary repetition.

Newspapers are cited in full in footnotes or occasionally in the text; a newspaper category is omitted from the bibliography. Sources not repeatedly used are cited by footnote, but in an abbreviated form that includes the last name of the first author, a partial title, and the specific page number; it closes with a parenthetical capital letter that identifies one of four *standard* categories in the bibliography. Categories *A* (articles) and *B* (books) are alphabetized by the last name of the first author, but the entry there provides the names of all authors, full titles, name of periodical, publisher, date, and any other pertinent information. The footnote thus keys to the bibliography, whose function is to enable interested readers to find the source of the information for themselves. Categories *G* (government documents) and *M* (manuscripts in other repositories) are less extensive, but footnotes again identify the full entry to be found there.

In the last two-thirds of the book, which covers the Gibbon and Custer campaigns in 1876, a multitude of participant accounts are quoted repeatedly on nearly every page; these participants become quite familiar characters. The lead-in to such quotations, *in the text*, includes the participant's name, the type of evidence (diary, letter, narrative, interview, etc.), and the specific page number (in parentheses), except that for diaries the entry date replaces the page number. This text information keys to one of two *special* categories in the bibliography. Categories *X* (Gibbon's men) and *Y* (Custer's men) are alphabetized by the *participant's* name, and the entries give the type (and interviewer's name) and date. The rest of the entry, like a footnote, gives the source in abbreviated form and its standard category letter. In short, a thousand footnotes are replaced by special categories.

Another thousand footnotes are eliminated for Custer's men who gave evidence at the Reno Court of Inquiry, held at Chicago in 1879, less than three years after the battle. This evidence is cited *in the text only*, by the name of the witness and the key words "testimony" or "testified," followed by the specific page number in parentheses. Most such testimony is taken from *Reno Court of Inquiry* (B), but it occasionally comes from Graham's *Abstract of the Official Record* (B), in which case the text reads "(Graham's *Abstract*, p. no.)."

PART I

The

Mitch Boyer

Story

DAKOTA ORIGINS

For the 1876 campaign against the Sioux Indians, Gen. John Gibbon employed for his Montana column a scout, half French and half Sioux, whom he called "Mitch Bowyer . . . next to Jim Bridger the best guide in the country." When later transferred to Gen. Alfred H. Terry's Dakota column, this same scout guided Gen. George A. Custer's famed 7th Cavalry to within gunshot of Sitting Bull's enormous Sioux-Cheyenne village on the banks of the Little Bighorn. Scorning orders to seek safety in the rear, he died with all those who fought with the ill-fated general on that afternoon of June 25, 1876.

So far as the public knew, the scout's career spanned only the day of his death. Nor has the passage of a century filled the biographical void, although his obvious courage and talents make him an attractive target for inquiry. Why was he fighting against his own tribesmen? Was he a grizzled veteran like Jim Bridger or a child prodigy like the publicity

The Northern Plains Country. Map by Bob Bolin.

image of "Buffalo Bill" Cody? Did his heritage of white and Indian blood endow him with the best, or the worst, of each? Had he spent his life in the isolation of Indian villages or among venturesome frontiersmen?

As it turns out, he moved easily and achieved full respect in both circles. And not surprisingly, the life story of this scout proved far more fascinating than the dramatic moment of his death, as a husband and father, at the age of thirty-nine.

The scout's march through life left an unexpectedly abundant trail, though sometimes elusive, because his name appears in a myriad of bizarre forms; some merely reflect a typesetter's struggle with illegible copy, but many manifest the usual frustration of Americans with the French language. The correct French name was Michel (for Michael, and Mich for short) Boyer (sometimes Boyé, in creole French). A Gallic tongue would sound this name, using the nickname, "Meesh Bwah-*yay*," but the English tongue prefers "Mitch" for the first and distorts the second to "Boh-yer," "Boy-yer," or even "*Boo*-yer," spelling the latter "Bouyer" or the whimsical, English-defying "Buoyer." A half-century after the scout's death, someone assumed Mitch to be the obligatory nickname for Minton (even Milton!), and punctilious mimics have ever since inflicted this indignity on his given name.

A former territorial judge of Utah, John Fitch Kinney, as a special commissioner investigating the shocking Fetterman Massacre, took testimony from "Michael Boyer" at Fort Phil Kearny on July 27, 1867, thereby extracting under oath the only biographical data ever secured directly from the scout. On conversion from question-and-answer form, the testimony revealed: "I am twenty-eight years old [born about 1839]. I have been in the mountains since 1849, trading with the Oglala Sioux, Snakes, Bannacks and Crows. I have been near the Yellowstone since 1864, and at Fort C. F. Smith for seven months [since January 1867]. I talk Sioux and Crow."[1]

However skimpy as an autobiography, these few words contain priceless clues. That Mitch was born by 1839, not in the mountains, to a French father and a Sioux mother, implies that his father was trading with the Sioux somewhere to the east, probably along the Dakota reaches of the Missouri River, where the American Fur Company dominated the

[1] "Michael Boyer's Testimony to J. F. Kinney, July 27, 1867," is given in full in Appendix A.

Sioux trade. The move to the mountains as a boy in 1849 was therefore westward and with his family. The tribes his father traded with there identify the place as present Wyoming. At the time, the trading head-quarters for the Oglala Sioux and Mountain Crows was Fort Laramie, on the North Platte River.

It has proved possible to trace an American Fur Co. employee named Boyer, with a son named Michel and who traded with the Sioux on the Missouri River from 1830 through 1848; soon afterward both father and son surfaced in the Fort Laramie region. From there, Mitch's later moves to the Yellowstone in 1864 and to Fort C. F. Smith in January 1867 can be documented in detail. The father is sometimes called "John" and sometimes "Baptiste" Boyer, but it should be noted that the French rarely used "Baptiste" without preceding it by "John" and were prone to address people by their middle names. Hence this man's full name was undoubt-edly John Baptiste Boyer.

This Boyer trail is first picked up in the American Fur Co. journal kept at Fort Tecumseh, the predecessor to Fort Pierre, located on the west bank of the Missouri at the mouth of Bad River (opposite present Pierre, S. Dak.). A journal entry for December 1, 1830, records the arrival there of "Mr. [Henry] Hay and Baptiste Boyer from White River," a western branch of the Missouri some distance downstream where the firm had another wintering post that served the Sioux. The next year, 1831, a roster of company employees again named "Henry Hay and Baptiste Boyer" as stationed at Fort Tecumseh.[2]

The Boyer name next appears nine years later in the baptismal records of Jesuit Father Christian Hoecken, who made a missionary trip from his Pottawatomie Mission at the Council Bluffs area up to Fort Union at the mouth of the Yellowstone and back again, baptizing mixed-blood children on the way. It seems not to have been recognized that he must have made this trip on the American Fur Co. steamboat, the *Antelope*, which in 1840 made its third and last upriver voyage, leaving St. Louis "about April 1." The dates and trading posts where he made baptisms provide an itinerary for this little-known voyage.[3]

---

[2] DeLand, "Records of Fort Tecumseh," 235 (A). The reader is urged to read A Note on Documentation, which follows the Preface. Footnotes are abbreviated, but the capital letter in parentheses identifies a category in the bibliography which fully identifies the source.

[3] Barry, *Beginning of the West*, 390 (B).

At Fort Pierre on June 13 and 14 Father Hoecken baptized thirty-six persons; for four of these children "John Boyé" is named as godfather. It is especially significant that four children of "John Boyé and his sauvagesse [Indian woman]" were also baptized there on June 13, with J. Baptiste Ortubise as godfather. The eldest of these children was "Michel Boyé, 3 years of age," thus born in 1837 (more reliable than Mitch's testimony). The other three were daughters, Marie, Anne, and Therese, each carefully noted as four and a half months old and thus that Indian rarity, triplets, born in late February 1840.[4]

Trader Boyer, with no given name, is again mentioned in the Fort Pierre Letterbook for 1848, on January 4, February 15, and April 3, in letters to Colin Campbell, who had charge of Fort Lookout, which served Yankton Sioux downriver near present Chamberlain, South Dakota. The second letter named Smutty Bear, second chief of the Yankton band, and Flying Bird, who owed Colin Campbell a debt. The third letter asked whether "Boyer's bro.-in-law, Flying Bird, has paid you his credit." This remark suggests that Boyer was then married to a sister of Flying Bird, who may have been a Yankton Sioux but, as will emerge, was not the mother of Mitch and his triplet sisters.[5]

It is probable that these numerous references to a Sioux trader on the Missouri from 1830 to 1848 are all to the same John Baptiste Boyer, the father of Michel Boyer by a Sioux woman. No mentions of other Boyers have been found in the fur-trade records during this period, and none at all after 1848 on the Missouri. These findings correspond nicely and uniquely to Mitch's own statements to Judge Kinney that he was born to an Indian trader named Boyer and a Sioux mother and moved while still a boy to the North Platte country in 1849. His probable birth year is thus 1837, however, instead of 1839.

One of Mitch Boyer's close companions in later years was another famous army scout, a Frenchman from St. Louis named John Baptiste ("Big Bat") Pourier. This surname sounded so nearly like Mitch's that some mistook them for brothers; this error may be the source of the "oo" sound conferred on Mitch's surname. Big Bat, in giving his life story to Judge Eli Ricker in 1906, recalled that Mitch had a half-brother, John Boyer, who killed an army scout near Fort Laramie in the fall of 1870.[6]

[4] Robinson, "Father Hoecken's 1840 Baptismal Journal," 230 (A).
[5] DeLand, "Fort Pierre Letterbooks," pp. 320, 223, 228 (A).
[6] Ricker, "Pourier Interview" (M).

The newspapers of Cheyenne, Wyoming, fully confirm that a John Boyer did indeed kill scout James McCloskey, as well as a John or Henry Lowry, at Six-Mile Ranch near Fort Laramie on October 27, 1870. John Boyer was tried before the first jury on which women served, and his hanging on April 21, 1871, was the first legal execution in Wyoming Territory. That morning the condemned man told a reporter that he was "a half-breed, about 26 years old," indicating a birth year of 1845. He added that his father and some brothers had already gone to the "Happy Hunting Ground," but he asked the reporter to "tell my mother I died brave, without a whimper." John's birth year implies that he had been born on the Missouri to the sister of Flying Bird, still living in 1871, though both of Mitch's parents were gone by that year.[7]

It is clear that Mitch had other half-brothers than John, but only one more has come to light. Walter M. Camp interviewed an Antoine Boyer in 1912, and among his edited notes appears the following: "Antoine Bouyer says Mitch Bouyer's name was Michel Bouyer. Mitch's father was a full blood Frenchman, who was killed by Indians while trapping. Mother of Mitch was full blood Santee Sioux. He [father? Antoine?] was married to three Sioux. John Bouyer, brother [?] of Antoine and Mitch, was hung for murder."[8] That Mitch's father may have had three wives presents no problem, and the clue that he was killed by Indians before 1871 will prove helpful. But Camp's editor states, citing no source whatever, that Mitch's father was named Vital Boyer.[9] This may represent a confusion with Vital Beauvais, a brother of the Platte trader Geminien P. Beauvais, whose surname was often pronounced "Boovay."

Other records of perhaps this same Antoine Boyer have been found. Among the signers of the 1889 Sioux Land Agreement at Pine Ridge, then the Oglala Sioux agency, appear "Antoine Boyer, aged 37 [b. 1852]," and perhaps his son, "John Boyer, aged 19 [b. 1870]."[10] In the Register of Enlisted Indian Scouts these same names again appear:

Antoine Bouyer, mustered in May 1, 1877, for 6 mo., by Lt. [Ira] Quinby [11th Inf.] at Cheyenne River Agency, aged 21 [b. 1855].

---

[7] *Cheyenne* d. *Leader*, Oct. 3, 1870 (for murder), Mar. 23 (for trial), April 21, 1871 (for hanging and interview).

[8] Hammer, *Custer in '76*, 126n (B).

[9] Ibid., 245 and n.

[10] Information from Harry G. Anderson, Milwaukee Historical Society, who also directed me to the article in note 4, above.

Johnnie Bouyer, mustered in Jan. 26, 1891, for 6 mo., by Lt. [Frank DeL.] Carrington [1st Inf.], at Pine Ridge Agency, aged 21 [b. 1870].[11]

These reappearances of the names Antoine and John may be significant, but more important, Antoine's probable birth year, 1852, indicates that he was the youngest "brother" and born after the family had moved to the North Platte region. He could have been a full brother of John but only a half-brother of Mitch.

No systematic genealogical search has been made for Mitch's ancestors; but there are hints that they had migrated from Canada to the early French settlement of Cahokia in Illinois. The first entry in the Fort Tecumseh journal (December 1, 1830), quoted earlier, carried the following editor's note: "Baptiste Boyer was of a well known family of Cahokia, probably [?] a son of Antoine Boyer." The first American census of Cahokia, made in 1778, lists this Antoine Boyer as living alone, an implication that all his children were adults and had already moved elsewhere.[12] This inference is borne out by the Cahokia Parish Records, which reveal that Antoine Boyer died there on September 7, 1790, aged over sixty and a native of Montreal, Canada, where he had married.[13] He had thus been born before 1730 and probably married before 1750. That he was a lonely widower in 1778 is not surprising. But if Mitch's father entered the fur trade in 1830 at about age twenty, he had been born about 1810, and if a descendant of Antoine, he was a grandson or great-grandson.

After the French and Indian War, France ceded to Spain her colonies west of the Mississippi (1762), and many of the French settlers in Illinois moved across to present Missouri to escape British rule. Jacques Boyer, a probable son of Antoine, married Elizabeth Chatillon in Kaskaskia, Illinois, and then moved across the river to become one of the first settlers of Ste. Genevieve, Missouri. Before long there were numerous Boyers in that area, with given names of John, Antoine, and Michel, and spread as far upriver as St. Charles, Missouri. This area supplied the majority of the fur-trade engagees during the first half of the 1800s. It is thus possible that Mitch's father was a descendant of the original Cahokia family, though it is by no means a certainty.

[11] *Register of Enlisted Indian Scouts* (G-M).
[12] Alvord, *Cahokia Records*, 624 (B).
[13] McDermott, *Old Cahokia*, 273 (B).

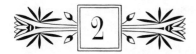

ADVENTURES ON THE NORTH PLATTE

Mitch Boyer was twelve years old when his family moved west in 1849, a year that brought significant changes in the Indian trade in the North Platte country. In June of that year Pierre Chouteau, Jr. & Company, still popularly called the American Fur Company, sold its venerable Fort John, better known as Fort Laramie, to the army for use as a military base to protect emigration over the Platte Road, suddenly swelled to a torrent by the California gold rush. The displaced firm moved 50 miles down the North Platte to Scott's Bluff and there erected a new Fort John. Scattered up and down the river were some constantly shifting independent trading firms, but much of the trade with the Sioux and Mountain Crows was conducted away from the trail in outlying camps that extended from the Dakota Black Hills in the east to the Big Horn Range in the west, and as far north as the Yellowstone River.

By July 1852 the Chouteau outfit, dissatisfied with its Scott's Bluff post, began erecting still another Fort John only 5 miles below the army's

Fort Laramie, of which John P. B. Gratiot took charge in September 1853. On August 19, 1854, Lt. John L. Grattan, taking a force of twenty-nine infantrymen from Fort Laramie, attempted to seize an Indian from a nearby Sioux village for having butchered an emigrant's stray cow. Not a soldier survived, but their rashness shattered a long reign of peace. On September 3, 1855, Gen. William S. Harney retaliated by slaughtering a Sioux village on Blue Water Creek, 75 miles below Scott's Bluff. The Indian trade was not only disrupted, but officially prohibited.[1]

Licenses to trade with Indians commonly named employees in upper, but not necessarily in lower, ranks, especially for the large Chouteau firm. Prior to 1857 father John Boyer is named on no licenses, and no other mentions of him have been found. Hence for the early years on the North Platte there is no certainty as to whom he traded for or with. But the family was there, for there are signs of Mitch's presence as early as 1851.

While Mitch was later guiding J. Hudson Snowden's party of army explorers to Pumpkin Buttes, northwest of Fort Laramie, he pointed out to his employer a pen built of poles and a deep pit, which the Arapahos had used to trap antelope, "last used in 1851." Mitch also related that "Sir George Gore, in the summer of 1855, took a large train of ox and mule wagons from the [North] Platte near the mouth of Box Elder Creek [90 miles up the North Platte from Fort Laramie] to Powder River, passing near the west side of Pumpkin Buttes."[2] There is confirmation of this clue that Mitch had been a guide for Sir George Gore, the wealthy Irish baronet.

Sir George left no known account of his three-year hunting excursion, the most lavishly luxurious the American West had yet seen. Several frontiersmen, who served as guides and hunters, have left reminiscent accounts that are vague or faulty, especially as to dates, but contemporary documents, some newly found, furnish reliable dates for the main events and clarify some confusion regarding the chief guides, Jim Bridger and Henri Chatillon.

Sir George outfitted at St. Louis with the aid of Pierre Chouteau, Jr. & Co., in the spring of 1854, and on May 24, 1854, Indian Superintendent

---

[1] For Gratiot's taking charge of Fort John, near Fort Laramie, see his affidavit in Chouteau's Indian depredation claim in *Upper Platte Agency*, 1855, R890 (G-M).

[2] Raynolds, *Exploration of Yellowstone*, 160 (for Snowden's references to Arapaho antelope trap and Sir George Gore) (B).

Alfred Cumming, at St. Louis, issued him a passport to the Indian country, leaving no doubt as to the starting year.[3] Two weeks later, on June 6, 1854, at Westport, Missouri (present Kansas City), a passing traveler marveled at the baronet's plush camp as it prepared to set out for distant Fort Laramie with a retinue of servants, campkeepers, guides, hunters, a pack of hounds, and an ox train of supplies and baggage.[4]

At this time Jim Bridger, who already owned a farm close to Westport, was in the area, for on August 26, 1853, the Utah Mormons had secured a warrant for his arrest in order to force him to sell them his ten-year-old Fort Bridger (in present Wyoming).[5] Bridger eluded the U.S. marshal and soon left with his Indian wife and half-blood children for his Westport farm, for in the forepart of October that fall, the eastbound Salt Lake Mail passed them at Devil's Gate on the Sweetwater River on their way home.[6] On March 11, 1854, when Sir George was outfitting at St. Louis, Father De Smet wrote a letter at St. Louis University, saying he soon expected to see Jim Bridger, who would visit his children in school at St. Charles, Missouri.[7] Since Bridger is usually named as Gore's chief guide, he may have been engaged at this time; evidence ties him to the party later that same year.

Henri Chatillon, of St. Louis, is also mentioned as starting out with Sir George. He was the famous hunter who had shepherded dyspeptic historian Francis Parkman on his classic trip to the North Platte area in 1846–47. Years later (Feb. 16, 1867) the hunter wrote the historian that he had, since then, made a trip west with "a very disagreeable 'Jonnie Bull'" and "was gone eleven months. . . . He put on any amount of airs, had 18 blood hounds to chase the antelope, and played smash in general."[8] Thus it is clear that Chatillon started out with Sir George in June 1854 but left in disgust the next spring to reach home in May 1855.

If the excursion left Westport on June 6 and followed the usual trail to Fort Laramie (about 650 miles), we can estimate its time of arrival. The

[3]Spence, "A Celtic Nimrod," 56–66 (for best account of Gore's hunting excursion) (A). At 59 it notes that in March and May 1854 Chouteau cashed drafts from Gore for 1,800 British pounds. For the passport date, see Vaughan to Cumming, July 1856, in McDonnell, "Fort Benton and Fort Sarpy," 192 (A).

[4]*New York Tribune*, June 23, 1854, excerpted in Barry, *Beginning of the West,* 1220 (B).

[5]Gowans, *Fort Bridger,* 50 (B).

[6]Barry, *Beginning of the West,* 1186 (B).

[7]Chittenden, *DeSmet,* 1483–89 (B).

[8]O'Leary, "Henri Chatillon," 137 (A).

ox wagons would limit its travel to 15 miles a day, implying an earliest arrival date of about July 19. If, however, by tarrying to hunt and see the country, it made only 10 miles a day, it might have arrived as late as August 10. In either case it would have arrived before August 19, the date of the shocking Grattan massacre, which no excursion account mentions. The implication is that Gore's party had already left Fort Laramie before this storm struck.

There are hints that when Sir George left Fort Laramie that summer, he proceeded up the North Platte to its great bend (near present Casper, Wyo.) and then followed it south into Colorado's North Park. At the southern margin of this elevated basin, the continental divide runs east and west and is crossed by Rabbit Ear and Muddy passes. From this point the Gore Range extends southward and 20 miles distant is crossed by Gore Pass, both named after the baronet. In August 1863 Maj. Edward W. Wynkoop's Ute Indian expedition followed this same route to the Gore Range, and the major reported: "We crossed the trail made by Sir George Gore, the English baronet, in 1854 under the guidance of Jim Bridger, this fact being established by the names of himself and party rudely carved on trees bearing the date, 1854."[9] There is a tenuous hint that Gore's party may have turned west to Utah and reached Uinta River; Bela M. Hughes in 1865 prospected for the stage line a possible new mountain route from Salt Lake City straight east to Denver and reported "finding an abandoned axle-tree left by Sir George Gore on Uinta River twenty-one [sic, eleven] years ago."[10] In any case, the hunting party returned to spend its first winter of 1854–55 somewhere on the North Platte.

Bridger left the party to spend that winter at his Westport farm, for he signed a deed of purchase for additional acreage there on April 2, 1855. He soon started west again, however, for on June 19 an eastbound Mormon missionary, John L. Smith, reported from just east of Fort Kearny that he had recently met Bridger "on his way to the mountains." Bridger is next mentioned at his former trading post, Fort Bridger, which he sold to Mormon agent Lewis Robison on August 3, 1854. He started east the next day, apparently to rejoin Sir George's party.[11]

[9] Wynkoop, "Report, Aug. 13, 1863" (M).

[10] Rocky Mountain News (Denver), Oct. 11, 1865.

[11] Alter, Jim Bridger, 260 (for farm deed) (B); Hafen, Fort Laramie, 217–18 (for John L. Smith) (B); Gowans, Fort Bridger, 66, 176 (for sale of Fort Bridger) (B).

Since Bridger had left in the fall of 1854 and Chatillon the next spring, someone had to pinch hit as the baronet's chief guide for some months. The substitute was Louis Vasquez, Bridger's former partner; Capt. John B. S. Todd, with Gen. Harney's punitive expedition, recorded in his diary at Ash Hollow on September 2, 1855 (the day before Harney destroyed the Sioux village): "The bearer of this message [from the Sioux across the North Platte] was Mr. Vasquez, who has for some time been attached to Sir George Gore's party as chief guide." [12]

All this evidence clarifies an uncertainty as to when Sir George left the North Platte in 1855. It was clearly not early in the spring, but in August, after Bridger had sold his post, which corresponds to Mitch's statement that it was in the summer. Mitch also said they had left the North Platte "at Box Elder Creek," which suggests that the party had wintered, not at the crowded and officious Fort Laramie, but in some quiet, inviting valley farther up the river on its south bank at the foot of the mountains, where shelter, wood, water, grass, and game were plentiful. If the Boyers were trading anywhere nearby, the eighteen-year-old Mitch could have found the camp in plenty of time to demonstrate his hunting skill and knowledge of the country and tribes to the north.

When the party left in August, Bridger was chief guide and other mountain men had signed on, including Mitch Boyer and Henry Bostwick, with whom Mitch would again serve in 1876. Mitch's service is vouched for in his death notice in the *Helena Herald* of July 30, 1876: "When the celebrated English hunter, Sir George Gore, came to the West, Mitch Boyer was selected as one of the guides to accompany him." Traveling leisurely and slaughtering game in prodigious numbers, the caravan trekked north, passing Pumpkin Buttes, picking up the head of Powder River, and following it down to its mouth on the Yellowstone. After working their way up the latter stream to the mouth of Tongue River (present Miles City, Mont.), the men began constructing elaborate cabins in which to spend the second winter, 1855–56.

In the spring of 1856 the caravan hunted southward up the valley of the Tongue, then veered west to the upper Rosebud and on to the Wolf Mountains, where they traded and socialized with a village of friendly Mountain Crows. Mitch, of course, knew these people, and a newspaper squib of 1878 indicates that he was still with the party:

[12] Mattison, "Journal of John Todd," 110 (A).

Paul McCormick [who had known Mitch well] and Mr. Sanborn have left Miles City on a prospecting tour to the Wolf Mountains, where gold was discovered . . . by a party of which Sir George Gore, Jim Bridger, Mitch Boyer and a Frenchman named Frazier made a part. At that time a nugget was picked up on the surface of the ground by one of the party . . . about ten miles from where Gen. Crook had his fight with the Sioux on the [head of the] Rosebud in 1876.[13]

The "nugget" feature of this quotation is undoubtedly apocryphal, but Sir George soon returned from the Crow village to his recent winter quarters at Tongue River, where he divided his party. He took one group, with a few wagons, on an overland hunt to Fort Union, a major Chouteau trading post at the mouth of the Yellowstone. The others lingered to build two flatboats for use in floating the heavy baggage downriver to the same point. Some wagons, left empty, the baronet ordered burned and the iron residue thrown in the river. A recent "find" reveals that this incident occurred at Tongue River, not at Fort Union as tradition has it, and that the canny expedition blacksmith cached the iron parts instead of tossing them in the drink. The evidence appears in a series of letters written by Henry W. Beeson, clerk for Sioux Indian Agent A. H. Redfield, in the form of a diary. They describe his cordelling trip up the Yellowstone with Crow annuities to Fort Sarpy, at the mouth of the Bighorn, in the summer of 1858. His entry for July 29, just above the Tongue, includes:

We also passed the winter houses of Sir George Gore, a wealthy Englishman who came to hunt the bison and grizzly bear. His expedition was conducted on a princely scale, he having a retinue of servants. Securing the services of experienced mountaineers at double the wages the trading companies could pay, he transported his own provisions, outfit, etc., built his own wintering houses and traveled perfectly independently of the trading companies. He armed and equipped his men in the most perfect manner so that his company could fire 248 shots without reloading. At this point he built his boats to come down the river in the spring, destroying his houses and ordering his wagons and carts burnt and the iron thrown in the river, determined that no one should reap any benefit from them. The present steersman of our boat was his blacksmith and instead of throwing the iron into the river, he cached it, and annually a portion has gone to Fort Sarpy to be worked into tomahawks, traps and other articles in

[13] *Rocky Mountain Husbandman* (White Sulphur Sprs., Mont.), April 25, 1878.

demand. We took on some wagon tires, the last remnant of Sir George's mammoth hunting expedition.[14]

After his men united at Fort Union, Sir George flatboated the Crow annuities, in the charge of Alfred Vaughan, Upper Missouri Indian agent, across the Yellowstone on July 24, 1856—and ran into some flak from Vaughan for wantonly slaughtering his wards' means of subsistence.[15] The baronet also sold some of his remaining wagons to explorer Lt. Gouverneur K. Warren, of the Topographical Engineers,[16] and discharged some of his mountain-man employees. Again dividing his remaining men, the baronet sent one party downriver with the baggage in the two flatboats to make another rendezvous at Fort Pierre, while he, with twelve men and the last of the wagons and livestock, headed south on another overland hunt. On reaching the Little Missouri River, he ascended it, still southbound, to its head just west of the Black Hills of Dakota. There a party of Sioux cheerfully ran off his livestock, forcing him to struggle back northward down the same stream.[17] A little below its mouth on the Big Missouri the weary party reached Fort Berthold, another Chouteau trading post, in the neighborhood of which it spent the third winter, 1856–57.

Meanwhile, the flatboat party at Fort Pierre was still anxiously awaiting news from Sir George as late as November 9, as reported from there by Agent Vaughan; by December 25 he could further report that Gore was wintering near Fort Berthold, as the Sioux had broken up "his traveling arrangements."[18] It is not clear whether Bridger had come down with the flatboats or had accompanied the overland party, but he apparently left that fall to spend the winter at home in Westport. The birth of his last child, William Bridger, near Westport on October 10, 1857, suggests that the father had been at home nine months earlier, in January 1857.[19]

In the spring of 1857 Sir George left Fort Berthold, presumably collected his baggage and mountain of trophies at Fort Pierre, and boarded the Chouteau boat, the *Spread Eagle*, captained by John Baptiste

[14] *Sioux City Register*, Dec. 30, 1858; Jan. 20, Feb. 3, 10, Mar. 17 (for quotation), 1859. All are signed "*B*" (Henry W. Beeson).

[15] McDonnell, "Fort Benton and Fort Sarpy," 174, 192 (A).

[16] Warren, "Explorations in Neb. and Dak.," 152 (A).

[17] Ibid., 158.

[18] Vaughan to Cumming, Nov. 9, Dec. 25, 1856, in *Upper Platte Agency*, 1856, R885 (G-M).

[19] Alter, *Jim Bridger*, 272 (B).

LaBarge, which docked at St. Louis on June 26.[20] Just when Mitch Boyer left the party remains unknown, but even a year of service under that master mountain man and guide, Jim Bridger, gave him priceless training and experience.

The North Platte Indian trade, to which Mitch returned, showed signs of recovering in 1857, though events would promptly rotate the kaleidoscope into a new pattern. From July to November the Platte Trail saw a continuous parade of supply trains and troop units marching westward to quell reported Mormon insubordination in Utah. Jim Bridger was chief guide for this Utah expedition, and numerous mountain men and traders were called on for service as scouts, guides, and couriers, though the Boyer name does not figure in these voluminous records. It may, however, have been the resulting disruption that persuaded the Chouteau firm that year to abandon the North Platte country entirely, thus leaving the trade to numerous French independents, including John Richard, Sr. (pronounced "Reeshaw" on the frontier), Joseph Bissonette, and Geminien P. Beauvais, the last-named turning independent on being released by Chouteau.

During this period the wilder northern divisions of both the Oglala and Brule Sioux hunted north of the river. Under the leadership of Red Cloud, a rising chief of the Oglala Badfaces, these northern Sioux were steadily pushing westward into Powder River buffalo country, ousting the Mountain Crows in the process. In the fall of 1857 the Upper Platte Indian agent, Thomas S. Twiss, moved his agency a hundred miles above Fort Laramie to Deer Creek, as he favored the migrating northern Sioux and hoped to add the Mountain Crows to his agency, despite the ongoing tribal conflict. Adjacent to this new agency, Bissonette erected a trading post, and 25 miles farther up, Richard had been trading and operating a toll bridge across the North Platte since 1853. Beauvais took over the former Chouteau post, 5 miles below Fort Laramie, to trade with the tamer southern divisions of the Oglala and Brule Sioux, who hunted south of the river.

On October 16, 1857, G. P. Beauvais applied for his first independent license, naming John Boyer (the father, as son John was only twelve) as one of his employees. A month later (November 24) John Richard, Sr.,

---

[20] Sunder, *Fur Trade*, 185 (for docking date) (B); De Trobriand, *Military Life*, 303 (for Capt. LaBarge's taking Gore to St. Louis) (B).

applied for his license, also naming John Boyer as an employee. Father Boyer probably traded for Richard with the northern Oglalas and Mountain Crows. These licenses may have been good for two years, for none at all was issued in 1858. When Richard applied for his next one on October 1, 1859, he named none of his employees, but Joseph Bissonette, applying the same day, named his, including Michel Boyer (now twenty-two) and Rafael Gallegos (a young New Mexican who will reappear in this chronicle); another name, hardly legible, was either John Boyer or John ("Popcorn") Myer. No later licenses in this area bear the Boyer name, though the family remained in the vicinity.[21]

In October 1859 Mitch was delighted to see his old friend Jim Bridger ride into Bissonette's trading post on Deer Creek, guiding the famed Yellowstone expedition of Capt. William F. Raynolds, of the Topographical Engineers. This scientific expedition had already explored the country from Fort Pierre northwest to the Yellowstone and south to the North Platte and would now winter at Deer Creek. Capt. Raynolds promptly detached his civilian topographer, J. Hudson Snowden, to take a party on a sidetrip to explore the Pumpkin Buttes area. It was undoubtedly Bridger who recommended Mitch Boyer as guide for Snowden's reconnaissance. On October 19, 1859, the party of eight men and five pack animals left on this trip of seventeen days and 247 miles. Snowden's frequent mentions of Michael Boyer reveal that he found his young guide not only competent, but endlessly knowledgeable and exceptionally congenial. It was at this time that Mitch told him of the antelope pit of 1851 and Sir George's route to Powder River, as earlier related.[22]

The Civil War was in full swing when father Boyer is next heard from in 1863, while living at Bissonette's post on Deer Creek. That spring John M. Bozeman and John M. Jacobs made their first attempt to conduct an emigrant train to the new goldfields of present Montana over what would become famous as the Bozeman Trail.[23] In late May, Bozeman and Jacobs were at Deer Creek, trying to induce emigrants to take their as-yet untried shortcut along the eastern base of the Big Horn Range. Diarist Sam Word, pulling in on June 30, decided to take the cutoff, and while

[21] *Register Books of Indian Trading Licenses* (G-RG75).

[22] Raynolds, *Exploration of Yellowstone*, 154–61 (for Snowden's report, replete with mentions of Michael Boyer) (B).

[23] Gray, "Bridger and Bozeman Trails," 23–51 (A).

waiting for more wagons to gather, he struck up a friendship with a local trader:

> An old Frenchman by the name of Bovier [John Boyer], who has trapped and traded through this country for twenty years, has furnished valuable information on the route, gold, etc. He seems to have taken quite a fancy to me while he talks little to others; presented me with a cradle, rocker, shovel and pick, worth $15–20—a handsome present. I shall ever remember old man Bovier for his kindness. He is an honest old backwoodsman and mountaineer, related to the Robidous in St. Joe.[24]

On July 6, 1863, Bozeman and Jacobs led the assembled wagons out on their new trail, taking Bissonette's young employee, Rafael Gallegos, to pilot them as far as the crossing of the Bighorn River (present Fort Smith, Mont.). When the train was only 125 miles along, angry Indians ordered it out of their buffalo country and back to the regular Platte Road. While the train halted to debate the proper course, Gallegos sped back to Deer Creek for military help. He did not return, but "Old John Boyer" reached the train on July 29, bringing military orders for it to retreat from Indian country. While Bozeman led a small horseback party on to Montana, Jacobs and father Boyer piloted the wagons back to the Platte Road.[25]

The next summer, 1864, the Bozeman Trail carried a heavy traffic of emigrant trains to the promising new Territory of Montana, Bozeman himself conducting the lead train, which Mitch Boyer would overtake and join. Let us postpone Mitch's departure for Montana, however, in order to complete his father's brief remaining career in the North Platte area.

Following several weeks behind Bozeman's lead train, the Townsend train assembled at Deer Creek, where it hired two guides to pilot it as far as the Bighorn crossing. This train had a lively fight with Indians on July 7, 1864, before reaching the Bighorn on July 20, when the two guides turned back, carrying the train's mail. Reminiscent accounts incorrectly name the two guides as Mitch Boyer and John Richard, Jr., but a diarist with the train identified them as "John Boyer and Raphael Gogeor." A contemporary newspaper account referred to the former as

---

[24] Word, "Diary, 1864" 57 (A).
[25] Gray, "Bridger and Bozeman Trails," 30ff (A).

"our old guide Boyer," indicating that he was Mitch's father, not half-brother. The other, of course, was Rafael Gallegos.[26]

Late in 1864 Indian hostilities on the North Platte so escalated that both Bissonette and Richard decided to move downriver to Fort Laramie for safety. They moved so slowly, however, as to suffer multiple Indian raids along the entire route. Bissonette's later Indian depredation claim enumerated five separate losses of stock that began at Deer Creek in mid-November and ended near Fort Laramie in April 1865. Father Boyer made this retreat, too, for he supplied an affidavit that detailed all these losses; it included the statement that "since 1863, he [John Boyé] has been living with Joseph Bissonette, a great part of the time in his employ." John "Boyé" signed this affidavit with his mark before the Upper Platte Indian agent, Vital Jarrot, at Fort Laramie on June 27, 1866—the very day the peaceful southern Sioux signed a treaty there that triggered "Red Cloud's War."[27]

The next year at Fort Laramie, on November 16, 1867, 144 white men with Indian families petitioned the government to set aside tracts of Indian land for themselves and their half-blood children. John Boyer makes his last appearance in the records as one of these petitioners.[28] Thus his death, at the hands of Indians, must have occurred at some unknown time between November 1867 and the execution of his son John in April 1871.

Father John Boyer was evidently illiterate, and there is nothing to suggest that Mitch ever learned to read or write. But intelligent he was, as demonstrated by his ready mastery of English, possibly French, and the Sioux and Crow tongues. He was a quick learner of wilderness skills, with a keen instinct for country and an indelible memory of its every feature. And to mingle easily and confidently among peoples with cultural backgrounds as contrasting as those of Indians and whites demanded an open, adaptable, perceptive, and understanding mind. Only respect and understanding of others can earn respect and understanding from others. That people could sense these qualities in Mitch is further revealed in a letter written on April 18, 1864, by Corporal Hervey Johnson, of Company G, 11th Ohio Volunteer Cavalry, then stationed at Deer Creek:

[26] Ibid., 48ff.

[27] Bissonette, *Indian Depredation Claim*, 5 (G-CSS).

[28] "Petition of White Men with Indian Families, Nov. 16, 1867," *Upper Platte Agency*, 1867, R892 (G-M).

There is a store just across the road from us . . . owned by one Bissonette, a Frenchman who has been in the mountains for forty years. . . . They all have squaws for wives, and are raising families of half-breeds. . . . One is Joe Bissonette, the son of our neighbor across the road; he dresses like white men and wants to be a white man, speaks English, wears fine shirts and fine boots like a real dandy, but he is not very talkative. Mitch Buazer [*sic*] is another, but he can talk and make himself free among whites as if he was one himself.[29]

[29] Unrau, *Tending the Talking Wires*, 115–16 (B).

ROAMING THE YELLOWSTONE VALLEY

Veteran traders, such as those on the North Platte, lived among the Indians and chose Indian women for wives. They understood their customers and knew that their lives and trade depended on maintaining peace. During the Civil War, however, the volunteer territorial troops inflamed the plains tribes to open hostility. To make matters worse, since 1862 the Upper Platte Indian agent, John Loree, had refused to issue trading licenses to anyone but his eastern friends.[1] Facing ruin, the traders began moving elsewhere and seeking other occupations. In 1864 one attractive "elsewhere" was sparsely settled Montana, which drew Mitch Boyer and some of his young trader friends.

Two new cutoff routes to Montana were opened in the summer of

[1] Gray, *Cavalry and Coaches*, 48–53, 74–78, and beyond (for provocations of Indians and resulting war) (B); *Upper Platte Agency*, 1863 (for traders' protests about licensing) (G-M).

1864. One was the Bozeman Trail, which coursed north along the eastern base of the Big Horn Range, crossing dangerous Sioux country to reach the crossing of the Bighorn River, where it turned west. The other was the Bridger Trail, which coursed north through the Big Horn Basin on the safer west side of the Big Horn Range and thus drew more traffic than the Bozeman Trail. On merging in Montana, the two trails continued westward to cross the Yellowstone River near present Livingston, Montana, and then surmounted the low continental divide into the Gallatin Valley at the site of the embryonic settlement of Bozeman. From there it joined an existing road bearing southwest to Virginia City, the territorial capital. Though Mitch's trading friends chose Bridger's Trail, Mitch would follow on Bozeman's.

On May 20, 1864, Jim Bridger pulled out from Richard's trading post at Platte Bridge with the first emigrant train to take his new trail. It was soon overtaken by a small party of traders that included John Richard, Jr., the quarter-blood Sioux son of the senior Richard, and Big Bat Pourier, a native of St. Charles, Missouri, who had been working for the elder Richard. Another wagon carried Jose Merival [Mirabal?], a veteran trader of New Mexican origins, and his family, including a daughter, Louisa. Bridger's augmented train wheeled into Virginia City about July 8, when young Richard and Louisa Merival paused to secure a marriage license before backtracking to the Gallatin Valley, where they found a preacher to marry them. The newlyweds then took up their residence in the newborn community of Bozeman. Big Bat, however, returned to winter on the North Platte with the elder Richard.[2]

Almost a month after Bridger's train, on June 15, Bozeman's lead train left Bissonette's post at Deer Creek to take his trail, followed three days later by the lone wagon of emigrant John T. Smith and family, hurrying to overtake. When Mitch "Bozier," riding alone on horseback, overtook the family, Smith asked him to have Bozeman wait for the wagon to catch up. On delivering the note, Mitch probably remained with Bozeman to assist his train. They all reached the Bozeman settlement about July 25, when Mitch joined his trading friends, the Richards and Merivals.[3]

Daniel E. Rouse, who had located a townsite on July 7, 1864, offered

<hr>

[2] Gray, "Bridger and Bozeman Trails," 42 (A); Richard (John, Jr.), "Indian Depredation Claim," No. 7651, U.S. Court of Claims (for wedding of John Richard, Jr.) (G-RG123).

[3] Gray, "Bridger and Bozeman Trails," 47 (A).

John Bozeman a free claim if he would settle there after conducting his train to Virginia City, which it reached by August 1. These earliest settlers, including young Richard and Jose Merival, organized a claim club on August 9 under the chairmanship of John Bozeman and gave the townsite the permanent name of Bozeman. By the end of that month another young man, Matthias ("Cy") Mounts, who had come out with a later train on the Bozeman Trail and had lingered briefly at the mines at Emigrant Gulch in Yellowstone Canyon, rode in to the new town. His biographical sketch reveals the intentions of the migrating traders: "For three years [1864–67], Mr. Mounts, with Michael Boyer and the Reshaws, traded with the Crow Indians and had some very narrow escapes from hostile Indians."[4]

That winter, while Mitch was trading with the Crows, the Montana legislature was holding its first freewheeling session and passed a law that would soon give Mitch extra employment. The modest legislators dealt their friends exclusive, twenty-year charters for a number of roads, with rights-of-way, as well as ferry, toll, and townsite privileges. Among the roads was that from Fort Laramie to Bozeman, which not only extended beyond the territorial boundaries, but claimed both the Bridger and Bozeman trails. The new business, promptly dubbed "The Broad Gauge Company" for its lofty ambitions, announced that both Jim Bridger and John Bozeman had been engaged to shepherd emigrant trains out to the Montana mines in the spring.[5]

In March 1865 the Broad Gauge Co. contracted with William J. Davies of Bozeman to build three ferryboats to be set up where the trails crossed the Bighorn, Clark's Fork, and Yellowstone rivers. Davies and his crew of six men left Bozeman on April 14 and took the Bozeman Pass to the Yellowstone Canyon, where they built a boatyard.[6] The company also hired Milo Courtright, one of the obliging legislators, to head another crew to operate the two ferries at the Bighorn and Clark's Fork. He arrived at Davies's boatyard about May 1, having picked up five men at Bozeman: M. "Bowyer," Col. Smith, John Donnelley, D. Shrike, and another who went nameless.[7]

[4]Leeson, *History of Montana*, 618, 620, and "Sketch of Matthias Mounts" (Gallatin Co.) (B); Houston, *History of Gallatin Co.*, 17–18 (B).

[5]*Montana Post* (Helena), Apr. 15, 1865.

[6]Davies, "Sketches of Early Days, No. 1," in *Bozeman Avant Courier*, Dec. 3, 1892.

[7]Courtwright, "Indian Troubles on Yellowstone," *Montana Post*, June 24, 1865.

In his lengthy and amusing reminiscences Davies well remembered Mitch, whose hunting skill kept the boatbuilders well fed for the next two weeks:

Mich Boyer [was] a half-breed French and Indian, rather a bad mixture as a general thing, but Mich was a very good fellow—when whiskey was an unknown quantity. He furnished us with fresh meat during the two weeks the party stayed with us. Mich was one of the best hunters I ever saw. . . .

I discovered a big band of mountain sheep on a flat about half a mile from the river. I told Mich about it, who was sitting at one side of the fireplace, mending his moccasins, a job he had to do every morning before leaving the house. He . . . reached for his gun and stuck a tall plug hat on his head, and asked me to put him across the river. I took a skiff and landed him on the other side. . . . He then worked himself up the river bank like a snake and when he got on top, stretched himself up like a pole, plug hat and all. Both arms and gun hung close to his sides, like a soldier on parade. His head and body were as rigid as a burnt stump, but his feet kept forging ahead all the time. It was the prettiest bit of acting I ever saw. The sheep were watching him with astonishment, debating what it was. Their curiosity was so aroused they couldn't withdraw their eyes from the tall plug hat until it was too late, and a dead sheep lay prostrate on the ground. Mich wheeled around and went back to his moccasin mending and I got one of the men to help get the sheep in.[8]

Courtright told about the subsequent misadventures of his crew and Mitch. Having fitted up their two ferryboats, the men shoved off on May 15, taking one pony. As such craft make 70 to 80 miles a day, they tied up the second day at the mouth of Clark's Fork and the next day towed one of the boats 15 miles upstream to its crossing, where they secured it. Returning to the other boat, all six men made the one-day float down to the mouth of the Bighorn, where they hitched the pony to the boat by rope and towed it about 70 miles up to the crossing (present Fort Smith, Mont.), arriving late in May.

Contrary to expectations, the ferrymen found no emigrant trains waiting to cross the river. Not knowing that the military had interdicted travel on both cutoffs to Montana that season and were planning to wage a major

[8] Davies, "Sketches, No. 4," *Bozeman Avant Courier*, Dec. 24, 1892.
[9] See footnote 7, above.
[10] Ibid.; Davies, "Sketches, No. 6," *Bozeman Avant Courier*, Jan. 7, 1893.

punitive campaign against the hostile Indians in the Powder River country, Mitch and crew waited patiently until their provisions ran low. Heading back on foot, they tramped the rugged 50 miles west to Clark's Fork, crossing it by the ferryboat they had cached there. The next day they reached Rocky Fork (near present Boyd, Mont.), where the Bridger and Bozeman trails merged, and there disaster struck on June 9.[9]

Both Courtright and Davies related stories of this encounter with a hundred Sioux warriors from the Platte. As the Sioux approached in friendly fashion, Mitch recognized their chief as a boyhood playmate and talked with them. Suddenly, the air was filled with bullets and arrows. One ball killed Col. Smith outright, another pierced a thigh muscle in Mitch's leg, and others riddled Courtright's clothing. Mitch instantly shouted, "Run for the brush; it's the only show for your lives!" and set a swift example himself. The five survivors streaked for the underbrush, crossed the creek, and scuttled south up a narrow coulee toward the mountains, eluding the pursuing warriors. Heading west for Davies's boatyard, they traveled as fast as each could go, which left the crippled Mitch behind. Courtright says "they" arrived June 13, followed by Mitch twenty-eight hours later; Davies recalled, however, that Courtright arrived first, famished, forlorn, and battered by the spring-flooded cataracts he had crossed by a succession of miracles. Two more arrived the next day and one the next, but not until the sixth day did "Mich come hobbling in," unperturbed. Having retained his gun, he had bagged plenty of game and, knowing the country, had crossed the streams by easy fords in the mountains.[10]

Pausing five days to help Davies cordell the third ferryboat upriver to a secure place opposite the gold diggings at Emigrant Gulch, Courtright and crew scattered in June. The limping Mitch reached Bozeman, where he found that young Richard had formed a trading partnership with William S. ("Mac") McKenzie and F. A. ("Al") Lund. McKenzie, a Georgian, had partnered with young Richard back in 1859 on the North Platte but in 1863 had come to Virginia City to try his luck at mining.[11] Already on their way out to join this outfit were Big Bat Pourier and Louis Richard, the younger brother of John, Jr.

[11] Undated news clipping (about 1903), in Mrs. Beal's "Scrapbook" (M). McKenzie had come to Montana and prospected for a time before settling at Bozeman in 1864.

Big Bat and the elder Richard, having spent the past winter at Platte Bridge, moved down to Fort Laramie in the spring of 1865 and then headed southwest for the high Laramie Plains. There they built a new trading post at Rock Creek on the busy Cherokee Trail, a little west of present Laramie, Wyoming. Joe Knight, a Canadian who had married a daughter of old Richard, arrived there with his freighting outfit bound for Montana. Both Big Bat and Louis engaged to Knight as mulewhackers and made Virginia City in thirty-five days, though not by a cutoff. Though Big Bat recalled that they had arrived in August, it must have been early in July, for by July 15 posters in that city were announcing that Joe Knight's train was about to depart for the States. Big Bat and Louis rode on to Bozeman, where they "went to work for John Richard, Jr., Mac McKenzie and Al Lund, all these being in partnership. This firm was trading with the Crows, John going out among them with goods to exchange for furs." All these traders, including Mitch Boyer and Cy Mounts, were in Bozeman in late August to experience their next adventure.[12]

On August 24, 1865, a small party of whites and five Crows under Chief Blackfoot was breakfasting at the eastern foot of Bozeman Pass, when thirty to forty Sioux warriors struck them. The party retreated to a boulder-strewn field, but in the melee Col. Kimball was killed and W. N. Buchanan wounded. Chief Blackfoot set out for Bozeman to bring help, but the others made so effective a stand among the boulders that the Sioux circled around and proceeded west toward the divide. After 8 miles they surrounded two hunters, killing a Mr. Smith but missing William Bunn, who dove into the brush. When just over the divide, the Sioux came on three wagons hauling lumber to the Yellowstone for use in building flatboats. This poorly armed outfit, led by Jose Merival, included his son Frank, Cy Mounts, and three others. The Sioux were set to overwhelm them when Chief Blackfoot's rescue party from Bozeman charged up.[13]

The members of this rescue party were Mitch Boyer, John and Louis

---

[12] Ricker, "Pourier Interview" (M). For more on the senior Richard's trading post on Rock Creek, see Gray, *Cavalry and Coaches*, passim (index) (B); *Montana Post*, July 15, 1865 (for Knight's departure advertisement).

[13] The story of these attacks is based on the following sources: *Montana Post*, Sept. 3, 1865; Topping, *Chronicles*, 34–38 (B); "Reminiscences of W. S. McKenzie," *Dillon* (Mont.) *Examiner*, Oct. 8, 1924.

Richard, Big Bat Pourier, Mac McKenzie, Al Lund, and Elliott Rouse. John Richard's rifle felled one Sioux, but the rest turned and fled. Once assured their friends were safe, the rescuers raced after their quarry, pursuing them across the Yellowstone, but lost them at nightfall. On their return they buried the dead. The citizens of Bozeman called on Virginia City to help guard the pass, but nothing came of it. On September 4 John Richard, Big Bat, and Jose Merival voted in Bozeman's first election.[14]

All this evidence of Mitch's presence in the Yellowstone valley in 1865 negates a claim that he served as guide, under Jim Bridger, for Gen. Patrick E. Connor's Powder River expedition, which sallied out from Fort Laramie late in July and returned in early October 1865. Capt. Henry E. Palmer, 11th Kansas Cavalry, the expedition quartermaster, made this claim in his diary on August 1.[15] It has always been accepted, as expedition records were lost by fire. It has recently been discovered, however, that the monthly reports of persons hired for this expedition were made by Capt. Samuel D. Childs, assistant quartermaster of volunteers, at Fort Laramie, and have been preserved. His reports for July through October identify the civilian scouts for Connor's expedition.[16] There were nine, with Bridger as "chief guide" and the others as "guide," but Mitch was not among them:

James Bridger, $10/day, July 6–Oct. 8; kept on duty at Ft. Laramie.
Nick Johnis [Janis], $5/day, July 6–Oct. 8; kept on duty at Ft. Laramie.
S. Iott [Cyfrois Ayotte], $5/day, July 6–Oct. 8.
Tony Dorio [Antoine Dorion], $5/day, July 6–Oct. 8.
Friday [Arapaho chief], $3/day, July 14–July 27.
C. Rulo [Charles Rouleau], $5/day, July 27–Oct. 8.
J. [James] J. Brannan, $5/day, July 27–Oct. 8.
A. LaDieu [Antoine Ladeau], $5/day, Aug. 5–Oct. 8.
Edward Lagennes [Lajeunesse, dit Simoneau], $5/day, Aug. 6–Oct. 8.

Mitch spent the winter and spring of 1866 trading with the Crows, for Big Bat recalled that a party composed of Mitch Boyer, John and Louis

---

[14] *Montana Post*, Sept. 2, 1865 (for petition and signers); Leeson, *History of Montana*, 619 (for Sept. 4 voters) (B).

[15] Hafen, *Powder River Campaign*, 109–10 (B).

[16] "Reports of Persons Hired by Capt. S. D. Childs, A.Q.M. of Vols., Fort Laramie, July–Oct., 1865" (G-RG92).

Richard, and himself took goods out to the Crows on the Musselshell River, north of the Yellowstone, and started back with a wagonload of furs and robes. "A war party of Sioux came upon them and they cut their horses loose from the wagon and escaped back to Bozeman. A month afterwards, they went back and got a part of the robes, such as were not cut up, or spoiled by rain. This was in the spring of 1866."[17]

That spring the Bozeman Trail saw heavy traffic, and Nathaniel P. Langford, president of the Broad Gauge Co., decided to reactivate his previous year's ferries. He wrote John Bozeman on May 25 to recruit him as operator of the ferry at the Yellowstone crossing, 51 miles east of Bozeman. A month later Bozeman reported that he had floated the old ferry from Emigrant Gulch down to the Yellowstone crossing, where he rigged it up as a pulley-and-rope affair. While ferrying the first wagon on June 24, the boat swamped, drowning a man, boy, and horse, but the next forty-five wagons crossed safely.[18] Trail diaries of 1866 confirm this report and add that he charged ten dollars a wagon until the flooded river subsided, when the toll dropped to six dollars; by September 9 the ferry had been abandoned. The deal had somehow soured, for the company sued Bozeman to recover the ferryboat and collect damages for its retention; in November the Helena District Court decided for the plaintiff and assessed princely damages of one dollar.[19]

Big Bat recalled that after their spring return with the robes, "Mitch Boyer, Louis and John Richard, Big Bat and Lew Wahn built [?] a ferry across the Big Horn for emigrant travel."[20] It is questionable that they built a new ferry, for this would demand a crew of boatbuilders; it is more likely that Nathaniel Langford, of the Broad Gauge Co., had recruited Mitch's party to repair and operate the ferry they had cached there the summer before. They must have left Bozeman about mid-June, for trail diarist Richard Lockey had proceeded 100 miles west of the Bighorn on June 26 when he "met a company of packers [i.e., with pack animals] . . . going . . . to make ferries—rough looking fellows." This un-

[17] Ricker, "Pourier Interview" (M).

[18] Burlingame, *John M. Bozeman*, 30–31 (B).

[19] *Montana Post*, Nov. 3, 1866 (letter to *Kearney Herald* on abandonment of the ferry), and Dec. 1, 1866 (for court decision).

[20] Ricker, "Pourier Interview" (M). Lew Wahn *may* have been Juan Jesus Luis, whom we shall meet again under various names.

named party should have reached the Bighorn crossing about July 1. It must have been Mitch's party, for trail diaries reveal that as late as July 3 there was no ferry in place at this crossing.[21] The crew would soon get the ferry into service, though not for long, as Red Cloud's War would erupt there in mid-July.

The early traffic on the Bozeman Trail this year of 1866 encountered no trouble with Indians, for the latter had been fighting for two years with troops and had just suffered a severe winter, isolated from supply sources. They were more keen to barter for necessities with emigrants than to harass them. Thus it was that the early trains occasionally met friendly Cheyennes, and all swapped freely with a large village of friendly Arapahos congregated on the west bank at the Bighorn crossing. Their chief even spoke English; his name appears as "Nave," "Davy," or "Old David." He was probably Neva, a well-known Arapaho chief. The first premonition of trouble came on July 3, when the last of the unmolested diarists recorded that these Arapahos abruptly became excited when runners brought news that hostile Sioux (Red Cloud's) were coming north.[22]

Big Bat's interview resumes with an account of events at the ferry site:

The charge for [ferrying] a team was $7.50; no charge for footmen, as they were required to help at the landings. This ferry was built [?] before Fort C. F. Smith was erected [on Aug. 12, 1866] right there. While they were operating the ferry, a train crossed and camped there [C. Beers's mule-team freighting outfit]. In the night, Red Cloud and his band [of Sioux with some Arapahos, suddenly hostile on July 17] dashed in and captured the horses [mules]. The man who was guarding them was wounded and died the next day. [Part of] the trainmen had to go to Bozeman and Virginia City to get horses to move the wagons. They bought the ferry from Big Bat and friends, who then went to Bozeman.[23]

The foregoing bracketed insertions come from newspapers and trail diaries, which identify the train that Mitch's party ferried across as a mule-team freighting outfit largely belonging to C. Beers. The *Montana Post* of September 15 noted its eventual arrival at Virginia City about

[21] Lockey, "Diary, 1866," June 26 entry (M); Haines, *Bride on the Bozeman Trail*, 56, 116–17 (B).

[22] Haines, *Bride on the Bozeman Trail*, 56, 116–17 (B).

[23] Ricker, "Pourier Interview" (M).

September 9, and that it had left Omaha June 6; on losing all its stock at the Bighorn, it had to send men ahead to the settlements to fetch fresh stock. Some of the trail diaries mention Beers's men guarding the wagons on the west bank at the crossing and reveal that one man had been killed and another wounded, but was recovering. One diary gave the accurate date of July 17 for the Indian attack, and another August 17 for the return of fresh stock from Montana.[24]

W. H. Norton, a member of the Beers train, furnishes the most detailed account:

> In the spring of 1866 . . . Mr. Norton started [from Illinois] for Montana with a freight outfit, and after three months of hard travel and several raids by Indians, but with no loss of stock or life, the outfit finally reached the Big Horn River, where it met 1500 Sioux, Arapahoes and Cheyennes. While camped almost in their midst, they neither molested nor annoyed the party, but soon broke camp and trouble began. Mr. Norton and a companion fought thirty-two of them for half an hour on the open plain over the stock herd before help came; they saved the stock and killed one and wounded two Indians. After two days and nights, the Indians succeeded in stampeding nearly all the stock [July 17]. Mr. Norton and ten others volunteered to stay and guard the property until help could arrive. For four weeks the little band of eleven men zealously guarded their trust, being over 200 miles from the nearest aid, possessing only 35 rounds of ammunition to the man and half their guns muzzle-loaders. Near the last of the fourth week, troops came up [Aug. 12] and established Fort C. F. Smith. Teams soon arrived [Aug. 17] and took the party on to Virginia City [about Sept. 9].[25]

The Sioux-Arapaho attack of July 17 put another small trading outfit out of commission at the crossing, an event that must be introduced because its three available accounts[26] give faulty information about Mitch's ferry party. This trading outfit belonged to Capt. Henry E. Palmer, who had mistakenly attached Mitch to Connor's Powder River expedition of the year before. Having been discharged from the Kansas Cavalry, he

---

[24] Sawyer, "Niobrara and Virginia City Wagon Road, 1866," July 29 journal entry (G-M95); Athearn, "Diary of Burgess," 61 (for meeting fresh stock, Aug. 16) (A).

[25] Leeson, *History of Montana*, 1365 (B).

[26] Topping, *Chronicles*, 51–52 (B); Coutant, *History of Wyoming*, 335–36 (B); Morton, *History of Nebraska*, 1:723 (B). These accounts are all brief and are cited in the text by author's name.

started out in March 1866 with four mule wagons loaded with goods to trade with the Indians on the Bozeman Trail. In mid-May he tarried ten days at Fort Laramie, where, according to the Coutant and Topping accounts, he picked up "three half-breed interpreters, John and Louis Richard and Mitch Boyer." This statement is irreconcilable with Big Bat's story, as well as its supporting evidence that the ferry party was still in Bozeman at this time.

In early June, Palmer halted again to trade at Clear Creek, but after five days a band of Cheyennes ordered him politely but firmly to move on to the Bighorn. Only the Coutant account mentions a second five-day halt at "Tongue River, near present Dayton," Wyoming, about 56 miles from the Bighorn crossing. The reason for this halt was undoubtedly nostalgia, for this is where Connor's expedition had routed and destroyed an Arapaho village under "Old David" and taken some women and children prisoner. Palmer, as expedition quartermaster, may have been given charge of these prisoners, who were well treated and soon released. While Palmer was reminiscing here, "Old David" appeared and mutual recognition followed. They made a satisfying deal for Palmer to come to the Bighorn crossing with his goods and trade with the needy Arapahos.

Independent confirmation of this account supplies precise dates. On June 15 diarist Lockey had come within 20 miles of the crossing, when he met "fifty Arapahoe warriors," coming from there in pursuit of Ute Indians who had just stolen some Arapaho ponies; their chief spoke good English. These warriors, continuing, met Palmer that day or the next. Then, on June 19, when Lockey was at the crossing, he recorded the arrival of "fifty Arapahoes and one white man," with no mention of half-bloods.[27] The English-speaking chief could only have been "Old David" and the white man with him, Palmer, coming to trade with the Arapahos. All three accounts of the Palmer venture agree that he went to the Bighorn and traded with the Arapahos for "almost a month," but when "Red Cloud's War broke out in July," Old David seized Palmer's goods and whisked him off as a captive for some weeks.

This evidence brings Palmer to the Bighorn on June 19, while the Arapahos were still peaceful and nearly two weeks before Mitch's ferry party reached the scene. It now becomes significant that the third ac-

[27] Lockey, "Diary, 1866," June 15, 19 entries (M).

count (Morton's) never mentions the "half-breeds" until after reaching the Bighorn: "He [Palmer] built the first [*sic*] ferry boat on that river [Bighorn] . . . while three half-breeds and 700 Arapahoe Indians were available for companionship." If we take this to mean that, when Mitch's party reached the Bighorn in early July, they found Palmer already trading there and that Palmer lent a hand in repairing the ferry, all contradictions vanish.

After Mitch's party sold the ferry, the friends left to reach Bozeman by early August 1866. They may have left as early as July 18 with Beers's trainmen in quest of fresh stock or as late as July 31 with James A. Sawyer's Niobrara Wagon Road Expedition, the next known arrival (July 29) at the crossing. This outfit paid Beers's guardsmen $7.50 a wagon to ferry them across (July 30) and the next day left with a locally hired half-blood who lived in Bozeman; they reached that settlement on August 13.[28]

For the second time a venture into ferrying emigrants across the Bighorn had proved a bust for Mitch and his friends, but there was still trading to be done with the Crows and a profitable prospect of freighting supplies to the troops who would be fighting Red Cloud's War.

[28]Sawyer, "Niobrara and Virginia City Wagon Road, 1866," July 31, Aug. 13 journal entries (G-M95).

A PEACE TREATY BRINGS WAR

The fever of belligerence that sustained the Civil War for four years, and provoked the plains Indians to war in its last years, began to subside after Appomattox, placing overwhelming pressure on the government to retrench on spending and demobilize the host of volunteer troops at once. Yet the ambitious Powder River campaign in the summer of 1865 had failed to terminate the war with the Sioux, Cheyennes, and Arapahos of the northern plains. Clearly, something had to be done to resolve this conflict before demobilization abolished the means to continue it.

As early as the fall of 1865 a few military officers, close enough to the scene to foresee the crisis, initiated peace overtures in order to seek some kind of accommodation with these Indians. They were making good progress until the government stepped in with a scheme to con the Indians out of the country that supported them and occupy it by troops. The refusal of the northern bands to accept such self-extinction transformed the occupation into an inept military invasion, ironically known as Red Cloud's War. These clumsy machinations, having been smothered in folklore, deserve a retelling, which also sets the scene for the adventures of our cast of characters during the coming years.

In the fall and winter of 1865 emissaries were sent out to the hostile Sioux, Cheyennes, and Arapahos in the Powder River country, inviting them to come to Fort Laramie for peace talks. The tribes proved receptive, for they, too, were weary of war, as continual fighting was crippling their livelihood. They could not hunt and gather enough to feed, shelter, and clothe their people, nor could they barter with traders for cloth, utensils, and arms. During the exceptionally severe winter of 1865−66 they could only watch their people suffer and die. For immediate survival they needed a truce; to expect a future they needed to reach an accommodation with whites that would leave them free to support themselves in their own way in their own country.

In response to the emissaries' invitation, a delegation of Sioux hesitantly appeared at Fort Laramie in January 1866. They received a warm welcome from a new Upper Platte Indian agent, Vital Jarrot, a former Indian trader, and from Col. Henry E. Maynadier, 5th U.S. Volunteer Infantry. The latter also had Indian experience under Capt. Raynolds on the Yellowstone Reconnaissance. He now commanded the West Sub-District of Nebraska from his headquarters at Fort Laramie. He relayed the good tidings of peace to his army superiors and the Indian Office. As a result, Edward B. Taylor, the northern Indian superintendent at Omaha, was appointed to head a special commission to treat with these Indians in the spring.[1]

On March 8, Spotted Tail, the prominent chief of the Southern Brules, came to the fort, and Maynadier, learning that the chief's favorite daughter had just died, arranged an impressive funeral, which soon won over the chief completely.[2] Three days later Spotted Tail brought in the hostile Red Cloud and one hundred fifty men. Uneasy at first in the colonel's office, Red Cloud soon began to speak, concluding, "We hope that when we see the commissioners, we may settle all our differences and secure a long and lasting peace." Jarrot distributed some immediate provisions, agreed to supply a little powder for hunting, and allowed them to visit the

[1]Maynadier to Cooley, Jan. 25, 1866, in Commr. Ind. Aff., *Ann. Report*, 1866, 205 (B).

local traders before sending them to gather their people in nearby good hunting country until the commission could come. A witness to this March 13 council was thoroughly impressed with the sincerity and resolve of both sides to find an accommodation that would support a welcome peace.[3] The Indians reiterated this theme at every meeting while awaiting the commission.

During the next two months large numbers of Oglalas and Brules, some Cheyennes, and a trickle of Arapahos paraded in and out of the fort. Though hard pressed to scrape up rations for them, Maynadier treated them with sympathy and friendliness, and Jarrot wired an urgent plea for the commission to hurry out by May 20. The colonel reported on May 9 that "it was not my intention that the [Indians] should come [so early], but they are forced by hunger and destitution." He added that he had succeeded in inducing a large band of Southern Cheyennes, who had been fighting in the north, to return to their home agency on the Arkansas River.[4]

One of the commissioners was Col. Maynadier, but its president, E. B. Taylor, and its two other members, Robert E. McLaren of Minnesota and Thomas Wistar, a Philadelphia Quaker, were still in Omaha on May 21, held up by bureaucratic delay in the delivery of their Indian presents and provisions. That was worrisome, for the indispensable lubricant for Indian negotiations consisted of filling long-empty stomachs. The commissioners had to leave without the shipment on May 22, but it reached Omaha the next evening and was soon loaded for the road. Unfortunately, part was sent by slow ox train and lagged far behind.[5]

Taylor reported on June 9 that his commission had reached Fort Laramie on May 30, planned its strategy on June 1, and held its first council with the Sioux on June 5. At this short session Taylor read a prepared speech that presented his demands to the respectfully silent chiefs:

The attendance of chiefs, headmen and people was very large. The commissioners read to them their opening address, setting forth the

[2]Ibid., Mar. 9, 1866, idem, 207 (B).

[3]"*D.C.*" to ed., Mar. 12, 1866, *Missouri Republican*, Mar. 24, 1866.

[4]Maynadier to Cooley, May 9, 1866, and Jarrot to Taylor, Apr. 30, 1866, *Upper Platte Agency*, R891 (G-M).

[5]Taylor to Cooley, May 21, 1866, and D. J. McCann (freighter) to Cooley, May 24, 1866, idem.

object of their mission, informing them that it was not the desire of the government to purchase their country, but simply to establish peaceful relations with them, and to obtain from them a recognition of the right of the government to make and use, through their country, such roads as may be deemed necessary for the public service and for emigrants to the mining districts of the West.[6]

Fortunately, there was a more forthright and knowledgeable witness present, whom the Denver *Rocky Mountain News* had secured as a correspondent: Capt. Ewell P. Drake, Company L, 11th Ohio Vol. Cav., who had served some years in the country and was now stationed at Fort Laramie. His dispatch of June 10 gave a fuller version of this opening session:

On June 5th the Peace Commission convened in front of headquarters under a very large covering festooned with cedar. At 10 A.M. the council was opened. . . . Nineteen chiefs in a circle fronted them: Red Cloud, Spotted Tail, Standing Elk, Red Leaf, Man Afraid of his Horses, Trunk, Fair Day, Tongue, Man that Walks Under the Ground, Sharp Nose, Two and Two, White Eyes, Big Mouth, Bad Wound, Sitting Bear, Bad Hand, Man that Looks to the Bottom, Fresh Beef and Greasy Nose.

After smoking the pipe of peace, the Post Chaplain, Mr. Wright, made a very appropriate prayer, which was replied to by Red Cloud, who prayed to the Great Spirit for peace, and then presented Taylor with a very fine redstone pipe with an embroidered tobacco pouch. Then, with a general hand-shaking, Red Cloud, through interpreter Charley Geneva [Guereu], said: "We have come to hear our Great Father."

Taylor replied by reading: "We have come here as special messengers from your Great Father. We are glad to see that what we have heard about you is true. You have kept your promise that you made in the winter and have done no damage to white people. We will talk to you freely and truthfully, and we are talking to you on important business. The Great Father desires to be at peace with you, also to make a treaty. You know that war brings trouble, and in war sometimes bad white men and bad Indians do bad things. What we want your people to remember is that this treaty is the last one, not made for a day, but for all time. We are willing to listen with patience, in council, to what you have to say. We will tell you all we have to say, keeping nothing back. You know that the Great Father, the Chief of Soldiers [Mayna-

6Taylor to Cooley, June 9, 1866, idem.

dier], has treated you well. He has given you provisions. All this he has told in letters.

In the mountains there are many people; they all get their provisions by trains. They want a road by which they can travel. White men will go about as they always have done. It is true they drive off game; therefore, we are willing to pay liberally for the damage done. The Great Father does not wish to keep many soldiers in this country. He will be satisfied if the mails and telegraph are not molested. We do not ask you to give up the country or sell it. We only ask for roads to travel back and forth, and no roads will be made except by orders from the Great Father, so as not to disturb the game; and whatever damage is done by the roads would be paid by the Great Father.

At the conclusion of the address, Red Cloud shook hands with the commissioners and said that "he had nothing to say, as he wished to get all the Indians together and have a talk." The council then adjourned.[7]

Note that Taylor demanded two things of the Sioux: to observe a lasting peace, yet to recognize the government's right to make and use roads through their lands as it deemed necessary for its people and soldiers. He also stated that the government did not desire to purchase the Sioux land. Capt. Drake confirmed all three of these points and added two more: the government wished to keep few soldiers in Indian country but was willing to pay liberally for damage done by the roads.

It was the lack of any trace of accommodation to the survival needs of the Sioux, for which they had been pleading, that struck the chiefs dumb. They knew that the whites, who had started the war, wanted the Indians to cease defending themselves; this they were eager to do, if left alone. The northern divisions of Oglala and Brule Sioux, however, knew that the Bozeman Trail was already destroying their last buffalo grounds, on which their lives depended. They were now asked to accept this destruction, and more of the same, as a government right, and clear out so that it could be held without purchase by a few soldiers. Since paying damages could not restore life to extinct Indians, the northern half of the Sioux understood that they were asked to commit peaceful suicide. The southern half, whose hunting grounds were south and east of the Platte, were not so directly menaced, but equally appalled. Still, they all politely promised to sleep on it and report an answer the next day.

[7]"*D*" (Drake) to ed., June 10, 1866, *Rocky Mountain News*, June 18, 1866. The June 13 issue had identified "*D*" as Capt. Ewell P. Drake, 11th O.V.C.

Oblivious to the Indians' desperation, Taylor continued his June 9 report with the next day's council, which was brief indeed:

On June 6th, Spotted Tail, Red Leaf, Man Afraid of his Horses and Red Cloud, four of the prominent chiefs of the Oglala and Brule bands, responded to the address of the commission. Their speeches were marked by moderation and good feeling, and at the conclusion of the council they expressed the opinion that a treaty could and would be made, and asked for time to bring in their people, who are encamped in large numbers on the headwaters of White River, some 50–60 miles distant. This request was acceded to.

Yesterday [June 8] all of these chiefs started for their camps, having first been supplied with provisions. They will return with their people on Tuesday, June 12. We hope to hold another council in the presence of the united bands of Sioux on Wednesday, June 13. Messengers have been dispatched [thus by June 9] to the camps of the Cheyennes and Arapahoes and the commission hope to secure attendance of the representatives of both tribes. These camps are 250 miles distant, however, and at least two weeks from this date must intervene before they can arrive [June 23]. The general feeling of all these tribes is very conciliatory and friendly, and I have no doubt that satisfactory treaties will be effected with each and all, if their attendance can be secured.[8]

Capt. Drake's June 10 dispatch also continues with more details on this second council and confirms the emissaries to other tribes, but although still hopeful, it expresses serious misgivings:

On June 6th the council met at 10 o'clock. Red Cloud said: "Yesterday we talked about small matters, and today we want to talk about *big matters*. My people on both sides of the road have [only] bows and arrows, and we came in here and told you all we wanted. We are 21 bands. All we want is peace. We have come here for you to give us instructions that *we may live*." [Italics added.] Spotted Tail then spoke, merely a repetition of Red Cloud's remarks. Standing Elk informed the commissioners of what he had done during the Indian war, and the council adjourned.

No council has been held since to enable the Indians to get all of the tribes in. This council has been principally with the Sioux, though a courier has been sent to the Cheyennes to come in, and in a few days the council will be resumed.

Nothing definite so far has been arrived at, but it is transparent that

[8]Same as footnote 6, above.

the Indians will with great reluctance consent to roads being made through the country. In fact, the young men of the nations are not for peace, but are here now merely from the force of circumstances, and as they are not actuated by any principle, they will observe a treaty only so long as it is policy to do so. It does not look reasonable that they will give up this western country to the white man and suffer a gradual extermination, for it is sure that wherever the white man goes, the game will disappear. The commissioners are sanguine that they will make a very satisfactory peace. I hope they will not be disappointed.[9]

This brief meeting with a few chiefs on June 6 was no council at all. Red Cloud and Spotted Tail politely asked the commission to talk about "big matters," but it simply adjourned the meeting. That was enough for Red Cloud; he left to marshal his Northern Sioux warriors for a desperate defense of their last hunting grounds and would not return to the councils. Spotted Tail left with his less menaced Southern Sioux to debate the thorny issue of joining their cornered cousins in war or accepting peace, a process that would consume two weeks.

Red Cloud acted on his decision within days. By June 10 or 11 his warriors had intercepted the emissary that the commission had sent by June 9 to bring in the Northern Cheyennes. They roughed him up and sent him back with an unambiguous message, which he delivered by June 14. On that date Corporal Hervey Johnson, about to leave Fort Laramie to be mustered out of the 11th Ohio Cavalry, hastily wrote a revealing letter:

> The Indian treaty has not met since it adjourned [June 6]. A messenger who was sent out to bring in the Cheyennes, came back with his head and face all bruised up, having barely escaped with his life. It seems that the old men and most of the chiefs are in favor of peace, but the young men are in favor of war; this is why the messenger was handled so roughly. . . . The general opinion is that there will be war again this summer.[10]

By conversing with individual Indians, the commission soon discovered that their instructions had sent them on a fool's errand. Easiest to contact were a few local Sioux, who were eager to sign any treaty. Often

[9]Same as footnote 7, above.
[10]Unrau, *Tending the Talking Wires*, 345 (B).

called Laramie Loafers, they had already abandoned the hunting and roaming life, had intermarried with whites, and were settling down in the environs of Fort Laramie. Leaving the commission to become disillusioned, we pick up the story of the military expedition, already nearby, which had been ordered to occupy the Bozeman Trail "in peace."

It had been only too apparent that demobilization of the huge volunteer forces of both the North and South would release a deluge of people from the re-United States to seek adventure and fortune in the West. Military planners faced the problem of protecting the trails and settlements with a few decimated regiments of regulars. On March 10, 1866, Gen. John Pope, commanding the vast Department of the Missouri from his desk in St. Louis, issued General Order No. 33 to implement his solution to this problem. Among other things, the order established a new Mountain District that stretched from the North Platte to Virginia City and charged it with erecting three new military forts to occupy and protect the Bozeman Trail. Pope was aware of the then-promising peace overtures to the trail's Indian owners, but counting on the Indian Office to secure its relinquishment, he made no contingency plans.[11]

Pope assigned Col. Henry B. Carrington to command the new Mountain District. An Ohio lawyer and politician, Carrington had been commissioned colonel of the newly organized 18th U.S. Infantry at the beginning of the Civil War but saw no field service until that conflict's end. He had been in the West only a few months, commanding Fort Kearny, Nebraska, when this new assignment came. Pope gave him a puny force of eight companies, comprising the 2nd Battalion of his three-battalion 18th Infantry. His marching orders were forwarded on March 28,[12] but it took nearly two months to ship out recruits to fill his skeleton companies. Jim Bridger was assigned to guide this occupation force and thus rejoins our cast for the next two years.

Back on November 30, 1865, Capt. S. D. Childs had discharged Bridger at Fort Laramie on orders from Gen. Grenville M. Dodge, then commanding U.S. Forces in Kansas and the Territories, to "discharge all citizen employees . . . not authorized by superior authority." Although complying, Col. Maynadier protested that soldiers could not re-

---

[11] Col. Carrington, *Indian Operations*, 51–52 (G-CSS).
[12] Ibid., 53–54.

place guides and interpreters. Bridger lingered for over two weeks, for Maynadier penned a letter on December 16, with Bridger at his side, describing the Bridger and Bozeman trails. The veteran guide then left for his Westport home but stopped at Fort Leavenworth to report the wholesale discharges to Gen. Dodge, who ordered the reinstatement of "needed" guides and interpreters on January 22. Capt. Childs rehired Bridger on January 25 but, since he was absent, dropped him again on January 31.[13]

Bridger boarded the westbound stagecoach at Atchison, Kansas, on February 26, to return to duty, and on March 5 Capt. Childs initiated a new contract with him as district guide at five dollars a day. Then, on March 31, the captain received orders to furnish Bridger with all tools and materials needed to build a new ferry across the North Platte, 52 miles above Fort Laramie, for military use. It would be known as Bridger's Ferry, although it was operated by trader Benjamin B. Mills. Finally, on April 13, the *Kearney Herald* announced that "Jim Bridger has been ordered to report to Col. Carrington as guide of the expedition which leaves Fort Kearney."[14]

Not until May 19, 1866, did Carrington's column begin its westward march from Fort Kearny, Bridger in the lead. Note that this date was eleven days before the commissioners left Omaha. A picnic atmosphere prevailed, as some officers' wives accompanied the column, feeling proud to open up new country. No one had warned of dire consequences, should the peace commission fail. Fortunately for history, among the women was Margaret Carrington, the colonel's wife, who kept a diary, on which she based a very readable book. Intelligent and perceptive, she observed more than her husband and regularly corrected the faulty dates that sprinkle his official letters. She alone recorded that on the evening of May 28, or the next morning, the fast-moving commission overtook the marching column 25 miles below Julesburg, Colorado, and called on the colonel. If not officially forewarned of the occupation force, the commission learned of its approach at this time.[15]

[13]"Persons Hired by Capt. D. S. Childs, A.Q.M., Ft. Laramie, 1865–66" (G-RG92); "Correspondence, West Subdistrict of Nebraska (Maynadier), 1865–66" (G-RG393).

[14]Ibid.; *Atchison Champion*, Mar. 1 (for coach departure), April 19, 1866 (quoting *Kearney Herald*, April 13).

[15]Mrs. Carrington, *Absaraka*, 48 (B).

Having completed an 18-mile march on June 13, the colonel halted his command for a few days a prudent 4 miles short of Fort Laramie, so as not to disturb commission proceedings. To make sure, he issued an order, which included: "Soldiers will attend to their duties like soldiers, and all intercourse with Indian lodges and individuals, while at Laramie or on the march, will be through headquarters." As Mrs. Carrington put it, he "kept his men at the camp" during their stay there.[16]

Mrs. Carrington revealed that on this June 13, when the column had settled into camp, she and her husband learned of a split between the Northern and Southern Sioux, and the reason, and that the troops would have to fight the Northern bands, who had not and would not return to the council:

> Just about sunset, Standing Elk, a [Southern] Brule, called on us for a talk. He asked us where we were going and was frankly told the destination of the command. He then told us that a treaty was being talked about with a great many Indians, some of whom belonged to the country to which we were going; but the fighting men of these bands had not come in and would not; but that we would have to fight them, as they would not sell their hunting grounds to the white man for a road. He said that he and Spotted Tail [Southern Brule] would sign the treaty and would always be friends.[17]

On June 15 the officers' wives were allowed to shop at the fort and visit the council grounds, as Mrs. Carrington wrote:

> Pine boards had been arranged as benches in front of one of the sets of quarters and over these boards were once-fresh evergreens [Capt. Drake's cedars, whose withering signaled no councils since]. . . . Under the eaves of buildings, by doorsteps and porches . . . were . . . hungry, masticating Indians of all sizes, sexes and conditions [Laramie Loafers]. . . . We had anticipated an attendance upon some of the deliberations, and the colonel had, without success, requested authority to remain at Laramie during the treaty. . . . The Indians who actually held possession of the route in dispute were not on hand when they were wanted. Man Afraid of his Horses and Red Cloud [northern Oglalas] made no secret of their opposition, and the latter, with all his fighting men, withdrew from all association with the treaty-makers,

---

[16]Ibid., 88 (for quotation); Col. Carrington, *Indian Operations*, 4 (for June 13 order) (G-CSS).

[17]Mrs. Carrington, *Absaraka*, 80–81 (B).

and in a very few days quite decidedly developed his hate and his schemes of mischief.[18]

On Saturday, June 16, Carrington reported: "All the commissioners agree that I go to occupy a region which the Indians will only surrender for a great equivalent; even my arrival has started among them many absurd rumors, but I apprehend no serious difficulty." This comment is the first sign that the commission had tumbled to its predicament and were now feeling out what the Laramie Loafers and Southern bands would demand for the road. On this day the colonel also noted that Maynadier and Taylor had introduced him to some chiefs as "the White Chief going out to occupy" the Bozeman Trail, which evoked a "cold" reception.[19] Mrs. Carrington, writing of the events of June 16, added confirmation:

> Some of the chiefs were seen by the officers, and when they knew that the command was going to Powder River country, in advance of any treaty agreement, they gave unequivocal demonstrations of their dislike. . . . One Indian said: "Great Father sends us presents and wants new road, but White Chief goes with soldiers to steal road before Indians say yes or no!" Some of us called this good logic.[20]

Capt. Drake's second dispatch, also dated June 16, states very specifically that the commission had been unable to resume councils and confirms the rough treatment of the emissary to the Cheyennes:

> Since I last wrote you, matters have to an extent remained in *status quo*, so far as peace is concerned. On the adjournment of the conference [June 6], of which I notified you in my last, the chiefs present had nothing to say in reply to the commissioners, and wanted to have a consultation with all their people. They left the post and have been anxiously looked for this week. Considerable doubt is expressed by many as regards the favorable termination of the treaty.
> A report is in circulation of an occurrence last week [ending Sat., June 9] not favorable to peace. It appears that Mr. William Rowland, an interpreter of the Cheyenne tongue, was sent out to have a party of Cheyennes come in, who were camped on Powder River, 65 miles from here [two days' fast riding]; he was met by some of the Bad Face Sioux [Red Cloud's band], who stopped him [before June 11?], and finding

[18] Ibid., 87–88.
[19] Col. Carrington, *Indian Operations*, 6 (G-CSS).
[20] Mrs. Carrington, *Absaraka*, 89–90 (B). Col. Carrington gave a similar account, misdated Aug. 16.

out his mission, informed him he could not proceed farther, as there was no desire for peace; when he insisted on proceeding, one of them knocked him off his horse. A circumstance like this does not seem productive of good . . . .

A battalion [the 2nd] of 18th Inf., under Col. Carrington, is now camped four miles down the [North] Platte. They start . . . for Fort Reno and a new post at the base of the Big Horn Mountains. As they go into the Indian country, a short time will develope the Indians' intentions.[21]

On June 17 Col. Carrington broke camp hurriedly and made a Sunday march of 13 miles up the North Platte, passing Fort Laramie. As they left, Mrs. Carrington revealed the gloom of the commissioners, who finally advised her of the treatment of interpreter Rowland: "Just as the troops left, one of the commissioners came to our ambulance and advised that very little dependence should be placed on the result of the deliberations . . . for a messenger sent out to the Indians had been whipped and sent back with contempt."[22]

Capt. Drake wrote his last dispatch from Fort Laramie on June 19 and noted that still no council had been held:

Since my last, nothing has occurred except the arrival of Indian goods. But few Indians are here to have a distribution, and we look anxiously for them, as their coming in peaceably will determine whether or not the white man can peacefully occupy and make roads through the country. As I told you in my last, it looked doubtful, but we do not yet despair. I could give you many rumors, but I can trace them to no source.[23]

The commission now realized it was in deep trouble. The effort to secure rights to the Bozeman Trail from that half of the Sioux whose livelihood depended on it had not only failed but had provoked them to violent hostility; now an inadequate military force was openly invading the trail. This was neither the first nor last time that two arms of government sabotaged one another. All the commission could do now was somehow induce some of the other Sioux, who had no interest in the trail, to sign away their cousins' rights to it. Such a fraud could not prevent war, but it

[21] Drake to ed., June 16, 1866, *Rocky Mountain News*, June 27, 1866.

[22] Mrs. Carrington, *Absaraka*, 90 (B).

[23] Drake to ed., June 19, 1866, *Rocky Mountain News*, June 25, 1866. Drake was mustered out Sept. 9, 1866.

could be sold to the public merely by claiming that whoever signed a treaty represented a vast "majority" of the Indians and by characterizing the tiny minority as renegades. That was the tack the commission chose to sail.

After his June 9 report Taylor remained silent until June 24, when he wired Washington for permission to purchase fresh beef to feast the Indians, necessarily the Laramie Loafers and Southern bands, who were then coming in. On July 30, in Washington, he submitted the bill, $4,645. To secure a few signatures, however, he was pushed to promise "$70,000 of annuities for 20 years," totaling $1,400,000.[24] Only Indian historian George E. Hyde seems to have established that the treaty was signed on June 27, with just a thousand Indians present. He named seven Brule and six Oglala signers, not one of whom was a Northern Sioux and several of whom were Laramie Loafers.[25] Congress, of course, would refuse to ratify the treaty.

From Fort Laramie on June 29, presumably the date of the commission's departure, Taylor sent a triumphant telegram to the Indian Office: "Satisfactory treaty concluded with the Sioux and Cheyennes. Large representation. Most cordial feeling prevails."[26] The representation, however, was fractional and the cordiality thin, indeed. Furthermore, no treaty had been concluded with the Cheyennes; a treaty was merely left for them to sign, as a few did in October. Worst of all, does a treaty that brings war qualify as "satisfactory"?

Some days later, on reaching Fort Kearny, Nebraska, Taylor told a local reporter that the chiefs had asked him for another three days to counsel among themselves, during which time they banished the rebellious ones and returned with only those committed to signing. At Fort Kearny, Taylor also complied with the chiefs' demand by publicly announcing to all whites, citizens, and soldiers "between Fort Laramie and the Missouri River" that the Southern Sioux had made peace and must not be treated as enemies while "they went on a big hunt in the Republican River Valley." Even Taylor knew what that meant: the Northern Sioux

---

[24]Taylor to Cooley, June 24 (for permission), July 30 (for bill), Sept. 15, 1866 (for annuities), *Upper Platte Agency*, 1866, R891 (G-M); Chandler to Denman, Jan. 13, 1867 (on promised annuities), Commr. Ind. Aff., *Indian Hostilities*, 11–12 (G-CSS).

[25]Hyde, *Spotted Tail's Folks*, 114–15 (B).

[26]Taylor to Cooley, June 29, 1866 (telegram), *Upper Platte Agency*, 1866, R891 (G-M).

were already at war, and the peaceful Southern Sioux did not want to be mistaken for them during their hunt on their own retained buffalo grounds.[27]

The western press was already condemning the treaty as a farce, fraud, and failure by the time Taylor reached Omaha. From there, on July 16, a telegram was fired off, in the names of Taylor, McLaren, and Wistar, to President Andrew Johnson: "Satisfactory treaties have been concluded with the Upper Platte Sioux and Cheyennes at Fort Laramie. Contrary reports are without foundation."[28] On reaching St. Joseph, Missouri, on July 19, Taylor gave the press a ridiculous blast against his critics and knowingly enticed emigrants into serious danger:

> Col. Taylor claims that a perfectly satisfactory treaty was negotiated at Fort Laramie, and that all reports to the contrary are made by freighters and others who are doing all in their power to create hostilities so as to make a good thing from transporting troop supplies to the plains. He further says that 3000 Indians were at Fort Laramie and that 14 out of 16 chiefs signed the treaty; that the two absent chiefs sent word that they concurred in all their brothers did. He says he is willing to stake his reputation that *there will be no trouble on the plains*, unless begun by whites. [Italics added.][29]

The brief published report of the commission, signed only by Taylor and Maynadier, is not even dated, although Taylor later referred to it as "the commission report of August 1," at which date Taylor was in Washington, but probably not Maynadier. The document is next to worthless, but it does admit that the Cheyenne treaty was left with Maynadier at Fort Laramie to be signed.[30] Taylor's annual report as superintendent, dated October 1, 1866, provided more misinformation about the treaty process and still pretended that he had secured a lasting peace with "seven-eighths of the Sioux."[31] The Bozeman Trail, however, had been running red with blood for months. And Red Cloud would win this war.

[27] *Rocky Mountain News*, July 18, 1866 (quoting *Kearney Herald*, July 10).

[28] Taylor, McLaren, and Wistar (telegram) to president, July 16, 1866, *Upper Platte Agency*, 1866, R891 (G-M).

[29] *Missouri Republican*, July 20, 1866 (dispatch from St. Joseph).

[30] "Report of Laramie Commission," in Commr. Ind. Aff., *Ann. Report*, 1866, 208 (B); Taylor to Cooley, Sept. 15, 1866 (for Aug. 1 date), *Upper Platte Agency*, 1866, R891 (G-M).

[31] Taylor to Cooley, Sept. 15, 1866, in Commr. Ind. Aff., *Ann. Report*, 1866, 210–11 (B).

FREIGHTING TO FORT C. F. SMITH

Mitch Boyer and friends, having sold their ferry at the Bighorn crossing, pulled into Bozeman sometime in August 1866. They did not long remain there, for Jim Bridger soon rode into their midst with full news of Red Cloud's War, which opened up new opportunities for the traders. Mitch stayed with his friends for some months before Bridger directed him to a service more to his liking and more suitable to his unique talents. To reveal how it all happened, and to set the scene for Mitch's future activities, let us return to Bridger and Carrington's column as it occupied the Bozeman Trail against growing resistance.

Bridger led Col. Carrington's column out of Fort Laramie on June 17 to march 52 miles up the North Platte and cross to its north bank at Bridger's Ferry on June 21. The day before, some of Red Cloud's warriors, left behind to spy and harass, had run off stock at the ferry. Another march of 113 miles up the Bozeman Trail brought the column on June 28 to Fort Reno on Powder River (near present Sussex, Wyo.), where it paused for nearly a week. On June 30, from right under the colonel's nose, the impudent warriors stole a large herd of sutler's mules. A party of mounted infantrymen boiled out on a pursuit of 70 miles but returned empty-handed. It was while they were still there on July 3 that the Arapahos at the Bighorn crossing had become excited at the news that Red Cloud's main party was coming north.

Having left one company to relieve the volunteer garrison at Fort Reno, Carrington's other seven companies left on June 9 to march another 63 miles, halting on July 13 at the point (near present Buffalo, Wyo.) where the colonel would erect new Fort Phil Kearny as his headquarters for the Mountain District. That very morning they had passed posted notices warning that civilian trains had suffered attacks on July 6 and 10. Although the column did not know it, Sawyer's wagon-road expedition, while traveling from the head of the Niobrara River toward Fort Reno, had also been attacked on July 8, 12, and 14.[1]

All these were gentle preliminaries, carried out by rear-guard warriors while Red Cloud was concentrating his main force farther north on Tongue River, as Carrington would soon learn. On July 16 some friendly Cheyenne chiefs came in to talk with him. They told him that Red Cloud, with a large force, was camped ahead on the Tongue; that the chief was kept minutely informed of the troops' every move and had just finished an ominous sun dance; that on July 13 his emissaries had come to the nearby Cheyenne camp to induce its young warriors to join the war, and others had proceeded on to the Arapahos at the Bighorn crossing to recruit that tribe.[2] It was this action that had turned the Arapahos so abruptly hostile against the outfits of Beers and Palmer at Mitch's ferry.

Early the next morning, July 17, Red Cloud's men ran off Col. Carrington's own mule herd from his camp and then ambushed a pursuit force of outraged soldiers, who paid a toll of casualties. On their return that evening, these chastened troops came on an appalling scene, the bodies

---

[1] This and preceding paragraphs are based on Mrs. Carrington, *Absaraka*, Chaps. 9, 10, 30 (the last giving tables of Bridger's mileages on the Bozeman Trail) (B); Col. Carrington, *Indian Operations*, 7–9 (G-css): Sawyer, "Niobrara to Virginia City Wagon Road, 1866" (G-M).

[2] Mrs. Carrington, *Absaraka*, Chaps. 11, 12 (B); Col. Carrington, *Indian Operations*, 9–10 (G-css).

of the six members of "French Pete" Gazeau's trading party, slain that morning. They had been trading with the Cheyennes and had ignored their warning that the Sioux were on the warpath. From that day on, the Sioux attacked citizens and soldiers alike all along the Bozeman Trail, from the North Platte to the Bighorn. Thus Red Cloud, who had waited so patiently up to June 6 to reach an accommodation, had by mid-July mobilized his forces for an all-out war.[3]

Carrington now realized that eight companies were too few to man scattered posts in wartime and escort the emigrant and freighter trains gathering so fast at his camp. Foregoing a third new post on the Yellowstone, he sent Capt. Nathaniel C. Kinney and Companies D and G to erect a second new post, Fort C. F. Smith, 91 miles farther out at the Bighorn crossing, and to escort the accumulated wagons at least that far. Fortunately for history, Lt. Templeton, of Company D, kept an invaluable diary. Also leaving with the column on August 4 were Jim Bridger and a fellow scout, Henry ("Hank") Williams, whom Carrington sent to lop off 25 miles of the Bozeman Trail between the Bighorn and Clark's Fork, to gather news from the Crows, and to deliver a letter to the territorial governor at Virginia City.[4]

On August 9, as Lt. Templeton recorded, Bridger rode ahead of the column to the Bighorn ferry, were he found the guardsmen of Beers's train still awaiting replacement stock. Capt. Kinney spent a few days prospecting for the best location for Fort C. F. Smith, which proved to be the ferry site, and on August 12 his troop column camped there to begin building. Bridger and Williams left with Hugh Kirkendall's freighting train about August 15 and after 210 miles reached Bozeman about September 1.[5] There Bridger must have met his protégé, Mitch Boyer, and his trader friends and given them the news of the failure of the peace treaty, the outbreak of Red Cloud's War, and the new posts, including Fort C. F. Smith, whose location was so familiar to them. Since the Kirkendall train here diverged north to Helena, Bridger rode on to reach

<hr />

[3] Ibid., chap. 12 and pp. 10–13, respectively.

[4] Lt. Templeton, "Diary, 1866–68" (M). This diary is quoted so frequently here that it is cited in the text by his name and date of entry. For the Bridger-Williams mission and "budget of news," see Col. Carrington, *Indian Operations*, 20.

[5] White, ed., "Letters of C. Millard," 54 (A). These letters slight dates, but other trail diaries often mention Kirkendall's train.

Virginia City with his letter to the governor by September 8, incidentally telling the *Montana Post* (Sept. 15, 1866) that the Fort Laramie treaty was a "farce."

While Bridger was gone, John Richard, especially, perceived that the isolated Fort C. F. Smith should provide a good market for the produce of the fertile Gallatin Valley and profitable freighting for his crew. They promptly began loading three wagons with prime Gallatin potatoes to haul out to the new post, confident that its garrison would welcome vegetables as manna from heaven. Thomas W. Cover, a partner in a local flour mill, also went along to secure supply contracts. This was the first of two potato trips, which Big Bat's memory telescoped into one, leaving us to assume that the crew he named—John and Louis Richard, Mitch Boyer, and himself[6]—went on both.

Either at Bozeman or out on the trail, Bridger and Williams joined Richard's train, and all paused at a Crow village on Clark's Fork to extract a budget of news for Col. Carrington, which may be summarized as follows:

> Chiefs Blackfoot, White Mouth and Rotten Tail insisted that their Crow village of 200 men, had rejected Red Cloud's offers to join the war and were friendly to the whites. They said it took half a day to ride through the hostile villages of Sioux, Cheyennes and Arapahoes on Tongue River, who were planning to attack the new Forts C. F. Smith and Phil Kearny, but not the old Fort Reno. The Sioux chief, Man Afraid of his Horses [northern Oglala] was considering accepting an invitation to visit Fort Laramie again.[7]

When Richard's wagons wheeled into Fort C. F. Smith on September 29, Lt. Templeton, the post adjutant, quartermaster, and commissary, recorded:

> Bridger and Williams came back, bringing John Richard, a half-breed Sioux, who has three wagonloads of potatoes for sale; also Mr. Koover [Cover], of Gallatin Valley, who owns extensive mills there and is looking for a chance to supply Government with timber and supplies. Bridger saw the Crows on Clark's Fork; they are not intending to come in this winter, but may. . . . They report the Sioux have been invited to Fort Laramie again.

[6] Ricker, "Pourier Interview" (M).
[7] Col. Carrington, *Indian Operations*, 20–21 (G-CSS).

On reaching the post, Mitch probably noted that for lack of assigned scouts it was trying to make do with transient or volunteer help. Its sutler, Alvin C. Leighton, had as partner John W. Smith, an experienced frontiersman and Indian trader with a half-Sioux wife, and late in August some friendly Crows wandered in bringing their own interpreter, Pierre "Shane" (Chêne?), an old American Fur Co. man who had traded and lived among the Crows. With the aid of this pair, the post had at least established friendly relations with the Crows, who furnished occasional intelligence regarding the hostile Sioux.[8]

The day after Richard arrived, the delighted Lt. Templeton, as commissary officer, bought all 6,450 pounds of his potatoes at 24 cents a pound, making a total of $1,548, paying by voucher. Highly pleased with their speculation, the entire party, including Mitch, started back for Bozeman on October 1, eager to haul out more vegetables to the grateful garrison. Probably because Richard could not get prompt payment on his voucher, the second potato trip was delayed, which leaves an interim to relate events at the Bighorn post.

At the end of October, when the Crows returned in considerable numbers, John W. Smith went out to trade with them in their nearby camps, frequently sending back news of the Sioux and the futility of their efforts to win the Crows to their side. Reassured, the garrison was pleased to have them hover around throughout November, thus sparing it from the continual raids that harassed Fort Phil Kearny and culminated on December 21, 1866, in the shocking Fetterman massacre, which snuffed out the lives of eighty-some soldiers. The Crows brought news of this disaster to Fort C. F. Smith on December 28.

Also during this interval Bridger and Williams had left Fort C. F. Smith on October 23 with an escorted party that reached Fort Phil Kearny on the 27th. They reported their news to Col. Carrington,[9] who, a month later, sent Bridger back with an escorted mail, the last to reach Fort C. F. Smith for the next two months. Lt. Templeton recorded Bridger's return on November 28, adding that the scout "is to stop at this Post." Contrary to the prevailing assumption that Bridger wintered at Fort Phil Kearny, he remained on duty at the Bighorn post until June 1867.

[8] For more on Smith and Leighton, see Gray, "Frontier Fortunes of John W. Smith" (A).

[9] Templeton gives departure date, and arrival date appears in "Post Returns, Ft. Phil Kearny, Oct., 1866," R910 (G-M).

On December 1, 1866, Lt. Thomas H. B. Counselman, who had relieved Lt. Templeton of his quartermaster duties, added James Bridger to his rolls as district guide at ten dollars a day and would so carry him through May 1867. The post returns so listed his position into June, noting that it was also carried on the quartermaster's reports at Fort Phil Kearny.[10] Bridger himself was at Fort C. F. Smith, however. During December and January, Indians and severe weather prevented anyone from passing between the two posts, yet Templeton noted on January 31 that "Bridger is uneasy about the lack of news from below." A single mail party did arrive in early February, but Bridger did not leave with it, for Templeton mentioned him again on February 14. For the next three months only Crow couriers dared the trip and certainly not the aged and rheumatic Bridger. Thus he was present when Mitch returned to Fort C. F. Smith, this time to remain.

Not until early January 1867 did John Richard, undaunted by weather or Indians, launch his second potato trip with four loaded wagons. Big Bat and Cy Mounts named themselves, Mitch Boyer, and Louis Richard as crew members.[11] The slow trip testifies to storms, snow, and delays, but Lt. Templeton registered the garrison's delight at their arrival on February 2:

> The garrison was all astir from seeing a party with two wagons coming from the direction of Virginia City. . . . They proved to be John Richard's with a party of ten men, bringing fresh vegetables and butter down for sale. They had been some 30 days on the road and were compelled to cache two wagons on Clark's Fork. . . . A man having a charter for a ferry across the river came along; also one wishing to settle and go into the farming business.

Again Richard had to accept vouchers for his vegetables, certified as "necessary to prevent scorbutic disease." Having already heard the Crow news of the Fetterman massacre, Richard and crew were still present on February 7, the day the first mail in two months brought official confirmation and details. Capt. Kinney gave Richard a message to a wavering

[10]"Persons Hired at Fort C. F. Smith by Lt. T. H. B. Counselman, 1866–67" (G-RG92); "Post Returns, Ft. C. F. Smith, 1866–67," R1190 (G-M).

[11]*Montana Post*, Mar. 16, 1867 (for Jan. 1 departure, which may have been from Virginia City); "Sketch of Matthias Mounts" (Gallatin Co.), Leeson, *History of Montana* (B); Ricker, "Pourier Interview" (M).

Sioux chief to be forwarded by the Crows, whom Richard expected to meet at Pryor Creek on his return; the captain also urged the trader to bring out ten wagonloads of flour, "as there was not a pound at the post and the hardtack was almost exhausted and so musty as to be unfit for use."[12]

Leaving Mitch behind at the fort, Richard and the others headed back for Bozeman on February 9, resolved to haul out the needed flour. Soon after they started, the Sioux ran off seven mules, but a spirited pursuit recovered them, most injured by the thieves. Forging on in the cold and snow, the party camped with the Crows, who had moved westward to Rosebud River, where all the mules gave out and died. Big Bat and others remained in the Crow camp, while Richard pushed on afoot to Bozeman. There, by March 1, he related his news of the Fetterman disaster and the spreading hostility of the tribes, thereby alerting the valley to the need for defense.[13]

Richard then continued through a blizzard to Virginia City, only to learn that army headquarters in St. Louis had refused to honor his vouchers, because the price was "exorbitant" and the officer "was not authorized to purchase potatoes," as he told the *Montana Post* (March 16) on March 12. This financial blow left him unable to deliver the promised flour to Fort C. F. Smith. He also told the paper of his second potato trip, gave the most accurate news yet received of the Fetterman massacre, and revealed the efforts of the Sioux to recruit other tribes as allies in the war, which threatened to spread into Montana.

Returning to Bozeman, Richard found the settlers in a state of alarm. Holding a war meeting on March 16, they resolved to build a stockade and delegated Tom Cover to go to Virginia City and procure arms and ammunition from Acting Governor Thomas F. Meagher. Richard advised Cover that, not having been paid, he could not deliver the promised flour but must rescue his stranded crew and trade to recoup his losses. He managed to scrape up some trade goods and two kegs of powder for self-defense and to augment his short rations by hunting. Leaving Bozeman about March 25, he finally found his crew with the Crows on the north side of the Yellowstone, to which they had struggled through snowdrifts in search of buffalo, as they had all been starving. Fortunately, a chinook

[12] *Montana Post*, Mar. 16, 1867 (for Capt. Kinney's requests of Richard).

[13] Ibid. (for early theft of mules); Ricker, "Pourier Interview" (for camping with Crows on Rosebud R. and departure of Richard) (M); *Helena Herald*, Mar. 7, 1867 (for Howie attending marriage, Feb. 25, and hearing Richard's news later at Bozeman).

had just cleared the snow, permitting a good buffalo hunt and a lively trade in robes.[14]

Cover had left Bozeman at the same time, as the *Montana Post* (March 30) recorded his arrival at Virginia City on March 28. It carried his story of the war meeting and announced that the governor would supply arms and ammunition. Cover also disclosed that Richard had taken two kegs of powder to trade with the Crows, who might pass it on to the Sioux. The editor cried foul and demanded that Richard's trading license be revoked. Before returning home, Cover made a sidetrip to Helena, where on April 1 he told the *Helena Herald* (April 4 weekly) of his intention to go to Forts Smith and Kearny "to arrange terms [presumably for reliable payment] on which the Gallatin settlements may supply them with flour, grain and beef."

Since Richard was still trading on the Yellowstone and Boyer had been left at Fort C. F. Smith, Tom Cover induced John Bozeman to conduct him to the Bozeman Trail forts in search of army contracts. This mission had not gotten far when Bozeman, whom everyone considered invincible, was killed by Indians, an event that brought both shock and panic to Montana. I summarize this event, with careful attention to dates, from the more reliable accounts.[15]

Mounted and leading a pack horse, the pair left Bozeman, probably on the afternoon of April 16, 1867, and reached the Yellowstone near present Livingston on the afternoon of April 17. Here they found the camp of Mac McKenzie and Nelson Story, both bringing in cattle herds from the Yellowstone valley. With McKenzie was his partner, John Richard, and his crew, who had completed their trading with the Crows. That night five renegade Blackfeet under Mountain Chief, who had left their tribe because of a quarrel to join some Crows, ran off twenty of McKenzie's horses. Richard's crew, expending some powder from their two kegs, succeeded in recovering all but one of the animals.

Despite warnings to travel only by night, Bozeman and Cover left the next morning, April 18, and rode 12 miles down the Yellowstone to camp

<hr/>

[14] Ricker, "Pourier Interview" (M).

[15] Bozeman's mission is reconstructed from the following, cited in the text by the name of the source person: T. H. Cover, Apr. 23 to Acting Gov. Meagher, *Montana Post*, May 4, 1867; W. P. Parson's news, Apr. 23, *Montana Post*, Apr. 27, 1867; W. W. Alderson, "Diary, April 1867" (M); W. S. McKenzie, "Death of John Bozeman" (Mont. News Assoc. insert), *Boulder* (Mont.) *Monitor*, Oct. 25, 1919. The last reminiscence was recorded years earlier, as McKenzie died in 1913.

for their noon meal on the south bank of the river near Mission Creek. There the same Blackfoot renegades, pretending to be friendly Crows, walked up to the campfire and suddenly shot Bozeman dead and wounded Cover in the shoulder. When the latter got his jammed Spencer working, he hit one and drove off the others, although they absconded with all the provisions and three horses.

Cover walked a wide circle that night, managed to swim the Yellowstone the next morning, April 19, and dragged into the McKenzie-Richard camp, which had moved 6 miles farther west. He told his story, presumably had his wound dressed, and got some rest before leaving for Bozeman on a borrowed horse. He was probably escorted home, but the only evidence points to Big Bat in this role. The timing is now vague, but it is likely that they left the camp late on April 19 and reached Bozeman late on April 20, dates that are compatible with ensuing events.

Cover's account, written at Bozeman on April 22, does not give his arrival date but does state that "a party started out yesterday [April 21] to bring in B[ozeman]'s remains." That is confirmed by W. W. Alderson's diary entry for April 21, at his farm outside Bozeman: "Just heard that J. M. Bozeman had been killed by the Indians and Cover was wounded. Indians supposed to be the Bloods or Blackfeet tribes. John [Alderson, a brother] started down to join in party to bring in Bozeman's corpse." If this group left early on April 21, the timing is compatible with Cover's arrival late on April 20. Mrs. Houston's account names the members of this retrieval party as "John Alderson, D. E. Rouse and John Baptiste." [16] The last-mentioned was Big Bat, who therefore must have brought Cover home, perhaps with others.

On reaching the McKenzie-Richard camp, the retrieval party may have been expanded, but by whom and how many is uncertain. The men found Bozeman's body but decided to bury it nearby. Their return to Bozeman was recorded by W. W. Alderson on April 24: "[Brother] John got back from the Yellowstone about noon. The party buried Bozeman near the place where he was killed." Richard and crew also came in to Bozeman at this time, for "D. W." (Davis Willson), a Bozeman schoolmaster and correspondent for the *Montana Post*, wrote a dispatch from there on April 27, from which the editor published one paragraph on May 4; Richard had brought in news that the Sioux were planning to invade the Gal-

[16] Mrs. Houston, *History of Gallatin Co.*, 16 (B).

latin Valley by three nearby passes as soon as the grass turned green, and even some Crows were showing signs of joining the hostiles.[17]

Not until the next issue did the paper publish the rest of this dispatch. Willson rebuked the editor for earlier jumping to conclusions about John Richard and made a vigorous defense of Richard's loyalty and his invaluable help to the settlers and army posts. As to trading powder, Richard invited anyone to examine his two powder kegs and verify that it was still all there, save the five pounds expended in hunting and in recovering the horses stolen by the Blackfoot renegades.[18] It would seem that the trader's reward for keeping the Fort Smith garrison alive, alerting the settlers to danger, and recovering stolen stock from Indians was to have his trading license jeopardized.

Even before Cover had ridden in with the news of Bozeman's death, the alarmed settlers of the Gallatin Valley had held another war meeting on April 19 (misdated April 29 in the paper of April 27), which resolved to send armed men to guard the passes and circulated a petition asking the governor to raise a militia and call for federal aid. One of the delegates, W. P. Parsons, left Bozeman on April 23 with this petition, signed by three hundred settlers, and delivered it as well as the first news of Bozeman's death to the capital on the evening of April 24. The *Montana Post* (April 27) published all this alarming news and the response it brought. At a mass meeting, held on the evening of April 25, Acting Governor Thomas F. Meagher called for volunteer companies to be organized immediately as the Montana Militia.

Despite the atmosphere of panic, Tom Cover was still eager to make contact with the Bozeman Trail posts. Perhaps to his surprise, John Richard, whom he had gotten into trouble, was still willing to help out, as a news item reveals: "Not intimidated by the recent mishap to Col. Bozeman and Mr. Cover, he [Richard] accepted the latter's proposition to carry a communication through to Fort Smith. Accompanied by two other men, he left for that place three days ago [April 30]. They depended upon their tact and skill to get through safely and will return immediately."[19]

John Richard, Big Bat, and party reached Fort C. F. Smith safely on May 6, 1867, but it is time to return to Mitch Boyer and bring his story up-to-date.

[17]*Montana Post*, May 4, 1867.
[18]Ibid., May 11, 1867.
[19]Ibid., May 4, 1867.

ARMY SCOUT AT FORT C. F. SMITH

When Mitch had arrived with his friends at Fort C. F. Smith back on February 2, 1867, he found that Jim Bridger was the only scout on duty. Age and infirmities, however, held him at the post, and no mail had been sent out or received for two months. It was Bridger, no doubt, who recommended young Mitch to Capt. Kinney as a skilled frontiersman who knew every inch of the country, was intimately familiar with both the friendly Crows and hostile Sioux, and spoke their languages. Thus Lt. Thomas H. B. Counselman, as quartermaster, contracted with Mitch "Buoyer," as he spelled it, as post guide and interpreter at five dollars a day on February 6.[1] Mitch was told to prepare to leave as courier for Fort Phil Kearny as soon as possible.

The very next day, however, Lt. Templeton recorded the arrival of a long-awaited mail from Fort Phil Kearny, carried by two daring sergeants,

[1]"Persons Hired by Lt. Counselman at Ft. C. F. Smith, Feb. 1867" (G-RG92).

Joseph Graham (Company G) and George Grant (Company E). They had started out on snowshoes with six days' rations of hardtack and lard, along a rugged but safer trail in the foothills in deep snow for the first day. Descending to the regular trail, they tramped on for three more days, with less snow underfoot but in falling snow and sleet, to reach the Bighorn post on the afternoon of February 7.

The garrison, so long starved for news, gave the couriers a rousing welcome. Besides officially confirming the Fetterman massacre, their dispatches revealed that the three-battalion 18th Infantry had been reorganized into three regiments, each expanded to the standard ten companies. As a result, the original eight companies (A–H) manning the Mountain District were now part of the 27th Infantry, under Col. John E. Smith and Lt. Col. Luther B. Bradley, though neither of these officers had yet reached the district. The original 1st Battalion retained the designation of 18th Infantry, under Col. Carrington and Lt. Col. Henry W. Wessells, but as Carrington had been recalled, Wessells now commanded the district at Fort Phil Kearny. The district also boasted a battalion of 2nd Cavalry.

Allowing the sergeants two days' rest, Capt. Kinney penned a letter on February 9 to Wessells, which included the following reference to his new employee:

> Within a few days I have been fortunate enough to employ a half-breed by the name of Mich Boyer, who would have started the day after the couriers from Phil Kearny arrived here; he will accompany them on the return. He is thoroughly acquainted with the country and will prove invaluable, if kept away from whiskey. After consulting with a party [Richard's] that came with Boyer from Virginia City, and with Mr. Bridger, who are more or less acquainted with the strength of our hostile Indians, I have made the following approximations of the several bands of hostile Sioux and Cheyennes. . . .[2]

That same day Kinney placed Mitch in the charge of Sgts. Graham and Grant, giving each a horse to ride and two mules to carry provisions and accumulated mail. At tattoo of that evening the trio set out for Fort Phil Kearny. The worried Lt. Counselman would be reduced to reporting Mitch "absent with the mail" at the ends of that month and the next two, but the

---

[2] Kinney to Distr. Adjt., Feb. 9, 1866, *Upper Platte Agency*, 1867, R892 (G-M). An extract was forwarded to the Indian Office.

story behind these laconic entries has been reconstructed in detail from official records and personal letters.[3]

Mitch and the sergeants urged their horses along for most of that first wintry night before taking a five-hour rest. The next day, on reaching the Little Bighorn at about 1 P.M., they came on a buffalo freshly killed by Indians, which prompted them to head for the foothills. After 5 miles Mitch cautiously approached the crest of a hill, from which he looked back and spotted fifteen Sioux warriors following their trail in the snow. The trio spurred on for 15 miles, climbing into the broken and timbered slopes of the Bighorn Mountains. Their already tired horses grew ever more exhausted and the pursuing Sioux gradually closer. What happened then was related by Sgt. Graham to a letter-writing officer:

> Grant, having disregarded the earnest appeals of Graham to relieve himself and horse of their heavy load, began to lag. When his horse was unable to proceed farther, Grant abandoned it and the surplus baggage, but overtook Graham and Boyer as they were ascending the mountain. Grant seized the tail of Graham's horse to assist himself up the hill. When Graham remonstrated, Grant let loose and disappeared, exhausted, behind a ledge of rocks. Graham perceived a good place for defense a little farther up the mountain and reached it, though exposed to constant fire from the Indians. The latter, not wishing to advance under a sharp fire from Graham and Boyer, retreated in the direction of Grant's disappearance. After the Indians disappeared, Graham returned to look for Grant, supposing him to be concealed behind some rocks or in some cave, thereby eluding the Indians. After a fruitless search, he began retracing his steps to Fort Phil Kearny.

Boyer and Graham then forged on, only to have their horses collapse; somewhere on the chase the pack mules, mail sacks, and provisions had also been abandoned, but Mitch had kept Capt. Kinney's dispatches safe in his pocket. Doggedly, the pair tramped up and down over the rugged foothills and snow-drifted ravines for several days on empty stomachs and in frigid weather. They struggled into Fort Phil Kearny on February 13, exhausted and frostbitten. The post surgeon promptly put them into his hospital for treatment and convalescence.

An hour or so later Sgt. Grant also straggled in to give his remarkable

---

[3]The condensed account that follows is based on Murray, "Long Walk of Sgts. Grant and Graham" (A); two letters to *Army and Navy Journal*, June 27 and Sept. 28, 1867 (the latter contains the quotation).

story. When he had fallen behind, he had run for some timber but fell through a snowdrift onto a narrow ledge on the steep side of a deep ravine. Soon an Indian fell nearly on top of him and was so startled at seeing the soldier that he dropped his gun and stumbled into the ravine. When a second Indian appeared, Grant shot him and hurled his body into the ravine. Near dark, a fog came up and the Indians all withdrew, allowing him to descend the mountain and plod on to the fort. He arrived in worse condition than the other two and spent considerable time in the hospital with pneumonia.

When Mitch failed to return to his home post, efforts were made to send Crows to find out what had happened to him, but the persistent cold and deep snow discouraged even these Indians. On March 16 some River Crows came in and gave Lt. Templeton the following news they had obtained from some Sioux:

> Last month the Sioux had a small war party out, who discovered tracks on the road from here to Fort Phil Kearny; they followed and came upon Boyer's party on Tongue River. The whites started for the mountains, leaving their pack mules, but while going up the mountains their horses gave out and they took to the pines. As they had thrown away most of their clothing and a storm was brewing, the Sioux concluded they would freeze to death, and so did not follow them. If this is true, my mail has all gone up.

Not until March 26 did a Crow courier come in and assure the officer that "Mitch Boyer got through, but they lost their horses and the mail." No one, however, specified why Mitch was so late returning; probably severe frostbite or pneumonia held him, or Lt. Col. Wessells retained him on some local duty. In any case, it was not until the end of April that the scout set out alone for his home post.

On reaching the upper Little Bighorn, Mitch found a Crow village, where he met a young Sioux, an old acquaintance. That night and next day and night he remained to pump his friend for all the Indian news he could extract. He obtained the Sioux's story of the Fetterman massacre and a recital of the reasons for the Sioux hostility, which he would later give to Commissioner John F. Kinney.[4] He also learned that the Sioux were recruiting other tribes into the war and were calling a grand sun

[4]See Appendix A.

dance on Powder River to generate unity and enthusiasm for all-out attacks; this news he would pass on to the Montana Militia. Lt. Templeton verified some of it:

> May 3: Mitch Boyer came in about 10 P.M. last night, all alone, and had traveled so all the way from Fort Phil Kearny. . . .
> May 4: Boyer talked with a Sioux in a Crow camp on his way up. The Sioux told him that the Sioux were collecting on Powder River to dance the sundance, after which they would come here [and attack us].

At this time Capt. Kinney, impressed with Mitch's service, promised him an extra five dollars a day for hazardous duty as courier, but not until August did the scout complain that he was not being credited with such bonuses. In response, an official order was made for supplemental payments, retroactive to May. On his return on May 2, Mitch found Jim Bridger still on duty at the Bighorn post and also learned that on April 1 Lt. Counselman had hired Pierre Shane as post interpreter at one hundred fifty dollars a month.[5] Pierre and Mitch would see years of service together at various places and in various capacities.

The post was seriously alarmed because no provisions had reached them for months and dwindling supplies had reduced the garrison to a diet of boiled forage corn. Even John Richard had not returned with the promised flour, for reasons no one at the post knew. It is thus not surprising to find Templeton noting in his diary, only days after Mitch returned to duty: "May 5: Boyer is to go to the Gallatin Valley tomorrow to send flour down." At daylight the next morning who should halloo the fort but John Richard, Big Bat, and others: "May 6: Mr. Richard, accompanied by three men, came in about daylight, having come to the river about 2 A.M. They left the Gallatin Valley six days ago [April 30]. Mr. Richard came as agent for Mr. Coover about supplying the post with flour."

Thus it was that on May 6, the very day Mitch was slated to leave for Bozeman after flour, Richard and Big Bat arrived as agents for Tom Cover, the flour contractor. The interests of all having so nicely converged, Capt. Kinney gave Mitch a letter describing the plight of the post and warning that without provisions he would have to abandon the post. On May 7 Templeton added that "Mr. Richard, Boyer and another man [Big Bat]

[5] See footnote 1, above, "April 1867."

started about 3 P.M. Mr. Richard says he will be back in sixteen days with a train of eight wagons."

Mitch and friends made a fast return to Bozeman, for Maj. Gen. Thomas Thoroughman, of the Montana Militia, reported from his camp there on May 11:

> I have just finished a lengthy interview with John Richard, Jr., Mitch Boyer and John Poiner [Pourier, or Big Bat], who got in last night [May 10] after dark from Fort C. F. Smith, having made the trip in three days, a distance of 210 miles. They all agree that there is an alliance formed between the Sioux, Arapahoes and Gros Ventres . . . [and] that those nations have already fixed a sundance for some time this month and will jointly commence their hostile work about the 1st of June. These statements they made with authority, for Boyer met a Sioux of his acquaintance, who gave him positive assurance of the alliances having been formed and the sundance. A sundance means, as he interprets, a war of extermination against the whites. . . . Fort C. F. Smith has but 200 men and they are without provisions, save a small quantity of corn, which they prepare for food by boiling. Nor do they have any hopes of getting anything better . . . and must depend upon others than themselves for relief.[6]

When Gen. Thoroughman announced to his militiamen that without provisions Fort Smith would be abandoned, they volunteered to escort a relief train. Richard and Cover promptly furnished three wagons apiece and others four more, to make a train of ten.[7] From Bozeman, Davis Willson soon reported that "the expedition in charge of stores for Fort C. F. Smith, in command of Col. [Walter W.] DeLacy [of the militia] moved out from headquarters at 2 P.M. yesterday [May 22]. There are forty-two men in the command, well armed and equipped."[8]

When the train reached Clark's Fork, Mitch sped ahead and at noon of June 12 informed Templeton that succor was at hand. The officer surprised Mitch with the big news that the long-awaited military supply train from the East had arrived the day before, escorted by Capt. John Green's two companies of 2nd Cavalry and bringing Company E, 27th Infantry, to swell the garrison to three companies. Sutler Al Leighton had also arrived

[6] Gen. Thoroughman, Bozeman, May 11, to Acting Gov. Meagher, *Montana Post*, May 18, 1867.

[7] *Montana Post*, May 25, 1867.

[8] Ibid., June 1, 1867.

with two wagonloads of wares, the remainder having been left at Fort Phil Kearny because of the loss of draft animals to Indians. Only hours before Mitch had arrived, the emptied train and escort had started back, taking his friend Jim Bridger and the retiring Capt. Kinney.

When Richard's train pulled in on June 14, Capt. Thomas B. Burrowes, the new post commander, refused to allow the undisciplined militia escort to cross the river. Richard, however, crossed his wagons on June 16, and Templeton promptly bought all his flour, beans, salt, and pepper, but none of his one hundred fifty bushels of potatoes. The train, with its militia escort, headed back for more provisions on June 18 and reached Bozeman on July 9,[9] but Richard did not accompany them.

Mitch later drew extra pay from May 7 to June 12 to cover this courier trip but earned no more bonuses for a month, implying no hazardous duty during that interval. John Richard left on June 17 for a fast solo ride to Fort Phil Kearny, for reasons the lieutenant did not disclose. Events had been taking place among the Crows and Sioux, however, that shed some light on the activities of both Richard and Boyer.

Back on February 18, 1867, the president had appointed a commission, often called the Sanborn Commission, to investigate the Fetterman disaster and the causes of Indian hostilities on the plains. It consisted of Gen. John Sanborn (retired), Gen. Nathaniel B. Buford (retired), Gen. Alfred Sully, Col. Ely S. Parker (aide to Gen. Grant), John F. Kinney, and Geminien P. Beauvais. Having promptly launched their investigation in the spring, they separated at Fort Laramie to continue their work in various other areas. John F. Kinney was assigned to Fort Phil Kearny, not only to gather testimony on the Fetterman massacre, but to contact the Mountain Crows and hold their allegiance to the whites. He left Fort Laramie May 13 with the first supply train, escorted by Capt. Green's 2nd Cavalry, and though molested by Indians, reached Fort Phil Kearny on May 31.[10]

The day after his arrival former Judge Kinney hired as special interpreter Rafael Gallegos, who had been serving as guide at Forts Laramie and then Phil Kearny since last mentioned. Kinney then sent out a Crow

<hr/>

[9] Ibid., July 20, 1867 (for dispatch of Davis Willson).

[10] Commr. Kinney, Ft. P. Kearny, June 4, 1867, to N. G. Taylor, *Upper Platte Agency,* 1867, R892 (G-M). With Kinney on this trip was N. S. Hurd, who sent dispatches to the *Rocky Mountain News,* May 29, July 3, 17, 1867.

chief, named "Swan," to bring the Crows down to counsel with him, as Templeton first learned from the Crows on June 6. The Crows were very reluctant to penetrate so far into Sioux country, and it may have been Mitch who helped persuade them to go. They appeared at Fort Phil Kearny on June 21, and on that day Kinney also hired John Richard, Jr., as another special interpreter.[11] Kinney had been forewarned of the approaching Crows by Jim Bridger when he arrived, on June 16, with the empty supply train escorted by Capt. Green.[12]

After counseling with the Crows on June 23–24, Kinney issued them presents on the next two days and on the 27th sent them back to the Bighorn country in the charge of Richard and Gallegos, assigned to watch over them and act as mediators should they meet any whites.[13] Templeton learned of these events when Richard came in to his post from the Crow camp on July 3 for a two-day visit, but there is no mention of Mitch. Protecting the Crows turned dangerous when the hostile Sioux exploded in anger at them for having treated with the whites. Both Richard and Gallegos took refuge at the fort on July 11, telling Templeton that "they were afraid to stay longer, lest the Sioux jump them and kill them." They also gave him ominous news, already forecast by Mitch: the Sioux, now camped only 40 miles away, were boasting that they would attack Fort C. F. Smith in force before troop reinforcements, which they already knew were nearing Fort Phil Kearny, could arrive.

On July 15 some Crows came into the post, acting in a puzzling way as though concealing bad news, as Templeton noted. That afternoon Richard took "Swan" aside and extracted the secret: three thousand lodges under Red Cloud and others were now close by on the Little Bighorn, prepared to send three to four thousand warriors, fired up by the recent sun dance, to attack the small garrison at the Bighorn post and "kill us all." This third warning was enough for Capt. Burrowes.

The captain wrote a warning note, and at dusk of July 16, Templeton sent Mitch Boyer to deliver the alarm to Fort Phil Kearny, under instruc-

[11] Charles King, by letter of April 1, 1869, filed Commr. Kinney's vouchers to Rafael Gallegos for $300 pay, June 1–Aug. 3, 1867, and to John Richard, Jr., for $180 pay, June 21–July 26, 1867, *Upper Platte Agency*, 1869, R894 (G-M).

[12] Kinney to N. G. Taylor, June 17, 1867, *Upper Platte Agency*, 1867, R892 (G-M).

[13] Kinney to Sec. Browning, Oct. 7, 1867, *Investigation of Ft. P. Kearny Massacre*, R1 (G-M).

tions to ride without regard for horseflesh.[14] At this moment began another period of hazardous duty pay for the courier, which would not end until July 29. With him rode Al Leighton's brother Jim to fetch the sutler wares that had been stranded at Fort Phil Kearny. By noon of July 17 Mitch had delivered the alarm to Col. John E. Smith, the new commander of the post, who had arrived there on July 3 with troop reinforcements and an army contractor's train carrying enough new breech-loading Springfield rifles to equip the garrisons of both Forts Phil Kearny and C. F. Smith.

Only hours before Mitch arrived, Col. Smith had sent the arms train on for Fort C. F. Smith escorted by Lt. Col. Luther P. Bradley and Companies E and H, 27th Infantry. Bradley was to take command of the Bighorn post and the two companies were to augment its garrison. In response to Mitch's warning, Col. Smith sent the scout back with orders for Bradley to halt his column at Goose Creek, 22 miles out, and wait to be overtaken by Maj. David S. Gordon and Company D, 2nd Cavalry, which would be needed to escort the emptied train back to Fort Phil Kearny. Mitch delivered these orders to Bradley that night, and he and another frontiersman, William S. Parker, left the next morning. They galloped into Fort C. F. Smith at 9 P.M. on July 20, as Lt. Templeton recorded, bringing the welcome news of approaching reinforcements and improved arms. Since Mitch's extra pay continued, he must have turned back to guide in Bradley's column.

Gordon's cavalry had overtaken Bradley's waiting column, and they proceeded together. Jim Leighton must have joined the column, too, for all accounts note that someone conducted a lively trade with eager Crows, who gathered all along the trail.[15] The column marched into Fort C. F. Smith on July 23, and the next day Lt. Col. Bradley assumed command of the fort, now a five-company post. On July 24 Lt. Counselman was relieved as post quartermaster and transferred Mitch and Pierre Shane to his successor, Lt. Edmund R. P. Shurly, one of the new arrivals.[16] Since Mitch was still receiving extra pay, it can be deduced that he left again on July 24, probably carrying Bradley's report of his safe arrival. In support of this inference, it was on July 27 that Commissioner Kinney

[14] Mattes, *Indians, Infants and Infantry*, 132 (B).
[15] "Lt. Wishart's Diary, 1867," Spear, *Bozeman Trail Scrapbook*, 7 (B).
[16] "Persons Hired by Lt. Shurly at Ft. C. F. Smith, 1867" (G-RG92).

corralled the fast-riding courier and took his testimony on the Fetterman massacre.

Mitch's testimony made crystal clear what young officers and seasoned frontiersmen knew to be the simple truth: the army invasion of the Powder River country was the sole cause of Red Cloud's War, and the Indians would fight desperately until the troops abandoned the posts and closed the Bozeman Trail, at which time, and not before, they would welcome peace.[17] That was the commission's chief finding, though it would take a more prominent peace commission to ram the obvious into the heads of army brass and civil bureaucrats. Mitch's extra pay stopped on July 29, signaling his return to his home post, where he earned two whole days of rest.

Well before daylight of August 1, Gordon's cavalry left to escort the supply train back, and with it went one of the garrison companies to meet an approaching ox train and escort it back to Fort Smith on August 4.[18] Since Mitch's extra pay also spanned August 1 through 4, he probably scouted out with Gordon and back with the ox train. Rafael Gallegos took this opportunity to return to his home post, for the empty train arrived there August 3, when Kinney discharged him as interpreter and then took his testimony the next day. Rafael must have reported that Richard had left the Crows to meet his own supply train coming out from Bozeman, for Kinney discharged Richard, too, backdated to July 26, presumably the day he had left for this purpose. Thus, only hours before the Sioux were to launch an attack on the Bighorn post, it lost one transient company of cavalry, one company of its infantry garrison temporarily, and all but Pierre Shane of its Indian-wise personnel.

As background for the imminent attack, confusion about the hay contract at Fort C. F. Smith needs clarification. The district quartermaster had let the contract to A. C. Leighton and John Richard to cut hay at Fort Phil Kearny and haul it to Fort Smith at a price of $58 a ton. This agreement was cancelled, however, in favor of cutting the hay at Fort Smith at $17 a ton. It must have been this second contract to the same pair that Lt. Templeton referred to on July 12: "Richard [and Leighton] got the contract for hay." When Richard left on July 26 to meet his train coming

---

[17] See Appendix A.
[18] "Lt. Wishart's Diary, 1867," Spear, *Bozeman Trail Scrapbook*, 10 (B); also Lt. Templeton's diary.

from Bozeman, Leighton hired Don A. Colvin's wagons and crew to start the haying operation.[19] Thus it was Colvin and his men who became involved in the battle a week before Richard and crew returned.

The attack by hundreds of fired-up warriors came between 9 and 10 A.M. of August 1, not on the well-stockaded fort, but 2½ miles north, at the camp of Colvin's haying party, consisting of nine citizens guarded by Lt. Sigismund Sternberg's squad of twenty infantrymen. The camp had a flimsy stockade, but it was solidly based at ground level on heavy logs; the workers had repeating rifles, and the soldiers carried their new breech-loading Springfields. Thus the standard Indian tactic of provoking a volley and then swarming in before muzzle-loaders could be recharged would meet with a rude and demoralizing reception.

At the first Indian charge, Lt. Sternberg ordered his squad to stand outside the stockade and promptly fell dead; soon afterward his sergeant was disabled by a bullet in the shoulder. It was the haymaster, Don Colvin, with Civil War and frontier service, who immediately took command, forcing all to lie behind the heavy foundation logs and limit their fire to sure targets. During lulls between attacks he kept them busy digging in and preparing breastworks for greater protection. Under Colvin's direction, they thwarted attack after attack all that morning and afternoon, inflicting heavy casualties on the Indians but suffering few themselves; one private was killed and two more wounded, but only one citizen was hit, although the wound proved fatal.[20]

In the meantime, early that morning Lt. George W. Palmer had taken a wood train out southward toward the mountains, from which elevation he saw heavy fighting at the hay camp. Hastening back ahead of his train, he informed Lt. Col. Bradley, who did nothing until the wood train got in, under harassment, at 1 P.M., when he locked the fort gates to prevent anyone from going out. A. C. Leighton, who had been in his sutler store just outside the fort that morning, also heard the firing and saw the smoke and thronging Indians, but Bradley called him in before locking the gates.[21]

---

[19]Camp, "A. C. Leighton Interview, Feb. 23, 1914" and "Don A. Colvin Interview," in Walter Camp Field Notes (M).

[20]This summary of the Hayfield Fight is based principally on the interviews in footnote 19, above, rather than on the inaccurate reminiscences of Finn Burnett (a Leighton employee), which were reworked by R. B. David in *Finn Burnett* (B).

[21]Lt. Palmer, "Diary," as quoted in Greene, "Hay Field Fight," 30–40 (A); Camp, "Leighton Interview" (M).

Lt. Templeton at the post recorded that the Indians appeared around the hayfield at noon, but he added that "some of them came this way and threatened the wood train coming in from the mountains." Thus Templeton had not seen the Indians appear at 9 or 10 A.M., but only the move toward the wood train at noon, for he "ran out and got two or three shots at them with the new gun [a howitzer] at long range, which caused them to pause." Lt. Palmer recorded the significant fact that "up to 4 P.M., not a man had been sent to the assistance of Lt. Sternberg, nor had anyone been sent to learn his situation."[22]

After six or more hours of continual fighting, with no sign of any response from the garrison, Colvin sent a soldier, whom he deemed worthless, to make a dash on horseback for the fort, carrying a message for Lt. Col. Bradley: "If he wants his soldiers, to come out and get them; if not, he may go to hell." By sheer luck, this courier did not fall off his horse until close to the fort. He undoubtedly edited Colvin's message before delivering it to Bradley, who at 4 P.M. sent out a platoon under Lt. Shurly to investigate, but a formidable array of mounted warriors blocked his advance. Capt. Burrowes then went to his aid with two companies and the howitzer, and together they forced their way to the beleaguered hay party. Bringing back all the survivors, including wounded mules, they marched into the post at 8:30 P.M.[23]

The Annual Record of the 27th Infantry states that the twenty soldiers and twelve (?) citizens defended themselves for eight hours before relief was sent but notes that Lt. Sternberg acted with great coolness and gallantry.[24] The "record of events" on the post return at Fort C. F. Smith gives a brief account:

> On August 1 a party of 19 soldiers and 6 citizens, under command of 2 Lt. Sternberg, 27th Inf., who were guarding a party cutting hay, were attacked by a force of Indians, variously estimated at from 500 to 800. The troops were partly protected by a brush and log corral and fought heroically for 3 or 4 hours until relieved by troops sent from the Post. The Indians were severely punished and sustained a heavy loss, estimated at 8 killed and 30 wounded. With the exception of one, they

[22]Templeton and Palmer diaries.

[23]Camp, "Colvin Interview" (M). Capt. Burrowes's Official Report, Aug. 3, 1867, is quoted in full by Vaughn, *Indian Fights*, 106–10 (B).

[24]"Annual Record, 27th Inf." is quoted in full by Mattes, *Indians, Infants and Infantry*, 135 (B).

carried off all their killed and wounded. Our loss was Lt. Sternberg, one private and one citizen killed, and one sergeant and two privates wounded.[25]

Capt. Burrowes made a detailed and honest report of this relief mission, but Lt. Col. Bradley's terse report claimed that "I did not know of the fight until it had been going on for some hours."[26] Only the citizen accounts and Lt. Palmer's diary reveal flaws in the day's action.

Nevertheless, the Hayfield Fight near Fort C. F. Smith on August 1, 1867, did chalk up the first signal victory over the Northern tribes in Red Cloud's War. Mitch Boyer missed not only this engagement, but the still greater victory, known as the "Wagonbox Fight," also won by a party of citizens and soldiers near Fort Phil Kearny the very next day, August 2.

Haying resumed on August 6, when Lt. Reuben N. Fenton, with fifty soldiers and the howitzer, was assigned to keep the Indians at bay. Richard, having met his provision train coming out from Bozeman, arrived on August 8 with his crew, including Big Bat and Cy Mounts, and his partners McKenzie and Lund. They would not only strengthen the haying party, but secure the contract to cut wood, both for winter fuel and lumber to expand the post, as Big Bat told Ricker.

Mitch, having returned soon after the Hayfield Fight, complained that he had not been credited with extra pay for hazardous duty. Adjutant Templeton, on consulting his records, found that such pay had indeed been authorized, but Lt. Counselman had neither noted it on his records nor informed his successor, Lt. Shurly. Accordingly, on August 9, 1867, Lt. Col. Bradley issued Special Order No. 12, which summarized the sequence of errors and concluded: "It is therefore ordered that Lt. E. R. P. Shurly pay Mich Boyer, guide, in addition to his regular salary, an extra $5 a day while traveling from this post to the Gallatin Valley and return in May last, and the same sum for all time employed in carrying dispatches between this post and Fort Phil Kearny in June and July and . . . hereafter."[27]

Mitch was still at the post, earning no extra pay, on August 24, when

[25] "Ft. C. F. Smith Post Returns, Aug. 1867," R1190 (G-M).

[26] Bradley's Official Report, Aug. 5, 1867, is quoted in full by Mattes, *Indians, Infants and Infantry*, 136–37 (B).

[27] This order was attached to Lt. Shurly's report of persons hired at Ft. C. F. Smith, 1867 (G-RG92).

a party from the fort crossed the Bighorn in search of more stands of hay to cut. Whether they found any, Lt. Templeton forgot to say, but they did spot an unexpected herd of buffalo, and his mouth began to water when Boyer, Richard, and McKenzie bagged four of the beasts as makings for a banquet.

On August 29 courier Rafael Gallegos rode in from Fort Phil Kearny carrying orders for Lt. Col. Bradley to send word to both the hostile Sioux and the peaceful Mountain Crows to meet with a new peace commission at Fort Laramie. Templeton immediately "started Boyer and Louis Richard to the Crow camp and from there have word sent to the Sioux." Nearly two weeks passed, but on September 10 the helpful diarist recorded that "Boyer, Louis Richard and Baptiste [Big Bat] came back, bringing about a dozen of the principal Crows with them."

That is the last mention of Mitch Boyer at Fort C. F. Smith. Sometime in September 1867 he vanished, not to surface again for six months. During this hiatus a strong peace movement gained momentum and would redirect Mitch's life.

RED CLOUD'S WAR WINDS DOWN

An act of Congress, approved July 20, 1867, authorized a new and prestigious peace commission, giving it a charge both praiseworthy and formidable: to remove the causes of war with the Indians, to provide them with reservations, and to devise a plan to civilize them. Nathaniel G. Taylor, the current commissioner of Indian affairs (not to be confused with Supt. Edward B. Taylor), was appointed president and became the leader of the civilian members: lawyer John B. Sanborn, Senator John B. Henderson, and Indian Agent Samuel F. Tappan. The high-ranking military members were led by Gen. William T. Sherman and included Gen. William S. Harney (retired); Gen. Alfred H. Terry, commanding the Department of Dakota; and, later, Gen. Christopher C. Augur, commanding the Department of the Platte.[1]

---

[1] "Report of Peace Commission, Jan. 7, 1868," in Commr. Ind. Aff., *Ann. Report*, 1868, 26ff. (B).

At initial meetings held in St. Louis on August 6–7, the commission resolved that Sherman should wire his field commanders, and Taylor his Indian agents, to send runners to the various tribes to bring them into grand councils, one to be held at Fort Laramie with the northern tribes on September 13, and another to be held on the Arkansas River with the southern tribes a month later. The commission also resolved that, while waiting for the Indians to gather, it would charter the steamboat *St. John* to carry the members up the Missouri into Dakota Territory, where they could consult with Indians and examine the country for suitable reservations. Most left on this mission on August 9.[2]

President Taylor, on August 8, also engaged two special agents to manage the challenging task of drawing in and holding the hostile Sioux and friendly Crows at Fort Laramie for the council. As special Sioux agent, he secured the veteran Indian trader Geminien P. Beauvais, then concluding his duties with the preceding Sanborn Commission. As special Crow agent, Taylor engaged Dr. Henry M. Matthews, about whom a word is in order, as he has been confused with another, better-known military surgeon, Dr. Washington Matthews.[3]

A St. Louis physician, Dr. Henry M. Matthews saw service in the Civil War with Union troops from Missouri. He was surgeon to the 12th Missouri State Militia Cavalry from May 17, 1862, to March 4, 1863, and to the 51st Missouri Infantry from May 9 to August 31, 1865.[4] During the interval between, save for beginning and end gaps of a week or so, Henry M. Matthews, probably the same person, served as major and then lieutenant colonel of the 4th Missouri State Militia Cavalry.[5] After his final discharge as surgeon, he became an acting assistant surgeon (contract surgeon) for the 2nd Battalion, 18th Infantry, and as such left Fort Kearny, Nebraska, on May 16, 1866, with Col. Carrington's Bozeman Trail column.[6] At Fort Phil Kearny on August 2 he was sent to Fort C. F. Smith as its first post surgeon, giving him a year of close contact with the Crows before he and

[2] Ibid.; *New York Times*, Aug. 11, 1867 (from *St. Louis Republican*).

[3] Beauvais to Sec. Browning, Dec. 14, 1867, *Upper Platte Agency*, 1867, R892 (G-M).

[4] *Battles of the War of the Rebellion and Roster of all Regimental Surgeons*, 123, 131 (B); *One Hundred Years of Medicine and Surgery in Missouri*, 120, 126 (B).

[5] *War of the Rebellion: Official Records*, Ser. I, vol. 22, Pt. 1, pp. 254, 264 (for first mention of Maj. Matthews, Apr. 16, 1863); vol. 48, Pt. 2, p. 35 (for last mention of Lt. Col. Matthews, Apr. 5, 1865) (B).

[6] Mrs. Carrington, *Absaraka*, 43 (B).

Jim Bridger were ordered on June 11, 1867, to report to Fort Phil Kearny.[7] From there he soon left for St. Louis, where Commissioner Taylor engaged him.

Leaving St. Louis by rail, the two special agents overtook the *St. John* at St. Joseph, Missouri, and when the boat halted a few hours at Omaha on August 16, they landed to start west on the new Union Pacific tracks, while the peace commission continued upriver to Fort Sully.[8] Reaching Fort Laramie on August 22, Beauvais remained to exert repeated but futile efforts to lure the hostile Sioux down for the council.[9] Dr. Matthews continued to Fort C. F. Smith, where on September 12, Lt. Templeton registered his return "as Special Agent of the Peace Commission to treat with the Crows."

It had been Gen. Sherman's wire from St. Louis to his commanders that had resulted in sending Mitch Boyer out to the Crow camp. Mitch had brought in a dozen Crow chiefs to Fort C. F. Smith on September 10, but the next day, when Lt. Col. Bradley formally invited them to proceed down to Fort Laramie to meet the new peace commission, "they declined on account of it being too far," as Templeton recorded. Dr. Matthews received this troublesome news on his arrival at the post the next day.

On that September 12 the doctor hired Pierre Shane as his interpreter, Pierre presumably being released for that purpose. It took a month, however, to persuade the Crow chiefs to make the long and dangerous trip through Sioux country to treat once again with a commission, for not until October 13 did Templeton record their departure for Fort Laramie. Pierre left with them, for Lt. Wishart recorded meeting him and the doctor on the trail the very next day.[10] John Richard apparently followed them, as he was now interested in freighting for the special agent.

Louis L. Simonin, a Parisian correspondent, described in detail the council the Crows held with the peace commission at Fort Laramie on November 12, naming both Pierre Chêne and John Richard, Jr., as Dr. Matthews's interpreters.[11] The hostile Sioux, of course, never made

[7] "Post Returns, Ft. C. F. Smith, Aug. 1866, June 1867," R1190 (G-M); "Post Returns, Ft. P. Kearny, June 1867," R910 (G-M).

[8] *New York Times*, Aug. 27, 1867 (from *Cincinnati Gazette*).

[9] Beauvais to Sec. Browning, Dec. 14, 1867. See note 3, above.

[10] "Lt. Wishart's Diary, 1867," Spear, *Bozeman Trail Scrapbook*, 17 (B).

[11] Simonin, *Rocky Mountain West in 1867*, 103 (B).

an appearance, and even the Crows refused to make a treaty, but their speeches nudged some of the commissioners one step closer to accepting the reality that peace was contingent on abandoning the Bozeman Trail forts and restoring the Powder River country to the Indians.

Sometime between September 10 and 24 Mitch Boyer vanished from the records, not to reappear for six months. The first date is when Templeton last mentioned him, and the second is when the lieutenant noted that Iron Bull, a Crow chief, had been hired to carry mail twice a month to Fort Phil Kearny, signaling Mitch's absence. The post returns had dropped Mitch's position by September 30, but not Shane's. The quartermaster reports should give dates of discharge or release, but on September 5 Lt. Shurly had transferred both employees to his successor, Lt. Walter Halleck, whose reports for 1867, unfortunately, are missing.

The 1868 reports of Lt. Halleck are preserved, however, and register Pierre's continuous employment, not on his original contract of April 1, 1867, but on a new one initiated on October 8, 1867.[12] Yet Pierre had left, for John B. Sanborn issued him a pay voucher on November 30, 1867, for services as interpreter at five dollars a day from September 12 to date, plus ten cents a mile for 327 miles of travel from Fort Smith to Fort Laramie (Pierre furnishing his own horse); Pierre signed the voucher by his "mark," witnessed by Dr. Matthews.[13]

Thus we know Pierre's whereabouts, but where was Mitch during this six months? One might presume that he, too, was serving the peace commission, but its records, which name a horde of employees, are utterly silent on Mitch. He could have wintered with the Crows, but nothing was there to draw him away from his job. A better guess is that he received news of his father's death at the hands of Indians (which *may* have occurred at this time) and, as the oldest son, left to look after the family.

Having left Fort Laramie on November 27, Dr. Matthews returned to Fort Phil Kearny on December 10,[14] bringing provisions and hoping to pull off the miracle that had eluded Beauvais—luring in the hostile Sioux. On January 2, 1868, he held a disappointing council with some semihostiles, which drew criticism from the post officers because he refused to tell the Indians that the army would abandon the military posts;

[12] "Persons Hired by Lt. Halleck at Ft. C. F. Smith, 1868" (G-RG92).

[13] Voucher, Sanborn to Shane, Nov. 30, 1867, *Mont. Suptcy.*, 1869, R489, fr. 741 (G-M).

[14] Matthews to Taylor, Dec. 11, 1867, *Upper Platte Agency*, 1867, R892 (G-M).

but as the commission had not yet agreed on this course, Matthews had no authority in the matter. He then left for Washington,[15] where he arrived in February, to receive instructions.

On February 19 John B. Sanborn wrote to Nathaniel B. Taylor, outlining instructions for Dr. Matthews. Sanborn wanted the doctor ordered back to Indian country, empowered to requisition provisions for the Indians from military posts, the costs to be borne by the commission. A key paragraph read:

> He should be instructed to induce all the Indians, if possible, in that section of country to attend councils to be held by the Peace Commission at Fort Laramie on or about May 11, 1868, and to attend them in person. He should be authorised to inform the Indians that the *military posts on the Powder River Road will be abandoned* in the spring, if they remain at peace and meet the commissioners as requested.[16] [Italics added.]

That is the earliest record found proving that the civilian members of the peace commission had fully determined to take the step needed to meet the congressional charge "to remove the causes of War." They apparently won over Gen. U. S. Grant, head of the army, for on March 2 Grant wrote Gen. Sherman to abandon the posts. On March 7 Sherman forwarded this letter, with his reluctant endorsement, to Gen. C. C. Augur, commanding the Department of the Platte.[17] This about-face by the military was announced publicly in the *Cheyenne Leader* of March 16.

About this time Matthews had reached Fort Laramie and would pull into Fort Phil Kearny on March 28. Two days later he left with a small escort and wagon train to reach Fort C. F. Smith about April 3. Armed with authority to announce the abandonment of the trail forts, he would encounter little trouble this time in gathering delegations of Crow, Cheyenne, and Arapaho chiefs. Templeton noted his departure for the Fort Laramie conference on April 12.

Many of the officers manning the Bozeman Trail posts had long recognized the counterproductive nature of their mission.[18] Since they had oc-

---

[15]Matthews to Taylor, Jan. 13, 1867, and Jan. 29, 1868 (from Ft. Fetterman), *Upper Platte Agency,* 1868, R893 (G-M); Greene, "Lt. Palmer Writes," 27–29 (A).

[16]Sanborn to Taylor, Feb. 19, 1868, *Upper Platte Agency,* 1868, R893 (G-M).

[17]Olson, *Red Cloud,* 71–72 (B).

[18]Bradley to Matthews, Jan. 10, 1868, *Upper Platte Agency,* 1868, R893 (G-M); "Lt. Wishart's Diary, 1867," Spear, *Bozeman Trail Scrapbook,* 25 (B); Greene, "Lt. Palmer Writes," 15n (A).

cupied the trail, the number of soldiers killed in the attempt to keep it open had exceeded the number of citizens who had ventured to use it. They had sacrificed more than one hundred lives and untold millions of dollars merely to *close* the trail. However eager they were to fight for gain, they had grown disgusted with fighting for loss. Now alerted to the concessions the commission would offer the Indians, they willingly cooperated in inducing the tribes, even the most hostile, to halt the mutual destruction.

At this hopeful moment, April 1, 1868, Mitch Boyer abruptly emerged from limbo as post interpreter at Fort Phil Kearny, still commanded by Col. John E. Smith. The date suggests that Mitch had come out from Fort Laramie with Dr. Matthews. The post quartermaster, Lt. Charles H. Warrens, was present to engage the new interpreter, but not Col. Smith to authorize it, for the latter would not return from a visit to the Bighorn post until April 3. The paperwork was still unfinished when Mitch was called on for his first duty. As related by Lt. George P. Belden, Company D, 2nd Cavalry, a large party of Sioux warriors, painted, feathered, and shouting defiance, appeared on a hill just north of the fort on April 8:

> Col. Smith ordered the cavalry to saddle up and stand to horse [inside the fort], and then taking Boyer, the interpreter, he rode out of the fort and approached the hill where the Indians were. He wished to go up to the savages, but Boyer advised him not to do so, and yielding to his advice, Col. Smith told him to call to the Indians to come down and talk, which he did, but for some time got no reply. Advancing a few steps, the colonel cried out, "How!" Someone on the hill answered, "How!" The colonel then directed Mitch to repeat that he wished to talk to them. A chief and three or four warriors rode down near the colonel and talked.

With Mitch interpreting, the colonel found that he was confronting some of Red Cloud's most hostile warriors, including that chief's own son. They had come, not in submission, but to ask why the troops had not kept the promise to evacuate the posts. Col. Smith could only reply that he was preparing to leave and would go as soon as ready, provided the warriors committed no further depredations. At that moment the cavalry began marching through the gates of the fort. The apoplectic colonel could only watch the untrusting warriors smirk and ride off.[19]

[19] Brisbin, *Belden, the White Chief*, 399–402 (B).

Apparently, this trial of Mitch's mettle and savvy reminded Col. Smith to issue Special Order No. 27, dated April 9, 1868: "The services of an Indian interpreter being indispensable for the present, Lt. C. H. Warrens, 27th Inf., a.a.q.m., is authorized to employ M. Boyer in that capacity at the compensation of $5 per diem and one ration; and as he has been employed since the 1st inst., he will be born on the rolls from that date."[20]

Most of the peace commission members (Pres. N. G. Taylor would not join them, because of family sickness) reached Fort Laramie on April 10, with a written treaty already in hand, not a word of which would be changed. The military and civil members had failed to reconcile their differences, as betrayed by the ambiguities and outright contradictions in the document. It set aside for the exclusive use of the Indians a permanent Sioux Reservation, covering all of present South Dakota west of the Missouri and an adjacent thin strip of North Dakota. Another article specified that no part of this reservation could be ceded in future, except with the consent of three-quarters of all adult male Sioux. This stricture would force the whites to launch a war eight years later.

The treaty detailed a plan to civilize the Indians, promising to ration them for four years while they transformed themselves from roaming hunters to dry-farmers. It promised to build an agency, staffed by an agent, engineer, farmer, teachers, and so on; to allot farms, animals, farm equipment, and seeds. Though the commissioners may not have known it, this plan was a brutal denial of reality. The Indian heritage made women the gatherers of supplementary plant food, while the men were the providers of the dietary staple, meat. If Indian men could become successful farmers of *prime* agricultural land in, say, five generations, they could become successful stockraisers in one or two, in the absence of buffalo. But in four years of being crowded close to an agency to receive rations, they would become demoralized beggars.

The treaty did make one concession by abandoning the military posts on the Bozeman Trail. It also promised to restore the Powder River country, west from the reservation border to the Bighorn Range, to the Sioux as their own "unceded territory," where they could roam and hunt without trespass or molestation by whites. A separate article, however, flatly con-

[20]"Persons Hired by Lt. C. H. Warrens at Ft. P. Kearny, April 1868," with attached Spec. Order No. 37 (G-RG92).

tradicted the "no trespass and molestation" clause. Of which article do you suppose the Indians were fully informed? And was it a mere oversight by sharp lawyers that the unceded territory lacked a northern boundary? Or that it carried no stricture on cedability? [21]

Gen. Sherman, who was not present for the councils with, nor the signings by, a single Sioux band, unilaterally decided that the army would not honor any treaty clause that he did not like. In direct violation of what the Sioux had so carefully been told, he issued orders prohibiting them from trading anywhere but on their permanent reservation and announced that the army would consider any Indian found off the reservation to be hostile and treated accordingly. [22] These violations and contradictions shape an excellent example of how a peace treaty can preprogram the next war.

The chiefs and headmen of only three bands of Sioux signed the Sioux Treaty of 1868 at Fort Laramie. The first to sign were the Brules (and Laramie Loafers) on April 29; some Oglalas signed on May 25 and the Miniconjous on the 25th and 26th. After the last of the commissioners had left (May 28), five more Oglalas signed about May 29 and June 4; their names, however, were added to those of the Yanktonais. The Yanktonais were one of the seven other Sioux bands that signed on July 2 at distant Fort Rice on the Missouri River, with no date or place given. [23] Red Cloud would not come in to sign at Fort Laramie until November 6, long after the trail forts had been evacuated. To him the evacuation signaled a victorious end to Red Cloud's War.

Dr. Matthews brought his delegations of Mountain Crows, Northern Cheyennes, and Northern Arapahos into Fort Laramie on May 1. Their treaties, though separate, were patterned after the Sioux treaty, so far as the civilizing plan was concerned, but with no concessions. The Crow treaty bounded the permanent Crow Reservation on the north and west by the Yellowstone River, on the south by the Montana border, and on the east by the 107th meridian, which runs just east of the Bighorn River.

---

[21] Kappler, *Indian Affairs*, 2:998–1007 (B).

[22] DeMallie, "Scenes in Indian Country," 47 (A); Spring, "Old Letterbook," 287, 291 (A); Manypenny, *Our Indian Wards*, 295–96 (B).

[23] A key to the confusion in signers, witnesses, dates, and places of these treaties may be found in Geren [Gereu] to Taylor, Ft. Laramie, July 1, 1868, in Commr. Ind. Aff., *Ann. Report*, 1868, 252–54 (B); Gray, "Mrs. Picotte-Galpin," 20 (A).

This area was only a portion of the country the Crows had roamed over, and they objected especially to losing the Powder River country, so recently seized by the Sioux. It seemed to the Crows that the whites granted concessions to their enemies, but not to their friends. Nevertheless, eleven Mountain Crow chiefs signed their treaty on May 7, 1868.[24]

It should be noted that the northern division of the Crow tribe, the River Crows, was not a party to this treaty. The Indian Office sent out a special agent, William J. Cullen, who made a treaty with the River Crows on July 15, 1868, at Fort Hawley, a trading post on the Missouri a little above the mouth of the Musselshell. Their reservation, shared with the Gros Ventres of Montana, was located north of the Missouri.[25]

The treaty for the Northern Cheyennes and Arapahos assigned them to no reservation of their own but left them free to choose that already granted to their southern cousins by the Medicine Lodge Treaty of October 1867 or the new Sioux Reservation. Eleven Cheyennes, but only two Arapahos, signed this treaty on May 10, at Fort Laramie, but on June 17 twenty-six more Arapahos signed. Somehow, these additional names were attached to the Sioux treaty, instead of the Cheyenne-Arapaho treaty, thus adding to the legacy of careless confusion.[26]

During these treaty activities, when the traffic of Indian parties passing Fort Phil Kearny must have been heavy, Mitch Boyer was undoubtedly called on often to act as interpreter. Troops and trains were moved frequently, and even into June the hostiles kept annoying the posts to speed evacuation. This activity should have kept Mitch busy, although no records have been seen that flesh out these bare bones. Fort Phil Kearny was evacuated at the end of June and Fort C. F. Smith at the end of July, but just prior to these events Dr. Matthews rescued both Mitch and Pierre from joblessness.

The commission had released the doctor from its service on May 27 at Fort Laramie but had ordered him out to the Crows while he awaited instructions from the Indian Office. Templeton recorded his arrival at Fort C. F. Smith on June 14 with Capt. Wishart and family; Templeton then left with Dr. Matthews on June 18 and reached Fort Phil Kearny on June 22, where they remained into July. Lt. Warrens discharged Mitch

[24]Kappler, *Indian Affairs*, 2:1008–11 (B).
[25]Cullen to Mix, July 18, 1868, *Mont. Suptcy.*, 1868, R488, fr. 978 (G-M).
[26]Kappler, *Indian Affairs*, 2:1012–15 (B).

Boyer there on June 25, and Capt. Wishart discharged Pierre Shane at Fort C. F. Smith on June 30. Before leaving for Washington, Dr. Matthews engaged both to live with the Crows, gather them on their new reservation, and keep them peaceful. Reaching Washington by July 25, the doctor requested instructions from the Indian Office, but since this is the last heard from him, he was undoubtedly discharged.[27]

The evidence for this new employment for Mitch and Pierre appears in a letter of November 30, 1869, from Gen. Alfred Sully, then superintendent of Indian affairs in Montana, to the Indian Office:

> He [Pierre Shane] also states that he and Mich Boyer were employed by Dr. Matthews, formerly Agent for the Mountain Crows, at $5 a day each, for the purpose of remaining with the Crow Indians and preventing them from joining the Sioux against the whites. They state they were employed for the months of July, August and September, 1867 [*sic*, 1868]. On the last of September they were employed by Maj. LaMotte; they were paid by him, but during the time they were employed by Dr. Matthews they were not paid at all; thus $460 is due each of them.[28]

Clearly, the pair had not been paid, because Dr. Matthews had been discharged, and this plea for delayed payment also failed, because of the erroneous year cited, for the government auditor found the commission voucher by which Pierre had been paid in the fall of 1867.

The reference to Maj. LaMotte, however, establishes the correct date as 1868. Bvt. Maj. Robert S. LaMotte, Capt., 13th Infantry, commanded Fort Ellis, established near Bozeman on August 27, 1867. To implement the 1868 treaties, Congress bypassed the Indian Office by appropriating funds to Gen. Sherman to be disbursed through military channels. By his Special Order No. 4, of August 10, 1868, Sherman assigned the management of the Mountain Crows to Capt. LaMotte.[29] The latter's appointment "to supervise the removal of the Crow Indians to their reservation" was announced from Bozeman on August 28, 1868.[30]

Mitch and Pierre were contentedly shepherding the Crows north and west onto their new reservation, but as fall of 1868 approached, with no

[27] Sanborn to Matthews, May 27, 1868, and Matthews to Taylor, July 25, 1868, *Upper Platte Agency*, 1868, R893 (G-M); "Persons Hired by Lt. Warrens and by Lt. Wishart, June, 1868" (G-RG92).

[28] See note 13, above, for letter and voucher.

[29] Gen. Order No. 4, in Commr. Ind. Aff., *Ann. Report*, 1868, 85–86 (B).

[30] *Helena Herald*, Sept. 3, 1868.

word from Dr. Matthews about establishing the promised agency, the pair rode in to Fort Ellis, seeking information and probably a little pay. On meeting Capt. LaMotte and learning that he was now in charge of the Mountain Crows, they promptly engaged to him as interpreters, with orders to carry on as before.

This outcome was revealed on October 21, when Capt. LaMotte appeared in Helena to purchase provisions for issue to the Crows:

> The Crow Indians, who are now on their reservation south of the Yellowstone, had dispatched two interpreters, Pierre Shane and Michael Boyer, to Fort Ellis to ascertain at what time the agent for the tribe would visit them. Capt. LaMotte has made an appointment to visit them on November 10, with a view of carrying out the provisions of his commission from Gen. Sherman.[31]

Later, in a letter of May 17, 1869, LaMotte reported he had employed Pierre "Chien" as interpreter "for about eight months past," confirming that the pair had come in on "the last of September,"[32] as Pierre had claimed, although he gave the date incorrectly as 1867.

Both Mitch and Pierre were now destined to live among the Crows, whom they would well serve.

[31] Ibid., Oct. 22, 1868.
[32] LaMotte to Parker, May 17, 1869, *Mont. Suptcy.*, 1869, R489, fr. 359 (G-M).

ADOPTION BY THE CROWS

Mitch Boyer and Pierre Shane dutifully assembled the Mountain Crows on the Yellowstone near the mouth of Boulder Creek (present Big Timber, Mont.), which the treaty specified as the location of their new agency, some 60 miles east of Bozeman. There Capt. LaMotte, commander of Fort Ellis as well as Crow agent, met his wards on November 11, 1868, with his train of annuity goods in the charge of Hugh Kirkendall. In council he arranged with them to meet again in December, but not so far out, and to send "Shane or Boyer" to notify him of the date and place. He added, "If you want a trader to come out, let me know, and I will bring one who will not cheat you." Chief Blackfoot promised to send Boyer in and undoubtedly asked for a trader, so necessary to the Crows' existence.[1]

[1] *Montana Post*, Nov. 27, 1868; *Helena Herald*, Dec. 3, 1868 (for Harry O'Neill letter from Ft. Ellis, Nov. 20).

On December 20 Capt. LaMotte, accompanied by Hugh Kirkendall and his supply train, as well as C. B. Clark, his presumed trading partner, again met the Crows, this time at the Yellowstone ferry, much closer to Fort Ellis. There he counseled with them, using Mitch and Pierre as interpreters, and then distributed his goods. His report enclosed two communications (unfortunately missing), one from Boyer and the other from a delegation of chiefs, both asking that Henry R. Horr, Capt. LaMotte's civilian clerk, be appointed Crow agent. As there was dissatisfaction with the choice of goods, C. B. Clark had to drive out some beef cattle to satisfy the Crows, with whom both he and Kirkendall spent another week.[2]

The request for Henry Horr as agent bore no fruit, for back on September 19 the captain had advertised for a Dr. Monroe Atkinson to contact him.[3] The contact having been made, LaMotte reported on January 8, 1869, that he had engaged Dr. Atkinson, an early Montana gold-rusher with experience as an agency physician to other tribes, "to live with the Crows" and provide them with medical care. But in effect, he became the captain's deputy to see that "my orders are carried out, especially as regards the intrusion of white men on the reservation." His explanation revealed who these intruders were, and more:

> Persons representing themselves as agents of the Northwestern Fur Co. have been endeavoring to persuade the Crows that they were badly treated by the government, and that their true friends were the traders at Fort Benton, trying to get them to leave the reservation and go there. The two interpreters, Shane and Boyer, are ignorant men, having no influence at all with the Indians and are distrusted by them. . . . I should have someone there to represent me that the Indians respect, which is the case with Dr. Atkinson. . . .[4]

The traders working out of Fort Benton, especially the many independent outfits, were notorious whiskey peddlers, but the fact that their customers were the River Crows, who were not LaMotte's responsibility, raises the suspicion that the captain was covering up an effort to enforce the trading monopoly of Kirkendall and Clark, with whom he may have

[2]LaMotte to Adjt. Nichols, Dec. 24, 1868, *Upper Platte Agency*, 1869, R894 (G-M); *Montana Post*, Jan. 25, 1869.

[3]*Helena Herald*, Sept. 24, 1868.

[4]LaMotte to Adjt. Nichols, Jan. 8, 1869, *Upper Platte Agency*, 1869, R894 (G-M).

had an interest. The tone of his reference to Shane and Boyer strengthens this suspicion; uneducated they were, but ignorant of trade monopolies that gouged Indians they were not. Their sin may have been to take the side of their friends, the Mountain Crows.

In mid-May of 1869 Capt. LaMotte issued another trainload of goods to the Mountain Crows on the Yellowstone, again accompanied by Kirkendall and Clark. Correspondent Davis Willson, who attended the distribution, mentioned Pierre Shane, Chief Blackfoot, and traders Kirkendall and Clark, whom "the Great Father" had sent to them. It is significant that for the first time there is no mention of Mitch.[5]

Although military supervision of the reservation terminated on June 30, 1869, this move only partially restored control to the Indian Office, for in May army officers, left unassigned by the consolidation of regiments, had been appointed as Indian agents. Lt. Erskine M. Camp, delayed by low water in the Missouri, would not reach his Crow agency until November. Gen. Alfred Sully, appointed superintendent of Indian affairs in Montana, traveled overland to reach Helena in July, but to cover the interim he had to appoint civilian agents. As acting agent for the Crows, he chose an enterprising merchant of Bozeman, Leander M. Black, whose previous contacts with Indians had been rather casual, but he would prove honest, perceptive, and diligent.[6]

The Crows had signed their treaty more than a year before, yet they still had no agency, resident agent, instructors, services, or equipment, and worst of all were rudely refused ammunition, much needed for hunting and to defend themselves, as well as the whites, from the continual raids by the Sioux and Blackfeet. In view of their long-standing friendship and loyalty to the whites, the Crows were not alone in failing to understand such treatment. Agent Black brought them their first ray of hope in mid-August, when he was introduced to a delegation of Crow chiefs at Fort Ellis by its new commander, Lt. Col. Albert G. Brackett, who had arrived on July 1 to reinforce the post with four companies of his 2nd Cavalry.[7]

Of this first meeting, Black reported that the chiefs had brought along their own interpreter, undoubtedly Pierre Shane, and continued:

[5] *Montana Post*, May 21, 1869.
[6] Sully to Parker, Aug. 4, 1869, *Mont. Suptcy.*, 1869, R489, fr. 516 (G-M).
[7] Brackett, "Trip through Rocky Mountains," 243 (A).

The principal chiefs handed me a copy of their treaty and asked why it had not been complied with. . . . They said they had come for the last time to see if they were to have a home and trader, as they had no powder or knives and had been told lies. . . . They say if they go to any of the forts to buy powder, they are ordered off and treated badly, which they have been . . . . They know the treaty just as well as you or I do. I was astonished at the good sense they manifested. . . .

Perceiving the validity of these complaints, Black reassured the chiefs by saying that their goods were on the way; that he would bring a sawmill and build their agency that fall; that he and Sully would come out to meet them in forty days; that he had been told that the Crows were good people, with whom he had been ordered to deal fairly. After the chiefs retired to ponder his words, they sent a message saying they were satisfied.[8]

At Fort Ellis on September 1, Sully contracted with Black to build the first Crow agency, and loading the sawmill, they crossed the Yellowstone on the 9th. Heeding the chiefs' protests that an agency at Big Timber would drive the buffalo from their best hunting grounds, Sully chose a site at the mouth of Mission Creek, 10 miles below present Livingston and 35 from Fort Ellis. Black's crew completed the buildings before winter weather, including a stockade with howitzers in two opposite bastions. Although officially called Fort Ely S. Parker, after the current Indian commissioner, the agency would be known as Mission Agency.[9]

Sully, accompanied by the belated Lt. Camp and his annuities, met the Crows at their new agency on November 23. Sully's report reveals that the Crows were learning how to educate whites; they refused to accept the selection of annuity goods until Sully promised to add what they really needed: "125 pairs of good blankets, some tobacco, knives, ammunition and brown sugar." Again, at none of these events of 1869 is there a mention of Mitch Boyer.[10]

Pierre Shane would remain as agency interpreter for years, but Mitch had obviously given up his job by the spring of 1869 to become inconspicuous for a year. This time, however, there is no doubt as to his whereabouts and activities. He was living with the Crows, courting a young full-

[8]Black to Parker, Aug. 21, 1869, *Mont. Suptcy.*, 1869, R489, fr. 128 (G-M).

[9]Sully to Parker, Sept. 1, 21, 1869, *Mont. Suptcy.*, 1869, R489, fr. 577 (G-M).

[10]Ibid., Dec. 8, 1869, R489, fr. 756; Camp to Sully, Aug. 1870, in Commr. Ind. Aff., *Ann. Report*, 1870, 197 (B).

blood Crow woman, whom he would wed before the year was out and live with for the rest of his life, thus making a permanent affiliation with her tribe. She was known to her people as Magpie Outside (or Magpie Out of Doors), but would become Mary Boyer to whites. They apparently married in the fall of 1869 and had their first child, also called Mary, within a year. Such preoccupation with matters of the heart and domesticity nicely accounts for Mitch's quiet year.

The available information on Mitch's marriage comes from the memoirs of Ohio-born Thomas H. LeForge, who had moved to Bozeman with his parents in 1864 and would become Mitch's close friend among the Crows. Tom, at age twenty (he became so on July 19, 1870), fell in love with another Crow woman, named Cherry, and married her, Indian style, soon after a new agent arrived (agent F. D. Pease, on Nov. 14, 1870). Thus Tom's marriage occurred about December 1870. The significance is that Cherry's close friend, Magpie Outside, *already married to Mitch*, was the matchmaker between Tom and Cherry. Mitch and wife made available to the newlyweds a spare room in their own house (not lodge). This recollection is consistent with Mitch's marriage by the fall of 1869 and might have confirmed it, had Tom mentioned that his hosts already had a baby at this time. He did mention that his own firstborn appeared in about nine months and that Mitch's firstborn was "older." [11]

There is another hint to support Mitch's approximate dates. On July 17, 1870, the former interim agent, Leander M. Black, applied for a trading license with the Mountain Crows, bonded by Bozeman merchant Lester S. Willson and Charles W. Hoffman, formerly with the Northwestern Fur Company but now interested in the Fort Ellis sutlership. The license named two employees, Michel Boyer and Carl Stanley. It is likely that Mitch accepted such employment the better to support his wife and newborn, or about-to-be born, daughter. It would also allow him to remain close to home for a time. [12]

Tom LeForge related an incident (undated, but probably spring of 1873) that is relevant here, for it provides a rare glimpse into Mitch's family feelings. Mitch and Tom were out together on an agency mission:

> We found a two-year-old Indian girl wallowing over the dead and decaying body of an Indian woman. The child was wild as a wolf. It

[11] Marquis, *Memoirs* (LeForge), 34–37 (B).
[12] *Register Books of Indian Trading Licenses*, (G-RG75).

ran, but we caught it. It hit, scratched and fought like a young tiger. It was starved to a pitiful skeleton. Its hands were like claws and its shrunken face resembled that of a sick monkey. The woman was evidently Sioux, as indicated by her decorations and beadwork, and the child kept screeching "mother" in Sioux, which the half-Sioux Mitch understood. We considered what to do, a hundred miles from the agency, with this sort of captive.

"By jolly, Tom, I'm not going to leave this baby here," Mitch finally declared. He petted the little one and finally got it quieted. Then he made some weak tea, soaked a cracker, and fed the starving midget.

"Mitch, my medicine tells me we'd better leave this country and go back to the agency," I announced. He agreed.

On the way back we encountered some white emigrants on the Yellowstone. A childless elderly couple begged us to give them this Sioux orphan. Mitch had made up his mind to keep it, but I persuaded him to give it to these white people.[13]

Mitch had chosen well when he married Magpie Outside, for she proved to be a fine wife and mother, big-hearted, loyal, generous, and respected among her people for the rest of her long life. The Boyer and LeForge families became very close, and both men were adopted into the tribe. They came to an understanding that, should anything happen to one husband, the other would look after both families. When that unfortunate day came, Tom would take Magpie Outside and her girl and boy into his family, and when Cherry died soon afterward, Tom would marry Magpie Outside and together they would raise all four of the children.[14]

Just as Mitch started working at the trader's store in July 1870, the Crow Reservation, like the others established in 1868, was restored to the control of the Indian Office, as army officers had been barred from filling civilian positions. On October 13 Joseph A. Viall arrived in Helena to replace Gen. Sully, and on November 14, Fellows David Pease, a former Indian trader with the Northwestern Fur Company and long married to a Crow woman, arrived to replace Lt. Camp.[15] Supt. Viall joined agent Pease at the Crow agency on November 25, bringing the following witnesses to his councils and the distribution of annuities: Maj. Eugene M. Baker, 2nd Cavalry, commanding Fort Ellis; William H. Wheeler, U.S. marshal of Montana; and the Rev. S. G. Lathrop, superintendent of Meth-

[13] Marquis, *Memoirs* (LeForge), 76–78 (B).

[14] Ibid., 279–80.

[15] Commr. Ind. Aff., *Ann. Report*, 1871, 409 (Viall to Clum, Sept. 15) and 423 (Pease to Viall, Aug. 31) (B).

Mitch Boyer. Courtesy of the Custer Battlefield National Monument.

odist missions in Montana. For once the selection of annuity goods met with the approval of the Crows.[16]

Mitch remained in the trade, for on October 26, 1871, Clendennin & Company, consisting of George Clendennin, Jr., former sutler at Fort Ellis, and Leander M. Black, applied for a new license, again naming "Mitz" Boyer, as well as Peter Koch, Clendennin's former clerk, as employees. Only five months later Charles W. Hoffman applied for a similar license on February 27, 1872, naming among his employees "M. Boyer and P. Shane."[17] This is Mitch's last appearance in the trading records, and within months he began serving the agency when not scouting for the army.

In the spring of 1872 George Owen and James Banks were trapping on Mission Creek, upstream toward the mountains. Banks was tending camp while Owen was checking traps on May 19, when Indians sneaked up on the camp, killed Banks, and stole the horses. On returning, Owen found his partner's body and set out for the agency, whence the alarm was carried to Fort Ellis. Lt. Edward J. McClernand led a platoon of 2nd Cavalry to the agency, where agent Pease engaged Mitch and Owen to guide them in pursuit of the miscreants. They started down the Yellowstone on May 22, but after a few days the trail faded and the cavalry turned back. Nonetheless, Mitch, under the agent's orders to identify the guilty tribe, soon picked up the trail again and with Owen followed it up Pryor Creek. Agent Pease's report continues:

> They came suddenly on a party of Indians, and on getting within hailing distance, they recognized them as Bannacks. The Indians, by refusing to have any communication with them, convinced them that something was amiss. Mr. Owen . . . discovered one of the Indians leading a horse which he recognized at once as his own; also a saddle and other articles taken at the time of his partner's murder.

> As the Indians were in superior numbers and well armed, the pair was compelled to let them pass. [Other accounts say Mitch questioned them as to where they had been and got the sullen answer that they had visited a Crow village; Mitch checked this claim on his return and found it false.] While passing, they recognized four additional horses stolen from Banks at the time of the murder. Mr. Bougier, an old

[16] *Mont. Suptcy.*, 1870, R490, fr. 783 (Viall to Parker, Dec. 3) and fr. 807 (for *Helena Herald* clipping on annuity distribution) (G-M).

[17] See footnote 12, above.

mountaineer, recognized the Indians as Bannacks and would know them anywhere.

Both furnished their own horses and subsistence and have been out 21 days [May 22–June 11] at an expense of $4 per day each, amounting to $84 each. I hope the department will sustain my action, undertaken . . . to convince the people of the Gallatin Valley that the Crows had nothing to do with the murder.[18]

That summer of 1872 the Northern Pacific Railroad sent out two parties of engineers, with military escorts, to the Yellowstone, one from Fort Ellis to survey eastward and the other from Fort Rice on the Missouri to survey westward; they planned to meet at the mouth of Powder River. This route, it may be noted, ran right through the Sioux's "unceded territory." The Fort Ellis party also intended on its return to strike north to the Musselshell River and survey its valley westward to its source. Its engineering party headed by J. A. Haydon (not to be confused with Dr. Ferdinand V. Hayden, who was simultaneously leading a geological expedition from Fort Ellis to Yellowstone Park). Maj. Baker commanded the military escort of four companies of his 2nd Cavalry from Fort Ellis and four companies of 7th Infantry sent down from Fort Shaw. Maj. John W. Barlow, staff engineer from Chicago headquarters, kept the expedition journal.[19]

The expedition camped on July 30 opposite the Crow agency, where Maj. Baker hoped to recruit a party of Crows to serve as volunteer scouts. When this attempt failed, he engaged "Mich Boyer, a half-breed Sioux, though living among the Crows at their agency, as guide to the expedition." It was the expedition quartermaster, Lt. Joshua W. Jacobs, 7th Infantry, who hired Mitch at one hundred dollars a month from August 1 to September 30.[20] A small group of citizens also joined as hangers-on, including Tom LeForge and George A. Herendeen,[21] both of whom would serve with Mitch in 1876 on Gibbon's campaign.

---

[18] Pease to Viall, June 19, 1872, *Mont. Suptcy.*, 1872, R493, fr. 157 (G-M); *Bozeman Avant Courier*, June 20, 1872.

[19] Barlow, *Journal of Survey, 1872* (G-CSS). Unless otherwise indicated, the account of this survey is based on this journal.

[20] "Persons Hired and Transferred by Lt. Jacobs to Capt. Forsyth, Sept. 1873, Ft. Ellis" (G-RG92). Incidentally, Forsyth had hired Peter Koch, whom we shall meet again, as guide at Fort Ellis from Nov. 1, 1871, to April 30, 1872.

[21] Marquis, *Memoirs* (LeForge), 83 (B); Noyes, "Interview with George Herendeen" (M).

The column traveled down the north bank of the Yellowstone, being forced occasionally to detour northward to circle bluffs and badlands. Maj. Barlow was much impressed with Boyer's knack for finding good water whenever needed and for locating easy passages for the supply wagons across rough terrain. On August 12 they reached a point opposite the mouth of Pryor Creek, near present Huntley, Montana. From this camp the next morning the engineers tramped 7 miles downstream, where they found the stakes left by a survey of the previous year before returning to camp.

About 3 A.M. of August 14 the crack of gunshots and the pounding of hooves startled the camp awake. Under cover of darkness, a war party of Sioux and Arapahos, estimated at four hundred to a thousand, had stolen up close to the camp, where most lay quietly in the brush while a small number dashed for the horse herd. The alert herders fired a volley and drove the animals into camp, and the twenty-six guards and nearly as many civilians rushed between the herd and the Indians. Their heavy fire drove the thwarted thieves back to cover.

It took half an hour to deploy the four infantry companies into good positions on the right front and a squad of cavalry to reinforce the guards and civilians on the left front. They were posted just in time to detect the main body of Indians sneaking from right to left through the thickets in a move to capture the entire horse herd. A devastating hail of bullets forced these Indians to hug the ground and, when it continued, to crawl for the bluffs in the background. There they stayed to deliver long-range shots and make defiant, brave runs along the troop lines. When this activity ceased by 9 A.M., a cavalry reconnaissance confirmed that the attackers were in full retreat, but no orders came to launch a pursuit.

The site of this lively engagement became known as Baker's Battleground. The Indian casualties, as usual, were unknown, but one sergeant was killed and three privates wounded; one civilian was fatally wounded. Some beef cattle, mules, and horses were also run off and killed. Rumors began to circulate that Maj. Baker had been so befuddled by drink that his delayed, indecisive, or absent orders had robbed his force of a decisive victory.[22]

[22]For more on Baker's fight, see *Helena Herald*, Aug. 22, 1872; *Chicago Tribune*, Aug. 31, 1872 (from *Helena Gazette*, Aug. 16); Lt. Bradley, "Journal of 1876," 167–71 (A); Topping, *Chronicles*, 92–93 (B).

That same afternoon, the surveyors resumed their work, but for the next five days they made slow progress, as the country became more rugged and bluffs crowded the riverbank. The infantry guarded the base camps, while the cavalry tried to protect the strung-out surveyors, who lost much time tramping to and from the base camps. These problems threatened to grow, for it would become necessary to ford to the south bank of the rising river. Although Maj. Baker insisted that his force could furnish adequate protection (*if* he could get his cavalry across the river), Haydon announced on the evening of August 19 that he would abandon further efforts to survey down the river and turn north to the Musselshell. To even the score, rumors circulated that Haydon was afraid of Indians, but Maj. Barlow sanctioned the decision as "just and wise, in consideration of all the circumstances."

On the morning of August 20 Mitch guided the column north over a barren divide to reach the east-flowing Musselshell three days later. At this camp a heavy rain fell, prompting a several days' rest to recruit worn stock. On the 26th Mitch led the cavalry and engineers downriver to the east, promising to show them that the great bend of the river, where it turned sharply north toward the Missouri, was not as far east as their faulty maps placed it. In 7 miles he showed them the valley where the river was already running north. The engineers promptly triangulated the several visible peaks in order to correct their defective maps.

While the surveyors were slowly working back up the Musselshell, an exhausted and starving courier from Fort Ellis rode into camp on September 5, without his mail. Expecting the column to have continued down the Yellowstone, he had proceeded to a point opposite the mouth of the Bighorn on the morning of August 29, when Indians surprised him in camp. Abandoning provisions and mailbag, he outran the pursuit by changing to and from his extra mount. Luckily, having fled back upriver, he spotted the expedition trail heading north and followed it to the Musselshell. This courier was Edmund Bradley, whom Capt. L. Cass Forsyth, the Fort Ellis quartermaster, had hired as courier at $7.50 a day from August 24 to September 12.[23]

[23]Capt. Forsyth, at Ft. Ellis, engaged Edmund Bradley by Spec. Ord. No. 119 to proceed to the command on the Yellowstone and return, Aug. 24 to Sept. 12, 1872 (G-RG92). The *Bozeman Courier*, Sept. 12, was concerned that Bradley had not yet returned.

On September 15 the surveyors started up the South Fork of the Musselshell (present Martindale, Mont.) and soon crossed the divide into the valley of the north-flowing Smith River. There, from what was dubbed "Camp Separation," the four infantry companies marched north for home at Fort Shaw on the 25th. The next morning three cavalry companies rode south and then west over Bridger's Pass to reach Fort Ellis on the 29th. The remaining company escorted the slower surveyors into the same post by October 1, the day Mitch Boyer was transferred to Capt. Forsyth as the post guide at seventy-five dollars a month. His service there with various scouting detachments, until discharge on October 31, was probably welcome, as a party of Sioux and Arapahos had raided the Crow Agency on September 21, running off all its stock and killing Dr. Frost, two Crow women, and a baby.[24]

Sometime during the week of October 6–12 Mitch guided a platoon of cavalry out to the apprehensive agency. As they were about to escort a party of civilians back to Bozeman, a "Sioux" alarm was sounded, though it proved to be a group of Crow women approaching the agency. Some wag wrote an unflattering description of the cavalry officer's attempts to control the mule he was riding but at least mentioned Mitch as the guide.[25] A real disaster struck at 2 A.M. on October 30, when fire destroyed Fort Parker and the agency employees' quarters.[26] Agent Pease jury-rigged quarters for the winter and then rebuilt the agency. Mitch may have resumed trading for Charles W. Hoffman that winter.

On March 4, 1873, Dr. James Wright, a devout Methodist, made his first visit to the Crow agency as the new Montana Indian superintendent. To his moral dismay, he found "several employees living with Indian women out of lawful wedlock." His orders to agent Pease to correct this situation within thirty days led to a flurry of nuptial ceremonies, including that of Tom LeForge and Cherry. The doctor also ordered that all unemployed whites hanging around the agency and Indian camps be banished from the reservation on twenty-four hours' notice. Pease did not fail to point out that this ban omitted the hundreds of gold miners, prospectors,

[24]Pease to E. P. Smith, Sept. 28, 1873, in Commr. Ind. Aff., *Ann. Report*, 1873, 248 (B).

[25]*Bozeman Avant Courier*, Oct. 19, 1872.

[26]See footnote 24, above.

and hangers-on who had preempted the southwest corner of the Crow Reservation.[27]

Wright also reported on March 13 that, because whiskey peddlers were demoralizing the River Crows on the Missouri, he had "ordered Pease to send a messenger to these Indians to come to . . . the Crow Agency, and to subsist them there."[28] Although Pease reported on March 31 that he had sent such a messenger, he may have wisely delayed the mission for better weather and the receipt of extra provisions to feed the River Crows. If so, the messenger may have been sent during Mitch's next spell of agency employment, which ran from April 22 to June 9, 1873.[29] His duties during this period are unknown, but he may have been the messenger. Tom LeForge, giving no date, said that he accompanied Mitch on a trip to bring in the River Crows but failed to find them. It was on this trip that the pair found the little orphaned Sioux girl, as earlier related.

[27] Wright to E. P. Smith, Mar. 10, 1873, *Mont. Suptcy.*, 1873, R496, fr. 317 (G-M); Pease to E. P. Smith, Mar. 31, 1873, *Mont. Suptcy.*, 1873, R495, fr. 469 (G-M).

[28] Wright to Smith, Mar. 13, 1873, *Mont. Suptcy.*, 1873, R496, fr. 351 (G-M).

[29] *Register Books of Indian Agency Employees* (G-RG75); Zed H. Daniels, as acting agent, discharged Mitch on June 9, during Pease's sixty-day leave in the East.

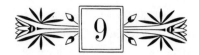

THE CROWS SURVIVE A REMOVAL THREAT

The invasion of the mountainous southwest corner of the Crow Reservation by gold miners and prospectors had drawn continual vocal resentment from the Mountain Crows. These complaints brought a special commission in the summer of 1873 to induce both the Mountain and River Crows to give up their separate reservations and accept one, much reduced in size, in the Judith Basin, lying to the north between the Musselshell and Missouri rivers. The three-man commission consisted of Felix R. Brunot (of the Board of Indian Commissioners), former Gen. Eliphalet Whittlesey, and Superintendent James Wright, with Thomas K. Cree as their secretary.[1]

On his way out, Brunot had apparently wired ahead to Agent Pease to send out messengers to assemble both divisions of the Crows at Mission

---

[1] "Report of Commission to Crows, 1873," in Commr. Ind. Aff., *Ann. Report*, 1873, 113–17 (B).

Agency for treaty councils. When Brunot and Cree reached Bozeman on July 7, 1873, they learned that Pease had already sent out Mitch Boyer and Tom LeForge to bring in the Mountain Crows and Barney Bravo (or Prevot) to bring in the River Crows, but that they probably would not arrive until July 22.[2] Leaving Cree to keep track of things, Brunot left on a vacation trip to Yellowstone National Park.[3]

Tom LeForge left a long account of his adventures with Mitch on this mission. Omitting the year, he said they started out "early in July."[4] The pair headed south (July 2) up Mission Creek toward the mountains, where rugged country and timber afforded concealment. Turning eastward along the foothills, they paralleled the Bozeman Trail. They spent one night (July 5?) on a peak of the Pryor Mountains and the next morning studied the country for Indian signs, such as agitated buffalo herds. By noon they had spotted the smoky haze of an Indian village far to the north near the Yellowstone. That afternoon they started in its direction down Pryor Creek. While resting in hiding, they were passed by a war party of Sioux, whose singing revealed to Mitch that they were after the Crows.

Turning northeast to avoid these Sioux, Mitch and Tom rode all night. The next morning, from a hilltop "where Toluca now stands" (now abandoned, but 20 miles west of Hardin, Mont.), Mitch again spotted some approaching Indians, who proved to be Nez Perces out hunting from the Crow village on the Yellowstone at Pompey's Pillar. Together, they all rode down a creek (apparently Fly Creek) about 20 miles to the Crow village they had been seeking (on July 7?, the day Brunot reached Bozeman).

When Mitch and Tom delivered to the Crows their summons to a council, Chief Blackfoot told them that his camp had earlier driven a large Sioux village from the Pryor Mountains eastward to and across the Bighorn River, and since then Crow war parties had been annoying and keeping track of this enemy village, as it moved down the east bank of the Bighorn. Mitch told of seeing the Sioux war party coming down Pryor Creek to attack the Crows. The next day Mitch and Tom moved with the

<hr/>

[2] Ibid., 115; Telegram Brunot to E. P. Smith, July 8, 1873, *Mont. Suptcy.*, 1873, R494, fr. 133 (G-M).

[3] *Helena Herald*, July 17, 1873 (Bozeman dispatch).

[4] The ensuing reconstruction of Mitch's mission is based on Marquis, *Memoirs* (LeForge), 84–98, with occasional attributions to Blackfoot's interview with the commission, in

two thousand Crows and two hundred Nez Perces up the Yellowstone to the mouth of Pryor Creek, as "a better place to fight the Sioux." All spent the next day preparing for the battle.

The next morning (July 9?) the expected large force of Sioux warriors made its appearance, both sides eager for a fight. For the first hour of combat the two forces made alternate charges, doing little damage. These attacks were then interspersed with lulls, during which individual warriors demonstrated their courage and skills by making brave runs. Both Mitch and Tom participated in these daring capers. Late in the afternoon the Sioux began to fall back, but detecting this withdrawal the Crows swarmed in and turned it into a rout. They pursued the disorganized Sioux for as long as ponies could run, far into the night and all the way to Fly Creek (according to Blackfoot). The triumphant Crows straggled back all that night and next day, flourishing scalps, captured guns, and ammunition, and driving captured horses.

Since the battle and the preceding weeks of conflict had interrupted the Crow's buffalo hunt for food, lodgepoles, and robes to trade, Mitch and Tom could only remain with the village while it completed these essential chores before starting for the agency. They all now moved up Pryor Creek to camp several days (July 14–16?) at the foot of Pryor Mountain, where they found buffalo, feasted on roast ribs, and swam in the "warm waters of the creek." They then moved southwest up Clark's Fork (even to Shoshone River in Wyoming, according to Blackfoot), where they made another buffalo hunt (July 21–22?). They were finally ready to make the long trek northwest to the Yellowstone and camped at the mouth of Boulder Creek (July 27?). Here the Crows in council decided to send an advance party of headmen, under Chief Blackfoot, to the agency, and with them went Mitch and Tom.

Meanwhile, Secretary Cree at Bozeman reported on July 24 that "two runners have now been out hunting the Crow Indians 23 days [and so had left early on July 2] and not a word has been heard from them or the Indians." By July 28 Brunot had returned from Yellowstone Park, and Gen. Whittlesey and Dr. Wright joined him the next evening. At Fort

---

Commr. Ind. Aff., *Ann. Report*, 1873, 123–25 (B). Dates are inserted in parentheses; the start on July 2 is firm, but others with question marks are estimated from map distances and travel times.

Ellis on July 30 the commission held its first meeting to plan its strategy.[5] The date and place of this meeting, at which Agent Pease was probably present, have special significance, as will emerge.

With George Herendeen as one of their drivers, the commission reached Mission Agency on the evening of July 31 to find that Chief Blackfoot's advance party had arrived, probably that morning. On August 1 the commissioners interviewed Blackfoot, who gave them an account of driving the Sioux off the reservation, Mitch's arrival at Pompey's Pillar, the victorious battle with the Sioux, and the delay to hunt, all confirming LeForge's story. Since the commission wanted all the Crows to attend the treaty councils, the chief agreed to return to Boulder Creek and bring them all in as quickly as possible. They all rode in on August 9.[6]

The following note that Agent Pease wrote to the Indian Office on August 5 completes the documentation of Mitch and Tom's mission:

> I transmit herewith for your approval triplicate vouchers in favor of Mitch Bougier, Tom LeForge and Bernard Bravo, amounting respectively to $150, $150, and $50, on which I have paid 50% on account, the men being in very modest circumstances and very much in need of money. . . . The men furnished their own riding and pack animals and traveled through a country infested with hostile Sioux.[7]

As Pease had no way of knowing how long these missions would take, he offered pay by the day, clearly the standard five dollars, confirming that Mitch and Tom were out thirty days (July 2–31, inclusive). As they received half-pay in cash on August 5, they must have returned with Blackfoot's advance party. Barney Bravo's lesser pay implies that he returned with the River Crows in ten days. A former private in the 27th Infantry, Bravo (or Prevot) had deserted from Fort Phil Kearny back on May 9, 1867, "painted and dressed in Indian costume" with a party of Crows.[8] He would not only spend his life with the Crows, but would also serve with Gen. Gibbon's Montana column in 1876.

Formal treaty councils opened on August 11 with a reading of the

[5] Cree to Clum, July 24, 1873, *Mont. Suptcy.*, 1873, R494, fr. 309 (G-M); *Helena Herald*, July 31, 1873 (for Brunot's return); *Bozeman Avant Courier*, Aug. 1, 1873 (for arrival of Whittlesey and Wright); "Report of Commission to Crows," 115 (for first meeting at Ft. Ellis), footnote 1, above.

[6] Noyes, "Interview with George Herendeen" (M); "Report of Commission to Crows," 113 (for arrival at agency) and 123–25 (for interview with Blackfoot), footnote 1, above.

[7] Pease to E. P. Smith, Aug. 5, 1873, *Mont. Suptcy.*, 1873, R495, fr. 317 (G-M).

[8] Murray, *Military Posts in Powder River Country*, 92 (B).

treaty, which proposed to buy the present reservation and move the Mountain and River Crows to the Judith Basin. Brunot daily told them that, since the whites would inexorably overrun the Yellowstone Reservation, the Crows would be better off if they sold it now and moved to the Judith Basin, where few white men came. The Crows daily protested that the basin was far too small to support both divisions of the Crow Nation. The impasse lasted for days, while Mitch Boyer and Pierre Shane, who had to interpret all the speeches, grew as confused as the Crows. Finally, Brunot authorized Agent Pease to conduct a delegation of chiefs to Washington, where loftier officials might apply verbal balm to the chiefs' wounds. On August 16 a large number of chiefs and headmen agreed to the still-mysterious document; Pierre and Mitch signed, as interpreters, by their "marks," and Nelson Story and Charles W. Hoffman, the Crow traders, as witnesses. At noon the commissioners hastily decamped, and George Herendeen, who drove for Brunot and Cree, later recalled that he had whipped his team into a lively pace to whisk them away from some resentful Crows.[9]

At the treaty councils the Crows had expressed their complete satisfaction with Agent Pease, but they did not know that back on July 22 the Indian Office had received orders "to suspend Fellows D. Pease as Crow agent, to be replaced by James Wright, whose former position as Montana Indian Superintendent has been abolished." Not until September 17 could Dr. Wright close out his Helena office and take over the Crow agency from Pease. He promptly installed Robert W. Cross, his son-in-law and former office clerk, as his right-hand man under the title of agency farmer and appointed Horace Countryman, a rather shady character, as agency miller. Retaining Pierre Shane as interpreter, he added two familiar names to his labor force: Tom LeForge (Sept. 20, 1873, to Mar. 26, 1874) and George Herendeen (Sept. 20 to Feb. 14).[10] These unexpected changes not only aggravated the dissatisfaction of the Crows with their treaty, but launched a comic opera rivalry between Pease and Wright.

Brunot had promised the Crows that Pease would conduct their dele-

[9] "Report of Commission to Crows, 1873," 119–25 (for Crow treaty and signatures) and 125–43 (for transcript of councils), footnote 1, above.

[10] *Mont. Suptcy.*, 1873, R494, fr. 211 (G-M) (Sec. Delano to E. P. Smith, July 22, 1873); ibid., fr. 473 (list of Crow agency employees, Sept. 20, 1873); Pease to E. P. Smith, Sept. 28, 1873, in Commr. Ind. Aff., *Ann. Report*, 1873, 248 (B) (for agency turnover date).

gation of chiefs to Washington, but rather than discharge him from the service, the Indian Office was allowed on September 20 to appoint him special agent to bring the Crows to Washington. On the 25th, Dr. Wright wired a plea that he deserved this honor, but two days later Pease spirited the delegation away, taking Barney Bravo and Samuel R. Shively as interpreters.[11] The first round thus went to Pease.

The removal of the Crows to a new reservation in the Judith Basin entailed selecting a location for a new agency within its confines. This became the second bone of contention, for since July 30, when Brunot had held his first strategy meeting at Fort Ellis, Pease had anticipated that he would carry out this mission in conjunction with Lt. Gustavus C. Doane, 2nd Cavalry, the fort's expert on the Judith Basin. The later Doane-Pease report reveals that "before the Crow Treaty was made, Lt. Doane, in conversation with Mr. Brunot at Fort Ellis, and in Dr. Wright's presence," described "the exact spot" he considered "the best place in the Judith Basin for an agency."[12]

Now that Pease had left for Washington, Dr. Wright decided to send his own party to choose the site he had heard Lt. Doane describe, and before Pease could return. Within days he arranged with the Crow traders, Nelson Story and Charles Hoffman, to establish a trading post in the basin. By October 2 the traders had engaged Peter Koch, the reliable and experienced young Dane, to build, stock, and manage this post. By the time Koch's party was ready to move out, Dr. Wright had also organized his agency party, with Robert Cross in charge and Horace Countryman as surveyor.[13]

Peter Koch's heavy bull train and Robert Cross's light outfit left the Crow agency together on November 6, and the next day Mitch Boyer appeared on the agency roll as laborer, to remain so until February 28, 1874.[14] Knowing the Judith Basin even better than Lt. Doane, Mitch

[11] *Mont. Suptcy.*, 1873, R494, fr. 266 (Delano to Smith, Sept. 20); R497, fr. 45 (Wright to Smith, Sept. 25); R496, fr. 210 (Pease to Smith, Sept. 22, for Sept. 27 departure date) (G-M).

[12] Doane and Pease, "Report, Feb. 19, 1874" (M).

[13] The ensuing account of the Cross mission and building of Koch's post is based on "Report of R. W. Cross, Nov. 26, 1873," and Wright's covering letter, *Mont. Suptcy.*, 1873, R497, fr. 719 and 715, respectively (G-M); Peter Koch, "Diary, Oct. 27, 1873–Mar. 18, 1874" (M); Cone, ed., "Trading Expedition among the Crow Indians" (Koch's letters to his fiancée), 407–30 (A).

[14] *Register Books of Indian Agency Employees* (G-RG75).

guided the caravan down the north bank of the Yellowstone, then turned north to skirt the eastern base of the Crazy Mountains to reach the Musselshell River. By this time the ponderous bull train had been left to follow, but the leaders passed into the basin through Judith Gap and then veered northeast. It was November 14 when they camped on a northwest-flowing branch of Judith River, known to the Indians as Trout Creek, but soon to the whites as Big Spring Creek. Mitch had led them straight to the spot suggested by Lt. Doane.

While awaiting the arrival of the slow bull train, the leaders spent several days exploring the valley before selecting and then surveying the exact agency location, adjacent to present Lewiston, Montana. It was on the west bank of Big Spring Creek, just north of the mouth of Little Casino Creek. Koch also chose a site for his trading post on the south bank of Little Casino Creek right opposite the agency. This post was sometimes referred to as "Story's Fort," although Koch called it "Fort Defiance" in a letter of December 24 and then "Fort Sherman" in a later one of February 28, 1874.

When the bull train pulled in on November 19, Koch lost no time in setting his crew to work cutting and hauling timber for a stockade and buildings for his trading post. On the 22nd, Cross and Countryman started back for Mission Agency, where the former prepared his official report, dated November 26, mentioning "Mitch Boyer" as his "guide, well acquainted with all the intervening country from here to the Basin, and with the Basin itself." Dr. Wright's letter of transmittal (Nov. 29) specified that Cross had been "accompanied by an intelligent half-breed guide." Since Mitch was still in agency employ, he presumably guided his party home, where he remained, though without mention, until the end of February.

Meanwhile, in Washington, Pease had succeeded in inducing the War Department to issue orders (via St. Paul on Nov. 6) detailing Lt. Doane to his service. He also persuaded the Indian Office to prepare a letter of instructions (dated Nov. 12) for him to lead some Crow chiefs to the Judith Basin and there examine its resources and select a site for the new Crow agency, and to submit a full report to the Indian Office. On returning to Bozeman from Washington on December 5, Pease found this letter awaiting him but probably also learned that Dr. Wright had already completed the mission. Pease had no recourse but to proceed with the task as instructed, however superfluous it was, but he and Lt. Doane did not get off until December 10.[15]

Dr. Wright was still one jump ahead of Pease, for on December 8 he sent a courier "to the Judith Basin and Missouri River as Messenger to the River Crows to inform them that their annuity goods were ready for them" at Mission Agency. These River Crows at this time were still in the charge of Special Agent William H. Fanton, whose agency was at Fort Belknap on Milk River north of the Missouri. The courier Dr. Wright had selected was Tom Stewart, an educated white man who had been filling contracts at the agency and had a Crow wife. He started out alone on a mule loaded with grub and a sack of mail for Koch's post.[16]

On reaching the Musselshell the fourth day out (Dec. 11), Stewart was attacked by hostile Indians and, losing his mule, had to foot it to Koch's post (arriving Dec. 14, by Koch's diary). Re-outfitting himself, he hired John Rogers and two horses and left (Dec. 17, by Koch's diary) for the River Crow camps on Judith River, where he learned that their ponies were too few and too winter-poor to come to the Yellowstone until spring brought new grass. Here he had a run-in with Agent Fanton, who threatened to clap him in irons for trying to steal his Indians, but standing his ground, Stewart discovered that the River Crows refused to go north of the Missouri with Fanton and instead asked that Dr. Wright deliver their annuities to them at Koch's post. Stewart left that post on January 1, 1874, but promptly met the approaching Doane-Pease expedition and returned to the post with Pease. When he left for Mission Agency is not of record, but not until January 27 did he finish his report, which Dr. Wright forwarded the next day. The agent would later act on Stewart's recommendation that some of the River Crows' annuities be delivered to the Judith Basin.

Although Mitch Boyer remained on the agency payroll until the end of February, there is no evidence whatever in Stewart's report, nor in Koch's writings for this period, that Mitch accompanied Stewart. It has been claimed, however, that Mitch did guide the Doane-Pease expedition, al-

---

[15]Doane-Pease report, note 12, above; *Bozeman Avant Courier*, Dec. 12, 1873 (for Pease's return to Bozeman).

[16]The ensuing account of Stewart's mission is based on "Report of Tom Stewart, Jan. 27, 1874," and Wright's covering letter, *Mont. Suptcy.*, 1874, R500, frs. 589 and 583, respectively (G-M); Peter Koch, "Diary" and letters (see footnote 13, above).

though its lengthy report never mentions Mitch, nor do the relevant Koch sources. The claim is apparently based on the assumption that the Cross and Doane-Pease expeditions were one and the same, despite the fact that they did not even overlap. Furthermore, the animosity between Pease and Wright fairly guarantees that the latter would not loan his own employee to serve the former. A brief outline of the Doane-Pease expedition will make all this clear.

The expedition personnel included Lt. Doane, an escort of seven 2nd Cavalrymen, and two teamsters; the civilians included Pease, trader Hoffman, Z. H. Daniels, Sam Shively, and for a portion of the trip, Barney Bravo. They left Fort Ellis on December 16 and spent the 19th to 22nd at Mission Agency, where they could induce only two Crow chiefs to accompany them, because of bitter antagonism between Pease and Wright. The party spent January 2 to 14 at Koch's post, exploring and confirming the agency site already selected by Cross. Bypassing the agency, they returned to Fort Ellis on January 30.[17]

A major event of February 1874 was the departure of the famous Yellowstone Wagon Road and Prospecting Expedition, which organized at Bozeman and left its rendezvous point at the eastern base of Bozeman Pass on February 11, already 125 men strong and growing. It passed Mission Agency about February 13 and picked up several recruits there, including George Herendeen, who resigned his position on February 14. Mitch Boyer and Tom LeForge, however, did not join the adventurers. The expedition proceeded down the Yellowstone beyond the mouth of the Bighorn, then cut a large circle south up the Rosebud and westward to the ruins of Fort C. F. Smith. On this circuit they encountered angry Sioux warriors in vastly greater strength than themselves but won a series of signal victories. The real objective was to find gold, but they saw no colors whatever. They straggled in to Bozeman again in the forepart of May, and on the 11th George Herendeen resumed his agency job until June 10, when he left to roam the Yellowstone National Park for the summer.[18]

By March, Nelson Story and Charles Hoffman had perceived that the

---

[17] Doane-Pease report, footnote 12, above.

[18] For the best account of this expedition, see Hutchins, "Poison in the Pemmican," 8–25 (A). For Herendeen's recollections of his summer in Yellowstone Park, see Noyes, *In the Land of Chinook*, 105–6, which misdates it 1873 but correctly names some of his companions from the Crow agency.

trading prospects at their Judith Basin post were fading fast, but they found a way to get rid of it while retaining their trade at Mission Agency, as recorded in the following news item: "T. L. Dawes, who has been engaged in business in Bozeman for the past eighteen months, has bought out Story and Hoffman at Judith Basin, and left for that place last Sunday [Mar. 1]. Mr. Dawes has been in the Indian trade for many years."[19] Other squibs reveal that William Dawes, a brother, who had spent the winter hunting and trapping on the Yellowstone, would later join T. L. in this trading venture.

Also on March 1, the day T. L. Dawes left to take over his new post, Mitch Boyer's employment status at Mission Agency was changed from laborer to messenger, and at this same time Agent Wright responded to Tom Stewart's earlier suggestion by sending Robert Cross to deliver a portion of the River Crow annuities to the Judith Basin. That Dawes, Mitch, and Cross reached Koch's post together is revealed in Koch's diary. The Dane was no less disappointed in his trade than his employers and so on March 12 recorded the unexpected arrival of "Coop [Cross], Dawn [Dawes], and Pick [Mitch] from the agency." The diary transcriber, here as elsewhere, was baffled by unfamiliar proper names written in Danish script.

For the next three days, while Koch was busy taking inventory, his diary turns blank, but it resumes briefly on March 16: "Left [Fort] Sherman in a dense fog and storm." He filled the gap and properly identified Dawes, however, in a letter to his sweetheart, written at Bozeman on March 24: "Story and Hoffman sold out their post in the [Judith] Basin to Mr. Dawes, and as soon as he came out, I turned everything over to him and came up [to Bozeman]." A newspaper item confirms this account and adds that Koch reached Bozeman on March 23.[20]

Before Koch had left on March 16, Cross, undoubtedly taking Mitch as his guide and interpreter, started on a 100-mile circuit of the River Crow camps along the Missouri to announce that part of their annuities were awaiting them at what had now become Dawes' Fort. Most of the camps began moving there, but not a most destitute one, whose chief confessed to a compelling addiction to the firewater peddled by the Missouri River traders. It was probably around March 25 at Dawes' Fort that

[19] Bozeman Avant Courier, Mar. 6, 1874; also April 3, 10 (for Wm. Dawes).
[20] Ibid., Mar. 27, 1874.

Cross issued his annuities and some much-needed provisions to the assembled River Crows. He also held councils with the chiefs, naming Mitch Boyer and A. P. Fox, Koch's former employee, as his interpreters.[21]

During Mitch's absence, trouble was brewing at Mission Agency, for Agent Wright had received a telegram warning him that some hostile Sioux, whom the army had driven north from Wyoming, might threaten his agency. As the Crows were then scattered all over the reservation, and the agent was scarcely the heroic type, he called on March 5 for a hundred troops and a generous supply of arms and ammunition to protect the agency.[22] When this appeal brought no response, he decided to call in all the Mountain and River Crows for a grand council to decide how best to thwart a Sioux onslaught. On March 14 he reported: "I this day dispatched two Indians to the Judith Basin to invite the River Crows to the council, and from there to return by the Mountain Crow camps and urge them to come in. These two, together with Mitch Boyer, the guide and messenger on the regular payroll, will, I hope, be able to collect the Crows on the reservation, at or near the agency."[23] The two Indians thus dispatched on March 14 were Bear Wolf, a Mountain Crow chief, and Pretty Lodge, a River Crow, whom Peter Koch had earlier sent to the agency with a mail. Apparently, they were to pick up Mitch, already in the basin, and bring in the Mountain Crows for the defensive council.

In the councils Cross and Mitch were holding with the River Crows at Dawes' Fort on our estimated date of March 25, Cross reported the presence of Bear Wolf and Pretty Lodge, who had brought Dr. Wright's invitation to join the Mountain Crows in fighting the Sioux. This prospect brought eager gleams to the eyes of the River Crows, but since their ponies were still winter-poor, they could not join their cousins on the Yellowstone until late spring. Cross also gave written authority to four of the chiefs to seize and destroy any whiskey brought to their camps, but not to injure the smugglers.[24] The final result was that Dr. Wright's grand defensive council never materialized, but neither did any Sioux threat to Mission Agency that spring.

Mitch presumably guided Cross back to Mission Agency, where the

[21] "Report of R. W. Cross, April 5, 1874," and Wright's covering letter, *Mont. Suptcy.*, R500, frs. 734 and 636, respectively (G-M).

[22] Wright to Smith, Mar. 5, 1874, *Mont. Suptcy.*, 1874, R500, fr. 652 (G-M).

[23] Wright to Smith, Mar. 12, 1874, *Mont. Suptcy.*, R500, fr. 679 (G-M).

[24] See footnote 21, above.

latter dated his report April 5 and Dr. Wright forwarded it ten days later, quoting Mitch as confirming Cross's charge that the clandestine traders who plied the River Crows with whiskey obtained it from the Missouri traders. As of March 3, Mitch's name was dropped from the agency pay-roll for nearly six weeks, during which time he may have joined Chief Blackfoot's band for a spring hunt, taking his family, probably numbering four by this time with the addition of a son named Tom.

On learning that the Judith Basin was to be reserved for Indians, Mon-tana citizens abruptly developed a keen interest in that country. Fort Ben-ton had never been a dependable head of steamboat navigation of the Missouri, because of long stretches of rapids and shallow water that started some 50 miles below the mouth of the Judith, above which the Missouri made a wide swing to the north. The long-neglected solution was to establish a steamboat landing a little above the mouth of the Mussel-shell and construct a wagon road across the Judith Basin directly to Hel-ena. Realizing that the new Crow Reservation would close out this option, the Diamond-R freighting firm was already laying out the Carroll Trail from Helena (and a branch from Bozeman) to a freight landing called Carroll (after Matt Carroll, a proprietor of the firm), located near the mouth of Little Rocky Creek. Both were completed in the spring of 1874, and the army detailed troops to protect the road and escort freighters over it.

Among these troops was Capt. Constant Williams's Company F, 7th Infantry, which marched out from Fort Shaw on April 18, 1874, and, picking up the Carroll Trail, reached Big Spring Creek in Judith Basin on May 10. There the captain established a summer post, called Camp Lewis, to guard the trail. His daily itinerary sketches show Camp Lewis located on the very meadow chosen by Cross for the new Crow agency, opposite Dawes's store.[25] William W. Alderson, of Bozeman, now Indian agent at Fort Peck and a faithful diary-keeper, traveled home from Carroll in a buggy driven by George W. ("Club-foot George") Boyd. He spent the night of May 12 and the next day at Fort Dawes being entertained by Mr. Dawes and noted that Company F, 7th Infantry, was camped close by.[26]

[25] Koury, *Guarding the Carroll Trail*, 13–14 (for Capt. Williams's report) and 41–50 (for Williams's itinerary sketches) (B).
[26] W. W. Alderson, "Diary, 1874" (M). For more on "Club-foot George," see Gray, "George W. Boyd" (A).

Blackfoot's band of Crows returned from its spring hunt in the forepart of May, and on May 12, whether by coincidence or not, Dr. Wright restored Mitch Boyer to his payroll as messenger, so to serve until well into August. Then, on June 8, the agent sent a notice to T. L. Dawes that the Indian Office had ordered that all traders whose posts were not adjacent to a functioning agency were to forfeit their permits to sell arms and ammunition.[27] He chose Mitch as the messenger and further ordered him to wait there for the delivery of the remaining annuities for the River Crows and then distribute them. The traveling correspondent of the *Helena Herald*, "Judge" Van H. Fisk, who spent June 23 to 26 at Camp Lewis, described the situation:

> Near Camp Lewis is Story's Fort, a trading post run by the Dawes Bros. The River Crows do considerable trading here, seldom going to their regular agency [Fort Belknap], even for annuities. Mitch Boyer, an intelligent half-breed, is now here, awaiting the arrival of a train of annuities dispatched hither by Agent Wright, which annuities Mitch is to distribute to the River Crows. . . . Camp Lewis is almost on the very site selected for the proposed new agency for the Crows, but the belief prevails that the change will not—as it certainly should not—be made.[28]

Fisk's account ends with the implication that Congress had not yet ratified the Crow treaty of 1873 and with the conviction that it should not. At the same time, Dr. Wright was reading the handwriting on the wall, for he reported on June 24: "The locating of the wagon road from Helena to Carroll is changing things. If the Government decides not to remove the Crows from the Yellowstone Reservation, immediate steps should be taken to move the agency farther from the reservation line. There are good locations 40 to 60 miles east of here."[29]

While Mitch was patiently waiting, George A. Beidler, young brother of famed "X" Beidler of early Montana days, passed west over the Carroll Trail to reach Helena by July 21 and reported:

> The country around Camp Lewis is alive with River Crows, their whole force being mustered there to receive annuities, which have been forwarded to that point for distribution. The Mountain Crows had

[27] Wright to T. L. Dawes, June 8, 1874, *Mont. Suptcy.*, 1874, R500, fr. 986 (G-M).
[28] *Helena Herald*, July 16, 1874.
[29] Wright to E. P. Smith, June 24, 1874, *Mont. Suptcy.*, R500, fr. 947 (G-M).

also begun to arrive, reporting all their bands en route from the agency. The entire absence of Crows from Mission Agency is doubtless the reasons the Sioux have recently been so bold and troublesome in that area.[30]

There had indeed been repeated Sioux raids about the agency throughout July, which kept Dr. Wright in a dither and may well have delayed the shipping of annuities to Mitch. The agent again called for troops and hired extra hands to guard the agency night and day. Among them were Tom LeForge (July 14 to Aug. 31) and John "Soos" Louis (Juan Jesus Luis? July 1 to Aug. 31, and Sept. 8 to 30), a member of a large family of mixed Indian and Mexican blood, all adopted into the Crow tribe.[31] The strait-laced Methodist agent was also annoyed by the white men living on the reservation with their Indian wives. He despised them and repeatedly asked authority to ban them from the reservation, naming names. Some were undesirables, but others were his trusted employees, whose Crow wives were the only Indians who would accept any of the blessings of his brand of civilization and whose children furnished the only pupils for his agency school.

Presumably, Mitch finally distributed the delayed annuities and returned to Mission Agency. There, on August 15, the River Crows began coming in, until they numbered eighty-nine lodges by August 22. On this date Mitch resigned, or was discharged, and Dr. Wright gave Addison M. Quivey, not then on his payroll, full credit for bringing in these River Crows; Tom LeForge, though an agency guard, said he accompanied Quivey on this mission and made no mention of Mitch.[32]

A clue to what may have befallen Mitch came on September 17, when Wright complained of four reservation whites whom he accused of smuggling whiskey, adding that "they get drunk themselves and give Mitch Boyer, a half-breed, whiskey and get him drunk."[33] This charge was particularly exasperating, for in contrast to the River Crows, the vast majority of the Mountain Crows shunned liquor. I have previously recited remarks that Mitch was no teetotaler, but this is the first specific instance in which

[30] *Helena Herald*, July 23, 1874.

[31] Wright's report of agency employees to Sept. 30, 1874, *Mont. Suptcy.*, R500, fr. 1234 (G-M).

[32] Wright to E. P. Smith, Aug. 22, 1874, *Mont. Suptcy.*, R500, fr. 1129 (G-M); Marquis, *Memoirs* (LeForge), 79 (B).

[33] Wright to Smith, Sept. 17, 1874, *Mont. Suptcy.*, R500, fr. 1176 (G-M).

he "fell from grace," as Dr. Wright might have put it. It was not a chronic problem, however, and I have sought but not found a single instance in which Mitch, drunk or sober, exhibited belligerence or meanness. His temperament must have been ever sunny and congenial, for he would soon be back in the good graces of the agent.

The Sioux were not the only horse thieves to plague the Crows. A party of Piegans made a fine haul at the agency on the night of October 2, 1874. Mitch was the principal victim, for he lost nine horses, worth five hundred dollars in all; John Soos Louis lost three; Tom Shane, son of Pierre, lost one; and John Downey, agency herder, lost an agency horse. Mitch and John Louis set out to trail the thieves and managed to follow them some 150 miles north to a Piegan village near the Blackfoot agency. There, on October 20, they spotted all the stolen animals and boldly entered the village, demanding the return of the stock. The Piegans admitted stealing them but refused to give them up, threatening the lives of the audacious pair if they did not leave pronto. The odds being pretty one-sided, Mitch and John discreetly withdrew and returned to their agency. Dr. Wright took affidavits from all the victims on October 29 to support claims submitted for their reimbursement. Whether these claims were paid is not divulged.[34]

Meanwhile, Congress had rejected the Crow treaty, making the Judith Basin reservation and its agency a thoroughly dead issue, which kept the old Treaty of 1868 in force. That left the Mountain and River Crows to crowd the Yellowstone Reservation and gold miners to overrun its mountainous southwest corner, annoyingly close to Mission Agency. The old treaty had promised the allotment of farmland, seed money, and farming equipment to any tribal member willing to work the land. Efforts to induce Crow men to demean themselves by farming when they could still live high on buffalo had gotten nowhere. But the Crow wives of the white men were now proving eager.

Thus on October 30, 1874, Dr. Wright was able to submit the names of fourteen of his charges who were willing to locate farms and begin tilling the soil. Only two were men, one a Crow in agency employ and the other an educated Oneida Indian of the Iroquois Nation, whom the Crows

---

[34]This account was assembled from the Oct. 29 affidavits of all the victims, *Mont. Suptcy.*, R500, fr. 1258–65 (G-M).

had adopted after his marriage to a Crow woman. The other twelve were Crow wives of white men and included some familiar names:

Mary Boyer, or Magpie Out of Doors (wife of Mitch Boyer)
Mary LeForge, or Cherry (wife of Tom LeForge)
Mary Prevo, or Sees Plain (wife of Barney Bravo, or Prevot)
Emma Shane, or Strikes Gun ⎱   (wives of Pierre Shane and
Mary Shane, or Goes Hunting ⎰   son Tom Shane, or Chêne)
Mary Stewart, or Goes Yellow (wife of Tom Stewart)
Sarah Shively, or Girl that Sees the Weed (wife of Sam Shively)
Mary Louis, or Medicine Pipe (widowed mother of John Louis, et al.)[35]

Tom LeForge remembered his venture into farming:

I tried farming for a few months while Dr. Wright was agent. He persuaded Barney Bravo, Tom Stewart and myself to locate on land. He gave us oxen, cows, implements, seed and rations. Marlow Collins [Marlo Seketer, the adopted Iroquois, already ranching a little south of Livingston, according to Dr. Wright] was making a success up the Yellowstone River at farming and stock-raising, and the agent wanted some more examples for the Crows to emulate. Cherry and I and our boy Tom found a cabin that had been built by a sawmill outfit at the mouth of Pine Cr. [east bank of Yellowstone, some 10 miles south of Livingston] and we settled there. I put in a garden and some field crops. But the trapping and hunting were too good to bother cultivating the land. After two months of this rural life, both Cherry and I were anxious to go back to the agency, where I went on duty again as blacksmith, watchman, interpreter and dispatch-bearer.[36]

The agency records confirm that Tom's farming proved short-lived, but the older Mitch would do somewhat better. Yet six years after the treaty had been signed, the first start had been made, thanks to the Crow women and their adopted husbands.

[35] Wright to Smith, Sept. 30, 1874, *Mont. Suptcy.*, R500, fr. 1273 (G-M).
[36] Marquis, *Memoirs* (LeForge), 50 (B). A paragraph on the "Suce" family appears at 44–45.

THE CROW AGENCY MOVES CLOSER
TO THE SIOUX

Dr. Wright, having asked to be transferred to another Indian agency, turned over the Crow agency to his successor, Dexter E. Clapp, on December 7, 1874. Agent Clapp, born in New York state and now forty-three years old, had been a Methodist minister until 1862, when he accepted a captaincy in the 148th New York Volunteer Infantry. In 1864 he raised the 38th U.S. Colored Infantry at Norfolk, Virginia, and became its lieutenant colonel until mustered out in January 1866, having been breveted a brigadier general of volunteers. He later entered the diplomatic service, holding the appointment of U.S. consul to Argentina from late 1871 to early 1873. He proved an able administrator, and his experience with other races and nationals had broadened his outlook. As agent he would win the respect of the Crows and his employees, for he acted promptly and with good judgment, instead of waiting interminably for

Indian Office approval. His correspondence is refreshingly free of verbosity and pious platitudes.[1]

Gen. Clapp's first pressing duty was to find a suitable site for a new agency on the old Yellowstone Reservation, farther removed than the existing one from invading gold miners and dubious traders on the reservation boundary over whom he had little control. Inevitably, it would be necessary to move down the Yellowstone closer to the enemy Sioux. Only three weeks after his arrival, on December 22, 1874, he was ready to report his choice:

> In obedience to instructions of October 4, 1874, to my predecessor to look for a new agency site, I left here December 16 and proceeded down the Yellowstone to the mouth of Bridger Creek and from there across to Stillwater River by the old Fort [C. F.] Smith road, and returned to the old agency yesterday evening.
>
> I found only two good locations: one on the Yellowstone at the mouth of Deer Creek, and the other at the junction of the Stillwater and the Rosebud. Both have good timber and water and sufficient tillable land. The first is 35 miles east of here and the second 58 miles.
>
> I recommend the junction of Stillwater and Rosebud Creek, for the following reasons: it is 20 miles from the reservation boundary and thus protected from whiskey traders; it has good farming land; it is away from the terrible winds of the Yellowstone Canyon.
>
> I wish to acknowledge the prompt and efficient escort furnished by Lt. Doane of Fort Ellis.[2]

How quickly Clapp perceived what his predecessors had not, appears in a brief letter of December 31, 1874: "As the Crows are as good herders as they are poor farmers, and as there is excellent grazing country available, I suggest that they should raise cattle, and propose that such should be purchased for this purpose."[3] He had not abandoned the farming program, however, for he reported on its progress on February 3:

> I enclose a list of Crows who have selected lands on this reservation with the intention of settling thereon. Several have built houses and begun farming, on the promise of my predecessor that they will receive

[1]"Dexter E. Clapp," in White, ed., *National Cyclopedia of Biography*, 5:526 (B); Heitman, *Historical Register, U.S. Army*, 1:302 (B); Wright to E. P. Smith, Dec. 7, 1874, *Mont. Suptcy.*, 1874, R500, fr. 500 (for agency turnover date) (G-M).

[2]Clapp to E. P. Smith, Dec. 23, 1874, *Mont. Suptcy.*, 1875, R501, fr. 347 (G-M).

[3]Clapp to Smith, Dec. 31, 1874, *Mont. Suptcy.*, R501, fr. 393 (G-M).

$100 worth of seeds and farming implements each. Most are married to whites. They ask for a survey and registration. They have a good location near the river about 20 miles above this [Mission] agency.[4]

The list of names no longer includes Mary LeForge or Mary Boyer, but the latter is replaced by Mitch Boyer, indicating that in the year of his thirty-eighth birthday Mitch was ready to accept this responsibility. The new names include "Emma Soos, wife of John Soos," and the latter's brother, "William Soos," further confusing the surname of this Indian-Mexican family.

Gen. Clapp spent the forepart of May 1875 in Bozeman, hiring a crew of mechanics and engaging White Calfee, a freighter, to help haul heavy equipment and building materials out to the new agency site.[5] On May 4 these men, supplemented by employees and an ox train from Mission Agency, were the first to start downriver, as rough parts of the trail would require roadwork. On the same day a small crew cast off in a flatboat loaded with provisions, while the Crows were preparing to leave for the mouth of the Bighorn on a long buffalo hunt. Soon Gen. Clapp started down overland, having consigned his wife, Susan Jane, to the care of his brother, Charles L., who remained in charge of the old agency. Tom LeForge recalled that he and Mitch also went down, probably guiding the agent on his trip to overtake the others.

Attached to the large wagon party was Deputy U.S. Marshal Frank M. Murray, who kept a daily record of his trip. On May 26 he learned that an accident to the flatboat had lost all of its provisions, but the crew was saved. The next day the train made the difficult fording of Boulder Creek, guided by John Soos Louis and Frank Ladeau, an agency blacksmith, a strong hint that Mitch, Tom, and the agent had not yet overtaken them. On May 29 the train camped at the mouth of Stillwater River, opposite present Columbus, Montana, and remained there the next day, when Frank Murray recorded: "Murray and [A. P.?] Fox start a fire on an old campground, when a cartridge goes off, followed at 400 miles an hour by Murray and Fox."[6]

It was May 31 when the combined parties ascended the Stillwater to

[4]Clapp to Smith, Feb. 3, 1875, *Mont. Suptcy.*, R501, fr. 381ff (G-M).
[5]*Bozeman Times*, May 7, 25, 1875.
[6]Ibid., June 8, 1875.

its junction with Rosebud River, and LeForge recalled that Clapp detailed him and Mitch to select the precise spot for the agent's new home. The workmen broke the first ground on June 2, at what was simply called the new agency. Later, however, adopting the Crows' word for their own tribe, it became known as the "Absarokee agency" and gave this name to present Absarokee, Montana.[7]

Early on June 4 Gen. Clapp started back on a fast, three-day trip to Bozeman with Marshal Frank Murray, arriving there on the evening of June 6; Mitch may have ridden with them to guide the agent on an equally fast return trip.[8] Before leaving, however, the agent had sent Tom LeForge and John Soos Louis to find the Crows and inform them of the location of their new agency. The pair soon located the Crow camp some 50 miles down the Yellowstone near and opposite the mouth of Pryor Creek. On June 6 they were puzzled by hearing the sound of a steamboat whistle, for none had ever before come higher than Powder River on this stream. But soon the *Josephine* rounded a bend and took the two couriers aboard. Tom remembered stowing away a sumptuous dinner spread by Capt. Grant Marsh, the boat's skipper, and meeting the son of President Grant.[9]

Capt. Marsh's *Josephine* had been chartered by Maj. James W. Forsyth and Lt. Col. Frederick Dent Grant, both of Gen. Sheridan's staff, with orders to make a reconnaissance up the Yellowstone in search of suitable locations for military posts near the mouths of the Tongue and Bighorn rivers, in the heart of Sioux unceded territory. At Fort Buford, at the mouth of the Yellowstone, the boat had picked up an escort of three companies of 6th Infantry and three quartermaster scouts. As the latter trio have usually been misidentified, they are here named: George W. Grinnell, A. W. Congdon, and W. D. Parshall, all hired from May 24 to June 10 by Lt. Charles G. Penney, post quartermaster. On reaching Tongue River on May 30, the boat scattered a frightened camp of hostile Sioux, and on June 2 she had steamed 12 miles up the Bighorn and back.[10]

[7] Marquis, *Memoirs* (LeForge), 110 (B); Clapp to Smith, Sept. 10, 1875, in Commr. Ind. Aff., *Ann. Report*, 1875, 301 (for ground-breaking date) (B).

[8] *Bozeman Avant Courier*, June 11, 1875 (for Murray); Eddie Alderson, "Diary," June 7, 1875 (for Clapp mention) (M).

[9] Marquis, *Memoirs* (LeForge), 107 (B).

[10] This and the ensuing paragraph are based on Forsyth, *Expedition to the Yellowstone* (B); *Bismarck Tribune*, June 16, 1875; Hanson, *Conquest of the Missouri*, 195–221; "Persons Hired at Fort Buford by Lt. Chas. G. Penney, May–June, 1875" (G-RG92).

On reaching a point about 8 miles above the mouth of Pryor Creek on June 6, the *Josephine* halted at the camp of 270 lodges of Mountain Crows and 20 of River Crows on a buffalo hunt. From this camp George R. ("Crow") Davis was hired to guide the craft as far upriver as she could get. She made only a few more miles, nearly to present Billings, Montana, when she was forced to turn back and Davis was discharged.

Tom and John, having delivered their message to the Crows, also headed back to report to Agent Clapp, who had just returned to the new agency, presumably guided by Mitch. Since Bozemanites had long been dreaming of the day when steamboats would ply the Yellowstone, Clapp wrote a letter on June 10 to the governor of Montana and sent Tom and John to deliver it to Bozeman, where it appeared in an "extra" of June 15:

> Two men that I had sent to the Crow camp, T. LaForgey and John Louis, have just returned and report that on June 6 they met the steamboat *Josephine*, Capt. Marsh in charge, carrying the expeditionary force of Col. Grant, about 6 miles below the mouth of Clark's Fork [*sic*]. They went on board. . . . On returning to the Crow camp, the two men again met the steamer going down the river [June 7].
>
> The men report they had great difficulty escaping from a large party of Arapahoes and Cheyennes; also, that they crossed the fresh trail of a war party of about a hundred Indians apparently bound for the upper Yellowstone country.[11]

This news brought excitement to many but a tinge of disappointment to others, for Fellows D. Pease was just about to start down the Yellowstone with a company of adventurers, hoping to meet the *Josephine* at the mouth of the Bighorn and there build a steamboat landing and "Fort Pease" to trade with the Indians and house a crew of trappers, hunters, and wolfers. At dawn of June 17 the initial force of the Pease expedition cast off from Benson's Landing in three mackinaw boats, paralleled by a mounted overland party. The thirty named adventurers included the three leaders, F. D. Pease, Z. H. Daniels, and Paul W. McCormick, and two other familiar names, George Herendeen and Samuel Shively.[12] That the party encountered a little difficulty is revealed by the first letter (June 27) of a series to the *Bozeman Avant Courier*, written by an observant employee at the new agency, William Y. Smith, who used the pen name "U

---

[11] *Bozeman Times*, June 22, 1875 (includes June 25 Extra and Clapp's letter).
[12] The best account of the Pease expedition is McLemore, "Fort Pease," 17–31 (A). An early roster appears at 20.

KNOW": "On June 19, Maj. Pease and his fleet of mackinaws landed at the mouth of the Stillwater, and on the 20th, Mr. Daniels visited us. He said they had swamped two boats on the way down, losing three guns and other goods. They started down again on June 21. So far we have not seen an Indian, but we are now close to their haunts." [13]

Around June 20 a three-day battle was raging at the mouth of the Bighorn between the buffalo-hunting Crows and the Sioux, whose camp near Tongue River the *Josephine* had earlier flushed up the river. The large Sioux force drove the Crows northward toward the Musselshell. [14] Thus when the Pease expedition reached the mouth of the Bighorn on June 24, it found the bluffs lined with belligerent Sioux, who spurned all peace overtures, an ominous sign for the future. They soon disappeared, however, and the next day the men began building stockaded Fort Pease 3 miles below and opposite the mouth of the Bighorn. On June 28 Pease, Herendeen, and one other skiffed down the river for Fort Buford; Herendeen would rejoin the expedition in October with Paul McCormick, but Pease went east, where he discovered that there would be no more steamboats on the Yellowstone that year. Disappointed, he would return to Bozeman but direct his energy toward mining ventures, leaving others to carry on the Fort Pease project.

Fort Pease would become an annoyance even to the friendly Crows, for its trappers and hunters poached freely on their diminishing game, and the wolfers spread strychnine-baited carcasses everywhere, a practice the Indians considered a crime against nature. More violent was the reaction of the Sioux, especially the winter roamers, who shunned agency rations and continued to support themselves by the chase in their own unceded territory. To them, Fort Pease was another threatening trespass that ranked with wagon roads, steamboats, and the Northern Pacific Railroad, which Sitting Bull and Crazy Horse were rallying them to resist. They attacked the post and the men who ventured out of it at every opportunity throughout its existence.

The new Crow agency, now temptingly closer to the outraged Sioux, drew its own share of attacks. The first came on July 2, as reported by Gen. Clapp to Capt. Daniel W. Benham, 7th Infantry, now commanding Fort Ellis:

[13] *Bozeman Avant Courier*, July 9, 1875.
[14] Clapp to Smith, July 5, 1875, *Mont. Suptcy.*, 1875, R501, fr. 503 (G-M).

I take first opportunity to inform you that on July 2, my camp of choppers and teamsters near the mouth of the Stillwater was attacked by thirty Sioux. They got away with one mule and several oxen, all but two of which I have recovered, some wounded. Soon afterward they waylaid the herder, Jose Pablo Trujio, or Mexican Joe, killed him and took his horse. The attackers left in fright, leaving numerous articles. Last night [July 4], the same or another party ran off from the agency 23 animals belonging to White Calfee [contractor], eight belonging to the agency and two to other parties.[15]

A dispatch from William Y. Smith told of a later assault on three men coming in from Fort Pease:

July 11, 6 A.M. Patrick Hyde and Nelson Weaver, of the Pease Expedition, have just come in to camp, reporting they were attacked yesterday morning at 10 A.M. by forty Sioux. Sam Shively was killed and Hyde was wounded in the right arm. They had left Fort Pease as messengers and lost everything. . . . The party was attacked on the divide, east of Beaver Cr., 10 miles [north] from the Yellowstone and 8 miles above [west] Stillwater.[16]

Mitch Boyer figured in the next two-day episode, which featured a raid on the agency, an ambush of an approaching supply train, and then a pursuit to recover stolen agency cattle. The following reconstruction of these events relies for timing on a letter by William Y. Smith, written concurrently in installments, and is supplemented by Clapp's later report and a news interview given by him and others, which are vague on timing.[17]

At 5 A.M. of July 21 about forty Sioux rushed the agency herd of forty-five oxen, driving off forty-three head. The lone herder dove for the brush, losing his saddled horse to the Sioux, but a party from the agency dashed out and found him unharmed. The raiders then gathered on nearby bluffs and for three hours poured long shots into the agency enclosure but inflicted no casualties.

During the next morning, July 22, Nelson Story was ascending Stillwater River with his supply train, which had left Mission Agency on

[15]*Bozeman Times*, Aug. 3, 1875. Clapp's letter from New Agency, July 5, was delayed in publication.

[16]*Bozeman Avant Courier*, July 16, 1875 (installment letter, July 8, 10, 11).

[17]Ibid., July 30, 1875 (another installment letter, July 21, 22); Clapp, Story, and Dusold interview, July 26, *Bozeman Times*, July 27, 1875; Clapp to Smith, Aug. 4, 1875, *Mont. Suptcy.*, 1875, R501, fr. 533 (G-M).

July 14, accompanied by "Captain" Andrew Dusold, U.S. Indian inspector for the Crow agency. When they were about 6 miles from the new agency, several shots rang out, the bullets whizzing by Dusold's head. Story, Dusold, and some train men charged the ambushers, but all they found were some personal effects that three Sioux had cached in a thicket. On hearing this action, a party of twenty-one men from the agency sped out to investigate and escorted the train in before 2 P.M.

By 2 P.M. a party of twenty men, including Gen. Clapp, Dusold, Bryan Goodwin, agency engineer, and certainly Mitch Boyer, left the agency to follow the trail of the stolen oxen. They tracked them for some 20 miles east toward Clark's Fork, noting eight head of dead oxen and gathering up nine others, all wounded but one. On spotting the smoke of a probable Sioux village on Rock Creek, the party turned back and reached the agency at 10 P.M.

All three accounts agree that at some point in this sequence of events Mitch held a sign-talk with one of the Sioux raiders who knew him and boasted that these Sioux were merely the van of a larger party that would come out and "give them plenty of fight." What remains uncertain is the date, which leaves indeterminate whether Mitch had come out with Story's train or, as I suspect, had been at the agency all along.

The last of the major attacks on the new agency came on July 27, when seven Sioux stampeded Story's cattle herd. The two herders put up a good fight, but James Hildebrand bled to death from a shot in the arm that tore an artery.[18] Earlier in July a series of raids between Mission Agency and Fort Ellis had resulted in several casualties and evoked serious alarm in Bozeman. Then, on August 2, a Sioux attack at Benson's Landing (near present Livingston) left John Soos Louis with a bullet hole through his chest.[19] There was also action near Camp Lewis in the Judith Basin, in which some unarmed army recruits were killed in early July; the angry Crows drove these impudent Sioux out of the country, but in the process Long Horse, a prominent Mountain Crow chief, was killed.[20]

During this summer Agent Clapp had made repeated business trips between the old and new agencies in spite of the danger of such travel.

[18] Bryant Godwin to ed., Aug. 1, *Bozeman Times*, Aug. 10, 1875.
[19] *Bozeman Times*, July 13, Aug. 3, 1875; Eddie Alderson, "Diary," July 1875 (M); Clapp to Smith, Aug. 4, 1875, *Mont. Suptcy.*, R501, fr. 533 (G-M).
[20] For more on events in Judith Basin, see Gray, "Long Horse Leads His Last War Party" (A).

His requests for military aid were largely ignored, primarily because there were simply too few troops to guard so vast a territory. Apparently, a little spite was involved, too, for the Fort Ellis officers were miffed by the removal of the agency to so distant a location. But none of these problems fazed Gen. Clapp; he recruited more mechanics to replace the faint of heart and bought them arms, including one high-powered rifle with telescopic sights for use in picking off Sioux snipers on the nearby bluffs.[21] As for traveling, he relied on Mitch Boyer to get him through safely, as he reported on September 27:

> Mitch Boyer, the most experienced and celebrated guide and scout of the Yellowstone and Fort C. F. Smith country, has been in my employ the past summer. He has frequently told me that the most dangerous portion of the route to Bozeman is the twelve miles this side of Fort Ellis [a dig at the military]. I have never hesitated to travel with him alone between the two agencies, but we were not willing to risk the road beyond towards Bozeman. In fact, for several weeks, no one crossed that range except with a large party.[22]

About September 6 Mission Agency was abandoned.[23] All the remaining employees and families, as well as usable equipment, were transported to the new agency, where they were installed in new and more comfortable quarters. Agent Clapp did nothing shabbily, for the buildings were adequate in number, some built of sawed lumber and others of solid adobes, both processed on the spot under his supervision.[24] In mid-September, when Col. E. C. Watkins, U.S. Indian inspector, made his official visit, he highly commended both the agent's management and his new facilities.[25] Nelson Story was also erecting a new trading post, to be managed by his brother, Elias Story; Mitch Boyer may well have taken employment at this store over the winter.

The Crows all came in on October 5 and expressed their satisfaction with the new agency and its location. When their annuities arrived, Clapp promptly issued them on November 4 and 5, as the Crows intended to leave on another buffalo hunt. As was customary, the chiefs expressed their gratitude by presenting robes to the agency heads as well as Elias

[21] Clapp to Smith, Aug. 13, 1875, *Mont. Suptcy.*, R501, fr. 558 (G-M).
[22] Ibid., Sept. 27, 1875, R501, fr. 594.
[23] *Bozeman Times*, Sept. 7, 1875.
[24] Clapp to Smith, Sept. 10, 1875, in Commr. Ind. Aff., *Ann. Report*, 1875, 302 (B).
[25] *Bozeman Avant Courier*, Oct. 1, 1875.

Story and his new clerk, Peter Koch. William Y. Smith's dispatch of November 6, which related these events, ended on an apprehensive note: "Gen. Clapp leaves this morning for Washington on leave of absence. There are rumors that he is to be relieved—a terrible pity, for he has done well."[26]

Leaving his brother, Charles L. Clapp, in charge as acting agent, the general and his wife left for their home in Kansas, but he soon appeared at the Indian Office in Washington, where his evident industry and competence won him another year as Crow agent.[27] The couple would return to duty at the agency by January 1. Meanwhile, William Y. Smith reported on December 20 that "nearly all buildings are completed and ready for winter" and added a social note: "Dancing is quite fashionable here. The squaws, who have white men for husbands, have learned to conduct themselves in a very becoming and graceful manner, and dress neatly."[28]

This type of entertainment was the prelude to a gala Christmas, of which Smith wrote on January 10, 1876:

> On Christmas Eve there was a grand ball, with Barney Bravo, general superintendent; Col. [Jerah I.?] Allen [who had been on the Pease expedition] and Maj. Yancey, floor managers; J. Mills, culinary department; and Mitch Boyer and Indian Joe, reception committee. The large attendance was half whites and half reds. A Christmas tree was greatly enjoyed, and Frank Murray [recently appointed U.S. detective for the Crow agency] played Santa Claus, distributing presents to the little ones. Capt. Ed Ball and Lt. McClernand [from Fort Ellis to inspect Indian rations] reached here Christmas day and aided in the entertainment.[29]

"Peace on earth, goodwill toward men" may have been the theme of this Christmas festival, but unknown to the celebrants, President Grant had already decided to launch an all-out war against the Sioux. Within months Mitch and many of his friends, both white and Indian, would be scouting for the army.

[26] Ibid., Nov. 12, 1875.
[27] Clapp to Smith, Washington, Dec. 4, *Mont. Suptcy.*, R501, fr. 637 (G-M).
[28] *Bozeman Avant Courier*, Dec. 31, 1875.
[29] Ibid., Jan. 14, 1876.

MOUNTING A WAR AGAINST THE SIOUX

It was now seven years since the Treaty of 1868 had guaranteed the Sioux a permanent reservation and unmolested occupation of their unceded territory and had promised a program to civilize them. The majority, now confined on the reservation, where they could no longer support themselves, had not become successful dry-farmers and so depended on government rations. A minority, less than 20 percent, were winter roamers sustaining themselves by the chase in unceded territory. It was this minority that so resented trespass on their hunting grounds by wagon roads, steamboats, railroads—and Fort Pease.

Lately, however, an even more serious threat to the agency Sioux had materialized. In 1874 Gen. George A. Custer's exploring expedition had broadcast the discovery of gold in the Black Hills, which covered the western portion of the Sioux Reservation. And now, in 1875, a government-sponsored expedition was prospecting the same area, and hordes of white citizens were swarming across the reservation and digging holes all over the Black Hills, from which their own laws barred them. Such ruthless violation of both law and decency angered even the agency Sioux. The government sent out another inept commission this summer to induce three-quarters of the adult male Sioux to sign away the gold-bearing portion of their reservation as well as their entire unceded territory. The councils held in September evoked bitter defiance from the winter roamers and forced the commissioners to flee ignominiously under the protection of a few cool and level-headed agency Sioux.[1]

The utter failure of this commission precipitated a crisis in Washington. The administration could send the army against the citizenry to enforce the law or against the Sioux and seize the coveted lands as the spoils of war. Other alternatives received scant consideration. At a secret White House conference, held on November 3, 1875, President Grant and a few carefully selected cabinet members and army generals made their decision: to launch a war against the Sioux.[2]

The White House conference decided to keep secret its war decision and the resulting mobilization of troops but to prepare propaganda documents and plan maneuvers to convince the public, when the time came, that the winter roamers were guilty of initiating an aggressive war against the whites. The misinformation program is too intricate to detail here, but the main document designed to shift the war onus onto the winter roamers was ready within a week of the conference. E. C. Watkins, the Indian inspector who had visited the Dakota and Montana agencies in 1875, was in Washington at the time of the conference and was induced to write, or at least sign, a report on Indian intransigence dated November 9, 1875. It contains no reference to the real issue, the rape of the Black Hills and the attempted seizure of the unceded territory, but concentrates for pages on "fiendish" Indians and "abused" whites. Though the account is remarkably nonspecific as to the time and place of depredations, one can discern that all the fiendishness refers to the resistance of the winter roamers to the whites' invasion of their unceded territory, including Fort Pease.

Gen. Philip H. Sheridan, commanding the Military Division of the

[1] For more on these councils on the Black Hills, see Gray, "Mrs. Picotte-Galpin, Sioux Heroine," Pt. 2, 15–16 (A).

[2] For a fuller analysis of the secret White House conference, see Gray, *Centennial Campaign*, esp. Chap. 3 (B).

Missouri, with headquarters at Chicago, was the most prominent officer at the secret conference, and it was he who was assigned command of the military campaign. His strategy was to launch promptly a winter campaign to strike the Sioux when they were most vulnerable. He chose as his target only the winter roamers, on the theory that to destroy this minority would thoroughly cow the majority. He planned a two-pronged offensive: Gen. George Crook, commanding the Department of the Platte, was to lead a Wyoming column northeast from Fort Fetterman on the North Platte, 80 miles above Fort Laramie; Gen. Alfred H. Terry, commanding the Department of Dakota, was to send Gen. Custer's Dakota column westward from Fort Abraham Lincoln on the Missouri, opposite the railhead at Bismarck. The two were to converge on the winter roamers in the Yellowstone country.

Unfortunately, Sheridan failed to reckon with the logistical problem of mounting such forces at isolated, winter-bound posts. Crook claimed he could get off at any moment, but that proved to be March 1, 1876. Terry confessed that Custer could not get off until steamboat and railroad service opened in the spring. In the meantime, politics would raise its ugly head and President Grant would depose Custer in favor of Terry, delaying his start until May 17, 1876. Sheridan's decisive winter blow thus shrank to a late and weak zephyr, March 17, by Crook's column alone on a small village, which merely alerted the winter roamers to prepare for more. The disastrous defeat of Custer's regiment on June 25 would shock the nation, and the demand of Congress for information from the secretary of war on how the unexpected conflict had started, would bring the release of the propaganda documents, including the Watkins report.[3]

It is now necessary to return to events that occurred at Fort Pease during the winter of 1875–76, for they significantly influenced the opening of the military campaign. Since mid-November, the freezing of the river had compelled its active proprietors, Paul McCormick and Newman Borchardt, to supply the post by slow and expensive wagon trains instead of fast and cheap flatboats. In December repeated conflicts with resentful winter roamers hampered hunting for meat as well as furs and skins for profit. In January the proprietors realized that their financial prospects were fading rapidly.

[3] Ibid., chaps. 4 (secret mobilization) and 6 (Custer's troubles in Washington).

On January 2, 1876, five men were wounded, one fatally,[4] but a party of Crows, led by Chief Bear Wolf, evened the score on January 9. Having spotted eight enemy Sioux spying on the post, the Crows ambushed them, killing all but one.[5] When the victors returned to enter the fort, one of them extended his hand from under his blanket to shake hands with H. M. ("Muggins") Taylor. It proved a grisly joke, for when the Crow walked away, Taylor was still grasping the hand—the severed extremity of one of the slain Sioux.[6] The last casualty came on January 29, when a wolfing party lost one man killed.[7] The Sioux then all disappeared to spend the winter along the Powder River.

Benjamin F. Dexter had become the leader of a growing number of men at the post interested in gold prospecting, for the air was filled with rumors of fortunes to be made in the gold diggings of the not-far-distant Black Hills. Companies of miners were forming at Bozeman, and temptation was preying on the employees at the Crow agency. A few hardy trappers and wolfers were anxious to remain at Fort Pease, but the others would soon succumb to the gold fever.

The exodus from Fort Pease began on January 22, when Benjamin Dexter left with seventeen men, some of whom he brought into Bozeman on February 8.[8] He carried an undated petition, signed by forty-four men at the post, asking the commander of Fort Ellis "to send troops to check the havoc of these hostile Sioux."[9] Then Paul McCormick, who had doubtless discussed the dwindling outlook with partner Borchardt, made a fast six-day trip to reach Bozeman with six others by February 15.[10] On the 18th McCormick and Dexter signed an affidavit at Bozeman that painted a lurid picture of the desperate plight of the fourteen men penned up in Fort Pease and about to be massacred, although these were the hardies satisfied to remain. To heighten the effect, the affidavit also

[4] J. S. Crain to ed., *Helena Herald*, Jan. 27, 1876.

[5] Clapp to Maj. Benham, Jan. 10, 1876, *Military Expedition against the Sioux*, 47 (G-CSS); *Bozeman Avant Courier*, Jan. 21, 1876.

[6] Topping, *Chronicles*, 103 (B); Gray, ed., "Capt. Clifford's Narrative of the Yellowstone Campaign of 1876," Pt. 1, 76 (for Muggins Taylor's story) (A).

[7] Wm. Y. Smith to ed., Feb. 14, 1876, *Helena Herald*, Feb. 24, 1876.

[8] *Bozeman Times*, Feb. 10, 1876.

[9] *Chicago Tribune*, April 4, 1876 (also *New York Times*, Apr. 6), "Fort Pease Disaster," datelined Ft. Ellis, Mar. 21, which gives the text of the petition and forty-four signatures. The article was probably prepared by Maj. Brisbin and/or J. V. Bogert.

[10] *Bozeman Avant Courier*, Feb. 18, 1876.

charged Agent Clapp with inciting the Crows to harass the post and drive its men from the country.[11]

That same February 18 a delegation of citizens, armed with petition and affidavit as well as newspaper and verbal testimony, marched to Fort Ellis[12] to confront Bvt. Brig. Gen. James S. Brisbin, Maj. of 2nd Cavalry, who had transferred from afar only a week before to assume his new command. The delegation was bent on persuading the major to send troops, not to protect Fort Pease, but to evacuate its doomed garrison. This appeal, of course, was pure bait; but if it worked, it would cost the government little extra to load the troop's supply train, half-empty on reaching the post, with all the remaining goods and accumulated furs and robes for the return trip. As the delegation no doubt pointed out to the major, whiskey and ammunition must not be allowed to fall into the hands of hostile savages.

With only a week's familiarity with his new post, Maj. Brisbin took the bait, for the next day he telegraphed for permission to lead an expedition to relieve Fort Pease. Apparently bypassing Gen. John Gibbon, who commanded the District of Montana at Fort Shaw north of Helena, he directed his request to Gen. Terry in St. Paul. Brisbin's report of his expedition reveals that Terry wired back permission that same day, February 19, and Terry's annual report confirms the rest:

> On the 19th of February, I was informed by a dispatch of that date from Maj. James S. Brisbin . . . that he had on the previous day received an appeal for help from a party who had established themselves for the purpose of trade, trapping and mining . . . at Fort Pease. It was stated that fourteen men were holding a stockade against the Indians who had surrounded them. Maj. Brisbin proposed to go to their relief. . . . The proposal was approved by me, and he was instructed by telegraph to proceed at once to carry it into effect.[13]

Terry had responded so promptly for several discernible reasons. He had been embarrassed by the logistical impossibility of fielding a Dakota column to cooperate with Crook's Wyoming column on a winter campaign and thus welcomed the opportunity to send Brisbin down the Yellowstone

[11]This affidavit was sent to Gov. Potts, who forwarded it to the Indian Office, *Mont. Suptcy.*, 1876, R505, fr. 726 (G-M).

[12]J. V. Bogert to ed., *Bozeman Times*, Mar. 2, 1876.

[13]Gen. Terry, Ann. Report, Nov. 21, 1876, Sec. of War, *Ann. Report*, 1876, 458–59 (G-CSS).

with even a token force. As will emerge, Brisbin was hoping to get a crack at Sitting Bull's hostiles and may have so hinted to Terry. Furthermore, at the moment Brisbin's telegram arrived, the energetic Custer was at Terry's headquarters helping to plan the coming campaign. While en route to Fort Abraham Lincoln from leave in New York City, Custer had been stranded at St. Paul because the Northern Pacific tracks were blockaded by snow.

On February 20 Maj. Brisbin wrote a letter to enlist the support of Agent Clapp for his relief expedition:

> Two men in from Fort Pease report that all but fourteen men have abandoned it and they are shut up and can't get out. . . . I have orders from Gen. Terry to go at once to relieve the besieged men at Pease and will start tomorrow [not until Feb. 22] with 200 soldiers and 50 citizens. This is hardly sufficient to go so far into Sioux country, and I have determined to call on you for aid in rescuing the men. I am informed . . . that you have some forty employees, and as your stockade is strong, you might spare 15–20 men to go with me without endangering your safety. . . . As he [Sitting Bull] has made his boast to attack all columns of troops that come into his country . . . it is possible he may give us a blast on this trip. Any setback he might get now, may save us trouble next summer.
>
> If you can, I want you to go with me down to Pease. Get all the Indians and white men you can together and join me on the road. . . . Do all you can to strengthen me and please tell your friendly Crows that if they go along and behave well, I will give them all the ponies captured on the expedition. Send runners [to the Crows] and do the best you can. . . . Put a white mark on them, so my scouting parties will know them and not fire on them by mistake.[14]

That same night, as further persuasion, Brisbin sent his adjutant, Lt. Charles B. Schofield, on ahead to talk with Clapp in person. Although Fort Ellis had long demonstrated reluctance to aid the agency, Clapp was no grudge-bearer. For diplomatic reasons, however, he decided not to go himself, but as he wrote the Indian Office, he allowed agency personnel to volunteer, and as to the Crows, "no influence would keep them back."[15]

---

[14]Brisbin to Clapp, Feb. 20, 1876, *Mont. Suptcy.*, 1876, R504, fr. 323 (G-M).

[15]Brisbin to Clapp, Feb. 20, 11 P.M., and Clapp to J. Q. Smith, Feb. 29, 1876, *Mont. Suptcy.*, 1876, R504, frs. 323 and 318, respectively (G-M).

As Maj. Brisbin stated in his report of the expedition, he left Fort Ellis on the morning of February 22, 1876, with Companies F, G, H, and L of his 2nd Cavalry and a detachment of 12 men from Company C, 7th Infantry, to serve a 12-pound Napoleon gun, making a total of 14 officers and 192 enlisted men. From Bozeman 15 citizens volunteered. A wagon train carried thirty days' rations for the men and one-third forage for the horses. After marching 98 miles, the column camped at the mouth of the Stillwater on the afternoon of February 27. There they found 25 citizens and 30 Crows from the agency waiting to join. At the next day's camp, 14 miles down the river, 24 more Crows joined the column.[16]

Two other diarists with the expedition were Pvt. William H. White, Company F, 2nd Cavalry, and William Y. Smith ("U KNOW"), from the agency.[17] The latter confirmed that the Crow volunteers totaled 54 but recorded that the citizen volunteers from Bozeman numbered 20 and the agency volunteers only 23. Only two of the agency employees are named, Wm. Y. Smith and Barney Bravo, Mitch Boyer's name being conspicuously absent. Of the Bozeman volunteers, only Paul McCormick, Z. H. Daniels, and Muggins Taylor, all having come in earlier from Fort Pease, are named.

At Baker's Battleground on March 1 Brisbin ordered two resentful wolfers to pack up everything and join the relief column; one was George Herendeen, who had built a pair of dugout cabins there, from which he had been operating since the preceding October. On March 5 the column reached Fort Pease, then garrisoned by 19 men, including Newman Borchardt and John W. Williamson, a former 2nd Cavalryman honorably discharged from Fort Ellis, who was destined to serve as a courier with Gibbon's Montana column. At this time William Y. Smith recorded in his diary:

> In council with Gen. Brisbin, the occupants of the fort concluded to evacuate the place, though some reluctantly, as they believed they could hold their position until spring boats arrived. Some claim their situation had been misrepresented and speak harshly of those who created the excitement. No Indians seen [here] since January 29 and they had no fear of them in the fort. They could walk out at any time,

---

[16]Brisbin to Terry, Mar. 21, 1876, *Military Expedition against the Sioux*, 50 (G-CSS).
[17]Pvt. White, "Diary, 1876" (M); *Bozeman Avant Courier*, Mar. 31, 1876 (Wm. Y. Smith letter of Mar. 20).

but could not pack three barrels of whiskey. The relief is a farce, a wild goose chase.[18]

The half-empty wagons having been loaded with everything worth moving, to the unanimous satisfaction of the proprietors, the column started back at noon of March 6, dragging the pouting post personnel. The whiskey barrels proved a mite heavy, for the men made devoted efforts on the return trip to lighten them a "wee drappie." On reaching the Stillwater on March 12, they apparently sold a barrel or two to dubious traders there, which created some havoc for Agent Clapp. The troops straggled in to Fort Ellis on March 17, but the overweight and arthritic Maj. Brisbin, who led from an ambulance instead of a saddle, received a frosty dunking while fording Boulder Creek.[19] During the entire trip not a single Sioux, or sign thereof, had been seen, for the simple reason that they had long since retired eastward to Powder River.

On the very day these troops returned to Fort Ellis, Crook's Wyoming column had struck a small village of Sioux and Cheyenne winter roamers on Powder River. Although a complete surprise, the attack was poorly executed and the Indians quickly rallied to drive the troops off. The entire force trudged back to Fort Fetterman to reorganize. This winter blow generated a storm of recriminations among the officers which led to a series of courts-martial, and, more significant, it fully alerted the winter roamers to the fact that they were marked for extermination and must consolidate their scattered villages in preparation for a determined defense.[20]

Although Brisbin's relief force made no fighting contribution to the futile winter campaign, it did prompt Gen. Terry to consider how he could use his Montana troops in the coming spring campaign. The first sign of this strategy came on February 21, the day before Brisbin had started, when Terry wrote Gibbon outlining his plan to send off Custer's Dakota column about April 1.[21] He followed this letter up with a telegram on February 25, directing Gibbon to ready all spare infantry in his district for a march down the Yellowstone from Fort Ellis.[22] On February 27

[18] See footnote 17, above, second reference.

[19] *Bozeman Times*, Mar. 16, 1876.

[20] Gray, *Centennial Campaign*, chap. 5 (Crook's winter campaign and its effects) (B).

[21] This letter is identified in Hughes, "Campaign against the Sioux," reprinted in Graham, *Story of the Little Big Horn*, appendix, 6 (B); Gibbon acknowledged receiving this letter on Mar. 7, in his reply to Terry on Mar. 8 (see footnote 24, below).

[22] Terry's Ann. Report (see footnote 13, above) misdates this telegram Feb. 27, but Sheridan to Terry (see footnote 23, below) dates it Feb. 25.

Sheridan wired his approval of Terry's "wire to Gibbon of Feb. 25" and urged that Gibbon "move as soon as possible."[23] On the 29th, Terry notified Gibbon of Sheridan's suggestion and authorized him to "enlist 25 Indian scouts and hire two interpreters"; Terry further suggested that Gibbon supply Brisbin in the field until joined by the infantry, but left this option to Gibbon's discretion.[24] Brisbin's column, however, would return to Fort Ellis before Gibbon could arrange to supply him.

While still at Fort Shaw on March 8, Gibbon outlined his plan of campaign to Terry:

> My first objective point will be [Fort] C. F. Smith, or, the mouth of the Big Horn, dependent upon whether we can cross the stream at its mouth. After crossing, my next objective will be any camps of Indians I can hear of; there must be some, though I hear most of them are on Tongue River. To get there I may have to go . . . down the Yellowstone. . . . The route to be finally adopted will depend upon the information to be derived from my guides, which I expect to employ at the agency and . . . to enlist my Crow scouts, and can possibly induce a good many more with the hope of sharing in the plunder. It ought not take long to finish up this matter satisfactorily.[25]

As ordered, Gibbon would assemble his Montana column at Fort Ellis, leaving only single companies of his 7th Infantry to garrison each of the four military posts in his district. Brisbin's four companies of 2nd Cavalry, on returning to Fort Ellis on March 17, learned that they would constitute the cavalry arm of the column. One infantry company left Camp Baker on March 14 and reached the staging base of Fort Ellis on the 20th. The remaining five infantry companies left Fort Shaw on March 17 and reached Fort Ellis on the 28th; Gibbon, having passed this battalion on its march, reached Fort Ellis on the 27th.

While there, Gibbon learned of Crook's fight of March 17 and the resulting information that the Sioux were farther east on Powder River. He therefore queried Gen. Terry by telegram on March 30: "In view of the information from Gen. Crook, am I not operating in the wrong direction by going south of the Yellowstone, instead of north? Brisbin thinks

---

[23] R. C. Drum (Terry's Adjt.) to Terry, Feb. 27, 1876 (telegram), Letters Sent, Mil. Div. of the Mo., 1876 (G-RG98).

[24] This letter is also in Letters Received, Mil. Div. of the Mo., 1876 (G-RG98).

[25] This letter is in Letters Received, Mil. Div. of the Mo., 1876 (G-RG98).

Sitting Bull is on the Big Dry [which runs north to join the Missouri at Fort Peck]. . . . May I strike Sitting Bull wherever I can find him?"[26]

The next day, March 21, Terry wired Gibbon his new instructions:

> I think you ought not to go south of the Yellowstone, but should direct your efforts to preventing the Indians from getting away to the north. I doubt that Sitting Bull is on the Dry Fork. All information here points to the Powder River as his present location, and Gen. Crook is positive of the fact. I think that if you move to the mouth of the Big Horn, by the time you reach it I shall be able to send information of the movements of Crook and Custer, upon which you will be able to determine your course. If, however, you find that you can strike a hostile band anywhere, do it without regard to reservations; but in doing it, be careful not to neglect the great object of keeping between the Indians and the Missouri.[27]

Since by this time the infantry had left to establish a field supply depot at the new Crow agency, Gibbon was compelled to send them orders to remain on the north side of the Yellowstone and wait for him and the cavalry opposite the mouth of Stillwater River. There he would pause to engage Mitch Boyer as chief guide and make a trip to the agency to enlist Crow Indian scouts.

These preliminaries to the Sioux campaign of 1876 provide a glimpse into the difficulties the frontier army faced in conducting a major campaign against the plains Indians in the formidable wilderness of the West. The problems stemmed not from army incompetence, but from the unusual conditions, especially alien to a force trained in the Civil War in the developed East. For the benefit of today's readers, these monumental problems deserve an explanatory note.

The West posed special problems in logistics, that is, the transport of troops and their essential supplies. Veritable mountains of rations, shelter, clothing, arms, and ammunition for the men, and forage for the animals, had to be delivered over long distances to the scene of action. Facilities for such transport were readily available in the densely populated East, but not in the forbidding, unsettled, and arid West. There, steamboats could ply only a rare river and then only in spring and sum-

[26] Ibid.
[27] Ibid.

mer. The Union Pacific was the only railroad west of the Missouri, and winter service was erratic indeed. Even wagon roads were few and rough, which translates to long and slow. Army contract trains, usually ox-drawn, made only 15 miles a day to allow grazing time, for to carry forage meant no payload. Quartermaster trains that supplied immediate needs of troops on the march were usually mule-drawn and could make 20 miles a day. As we have seen, even the assembling of troops and supplies at a staging base was time-consuming and often impossible in winter.

After the staging base was left, transport problems intensified, for there were often no roads whatever. Yet a trail suitable for heavily laden wagons simply had to be found, with essential wood, water, and grass at each night's bivouac. In unfamiliar country these requirements called for expert guides. For any prolonged operation, supply depots had to be established in the field and then replenished by successive supply trains; troops, usually infantry, had to be detached to guard such depots.

Another problem in the field was communications. Mounted couriers were the fastest means available but were still slow and uncertain. Soldiers could be used as couriers only when the route was both familiar and safe; otherwise, this duty demanded skilled frontiersmen. The slowness, however, meant that supplies had to be arranged far in advance and could not be adjusted as needed. Another consequence was that concerted action between far-separated columns was nearly impossible.

Locating the elusive Indian enemy and striking him effectively were the most frustrating problems of all. Success demanded expert scouts with frontier skills, knowledge of the country, and an understanding of the nature, habits, and tactics of the Indians—and the knack of getting through to officers not so gifted. The cavalry was the most mobile, but its range was inversely proportional to its speed. The range could be extended and speed still maintained if the column was supplied by a pack-train, but only Gen. Crook had developed an efficient one that could keep up with the cavalry it served. It consisted of specially trained mules managed entirely by expert civilian packers and therefore too expensive for general use. Others had to rely on draft mules and novice soldier-packers that both slowed and weakened the cavalry column.[28]

---

[28] For more on the logistics problem and army packtrains, see Gray, "Packtrain on Custer's Last Campaign," 53–58 (A).

Contrast this immobility of the army with the mobility of the plains Indians. They had herds of swift ponies that subsisted on grass alone. They were accustomed to living off the country, and what little they had to carry went on spare ponies. They knew every landmark and trail, every plot of grass, stand of timber, and waterhole. They could cross any terrain, and as both they and their ponies were expert swimmers, rivers were no obstacle. If pressed, a whole village, including women and children, could travel faster and longer than cavalry; if necessary, it could instantly break up into families and scatter in all directions. The cavalry, however, resembled nothing so much as a tortoise tethered by a string. Knowing this, the troops could only pray that persistence would bring a lucky break.

No means were then available to give the army the mobility comparable to that of the Indian, but it was possible for the army to hire, through the quartermaster, knowledgeable frontiersmen, half-blood and even full-blood Indians to serve as expert guides, scouts, couriers, and interpreters and to provide insight into Indian ways. In 1867 Congress had authorized the army to enlist groups of Indians as scouts, for short but renewable terms of service, subject to modified discipline and eligible for the same pay as regular soldiers. They were known as Enlisted Indian Scouts and placed in charge of a junior officer sometimes designated Chief of Scouts. Such quartermaster and enlisted auxiliaries were common, but how many, how well chosen, and how effectively used varied widely. A commander who ignored their Indian savvy was apt to meet frustration and even disaster, as exemplified by Braddock's defeat in colonial days.

GUIDING THE MONTANA COLUMN

Gen. John Gibbon's Montana column departed from its staging base at Fort Ellis not as a unit, but in several sections.

Capt. Walter Clifford (diarist) took the advance on March 23 with his Company E, 7th Infantry (from Camp Baker), and a contract supply train; on reaching the new Crow agency on April 1, he established a field supply depot. On March 30, Capt. Henry B. Freeman (diarist) departed in charge of the other five infantry companies (from Fort Shaw), which included Lt. William L. English (diarist) and Lt. James H. Bradley (diarist), and was soon overtaken by Mr. Powers's contract supply train. After crossing to the south bank of the Yellowstone, Freeman reached Deer Creek, 70 miles out, on April 4, when a courier from Gibbon brought him orders to remain on the north bank and wait opposite the mouth of the Stillwater. Recrossing the river, Freeman's battalion halted at this rendezvous on April 6. On April 1 Capt. Lewis Thompson left Fort Ellis in charge

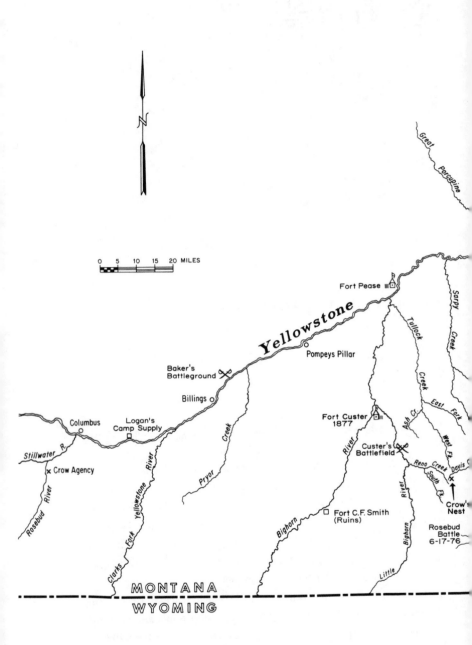

The Yellowstone Country. Map by Bob Bolin.

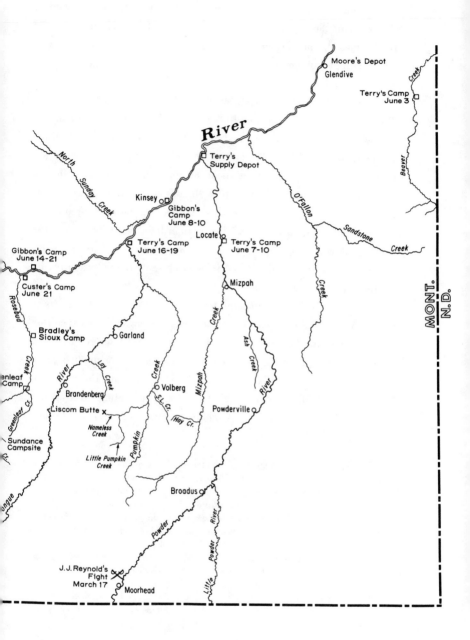

of the four companies of 2nd Cavalry, which included Lt. Edward J. McClernand, the expedition engineer and official itinerist (diarist), and Dr. Holmes O. Paulding (diarist), assistant surgeon and the sole medical officer with the column; the cavalry then joined Freeman's halted battalion at the rendezvous on April 8.[1]

Not until April 3 did Gen. Gibbon wire Terry from Fort Ellis: "Expedition finally off today. Total of 409 men and 27 officers."[2] That morning he and Maj. Brisbin, accompanied by Lt. Levi F. Burnett, the expedition adjutant, and Lt. Joshua W. Jacobs, the expedition quartermaster, left Fort Ellis and at 5:30 that afternoon overtook the cavalry battalion in bivouac 30 miles out at the mouth of Shield's River. That afternoon Dr. Paulding recorded that Gibbon's party "struck [our cavalry] camp like a percussion shell in a woodpile." It was from here that Gibbon sent the courier ahead to hold Capt. Freeman to the north bank. Gibbon's party then sped ahead to join the halted infantry opposite the Stillwater on the afternoon of April 7.

The purpose of these mundane details, assembled from diaries, is to identify where Quartermaster Jacobs was when he engaged the expedition scouts. Henry S. Bostwick, who had served as post interpreter at Fort Shaw since July 12, 1870, had been brought from there as the first guide and interpreter at fifty dollars a month.[3] This was the same Bostwick who had served with Mitch Boyer on Sir George Gore's hunting extravaganza back in 1855–56. Since he was relatively unfamiliar with the Yellow-

---

[1] This chapter and the next three deal with the march of the Montana column down the Yellowstone to make a junction with the Dakota column. From now on, footnotes are used only for occasionally cited sources. The bulk of evidence comes from repeatedly cited accounts of participants with the two columns, who will become familiar characters. In the text they are adequately identified to enable the reader to turn directly to a *special* category in the bibliography that replaces footnotes; Category X is for participants with the Montana column, Category "Y" for participants with the Dakota column.

These special categories are subdivided into military and other (scouts and civilians) personnel and are alphabetized by the participant's name. Each entry identifies the kind of account (diary, journal, official itinerary, letter, narrative, or interview), provides an abbreviated source, and ends with a capital letter, keyed to the standard bibliography. The text similarly identifies the participant and the kind of account, as well as the page number (in parentheses), except for diary-like accounts, for which the entry date replaces the page. (See A Note on Documentation, following the Preface.)

[2] Gibbon to Terry, April 3, Telegrams Sent, Distr. of Mont., 1876 (G-RG98).

[3] "Persons Hired by Lt. J. W. Jacobs, expedition quartermaster, 1876," lists all employees for the Montana column (G-RG92).

stone country, Bostwick remained rather inconspicuous on this campaign. It must have been he that Freeman recorded at the crossing of the Yellowstone on April 3: "Saw our Yellowstone guide at work."

The next person Lt. Jacobs engaged was John W. Williamson, as scout, at fifty dollars a month on April 3, the date indicating that he was hired at Fort Ellis. He was the former 2nd Cavalryman that Brisbin's relief column had brought back from Fort Pease. He came out with Gibbon's party, and when it overtook the cavalry, he was sent ahead to alter Freeman's route. He would see much service as a reliable courier. Gibbon also tried to hire George B. Herendeen at Fort Ellis, but that worthy told Noyes (1917, p. 107) that he had spurned the paltry offer of sixteen dollars a month as teamster. A month later he would come out with Paul McCormick, prove his worth, and then be hired as scout.

When Gibbon and staff reached the infantry camp opposite the Stillwater on April 7, Lt. Bradley, detached from Company B to command a mounted infantry detachment of thirteen men, recorded in his invaluable diary that the general was anxious to employ "Mitch Bouyer, noted guide." Gibbon elaborated on this comment in his narrative of the campaign (1877, p. 275):

> I had in the morning [April 7] sent forward a courier to the Crow Agency, calling a council with the Crows to obtain some of them to accompany the troops as scouts, and had requested Mitch Bowyer, a noted guide and interpreter, to meet me that night in my camp. This man I had never seen, but he had served with troops before and bore the reputation of being, next to the celebrated Jim Bridger, the best guide in the country. While seated in my tent the next morning [April 8], a man with the face of an Indian and the dress of a white man approached the door, and almost without saying anything seated himself on the ground, and it was some moments before I understood that my visitor was the expected guide. He was a diffident, low-spoken man, who uttered his words in a hesitating way as if uncertain what he was going to say. He brought the news that the Crows were waiting to see me. . . .

Gibbon ended his story in midsentence, but Lt. Jacobs's report for April furnishes a proper conclusion. On that April 8 the quartermaster engaged Mitch "Bouyer" as guide at five dollars a day (one hundred fifty dollars a month), the highest salary of all. That same day Jacobs also engaged H. M. ("Muggins") Taylor, who had been on the Pease expedition, as scout at one hundred dollars a month. Tom LeForge told Marquis (1928, p. 210) about Mitch's employment:

> [He] had been hired, not enlisted . . . as guide and his duty kept him at all ordinary times with the wagon train. At various times prior to this he had served in like capacity for both army and civilian travelers. As a reliable guide anywhere in this part of the West he had a high reputation and he fully deserved it. He knew minutely every local region from the Platte to Bozeman and he could talk Sioux, Crow and English.

When the cavalry pulled in about 10 A.M. of April 8, Gibbon and Capt. Freeman, escorted by Bradley and his mounted infantry detachment, plowed through a wet snowstorm to the Crow agency, where Agent Clapp received them hospitably. On the morning of April 9 they held a two-hour council with the Crow chiefs, with Pierre Shane as interpreter, though Gibbon and Bradley could scarcely understand his "English." Gibbon asked for twenty-five Crow warriors to enlist and serve as "eyes" for his column. As the Crows had never enlisted before, they showed hesitation, for they were not great admirers of the army's discipline nor its clumsy manner of campaigning. The chiefs actually gave their consent but tried to explain that by their custom each Crow was to make his own decision. Even with Agent Clapp's support, the officers feared the council had failed.

That afternoon the Crows entertained their guests with a dance, and in the evening some warriors expressed their eagerness to enlist against the Sioux. As Tom LeForge told Marquis (p. 206), Bradley offered him an extra dollar a day if he would enlist and not only help manage the Crows but act as interpreter. Clearly, Bradley perceived that ignorance of Indian ways and inability to speak Crow were obstacles to be overcome. The result was that both Tom LeForge and Barney Bravo, although technically ineligible, accepted enlistment, thereby initiating the lieutenant's education. Maybe that was a better arrangement than if Gibbon had loosened his purse strings and hired them, as he had been authorized to do.

Gen. Gibbon was nursing a hunch that hostile Sioux were still lurking in the Bighorn valley, where he could strike them. That evening he talked with a party of two hundred miners from Bozeman, now bound for the Black Hills and whom the troops had noted on the march out. Gibbon was happy to learn that they were heading first for Fort C. F. Smith on the

Bighorn, and he hoped they might flush some Sioux northward toward the altered route of his column. He had also hoped to induce some Crow war parties to volunteer to go after the Sioux. He apparently succeeded, for a few would accompany his force and others would leave the next day with the miners' party.[4]

On the morning of April 10 Lt. Bradley, now assigned charge of the Crow scouts, mustered in the full authorized quota of twenty-five, including Tom LeForge ("Horse Rider") and Barney Bravo ("Big Nose"). The *Register of Enlisted Indian Scouts* lists them all in phonetic Crow and translated English names, but for some reason without the usual height, weight, color, and age.[5] Bradley recorded, however, that two were over sixty, far beyond warrior age; they would serve as advisers to the young men. These elders were "Shows His Face" and "Little Face."

On April 11 Gibbon's party left the agency early so as to avoid being drifted in by a heavy snowstorm and found the troops had all moved 14 miles downstream to a new camp. The next day was spent in preparing to resume the march. Capt. Clifford's company had already come out from the agency, and Lt. Jacobs had taken empty wagons there to remove the supply depot to the new troop camp, which would be called Camp Supply (111.5 miles from Fort Ellis)[6] and was left in the charge of Capt. Logan's Company A, 7th Infantry. That evening Barney Bravo brought out the enlisted Crow scouts, but Tom LeForge was delayed a day by personal business.

From Camp Supply on the morning of April 13 the Montana column, save for Logan's company, stretched out on the trail down the north bank of the Yellowstone, bound for Sioux country, but muddy roads held them to 12 miles. Having been given the permanent duty of scouting the van and flanks, Bradley sent Bravo ahead with ten Crows and then followed with the remainder and his mounted infantry. It proved a day of frustration, for with no interpreter at hand, Bradley could not control his own Crows; he was greatly relieved when Tom LeForge overtook him in camp that night.

Mitch Boyer was a good interpreter and wielded considerable influence

[4] Dispatch from J. V. Bogert, Bozeman, April 14, to *Chicago Tribune*, May 2, 1876.

[5] *Register of Enlisted Indian Scouts*, 1866–77 (G-M).

[6] Lt. English's diary and Lt. McClernand's official itinerary recorded odometer mileages systematically, but others less so.

over the Crows, but neither he nor the other quartermaster scouts were under Bradley's command. That is the reason the latter's diary does not bristle with references to Mitch. Boyer was answerable to Gibbon, who kept him on guide duty while the column was on the march, not because the troops could not follow a river, but because the heavily laden wagon train needed a far smoother trail than horsemen or footmen. When bluffs crowded the river, sometimes on both sides, it became necessary to ford or circle away from the stream by a negotiable trail affording wood, water, and grass. At these times Mitch's knowledge became invaluable. Later his duties would expand, and vastly more than LeForge told Marquis (p. 224): "His [Mitch's] regular place was with the train when it was on the move, but when a base camp would be established, he would go out at times with us, or with the soldiers, perhaps as guide, more likely for the pure love of adventure. He was my regular choice associate when we were together in the same camp, as we had been friends and companions on many an adventure."

On April 14, with the aid of LeForge, Bradley got all his ducks in a row, for he recorded: "Crows scouted excellently today, scouring the country for a breadth of 10–12 miles, keeping well ahead. No sign of Sioux." That phrase would make a constant refrain all the way to the Bighorn. The next day, encroaching bluffs forced the column to climb to a plateau for a stretch and then descend to camp on the bottom at Baker's Battleground, 43 miles out. Mitch had chosen the trail well, for they made 17 miles that day. On April 16 they made only 7 miles to camp on Pryor Creek, as they were compelled to make a difficult fording to the river's south bank, nearly drowning Lt. Charles B. Schofield, Brisbin's adjutant. They followed the south bank on April 17 down to Pompey's Pillar, 66 miles out, where they would lay over a day while scouts were sent out.

As Bradley recorded that evening, Gibbon sent Muggins Taylor and a Crow southeast toward the mouth of the Little Bighorn, some 30 miles distant, to scout for hostile Sioux; they returned to the camp the next day, reporting that they had seen nought but quietly grazing buffalo. Gibbon had sent another party that same evening northwest down the Yellowstone, which gave Bradley a little concern:

April 17: Have been annoyed by fourteen Crow volunteers who seduce my Crows from duty. Gibbon gave them three days' rations to scout downriver. They left at dark, accompanied by two of my Crows, who are to return and report findings.

April 18: Some [of my Crows] went up the river to look for Sioux on our [back] trail. All but one returned in the evening, seeing no signs of Sioux; the absentee deserted to join the Crow Volunteers who went downriver last night.

These three scouts, who joined the volunteer Crows heading downriver on April 17, were three of Bradley's best: Curley, White Swan, and Hairy Moccasin, as Curley told Dixon (1909, p. 143):

After we started [from Camp Supply, April 13] my brother, who was then on the warpath [against Sioux as a volunteer Crow] approached me and took me, Hairy Moccasin and White Swan and said he had a secret mission in another district. We went with my brother as far as Tongue River, but not seeing what we were searching for [Sioux], we came back home [to the Crow village at the agency, as will emerge].

Scouting as far as Tongue River could not have revealed any Sioux, for following Crook's attack of March 17, the winter roamers were consolidating their villages on the lower Powder River. But instead of reporting back to Bradley, the trio headed for the Crow village. (Bradley will soon reveal more about his presumed "deserters.")

Resuming the march on April 19, the column made 19.6 miles, despite having to ford the Yellowstone to the north bank and, within 2 miles, ford back again. In the middle of the 17-mile march of April 20 came the final crossing that left them on the north bank; it was the most difficult fording, for the river was now rising, as Gibbon related (1877, p. 281):

Our guide, Mitch Bowyer, is of inestimable value now, for he rides forward to search for a crossing and is an indefatigable worker, riding his hardy little pony into the ice-cold water sometimes to a swimming depth, testing the crossings where anybody thinks there is a chance to get our wagons over. At last the shallowest point is found, and although deeper than is comfortable, we must take to the water, for we cannot afford to wait another day.

Mitch led the dripping wagons up onto the bluff and then downstream, passing opposite the mouth of the Bighorn before descending into Pease Bottom, where they bivouacked two miles short of Fort Pease. Its flag still fluttered, and discarded things useful to Indians lay scattered around as mute evidence that no Sioux had been there since its evacuation back in early March. Rumors of "Indian tracks" circulated that day, but the careful Bradley and his Crows found that they had been made by two wild horses.

143   *Guiding the Montana Column*

The next morning Gibbon began a letter to Terry, dated at Fort Pease, April 21, to report his progress and supply problems:

We reached here yesterday in good shape, but have been delayed . . . by the roads and weak animals, especially those of hired teams, which are very poor, but the best we could get for the price. We are now north of the Yellowstone and must stay here with our wagons, though the cavalry can no doubt cross for some time yet in case an opportunity should present itself for striking Indians.

I left Logan's company with the supplies left behind and shall have to send wagons back for them as soon as I can get enough empty ones to send, which will take another of my infantry to guard, hence it becomes an important question as to whether I am going to meet supplies on the boat below, of which I telegraphed you today. Logan will have to come down north of the river by a longer and more difficult road than the one we followed and additional supplies will have to follow the same route. Should you deem it necessary to have more supplies come to us by this route, I hope you will telegraph to this effect to . . . Fort Ellis, as I am too far away to get the necessary information about freight contracts, etc., with certainty. . . .[7]

At this point the letter was interrupted by the arrival of a dispatch from Terry. The soldier-courier from Fort Ellis had picked up Will Logan, the young son of Capt. Logan, at the latter's Camp Supply, and the pair had made a fast trip. Terry's dispatch, dated April 15 at St. Paul, informed Gibbon that Crook's Wyoming column could not take the field again until mid-May (actually May 29) and the Dakota column had not yet started; it also directed Gibbon to proceed no farther than the Bighorn, "unless sure of striking a successful blow." That was unwelcome news, for it left Gibbon's small force stranded alone in Indian country to wait a month or more for support. After reading the dispatch, Gibbon resumed his letter to Terry:

10:40 A.M. I had just got this far when a courier arrived with your dispatch of the 15th. I have, in accordance with directions, moved my camp along side of Fort Pease [104 miles out], where I am strong enough to defy the whole Sioux nation, should they feel inclined to come this way, but I think they will be felt in the direction of the Black Hills first, whatever they do afterwards. The position here is so strong that one company can easily hold it and let all the rest loose in case

[7]Gibbon to Terry, April 21, 1876, Letters Received, Dept. of Dakota, 1876, Box 19 (G-RG98).

we see a chance to strike. In the meantime I will send back for Logan's company and the supplies left with him, and make requisition on McClay & Co. [the Diamond-R firm] for freighting another month's supplies down and make this my depot.

I have today sent scouts to the north of us, where some signs were seen yesterday [which Bradley had already found to be wild horses]. Will keep my scouts busy every day in various directions and think also I will send a company of cavalry with good scouts in the direction of [Fort] C. F. Smith to communicate with that citizen party on the road. If there are any Sioux in that direction, I imagine I shall hear of it. Hoping we shall be able to settle this Sitting Bull matter. . . .

At 1 A.M. of April 22 four cavalrymen rode out of Fort Pease to deliver Gibbon's letter to Fort Ellis for relaying to Terry. On the morning of the 23rd, Gibbon sent Capt. Freeman's Company H, 7th Infantry, to escort the now-empty wagons of the Powers contract train back to Camp Supply. He sent Mitch Boyer as guide to locate a new wagon road along the north bank and thus reduce the number of crossings of the still-rising river.

Capt. Freeman's diary, which covers this eighteen-day round trip, mentions Mitch several times; it also tells of road work, game being brought in, talking with Crow Indians, and finding good spring water, all of which attest to Mitch's presence. The party reached Camp Supply on April 28, Mitch and young Will Logan having been sent ahead the evening before to notify Capt. Logan to evacuate the depot, for both the supplies and Company A were ordered to Fort Pease. During the return trip, which began on the afternoon of April 29, Freeman recorded some items that shed light on events at Fort Pease.

Gibbon's long letter had indicated that he was confident in the strength of his base camp at Fort Pease and eager to find the Sioux and strike a blow. On the morning of April 24 he sent out not one but two companies of 2nd Cavalry, Capt. Ball's (Co. H) and Lt. Roe's (Co. F), on the promised reconnaissance up the Bighorn River in search of Sioux, or at least news of them from the Black Hills mining party. The only scouts to accompany this eight-day mission were Tom LeForge and a Crow, Jack Rabbit Bull. Then, on April 27, Lt. Bradley dispatched six other Crows to scout down the Yellowstone as far as the Rosebud, nearly 60 miles distant; they would return on the 30th, having seen plenty of buffalo but no Sioux.

On the 29th, Bradley had discovered to his dismay that three more of his Crow scouts had stolen away with their horses and personal effects,

raising the total of apparent deserters to six. But the sextet that had returned from the Rosebud on the 30th must have encountered Curley,
White Swan, and Hairy Moccasin coming back from Tongue River with
the volunteer Crows (who had left April 17 from Pompey's Pillar), for
Bradley recorded on May 1: "We hear that the party of volunteers had
scouted to the Rosebud [sic, Tongue] and then returned to the Crow camp,
my three scouts going with them, instead of rejoining us as ordered."
Capt. Freeman, who met the trio and volunteers on dates that fit during
his return from Camp Supply, added confirmation: "April 30: Met party
of Crows who had left us at Pompey's Pillar on April 17. They report going
to Powder River [sic, Tongue] and seeing no Sioux sign. The Crow camp
is coming down to hunt buffalo. May 1: Met balance of Crow war party
which had been nearly to Powder River [sic, Tongue], but found no
Sioux."

That same evening of May 1 Bradley sent Barney Bravo and elderly
Little Face to the Crow agency with a letter to Agent Clapp, asking for his
help in getting all six of his missing Crows to return to duty. This fact
amply establishes the veracity of Curley's statement to Dixon (p. 231),
which concludes: "Then we Crow scouts left the agency and camped at
Clark's Fork, and Barney Bravo and Little Face, Crow scout and interpreter, met us there. These two took us down to Gibbon's camp [reached
May 12]."

Also on May 1 Ball and Roe's reconnaissance up the Bighorn returned
with Tom LeForge and Jack Rabbit Bull. They had marched to the adobe
ruins of Fort C. F. Smith and back, for a total of 178 miles. They had
seen no trace of Sioux, nor picked up any news of them, for they found
only the deserted camps of the Black Hills miners. While this second
negative report was setting the entire camp to buzzing with speculation
on the whereabouts of the Sioux, Gibbon composed a telegram to Terry,
dated May 1 at Fort Pease: "Capt. Ball just in with two companies from
Fort C. F. Smith. Went on Phil Kearny road as far as Rotten Grass Creek,
thence over on Little Big Horn to Tullock's Fork and down that. He saw
no sign of Indians. My [Crow] scouts report none on Rosebud. As soon as
my supplies reach here, say in ten days, I propose, if no news comes from
you, to move downriver."[8] That night, courier John W. Williamson sped

[8] Ibid., May 1, idem.

from Fort Pease to deliver this dispatch to the Bozeman telegraph office, meeting Capt. Freeman's returning column on May 3.

The Montana column, now three weeks in the field, had failed to find any trace of the Sioux, but before dawn of May 3, alas, the Sioux managed to find the column at Fort Pease, asleep, as all participants noted. Henry S. Bostwick went out early to bring in his horse and mule, only to find mere picket pins and knife-cut ropes. The Crows rushed out to where they had left their ponies grazing on an island and found nothing but Sioux moccasin tracks. After a good cry they started out on foot to follow the thieves' trail, but 8 miles downstream the sound of shots drove them back. They did learn, however, that the Sioux numbered fifty, of whom twenty had purloined the ponies while the rest had waited in reserve, as Bradley recorded.

The troops, mystified again, wondered how these raiders had so suddenly materialized from nowhere. It is known today that the winter roamers, consolidated under Sitting Bull and Crazy Horse, had moved leisurely down Powder River almost to its mouth, where they turned west. On this May 3 their village, approaching four hundred lodges and eight hundred warriors strong, stood a little up from the mouth of Tongue River.[9]

Leaving speculation to others, Bradley resolved to find out whence these raiders had come. He managed on May 5 to persuade all the Crows to set out again to follow the Sioux back trail, unaccustomed though they were to scouting on foot. They soon returned, having ventured little farther than on their first pursuit. So on May 6 Bradley mounted Half Yellow Face and Jack Rabbit Bull on his own horses and sent them out. The pair followed the trail 15 miles downriver, where they spotted three Sioux warriors, whom they charged recklessly at full speed. The startled Sioux broke and fled, abandoning their three mounts to the two Crows, who rode their prizes back to camp in triumph. Armed with this information, Bradley requested permission to lead a strong and determined party to where the raiders had come from, whether north, south, or downriver to the east. Reluctantly, Gibbon granted the request, but he delayed the start until the evening of May 7.

Another event of May 6 came as a pleasant surprise to the Fort Pease

[9] Gray, *Centennial Campaign*, chap. 27, which reconstructs the movements of the winter roamers; Table 11 (pp. 326–27) summarizes locations day by day.

camp. A small boat bearing the name *Fleetfoot*, which had left Benson's Landing on May 2, landed in their midst and disgorged its crew— "Commodore" Paul W. McCormick and "Captain" George B. Herendeen.[10] Since Gibbon had brought no sutler into the field, McCormick had come to seek the privilege of acting as a free-lance sutler to the column. He would soon return to Bozeman to bring down a good load of sutler wares. Herendeen, however, had come to stay and, anticipating the column's move downriver, began repairing some of the small boats still there that he had helped build for the Pease expedition, claiming them as his own property. In a little argument with Gibbon, George won the right to operate the boats in the interest of the column but with no remuneration, as he told Noyes (n.d.). His competent services would later bring him quartermaster employment.

At dusk of May 7 Bradley rode out of this base camp at the head of a sizable scouting party, consisting of seventeen mounted soldiers, Henry Bostwick, Tom LeForge, and four of his Crows. Probably the Crows included Half Yellow Face and Jack Rabbit Bull, riding their captured Sioux ponies, but the other two are unnamed. Tom LeForge gave Marquis (pp. 230–31) an account of what can only be this mission, but it is so garbled as to be useless (he claimed they went to Powder River and named Boyer as present, though the latter was still absent with Freeman).

At 3 A.M. on May 8, when 15 miles downriver, the scouts discovered three warlodges that had sheltered some thirty Sioux the day before. Half Yellow Face and Jack Rabbit Bull, who had so recklessly charged three Sioux near this point, thus learned just how good their medicine had been. Later that morning, having found where a Sioux party had crossed to the south bank, Bradley retired to the bluffs, while the sharp-eyed Crows scanned the country beyond the river for the smoke of a village but could see only quietly grazing buffalo. On returning to the bottom, the scouts soon found more Sioux signs, including the tracks, now two days old, made by Bostwick's stolen mule.

Proceeding down the valley, they came on a larger and older camp of warlodges and then made a long noon halt. It was probably at this halt that the scouts spelled out their findings in detail to the eager Bradley, interpreting them to make a coherent and dated story of the Sioux raid.

[10]The boat departure and "ranks" appeared in *Helena Herald*, May 18, 1876.

All the movements of the Sioux had been up and then back down the Yellowstone. On reaching the Great Porcupine late that afternoon, some 40 miles out, the Crows spotted a herd of buffalo and bagged several; even Bradley welcomed the meat, but not the heavy firing. From there the party turned back and, after camping for the night, rode in to the Fort Pease base camp at noon of May 9.

This mission was Bradley's first independent scout, and although it had located no hostile village, the lieutenant now knew that the Sioux were down the Yellowstone and not in the interior, north or south. The operation gave him confidence not only in himself, but in the ability of the Crows to read and interpret "sign" and thus provide invaluable military intelligence. Some of his fellow officers, including Gen. Gibbon, who soldiered "by the book," considered the chief of scouts to be merely foolhardy and would remain skeptical of his findings and ignore their implications.

BRADLEY FINDS AND GIBBON LOSES THE SIOUX

When Lt. Bradley returned from his scout on May 9, he found the Fort
Pease base camp bustling with activity. The day before, Mitch Boyer had
brought in the supply train, escorted by the companies of Freeman and
Logan, thus restoring the Montana column to full strength and supplies.
All were now preparing to move down the north bank of the Yellowstone
in the direction from which the Sioux raiders had come and where there
were good river crossings that Gibbon must prevent the Sioux from using
to escape north to the wilderness. Clifford's company was slated to float
down the river in Herendeen's flotilla but to camp each night with the
overland column. Bradley assigned them two unmounted Crows to scour
the riverbanks for evidence of Sioux crossings.

Also on May 9 Gibbon wrote another telegram to Terry, which Paul
McCormick carried that evening on horseback to Bozeman:

> Leave here tomorrow with my whole command. Small war parties
> have been in our vicinity and this place is too far up the river to

produce any effect. A scouting party under Lt. Bradley, just in from the Porcupine, 40 miles below, saw no Indians, but found the fresh trail of a war party of thirty Indians leading down the river. This party ran off some Crow ponies from this camp on the night of May 2nd. We shall be short of rations before our [next] train [Diamond-R train] can reach us, but buffalo are plenty and we shall not suffer.[1]

The march from Fort Pease began in rain and mud on May 10 and, with layovers on the 11th and 13th, would end in a severe evening hail-storm on May 14, 52 miles down and 1 mile above the Little Porcupine and 6 miles above the Rosebud, where the column would halt for six days. For this entire movement Mitch Boyer guided the wagon train in the company of Lt. McClernand, official itinerist. On the first day's march McClernand spotted a sharp butte far ahead, which Mitch told him marked the east bank of the Great Porcupine. When they passed it on the last day's march, it could only have been Mitch who told Bradley that it served the Sioux as a favorite lookout point. That same day water proved desperately short, but Mitch discovered a spring, which on being dug out yielded a generous flow of water, clear and sweet, to everyone's satisfaction, both then and later.

In the middle of this move, on the evening of May 12, Bradley welcomed the return of Barney Bravo and Little Face as they brought back to duty all six of the missing Crow scouts, including Curley, White Swan, and Hairy Moccasin. Curley told Dixon (p. 143) that on rejoining the column he found the scouts with Gibbon "had no horses. We had eight horses with us." Bradley's account agrees and adds that the returning eight now gave him a total of ten mounted Crows. White Man Runs Him also told Dixon (p. 153) that he was among those who had lost horses to the Sioux, and "I was left to go on foot, so I put my gun on my shoulder and marched with the soldiers."

Little had been seen of Sioux on this march, and only one downriver scout had been completed and another launched. On the evening of May 12 Quartermaster Jacobs, Muggins Taylor, Henry Bostwick, and Engineering Sergeant James Wilson were skiffed across the river to scout down to the Rosebud; they returned the next day, having seen nothing and not sure they had reached the Rosebud (Bradley and Freeman diaries). To settle the matter, Bradley sent four unmounted Crows across the river on

---

[1] Gibbon to Terry, May 9, 1876, Telegrams Sent, Distr. of Mont., 1876 (G-RG98).

Bradley Finds and Gibbon Loses the Sioux

the evening of May 13, in hopes that they could steal Sioux horses. They returned on the 15th, disheartened but with news. They had been below the Rosebud on the 14th, when they struck the tempting trail of thirty well-mounted Sioux leading up the Yellowstone from the Tongue. Eager for remounts, they followed it, only to have the heavy hailstorm of that evening obliterate the trail. Bradley promptly asked Gibbon for permission to lead a strong scouting party to locate this suspected village on the Tongue. With some reluctance, Gibbon consented.

Bradley's second independent scouting mission would hit the jackpot. He started out that evening of May 15 with twelve of his mounted infantry detachment, swelled by eight volunteer soldiers and Barney Bravo with five Crow scouts. Bradley did not name the Crows, but Curley told Dixon (p. 143) that he was one and gave a sparse but accurate account of the mission. Barney Bravo told Walter Camp (1911, p. 244) that he was also present and gave a more detailed and equally accurate account. It is unlikely that Mitch Boyer was present, for Bradley usually named scouts who were not his own, and Gibbon was hoping to resume the march and would thus want to keep Mitch on hand as guide.

After crossing the river in Clifford's boats, Bradley headed southeast, crossing the Rosebud 5 miles out and then resting for the night 14 miles out. The next morning, May 16, they advanced 5 more miles to a sheltered ravine, from which they climbed to a high peak, or lookout, in the Wolf Mountains. From this point they could see Rosebud Creek, now behind them, for 30 miles above its mouth, but saw no Indians or signs of a camp. Proceeding easterly again, they examined the very trail of the thirty Sioux seen by the unmounted Crows on the 14th; it appeared to have originated from the Tongue, 15 to 18 miles above its mouth. Bradley halted on the brow of a ridge and glimpsed Tongue River 5 to 6 miles ahead. In its valley, buffalo herds were running, as though driven by Sioux, which made the Crows nervous.

According to Curley, Barney Bravo was the first to spot a haze of smoke drawing up from a Sioux village strung along the bank of the Tongue. Bravo confirmed Bradley in saying that the officer was eager to descend close to the village and count the lodges, but the scouts vetoed the idea as both suicidal and unnecessary, as they could easily tell that it was a very large village of about two hundred or three hundred lodges. It would later be counted as probably four hundred lodges, thus representing nearly all the winter roamers gathered in one camp—the very target of the campaign. Bradley reported it as only 35 miles in a beeline from the Little Porcupine base camp; his distances, bearings, and geographical features, when applied to topographical maps, define the site of the village as very close to present Garland, about 30 miles above the mouth of the Tongue.

Bradley reluctantly started back at 6 P.M. that day and, aside from two rest periods, rode hard all night to reach the Yellowstone opposite the Little Porcupine base camp at daylight of May 17. On skiffing across, he learned that the camp had experienced an alarm the evening before. The pickets at the river had seen Indians on the south bank and fired on them. The whole camp had turned out to resist an attack but soon returned to bed. Some of these Sioux were probably still around, and others may have picked up and followed Bradley's trail, for there were many that day on the south bank.

When Bradley reported his discovery of the hostile village, Gibbon promptly decided that this was his opportunity to strike a successful blow. Holding back only Capt. Sanno's Company K, 7th Infantry, to guard the camp and supply train, he ordered the rest of his force to cross the river, make a fast night march to Tongue River, and there launch a surprise attack in the morning on the Sioux village. [2]

Crossing the Yellowstone at high water in Herendeen's boats was no problem for the infantry, but swimming cavalry horses across was a formidable task. By the time preparations had been completed, at 9 A.M., some Sioux were already visible on the bluffs, watching the process. The cavalry horses again and again refused to take to the deep water. Offers of the Crows to swim them across were ignored. Capt. Ball then tied them in a long string and tried to lead them across from a small boat. On striking the swift current in deep water, the lead horse turned back in fright, pulling the others under. By 5 P.M. very few had made it and four or five mounts had drowned. This was by no means the first time a cavalry force had been thwarted by a river. Gibbon had to order the attempt abandoned, for the advantage of surprise was already lost. [3]

---

[2] In his official report of the campaign, Oct. 17, 1876 (x), Gibbon located this village on the Rosebud, instead of the Tongue, an error that will receive later comment.

[3] All diaries and accounts describe this aborted attempt to cross the river; Barney Bravo told Camp (1911, 245) about the Crows' offer and Capt. Ball's disastrous maneuver.

Up to this moment Gibbon had displayed some eagerness to find and strike the enemy, hoping for a short campaign. But this day of frustration apparently demoralized him, for his next report to Terry did not refer to this reverse, nor even to the discovery of a huge Sioux village on the Tongue, and he would remain dispirited for the rest of the campaign. It is hindsight, of course, that reveals a second and greater opportunity within Gibbon's grasp: circumstances had forced all the winter roamers into one large camp, which Bradley had just located and *could keep track of*, thereby furnishing invaluable intelligence to guide the coming heavier operations. To reap this harvest, Gibbon had only to persevere in the path he had been following, but he would fail to do so.

Dr. Paulding recorded in his diary that both Gibbon and Brisbin turned up sick on May 18 and 19, but nonetheless, several scouting parties set out, in the rain, on the 18th. At noon Capts. Thompson and Wheelan, with their companies L and G, 2nd Cavalry, guided by Mitch Boyer and two Crows, launched a three-day scout down the north bank as far as Tongue River to look for evidence of Sioux crossings. Then, that afternoon, Bradley sent four unmounted Crows down the south bank, again to steal horses. At dark Bradley led his mounted infantry, Tom LeForge, and five Crows upriver to meet expected couriers from Fort Ellis. This party returned the next day with two soldier-couriers and a heavy mail, including a letter from Terry with information, but no orders, for Gibbon. Apparently, the Dakota column had been delayed, partly by Custer's troubles in Washington, but Terry hoped to get off by May 10 and reach the Yellowstone at Glendive Creek about May 28.

At 8 A.M. of May 20 the four horse-stealing Crows returned to camp, empty-handed but brimming with news for Bradley. At noon of the 19th, from Bradley's former lookout point in the Wolf Mountains, they had discovered several hundred Sioux warriors approaching from the direction of the Tongue. From concealment they had watched this party, mounted and equipped for war, file by within a few hundred yards and proceed into the Rosebud valley not far from its mouth. Other diarists implied that these Sioux had crossed or intended to cross the Yellowstone, and Dr. Paulding recorded that the Crows had heard firing all day downriver in the direction Mitch had led the Thompson-Wheelan party.

Gibbon immediately detached Capt. Kirtland's Company B, 7th Infantry, to guard the camp and supplies, while he led the rest of his force to the relief of Thompson and Wheelan, taking Bradley's mounted infantry and the Crows to scout the riverbanks for signs of Sioux crossings. Having found no such signs in a march of 8 miles, Gibbon went into camp 2 miles below and opposite the Rosebud. Bradley's scouts, however, continued for another 13 miles downstream but turned back when they found the trail of the cavalry party that had also turned back with Mitch. As Gibbon's new Rosebud camp proved superior to the one at the Little Porcupine, the latter was moved down the next day, and there the command remained for the next two weeks.

Just as Kirtland and the supply train joined the Rosebud camp on the afternoon of May 21, the members of the Thompson-Wheelan scouting party returned with a story to tell.[4] On the morning of May 19 they had detected forty to fifty Sioux ascending the south riverbank, apparently aiming to cross it 3 miles upstream. The troops sneaked back to that point and set an ambush, but the Sioux merely tested the water and then continued upstream, concealing some spare ponies in the timber. Noting this tempting pony herd, Mitch Boyer and one of the Crows, Hairy Moccasin, swam the river, stripped and weaponless. They stalked toward the prize but found that the last hundred yards offered no cover. Seeing only two or three Indian boys guarding the herd, the two scouts risked a dash across the open ground, but the boys responded instantly by driving the herd off at full speed. Foiled, the two scouts could only swim back in disappointment. The cavalry party then continued on to Tongue River but found nothing except the trail where Lt. Bradley had turned back.

Since rations were now running short, Gibbon reduced the issue by one-half on May 22 but encouraged selected soldiers to go hunting for meat. The result was that three cavalrymen, while so hunting that day, were fired on by Sioux but escaped unharmed. The expected Diamond-R train, in the charge of Matt Carroll (another diarist), had left Fort Ellis on May 15, but Gibbon needed to replace its temporary escort by one of his own. For this reason, early on May 23 he sent back Lt. English's Company I, 7th Infantry, reinforced for the first two days by Lt. Roe's Company E, 2nd Cavalry. With them went the Powers contract train, now empty, for discharge at Fort Ellis.

[4] The "story" that follows is from the diaries of Bradley, Freeman, and Dr. Paulding and Gibbon's narrative (1877, 286); all name Boyer, and Freeman names Hairy Moccasin.

Bradley seized this opportunity to dispatch Barney Bravo and two Crows to the Crow village to secure ponies to remount his scouts, still crippled without them. On reaching Pompey's Pillar on May 27, Lt. English recorded in his laconic diary: "Bravo and the two Crows swam the river and struck out for the Crow camp." In telling Camp (1911, p. 244) of this duty, Bravo failed to mention his Crow companions. On May 28 English met the Diamond-R train a little below Baker's Battleground and would escort it back to Gibbon's Rosebud camp on June 4. Neither Lt. English nor anyone else even hints that Mitch Boyer accompanied this mission.

Meanwhile, at the Rosebud base camp English's caravan had scarcely faded over the horizon on the morning of May 23 when George Herendeen galloped in from a hunt, reporting that he had heard firing and seen a fleeing party of Sioux. Bradley's mounted infantry and some cavalry companies dashed out in futile pursuit but found the bodies of three other hunters. Other Sioux were seen on the south bank but, being inaccessible, were left alone. Dr. Paulding, driving an ambulance, brought in the mutilated bodies of the three slain hunters: Pvts. Raymeyer and Stoker, Company H, 2nd Cavalry, and Matt Quinn, a civilian teamster.

While the doctor was performing autopsies that afternoon, a mackinaw dubbed *General Brisbin,* which had sailed from Benson's Landing on May 16 under "Commodore" James D. Chestnut,[5] another free-lance sutler, reached camp, bringing a full load of butter, eggs, and fresh vegetables to cheer the troops on half rations. At 7 P.M. the three slain hunters were ceremoniously buried. The most affected mourner was one of the elder Crows, Little Face (according to Bradley) or Shows his Face (according to Dr. Paulding). Sioux lined the bluffs across the river, solemnly watching the ceremony. Chestnut's mackinaw had delivered more than vegetables, for Dr. Paulding told of a "jamboree" held that evening over eight gallons of beer.

Gibbon took the loss of three men seriously, for during the next dozen nights at his camp, he rousted out all troops to lay on their arms along the picket line until dawn, prepared for attack. To everyone's disgust, the precaution proved unnecessary, for the Sioux abruptly and completely disappeared, a phenomenon that drew much speculation. Just three

[5]The departure of Chestnut's mackinaw was announced in the *Bozeman Times,* May 18, 1876.

nights of such sleepless peace and quiet so aroused Bradley's curiosity that he prepared to make another independent scout to find out what had become of the Sioux village. He rounded up his mounted infantry, Tom LeForge, and five Crows; Curley told Dixon (1909, p. 143) that he was one of the five Crows, and Tom LeForge told Marquis (pp. 229–30) that White Man Runs Him was another.

At 5 A.M. of May 27 Bradley's party skiffed across the river in Clifford's boats, swimming their horses without trouble. While heading south toward the Wolf Mountains, they crossed some open country, which they found strewn with recently killed buffalo and laced by hundreds of pony tracks. As they approached Bradley's old lookout point, 14 miles out, they came on the warrior trail leading toward the lower Rosebud, seen by the Crows on May 19. The Crows concluded that the warriors had been the vanguard of a movement of the entire village from the Tongue to the Rosebud.

On scanning the valley of the Rosebud from the lookout, they beheld a heavy smoke and with field glasses saw lodges and surrounding herds of ponies representing an immense Sioux village, perhaps four hundred lodges, only 8 miles distant and 18 miles from the Rosebud base camp. One letter writer from the camp made it five hundred lodges; he also revealed that Bradley's hard-riding infantry detatchment had earned the sobriquet, "The Shoo-flies."[6] To the scouts the signs were unmistakable; the Sioux village they had seen on May 17 on the Tongue had moved westward to the lower Rosebud about May 19 and then leisurely up the latter to where it now stood. Obviously, such movements so near the Montana column meant it stood in little awe of the troops it had been raiding.

Bradley, anticipating more skepticism from his fellow officers, was anxious to have every one of his soldiers ascend the peak and verify his observations, but before he could do so, the scouts discovered that the villagers were driving in some ponies, as if they had spied the Crows and were about to investigate. Reluctantly, Bradley withdrew and led his party on a fast ride back to the Yellowstone, where Clifford's boats awaited them. By noon of that May 27, he had skiffed across to report his startling news to Gibbon.

Bradley's fear of skepticism was not without foundation, for Freeman

[6]"Long Horn" to ed., May 28, in *Helena Herald*, June 15, 1876. The author appears to have been an enlisted 7th Infantryman, who wrote a number of letters from the expedition.

recorded that Bradley reported "a big smoke and a large band of horses—thinks it a village." Dr. Paulding, more perceptive but no admirer of Gibbon, recorded that Bradley had

> seen a large village on the Rosebud, 18 miles away. Don't know whether Gibbon's instructions, or disposition, will allow us to go for them. . . . I suppose we will wait for Crook and Terry, hoping our untutored friends across the river will await their arrival. Meanwhile, Bradley can go over and take a look every day or so to see that they are still there. His party will be accommodated by a small grave, 30x8x4, some day.

The information Bradley reported at this time was the most valuable Indian intelligence discovered during the campaign. It established the present location and direction of movement of the consolidated force of winter roamers. Bradley would have been eager to keep track of the village, despite the danger, but since he did not know that he had just made his last independent scout, he merely commented: "Everybody wondered why we were not ordered over to attack the village; but the general probably had good reasons."

It is only fair to say that Gibbon had several reasons. His orders were to keep the Sioux south of the river and to attack only if certain of success. He was still smarting over his failure to get the cavalry across ten days earlier, and the river was now higher. He was concerned about his supply train and was already planning to send back two more companies to reinforce its escort, thus reducing his offensive force. His decision not to attack may have been wise, but his decision to ignore the enemy village is incomprehensible. He tried to conceal this blunder, for neither in his official report nor in his narrative of the campaign did he even hint at Bradley's discovery of the movement of the hostile village to the Rosebud, only 18 miles distant.

That very afternoon Gibbon penned another letter to Terry, dated May 27, opposite the Rosebud, which betrays how faint an impression Bradley's momentous discovery had made on his mind:

> I have reached this point and have scouted the country on both sides of the Yellowstone. *No camps have been seen*, but war parties from 20 to 50 have been seen to the south of the river and a few on the north side. One of these latter murdered three of our men whilst out hunting on the 23rd inst.

As soon as my train arrives from Fort Ellis, which is expected about the 1st of June, I will resume the march down the Yellowstone with supplies that will last till about July 10, and I can draw no more from there, the supply being nearly exhausted. In the meantime, I will keep scouting parties out, up and down the river, and watch closely for any movement of the Indians to the northward.

A steamboat, if you have one at your disposal, will be of great assistance in passing troops across the river for effective cooperation if necessary. I have a few small boats which can be used, but they require, of course, a good deal of time. I send this by men in one of them. The three are Pvts. Evans and Stewart, Company E, 7th Inf. (volunteers), and Williamson, a citizen scout, and if they get through successfully will deserve commendation. The danger by river is less than by land.

P.S. A *camp some distance up the Rosebud* was reported this morning by our scouts. *If this proves true*, I may not start down the Yellowstone so soon.[7]

The added italics mark the sole references to Indian camps; the first flatly denies seeing any, and the second reports an "if true" camp up the Rosebud. Neither the earlier Tongue River camp nor the aborted effort to attack it is mentioned.

At dark of that May 27 courier John W. Williamson and the two soldier volunteers pushed off in a frail skiff, risking their lives to deliver this sour note. Apparently, all that Gibbon could tell them was that Terry intended to march the Dakota column overland to a field depot at the mouth of Glendive Creek on the lower Yellowstone. At the same time, Capt. Ball's Company H and Capt. Thompson's Company L, 2nd Cavalry, started down the north bank to Tongue River to check possible Sioux crossings and to give the three couriers-by-skiff some moral support. This was a Gibbon-ordered mission, for Bradley provided no Crow scouts, knowing it was pointless. Perhaps Gibbon assigned Boyer to guide them, as on the earlier Thompson-Wheelan scout.

At noon of May 28 Paul McCormick floated into Gibbon's camp with another load of vegetables and a dispatch from Terry to Gibbon, dated at Fort Lincoln, May 14. Terry expected to get off with the Dakota column the next morning (but a rainstorm delayed departure to May 17). He also

[7]Gibbon to Terry, May 27, 1876, Letters Received, Hqtrs. Dept. of Dak., 1876, Box 19 (G-RG98).

expected to encounter Sitting Bull's force assembled to fight him on the Little Missouri, but these were merely some agency Sioux preparing to spend the summer hunting buffalo, and Terry would find no trace of Sitting Bull's warriors. This news, however, may have reinforced Gibbon's skepticism of Bradley's findings. Terry's dispatch also ordered Gibbon to march immediately downriver to the Glendive depot and then across country to cooperate with the Dakota column in dealing with the supposed hostiles on its front.

On the morning of May 29 Gibbon sent Capt. Sanno's Company K of infantry, Lt. Roe's cavalry company, and twenty-four empty army wagons back on the trail to meet Lt. English and Matt Carroll's supply train and share the latter's load. With them went Paul McCormick, heading for Bozeman for more sutler wares; he would complete the major portion of the trip alone. Bradley also sent down two Crows (Curley told Dixon he was one of them) to meet Barney Bravo and his two Crows on their return from the Crow village with the expected remounts for the Crow scouts.

On that same afternoon the Ball-Thompson scout returned from Tongue River, having seen no Sioux crossings nor any trace of the three couriers-by-skiff. If Mitch had guided this outfit, he returned with it, in which case he had not joined the parade of upriver escorts. That evening Dr. Paulding recorded a squabble among the officers, in which Bradley branded as "a liar" anyone who denied he had seen the Sioux village on the Rosebud. Since he had accomplished more than all the others put together, he had a right to be miffed.

Many diarists recorded an event of the evening of May 30 which involved "two Crows" who were put across the river for another attempt to steal ponies from a party of Sioux. LeForge told the same story to Marquis (pp. 223–34), without date, but names himself and Mitch Boyer as the pair involved. Having spotted some Sioux warriors across the river, they alerted the pickets and asked to be rowed across to go after the horses. They managed to rope four of the animals and were stealthily working their way to freedom when the Sioux found their ponies missing and showered the thieves with bullets. The pair had to release their prizes, dash for the river, and push off in the skiff. Bradley observed that they had decided their "medicine was bad" that night. If Tom's identification is correct, his story indicates that Mitch was with the command at this time.

Tom also told Marquis (p. 262) that he and Mitch held a sign-talk one morning from the Rosebud base across the river with some agency Sioux on the south bank, who had come out to hunt buffalo because agency rations kept them starved, a plausible enough reason. Tom gave no date, and his credibility is undermined by the naming of Lt. Roe, who was absent. This incident is mentioned because some have embroidered it to indicate that Mitch, though not Tom, was treacherously dealing with enemy Sioux. There was nothing treacherous about the conversation, but if it occurred at this time, it further supports Mitch's presence at the Rosebud camp, rather than with supply train escorts. On May 31 Capt. Wheelan's Company G made another scout of 16 miles downriver and back with LeForge and five Crows, but found nothing.

June opened with an unseasonable, two-day blizzard that covered the plains with a blanket of snow and then vanished on June 3 in a fast and sloppy thaw. At 2 P.M. of June 4 the long-awaited Diamond-R supply train pulled in to the camp with its three-company escort, thus restoring full troop strength. With them came Barney Bravo and all the absent Crow scouts, driving a herd of remount ponies from the Crow village, much to Bradley's satisfaction. All the Crows were now mounted, except two who had refused to send to the village for remounts. Gibbon promptly ordered the column to resume the march the next morning and cheered his men by terminating the full-strength nightly picket lines.

At 9 A.M. of June 5 the column started down the north bank to make a union with the Dakota column, ignoring the Sioux village on the Rosebud which no one had seen for a week. Bradley's Crows rode the van and flanks, while Mitch Boyer guided the wagon train on the still-muddy road. Clifford's infantry company again floated down in Herendeen's skiffs. That day and the next slow going held the column to 19.5 miles, but on June 7 they made 21.5 miles, despite a climb up onto the bluffs and down again. That evening they camped 41 miles out, 2 miles below and opposite the mouth of the Tongue, and Gibbon noted (1877, p. 288): "Mitch Bowyer informed us that the roads passed over heretofore were good compared with those we should have in the next few days, when we should be compelled to enter a terrible section of the Mauvaise Terre."

Early on June 8, just after leaving camp, the Crows discovered the trail of two shod horses leading upriver and then turning back, and on it a sack containing ammunition and some rations wrapped in newspaper. They decided that two couriers, sent up by Gen. Terry, had turned back when they had sighted the Crows, whom they mistook for hostile Sioux. One, it would prove, was John Williamson, whom Gibbon had sent with two soldiers down to meet Terry by skiff on May 27. This day's march of 16 miles entailed a rugged detour away from the river, requiring an afternoon rest, but at 8 P.M. bivouac was made 18 miles below the Tongue.

Another departure from routine on this day concerned Capt. Clifford's flotilla. He had been ordered to take two days' rations, as the overland marchers might not be able to camp on the riverbank, but the captain misunderstood and thought he was to make two days' run in one. Taking Maj. Brisbin and Lt. Doane aboard, he ran all the way down to Powder River, where he found Capt. Grant Marsh's steamboat, the *Far West*. Curley told Dixon (p. 144) that White Man Runs Him and another Crow were sent down in the boats because they lacked horses, and White Man Runs Him also told Dixon (p. 154): "Gibbon moved to Tongue River. . . . We heard that Custer [*sic*, Terry] was coming, and I and 30 soldiers went down the river in boats [June 8]. Two Crow scouts, Elk and Two Whistles, were with me. At the junction of the Yellowstone and Missouri [*sic*, Powder], we met Custer [*sic*, Terry]. We went aboard the steamboat." Herendeen gave some pertinent details to Noyes (1917, p. 108):

> One morning [June 8] we took a boat to go downriver; Maj. Brisbin, a soldier or two and a couple of Indians were in the boat. We soon found out that the object was to see if a steamboat was downriver, as it was about time that the forces were getting together. We ran Wolf Rapids [just below Powder R.] and found a steamboat just landing. We went on the boat and [soon] Terry and staff [arrived]. . . . Terry, the day before, had sent scouts out [to Gibbon], but they were driven back and he was worried about how to get word to Gibbon. He told me he would give me $300 if I would take a dispatch to Gibbon that night. I [and a Crow] started out and got to the camp about 3 A.M. [of June 9].

Other Montana column sources agree that it was 2 A.M. of June 9 when Herendeen and a Crow from the flotilla rode into Gibbon's camp, bringing orders for Gibbon to leave his command in camp but to come down himself to meet Gen. Terry, who would steam up in the *Far West* to meet him in the morning. About 7 A.M. of June 9 Gibbon left his camp, escorted by Capt. Ball's company of cavalry and Bradley's mounted infantry and Crows to keep an eye out for the boat. On this ride Gibbon (1877, p. 289) "saw some badlands referred to by Mitch Bowyer." They had made 8 miles when they met the *Far West*, and Gibbon boarded her to confer with Terry as she steamed up to the camp.

While Gibbon's escort and scouts were plodding overland back up to camp, Tom LeForge was thrown from his horse, breaking his collarbone. Dr. Paulding had to drive an ambulance down to bring him in, and poor Tom would ride in a wagon or lie in hospital for the next week or two. Nonetheless, it is probable that LeForge's misery that morning was minor compared to that of Gen. Gibbon during his long conference with Terry aboard the *Far West*.

THE GIBBON-TERRY CONNECTION

Of the three columns comprising the spring–summer campaign against the Sioux, Crook's was the strongest but the least inclined to seek communication with the other two for purposes of cooperation. Terry's column, however, started farthest from the field and expected that Gibbon's column, already there, had gathered intelligence about Indian movements which would permit coordinated action. Thanks to Lt. Bradley and his Crow scouts, information of the kind Terry needed had been obtained. Gibbon sent a long dispatch to Terry, and Terry came in person to confer with Gibbon, but on both occasions communications would fail, with dire consequences. This chapter attempts to reconstruct the intricate details of this double failure in communication.

The story begins at the Rosebud camp on May 27, when Gibbon prepared his dispatch to Terry, which we have seen concealed Bradley's discoveries. That evening Gibbon placed the letter in the hands of scout

John W. Williamson and Pvts. William Evans and Benjamin F. Stewart, both of Clifford's Company E, 7th Infantry, and sent them by skiff down the Yellowstone to deliver it to Terry at Glendive depot, 150 river-miles distant. Pvt. Evans left an account of this mission, and scout Williamson gave a newspaper interview that rather sensationalized his exploit.[1]

The trio pushed off in their frail craft after dark of May 27, intending to travel only by night, without using oars because of the Indians' keen ears. That first night they glided safely downstream and then slept the next day, hidden in some willows. The second night (May 28–29) they had to run Buffalo Rapids (47 miles out and 13 below Tongue River) but in the dark swamped their skiff on some rocks. They managed to land it and themselves but saved only their rifles and one lonely can of peaches, which they promptly devoured. Having made only a third of their voyage, with no provisions left, they decided to travel faster with oars during the longer daylight hours. Here narrator Evans simply skipped ahead to their arrival at "3 P.M." (no date) at Glendive depot, where they found only Maj. Moore's battalion of 6th Infantry. By traveling longer and faster in daylight on both May 29 and 30, they could easily cover the remaining two-thirds of this trip by 3 P.M. of May 30, which is thus the missing date.

As for the Glendive depot, back on April 21, Gen. Terry had notified Maj. Orlando Moore, then commanding Fort Buford, that when the *Josephine* arrived with expedition supplies, he was to embark Companies C, D, and I of his 6th Infantry and steam up the Yellowstone to meet Gen. Custer's column marching out from Fort Abraham Lincoln. Then, on May 4, after Terry had assumed command of the Dakota column, he directed Moore to establish a field supply depot on the river at the mouth of Glendive Creek (present Glendive, Mont.), to which point Terry would march overland to renew his supplies.[2]

Accordingly, the *Josephine*, Capt. Mart Coulson, left Bismarck May 9 and docked at 6:45 P.M. of May 13 at Fort Buford, where part of the cargo was unloaded to make room for Moore's battalion. At 3:30 P.M. of

---

[1] Pvt. Evans's account is in Rodenbaugh, *Sabre and Bayonet*, 315–18 (B); scout Williamson's interview of June 24 is in *Bozeman Times*, June 29, 1876. Each is cited in the text by the informant's name only.

[2] Terry's instructions to Moore, April 21 and May 4, are in Letters Received, Mil. Div. of the Mo., 1876 (G-RG98).

May 14 she pushed up the Yellowstone to unload troops and cargo at Glendive on the morning of May 18. Returning to Fort Buford for the cargo left there, she started up again on May 21, delivered this load about May 23, and then turned back to the States for more supplies.

A second supply boat, Capt. Grant Marsh's *Far West*, left Bismarck on May 26, and on the 30th part of her cargo was unloaded at Fort Buford and Lt. Nelson Bronson's detachment of his Company G, 6th Infantry, was taken aboard as boat guard. Leaving the same afternoon, she reached Glendive at 10 P.M. of June 1. She did not return to fetch up the residue of her cargo, for she and her boat guard were retained to serve the Dakota column, which had not yet been heard from.[3]

These details explain why Gibbon's three couriers, when they landed at the depot on May 30, found only Maj. Moore and his three companies, but neither a boat nor Gen. Terry. Of the depot garrison, only three officers, but all three of its auxiliary personnel, are especially important to what follows. Besides Maj. Moore, two other officers must be named: Capt. James W. Powell and Lt. Bernard R. Byrne, both of Company C; Byrne was also the depot quartermaster and commissary officer. Moore and Powell both wrote valuable official letters and, as we shall see, Byrne was the author of a series of unsigned news dispatches. One of the auxiliary personnel was Charles Sargent (or Sergeant), whom Lt. Byrne had engaged as scout at Fort Buford on May 14, the day they left that post; the other two were already in service there: George P. Mulligan, interpreter, and Crow Bear, a Gros Ventre enlisted Indian scout.

Lt. Byrne's first two news dispatches were datelined, "On the Yellowstone [at Glendive depot], June 1," and "On the Yellowstone, near Powder River, June 10."[4] They were published together under a single headline, do not overlap, and were written in installments that violate the datelines. These features indicate that they were written by the same person. Fortunately, internal and external evidence establishes a correct dateline for each entry. The writer's movements during these ten days correspond to those of Lt. Byrne only. His June 1 dispatch tells of the arrival of Gibbon's couriers:

[3] The accounts of the trips of the *Josephine* and *Far West* are based on official records of Fort Buford, 6th Infantry, and *Bismarck Tribune*.

[4] Byrne's dispatches, June 1 and June 10, *New York Times*, June 29, 1876. They are cited in the text as "Byrne's dispatches."

[Glendive depot, evening of May 30]: Three soldiers [*sic*, two soldiers and one civilian] came down the Yellowstone today [3 P.M., May 30], to [*sic*, for] Fort Buford with important dispatches for Gen. Terry from Gen. Gibbon. It was a hazardous adventure in an open boat with Indians on both sides of the river. They report that Gen. Gibbon is on the Yellowstone near Rosebud Creek with . . . troops and some Crow scouts, living on half-rations and constantly menaced by hostile Sioux. Three men were killed on May 23 [gives names and details omitted by Gibbon].

At this time Lt. Byrne thought the couriers would continue to Fort Buford, for reasons that will soon emerge.

In his June 10 dispatch Byrne picked up the story as of June 1, in an unseasonal blizzard, but he does not mention the couriers nor the arrival of the *Far West* that night:

[Glendive depot]: When we were awakened by reveille on June 1, we did not enjoy the sight of a severe snowstorm [beginning at midnight, May 31] on a summer campaign. . . . The snow continued all that day, completely covering the ground, as our camp was at the field supply depot. We did not have to march, but standing around our blazing campfires, we commiserated with Gen. Terry's battalion, who must have suffered severely in marching [they were snowbound, June 1–2]. . . . After two days' storm, the weather is bright and warm again [on June 3].

Maj. Moore now extends the story of the couriers in a letter to Terry's adjutant, dated at the depot June 1, but he began writing before midnight and finished in the morning:

I forward dispatches from Gen. Gibbon, which I had sent down the river in anticipation of reaching Gen. Terry on the *Far West*, which arrived this evening at 10 P.M. [June 1], bringing back the dispatches. I now start them by scouts this morning [June 2] to meet the [overland] expedition.

The freight of the *Josephine* entire is at this camp, and all but 100 tons of forage on the *Far West* which was left at Fort Buford, has been received. I detain the *Far West* at this point, as instructed, until the command arrives. The river is in fine condition, the stage of water being such that the boat can proceed higher without difficulty and serve the interests of Gen. Gibbon's command, now near the Rosebud.

I have no news of hostile Indians in addition to what Gen. Gibbon gives in his dispatches. If you deem it proper for the *Far West* to return to Fort Buford for the balance of her freight before the command arrives at this point, please inform me and the boat will be sent at once.[5]

Each of the dates inserted above has confirmation: the *Far West* could not have arrived a day earlier, nor could the couriers have left overland a day later and still reach Terry's marching column on the morning of June 3. What is puzzling is why Moore lost several days by sending the couriers downriver when he had been forewarned that Terry would march overland directly to the depot. That Moore had indeed sent the couriers downriver promptly on their arrival is supported by Byrne's impression that they were bound for Fort Buford. That is reinforced by a cryptic sentence in Pvt. Evans's account: "Col. Moore kindly sent his own scouts on [downriver] with the dispatches, who returned two days later [10 P.M., June 1] on the *Far West* with the answer [*sic*, the original letter]."

Assembling these time-motion features yields a consistent scenario: the couriers first reached the depot at 3 P.M., May 30; Moore replaced them, wholly or in part, and sent them downriver that same evening; as this was also the time the *Far West* left Fort Buford, the skiff and steamboat had to meet somewhere in the middle; knowing that Terry had been marching for the depot since May 17, Marsh took the couriers aboard and returned them to the depot, in the snowstorm, at 10 P.M., June 1; the next morning Moore sent them overland to meet Terry's column. This scenario is reasonable and fits.

But *who* were the couriers? Evans's sentence says that Moore sent his own scouts, presumably to give Gibbon's tired and hungry men a rest. But John Williamson's newspaper interview indicates he was not replaced: "Williamson went down the Yellowstone [from the Rosebud] to [towards?] Fort Buford . . . and not finding Terry on the river. . . . " That suggests that Gibbon's two soldiers were replaced by two of Moore's scouts, of which he had only two, Charles Sargent and Crow Bear, for Mulligan was an interpreter.

Apparently, it was this same trio that Moore sent overland on the morning of June 2 with both his own and Gibbon's letters on a ride of some 45 miles, partly through falling snow, to meet the Dakota column. Gen. Terry recorded in his diary on June 3 that he received the dispatches at

[5] Moore to Terry's Adjt., June 1, 1876, Letters Received, Dept. of Dak., 1876, Box 19 (G-RG98).

10 A.M., while on the march. In an unsigned news dispatch of June 12 Gen. Custer identified the couriers as two white men and one Indian, all mounted, but none a soldier. Two of Custer's Ree (Arikara) scouts, Red Star (p. 18) and Running Wolf (p. 138), told Libby (1912) that the Indian was Crow Bear, a Gros Ventre.[6] Williamson's interview makes himself one of the whites: "Not finding Terry on the river, Williamson set out on foot [sic] by land to find him. He travelled . . . solitary and alone [sic] and encountered the terrible snowstorm, but found Gen. Terry." Despite the heroics, the identification fits; the other white scout was undoubtedly Sargent.

Gen. Terry could only have been gratified to learn that his column's supplies had reached the field depot, that the Yellowstone afforded excellent navigation, and that the *Far West* was waiting to serve him. Gibbon's dispatch, however, must have brought deep disappointment. After a month in Sioux country Gibbon was still at the Rosebud, awaiting a supply train, and had seen no hostile camp and only a few warriors. Moore had learned nothing from the couriers, but Custer had learned (undoubtedly from Williamson) one additional fact, useless though it was, which he included in his June 12 news dispatch: "The Indians had run off all the ponies belonging to Gibbon's twenty-five Crows, though Gibbon had not mentioned this." Had Gibbon cautioned his couriers against revealing Bradley's discoveries?

Terry must now have felt that the batting call on his campaign stood at three strikes. Custer had spent May 30 scouting up the Little Missouri, where Sitting Bull's army was expected to make a stand, and had found nothing whatever; Moore and his scouts had found no signs around the depot nor on the trail to Terry's column; and now Gibbon had nothing to report from the upper Yellowstone. Terry could only draw the obvious conclusion that the hostile Sioux were still south of the Yellowstone and east of the Rosebud. This error was the first consequence of Gibbon's concealment.

Having completed a good march of 25 miles to camp that evening of June 3 on Beaver Creek, Terry altered his plan of operation, as there was

[6] At this point, attention is called to Special Category Y, Participant Accounts, Custer's column, in the bibliography, which reduces the need for notes in this and remaining chapters. It is more extensive than Category X but is organized and functions in the same way (see Chap. 12 note 1).

no longer any point in joining Gibbon at the depot where there were no Indians. He decided to move the depot farther upriver in the direction the Indians must be and to lead his column south up Beaver Creek, then circle west to the head of O'Fallon's Creek, descend it northward to the Yellowstone, and follow up the latter to the mouth of Powder River.

Accordingly, Terry prepared dispatches for Moore and Gibbon, advising them of his change in plan. He directed Moore to send the *Far West*, loaded with supplies, to the mouth of Powder River and there await the arrival of the Dakota column; he also instructed Moore to forward to Gibbon another dispatch countermanding the earlier order to march to Glendive. Custer's June 12 news dispatch added: "As there was risk to the two scouts who were to deliver the orders to Gibbon from the [Glendive] stockade, they were promised $200 extra compensation." The three couriers left that evening, and as the day's march had shortened the distance to about 30 miles, they undoubtedly made delivery to Moore sometime the next day, June 4, having been absent over three days.

In the forenoon of June 5 Moore answered Terry's instructions, but since he sent the reply up by the *Far West*, it did not reach Terry until June 8.

> I acknowledge the receipt of your communication by the scouts. Today the *Far West* starts [at 1:05 P.M.] for Powder River in compliance with your instructions. The boat is loaded, as directed, with 75 tons of forage and 15 days' subsistence stores for 1200 men, hospital stores, private packages for officers and . . . ammunition, including the 10,000 rounds of half-inch Gatling, which I brought from Buford. . . . Capt. Grant Marsh is fully assured that the *Far West* can make the trip with his present freight without difficulty. I sent Capt. Powell with his Company C, 6th Infantry, on the boat with orders to report as soon as practicable.
>
> I forward [by the *Far West*] your dispatches to Gen. Gibbon by two scouts, giving them the benefit of the authorized extra pay for the trip. They will make it with dispatch at all hazards. One of them belongs to Gen. Gibbon's command [necessarily Williamson], who came down with the late dispatches which you received forwarded by me. I have no information of Indians in this vicinity and the scouts report no Indians on their return from your command. [7]

---

[7] Moore to Terry's Adjt., June 5, Letters Received, Dept. of Dak., Box 19 (G-RG98).

Capt. Powell likewise reported to Terry under the heading, "On the *Far West*, near Powder River, 8:45 A.M., June 8," which provides key facts about the boat trip up to the Powder and the fate of Terry's dispatch to Gibbon. Here quoted are the last paragraphs, reversed in order to preserve chronology:

> This boat, with the supplies ordered, left the stockade June 5, 1:05 P.M., and arrived at Powder River June 6, 9:15 P.M. Running time, 14 hrs. and 38 min. No trouble at Powder R. Rapids [Wolf Rapids, 6 miles below the Powder]. Minimum water, $5\frac{1}{2}$ ft. River rising rapidly.
>
> The two civilian scouts [Williamson and Sargent] were disembarked on the north side of the Yellowstone on the evening of June 6 at Custer's Creek [4 miles above the Powder] with your dispatches for Gibbon. They returned here this morning [June 8] at 6 o'clock, reporting they [had] proceeded to within a couple of miles of Tongue River yesterday afternoon [June 7]; that they there observed a party of about 40 Indians, on the same side of the river, and claiming to have been discovered, determined to return here. Believing this information of importance to the command, General, I immediately sent a small boat down the river, anticipating that your command would be met at O'Fallon's Creek.[8]

With these facts in hand, it can now be established that, besides Lt. Bronson and the boat guard, Lt. Byrne also went up on the *Far West* as Powell's company subaltern and as quartermaster and commissary officer to oversee the pending transfer of Terry's supplies. Lt. Byrne's June 10 dispatch reveals:

> [Powder River, June 7]: An offer of $200 reward to carry important dispatches to Gen. Gibbon on the Rosebud secured [at the depot] two scouts as volunteers [Williamson and Sargent]. They started from here [Powder R.] last night [June 6, proving this was written June 7] and will reach Gibbon in two nights' hard travel, if they succeed. There is great peril in the adventure. . . . Such men have grit . . . and knowing the men [Byrne had hired Sargent], I am sure that the love of adventure . . . is even a more powerful incentive than the pecuniary reward.

It is now possible to extract some further information from Pvt. Evans, who has been silent during his stay at the depot:

[8]Powell to Terry's Adjt., June 8, 8:45 A.M., idem.

We [Evans and Stewart] volunteered to carry the [Terry's] answer [on to Gibbon], but Col. Moore sent his own scouts [only Sargent was Moore's], as he seemed to lack confidence in soldiers as couriers. . . . The *Far West* coming up [having come up June 1], we all [Evans, Stewart, Williamson, and Sargent] boarded [at 1:05 P.M., June 5] and went up to Powder River [reached June 6, 9:15 P.M.]. Capt. Powell and the Sergeant Major were present and I offered to bet that they [Williamson and Sargent] would be back before morning, and the Sergeant Major lost. The first thing we saw at reveille [June 8] was the scouts returning with neither ammunition or rations; they said they had run into Indians and had thrown everything away.

These accounts establish that Williamson and Sargent, carrying Terry's orders to Gibbon, had turned back on sighting Indians on the afternoon of June 7 from a point a little below the Tongue and reappeared at the *Far West* at 6 A.M. of June 8, having lost their rations and ammunition. These events precisely fit the story that Gibbon's Crow scouts had read from trail signs, as related in the last chapter. As the only difference, the couriers reported being seen by Sioux, whereas the Crows reported seeing only the couriers' trail. Whichever it was, the couriers' bonuses were practically in hand when they turned back.

It will be recalled that, the moment these couriers returned unsuccessful so early on June 8, Capt. Powell sent the bad news by small boat down to inform Terry at O'Fallon's Creek. This effort also failed, for Terry's column had struck the middle reaches of O'Fallon's Creek on June 6, intending to descend it, but the column's guide, Lonesome Charley Reynolds, misidentified the branch and led it astray, south instead of north. In conference that night Terry, Custer, and Reno decided to strike due west over the badlands to the Powder, as Terry wrote in the June 6th entry of his June 12 letter to his sisters (p. 15). After a long and grueling march on June 7, the column bivouacked on the east bank of the Powder, some 24 miles above its mouth (present Locate, Mont.).

That evening of June 7 Terry wrote in his diary: "Sent scouts to the mouth of [Powder] river at 10 P.M." These scouts were enlisted Rees, about whom Red Star told Libby (1912, p. 72) in a sentence buried in a confusing paragraph: "Two Ree scouts were sent ahead, Stabbed and Goose, and they were given a letter to take to the camp across the river." Libby misidentified this camp as Gibbon's, although Gibbon was far distant and no one with Terry knew where. It was Lt. Byrne's camp opposite the mouth of the Powder, which guarded the supplies put ashore, as the lieutenant confirmed in his June 10 dispatch: "Early on the morning of June 8, the pickets on a high bluff or butte made the signal, 'Indians,' but relieved our anxiety as to numbers a few minutes later with the signal, 'supposed to be friendly.' They proved to be Indian scouts from Gen. Terry."

These Ree couriers reined up at the mouth of Powder River just before 8:45 A.M., for their arrival was the event that prompted Capt. Powell to write his letter to Terry at this early hour. There remains to be quoted only its opening lines: "Your scouts just arrived here. The *Far West* is cutting wood a mile below Powder River—will be at its mouth in an hour. Have not seen any Indians or trace of Indians." Powell then sped the two Rees back up to Terry's camp to deliver his letter, as well as Moore's letter of June 5 and some mail brought up by the steamboat.

Early on that morning of June 8, before Terry had received any response from the boat, he began preparing a major operation, based on his inferences from Gibbon's old dispatch. In the June 12 letter to his sisters Terry's account of June 8 begins: "This day was devoted to organizing a packtrain for rapid movement." Other accounts noted that each of the twelve cavalry companies received pack mules as support for a trip of eight to ten days, to leave the next morning. One of Terry's staff officers (almost certainly his adjutant, Maj. Ed. W. Smith) wrote an anonymous news dispatch that day that read: "Gen. Terry intends to start on the 9th with the cavalry and packmules to beat up the country west of Powder River. He will probably be absent for ten days or two weeks. The wagon train [as well as infantry companies] is to be dismissed here and sent to the depot at the mouth of Powder River."[9] For Terry himself to lead Custer and the entire 7th Cavalry on a ten-day operation that could cover 300 miles represented no minor scouting sortie, but a hopeful strike against Indians thought to be south and west of the Powder.

Before the morning was over, however, the two Ree couriers dashed in with Powell's and Moore's dispatches, as well as the mail. Lt. Godfrey noted in his diary that "we got mail about 11 o'clock, one brought by the *Far West*." Reporter Mark Kellogg also noted in his diary the return "of the scouts sent last night by Gen. Terry," bringing news that the couriers

[9] News dispatch (unsigned), June 8, *St. Paul Pioneer Press & Tribune*, June 24, 1876.

sent to Gibbon with Terry's order "were unable" to deliver it. Red Star told Libby (1912, p. 73) that "Stabbed and Goose came back and reported to Custer's camp."

Without mentioning either couriers or dispatches, Terry resumed his June 12 letter to his sisters with an abrupt and startling decision:

> I determined to proceed to the mouth of the river with three objects in view. I wish to ascertain whether there were any Indians below us; find out whether the *Far West* was up with supplies; and to examine the valley and its practicability for sending our train down to the depot, which is to be established at its mouth. I started at 12:30 with two companies of cavalry and Capt. [Eugene B.] Gibbs, who alone of my staff [aide de camp] was sufficiently well mounted to be able to go with me.

Custer's news dispatch of June 12, also with no mention of couriers or dispatches, adds a fourth objective to Terry's list: "Terry, taking [Myles W.] Keogh's and [Myles] Moylan's companies [I and A, 7th Cavalry] as escort, proceeded down the valley of the Powder to its mouth . . . to ascertain if the scouts had succeeded in reaching Gibbon."

The return of the couriers at 11 A.M. and Terry's departure at 12:30 P.M. make it certain that the dispatches triggered Terry's abrupt decision to ride in person to the Powder's mouth. Not one of the four stated objectives, however, is acceptable, and it should be noted that all were enumerated days later, when hour-by-hour events had become blurred. The three important questions had all been *answered in the dispatches* just received; in fact, they had to be the reasons Terry sent off the couriers the night before. What, then, was the true reason for the sudden decision?

The answer can be found in a revelation in Powell's dispatch, that the two bonused couriers had been turned back by *hostile Indians near the mouth of Tongue River*. On reading this, why would Terry lead the 7th Cavalry far south and west, when the hostiles were nearby and due west? He may have recalled that Gibbon mentioned, as an afterthought, a village on the Rosebud, which if verified might delay his move downriver beyond June 1. Delayed he must have been, for a week had passed, yet Powell had not seen him. Had Gibbon found the Sioux and attacked? or been attacked? If not, he must be very close, and the boat was now available at the mouth of the Powder. By going down now, Terry could contact Gibbon in person, save time, get the latest information, and arrange a concerted action against a possibly known target. This construal makes a sound explanation for both the timing and the nature of Terry's sudden decision.

While Terry and escort were forging down the rugged valley of the Powder, another event transpired at its mouth, as Lt. Byrne wrote in his June 10 dispatch: "In the afternoon [June 8] the pickets reported a large party approaching. From their direction and movements, they seemed to be hostile, and the trumpeter sounded 'To Arms.' Our troops, consisting of about 60 men, were arranged in a ravine. As the visitors came nearer, they proved to be from Gibbon's command." Pvt. Evans added that he saw a skiff coming downriver, "the advance of his own command." It was indeed Clifford's flotilla, carrying his company, Maj. Brisbin, Lt. Doane, George Herendeen, and the two or three Crows, as related in the last chapter. Clifford wrote in his narrative that they boarded the *Far West*, where they "met Capt. Powell and Lt. Bronson."

Terry's diary says his party reached the *Far West* on June 8 at 8 P.M. He then wrote a note to Gibbon, ordering him to leave his troops in camp and ride down himself the next morning to meet the boat steaming up. Pvt. Evans again volunteered to deliver this note, but Terry forbade it, as Clifford noted. Instead, Clifford recommended George Herendeen for this duty, as he had found him exceptionally competent and thoroughly reliable. That evening Herendeen and one of the Crows slipped into the night and safely delivered the note to Gibbon at 2 A.M. of June 9.

At 4 A.M. of June 9 Terry and his aide, Lt. Gibbs, started upriver on the *Far West*, taking all the military and auxiliary personnel of the Montana column back to their command. Incidentally, Lt. Bronson and the boat escort were still aboard, and Capts. Powell and Keogh went along for the ride, but the June 10 dispatch of Lt. Byrne reveals that he remained behind in charge of Company C and the supply camp. Thus he was the only officer who could have authored the "Byrne" dispatches.

It was 11 A.M. (Terry's diary) when the *Far West* met and took Gibbon aboard, leaving the rest of his escort to turn back overland, including Bradley, the best intelligence officer on the campaign and the one who knew most about the Sioux, their whereabouts, and movements. During the hour and a half it took the boat to push her way up to Gibbon's camp, the two generals held an important conference, of which, alas, little record remains.

The burning question is: Did Gibbon comprehend the value of Bradley's finding? And if so, did he convey the information to Terry at the conference? If he did, certain key bits should surface in available accounts, namely, the *size, locations, dates,* and therefore *movements* of the Sioux village sighted by Bradley. But none did, and the plan Terry devised at the conference was based on woefully defective knowledge of the village. Furthermore, Gibbon never did admit Bradley's findings.

Gibbon's annual report (Oct. 17, p. 472) says of this conference only that "I met Terry on the *Far West.* In accordance with his instructions, my command was at once prepared to move up the river again, but a furious rainstorm that afternoon delayed the movement." Terry also gave it the silent treatment, for the most he ever divulged was to his sisters in his June 12 letter (p. 17): "I met him [Gibbon] personally . . . took him aboard and had my talk with him on the way up. We arranged our plans. I gave him orders, which were substantially to return at once to his old position."

Gibbon must have revealed only one bit of garbled information that led Terry to believe that the Indians were south of the Yellowstone and on the Rosebud. In his annual report of October 17 (p. 472) Gibbon did tell of his futile attempt (on May 17) to cross the Yellowstone and attack a village, which he *mislocated* on the "Rosebud" (instead of the Tongue). This error was not just a slip of the pen, for when Terry returned to his command the night of the conference, he apparently relayed this same garbled item to Custer, who incorporated it into his news dispatch (June 12), intermixed with Terry's new plans:

> [At the conference on the boat] it was arranged that . . . in view of the movement of the 7th Cavalry on this side of the Yellowstone, Gibbon should retrace his steps and post his command on the Yellowstone nearly opposite the mouth of the Rosebud, thus to prevent the forces of Sitting Bull from escaping across the Yellowstone, in case they were pressed by the 7th Cavalry. . . .
>
> Gibbon's scouts report that they swam the Yellowstone near the mouth of the Rosebud and advanced to within five miles of the immense Indian camp along the valley of the Rosebud [*sic,* Tongue]. Gibbon attempted to cross his command [May 17] for the purpose of attacking the village, but the rapidity of the current, some 8 mph, prevented it, but not until he had drowned six horses. It is against this camp that Custer will soon move.

Lt. Bradley's journal for June 9 confirms these planned movements of the two columns:

The 7th Cavalry under Custer will scour the country south of the Yellowstone, while we return up the north bank to prevent the Indians from escaping to this side. As it is feared they may attempt to do so, the . . . 2nd Cavalry were ordered to move back up at once and would have got off today, had not a heavy rain set in, accompanied by hail, which caused the movement to be suspended until tomorrow.

Bradley's scouts had last seen the village on the Rosebud on May 27; by June 14, when Gibbon's command took its position opposite the Rosebud, the village had moved far up the Rosebud to its Busby bend, some 70 miles distant.

Only one officer of the Montana column registered his conviction that Gibbon had blundered. Dr. Paulding confided to his diary (June 9) that Maj. Brisbin, by skiffing downriver with Clifford, had "succeeded in getting in the first word with Terry; Gibbon is hot about it, apparently." He was more critical in a letter to his mother:

> A large camp was found on the Rosebud about 18 miles off, but our genial C.O. did not deem it advisable to attack it. . . . After laying there for 10 days, with the Indians showing themselves every day as though they knew what a harmless command they were dealing with, he began to do something . . . go away . . . until we met Terry and were turned back as soon as he heard of it. Our C.O.'s excuse was that he had rec'd orders to guard *this* side of the Yellowstone. There's literal obedience for you.[10]

When Gibbon confronted the problem of telling about the conference in his narrative (1877, pp. 289–90), his tortured soul composed a logic-defying masterpiece of incoherence and irrelevancy:

> The existence of any large camp of hostiles in this region was now more than ever a matter of doubt, for Gen. Terry discovered no trace of any on his march from Fort Abraham Lincoln . . . and had heard nothing from Gen. Crook. He intended on his return to Powder River to send a cavalry command on a scout up that river and cross it west to the Tongue and Rosebud. If no Indians should be discovered, then the only remaining chance would be higher up the Yellowstone, where from my observations there must be some Indians, and if Gen. Crook should strike them from the south, it would be all the more necessary for us to guard the line of the river and prevent any escape to the

[10]Dr. Paulding to mother, June 14, 1876, Buecker, ed., "Letters of Dr. Paulding," 39 (A).

northward. He therefore instructed me to retrace my steps and await his arrival at the mouth of the Rosebud, and as dispatch was now more important than ever, I agreed to start the cavalry . . . that afternoon.

The conference terminated by 12:30 P.M. of June 9, when the *Far West* tied up at Gibbon's camp. Terry held a half-hour reception for Gibbon's officers, at which Lt. English met Gen. Terry, Lt. Gibbs, Capts. Powell and Keogh, and Lt. Bronson. At this time a chain of events was set in motion that would ultimately prove fatal to Mitch Boyer, as Gibbon related (1877, p. 290): "Terry had no guide at his disposal acquainted with the country south of the Yellowstone, and I suggested he take Mitch Bowyer, who had proved so valuable to us, and was, I knew, familiar with that country. Mitch, always ready and willing, assented at once, and as soon as his horse and he were aboard, the boat started downriver."

The *Far West* nosed about at 1 P.M. and, aided by the fast current, tied up again at the mouth of Powder River at 2:45 P.M. (Terry diary). Terry left orders for Maj. Moore to transport by steamboat all the troops and supplies left at Glendive up to Powder River and there establish a new depot closer to the scene of operations. Then, taking Mitch and the cavalry escort, Terry began the long and arduous ride back up Powder River at 3:40 P.M. Twenty minutes later, a heavy downpour started and never let up during the 24-mile march, turning the trail treacherous underfoot, especially after darkness descended. Though fit and vigorous, Terry had experienced more deskwork than field service since the Civil War and was grateful to have Mitch Boyer leading the way, as he confessed to his sisters (June 12, pp. 17–18): "If left to myself, I could only have halted and waited for day, but we had a first-rate, half-breed guide, whom Gibbon had lent me; he kept us on the road and finally detected the camp by his nose; he smelt the smoke. We got in at 10 o'clock."

The storm that Terry and escort splashed through that evening was the same that held Gibbon's command in camp. Not until 10 A.M. of June 10 would the 2nd Cavalry start upriver, followed the next morning by the 7th Infantry. They had only twice as far to march as Terry had covered in half a day, but the Montana column would not reach its assigned position below and opposite the Rosebud until the afternoons of June 13 and 14.

The Gibbon-Terry connection had been made, with some days of unnecessary delay, but little current flowed and practically no signal. Mitch Boyer would see no more service with Gibbon's column.

PART II

Custer's

Last

Campaign

GUIDING THE RENO RECONNAISSANCE

On June 9 Gen. Terry had initiated a solution to the problem of supplying Gibbon's column as well as his own, by moving his supply depot up from Glendive to the mouth of Powder River. This action would be completed by June 14, freeing the *Far West* to ferry personnel as needed and transport supplies anywhere along the river.

At the conference Gibbon had given Terry a garbled clue that a Sioux village had been seen on the lower Rosebud. Unfortunately, no one thought to question Mitch Boyer, who could have furnished full information about the size and movements of this village. Nevertheless, Terry had promptly chosen this vague village as the target of attack, as implied by the forewarning he gave Gibbon; Montana column accounts reveal that on June 16 Gibbon ordered his troops to keep three days' cooked rations on hand in expectation of the arrival of the *Far West* and a march up the Rosebud.

By noon of June 10, after consultation with Custer, Terry had also discarded his plan to take the entire 7th Cavalry far south and west in a blind search for Sioux. He replaced it with a two-stage plan and immediately set in motion the preparatory stage. That very afternoon he sent Maj. Reno, with only half of the 7th Cavalry, on a reconnaissance far up the valley of Powder River and back and then diverging terminally to the mouth of Tongue River, as a rendezvous point. On June 11 Terry led the rest of the column down to the new depot, where he detached the wagon train and two companies of 17th Infantry to reinforce Maj. Moore's depot guard. On June 15 Custer led the other half of his cavalry, supported by packtrain, up the south bank of the Yellowstone to reach the rendezvous at the Tongue on June 16. Concurrently, Terry and staff made the same move on the supply-laden *Far West*, taking as boat guard Capt. Stephen Baker's Company B, 6th Infantry (Terry's headquarters company). The arrival there of Reno's reconnaissance completed this preparatory stage.

The second stage was to consist of a two-prong attack on the Sioux village on the lower Rosebud, which was outlined on June 12 by both Terry (official letter)[1] and Custer (June 12 news dispatch). Custer was to lead nine companies of his cavalry up Tongue River, cross west to the Rosebud, and descend it to strike the village from above. Terry was to take the other three cavalry companies on the *Far West* up to Gibbon's camp, there ferry Gibbon's four cavalry and five infantry companies across the river, and lead all twelve companies up the Rosebud to strike the village from below, thus trapping it between the two forces. Clearly, for this plan to succeed, the Sioux would have to remain on the lower Rosebud for more than three weeks, an unlikely behavior for nomads.

With Terry's plan in mind, let us return to Reno's reconnaissance, which Mitch Boyer would serve as the sole quartermaster scout and guide. This move reflected a compromise between the opposing views of Terry and Custer and so ended up neither fish nor fowl. Reporter Mark Kellogg's June 12 news dispatch gives one clue to the problem: "Gen. Custer declined to take command of the detachment, which Maj. Reno now heads, not believing that any Indians would be met with in that direction." Custer, in his June 12 news dispatch, discreetly contrasted Terry's views with his own:

[1] Terry to Sheridan's Adjt., June 12, 1876, *Military Expedition against the Sioux*, 57 (G-CSS).

Feeling that he ought to send a scout up Powder River to clear it of any small detached band of Indians lurking away from the larger village, Terry decided to send six companies of 7th Cavalry and one gatling gun . . . all under Maj. Reno, to scout the Powder River as far as the Little Powder. . . . It is not believed that the . . . [party] will find the Indians, as their present abiding place is . . . on the Rosebud.

In his June 22 news dispatch Custer added that "Terry explicitly and positively ordered Reno not to move in the direction of the Rosebud, for fear it would 'flush the covey' prematurely."

These passages reveal that only Terry, for undisclosed reasons, felt it necessary to scout for stray Indians up the Powder Valley and back, while avoiding the only areas where a village had been seen. It was Custer who perceived that such a move was futile at best, delaying in any case, and at worst might drive the Indians to scatter in flight. He thus declined to command it. One wonders what purpose Terry saw in the operation.

Terry gave Reno his instructions in Special Field Order No. 11, June 10:

Maj. Marcus A. Reno, 7th Cavalry, with six companies (right wing) of his regiment and one gun from the Gatling battery, will proceed to make a reconnaissance of Powder River from the present camp to the mouth of the Little Powder. From there he will cross to the headwaters of Mizpah Creek and descend it to its junction with the Powder. Thence he will cross to Pumpkin Creek and Tongue River and descend the Tongue to its junction with the Yellowstone, where he may expect to meet the remaining companies of the 7th Cavalry and supplies of subsistence and forage.

Maj. Reno's command will be supplied with subsistence for twelve days and with forage for the same period at the rate of two pounds of grain the day for each animal. The guide, Mitch Boyer, and eight Indians to be detailed by Lt. Col. Custer will report to Maj. Reno for duty with this column. Acting Assistant Surgeon H. R. Porter is detailed for duty with Maj. Reno.[2]

These orders shed no light on the purpose of the operation nor suggest what Reno should do if he saw any Indians. They sanction no deviations but do define a very precise route, which runs south about 77 miles along the east-bulging arc of the Powder and reverses north down Mizpah

[2] *Orders, Dept. of Dakota* (a small booklet, National Archives). Because of a "typo," this order is often reprinted as "No. 2."

Creek, a branch of the Powder, to its mouth, this entire distance lying within the valley of Powder River. From there the route turns west for a short distance to the mouth of Pumpkin Creek on the Tongue and descends the latter 14 miles to its mouth; this final segment is merely the most direct route to the rendezvous and strikes the Tongue *below* the site of the Tongue River village. Clearly, this narrow route was designed not to check out Bradley's Sioux campsites, but merely to examine the upper valley of the Powder. The standard cavalry march of 25 to 30 miles a day would cover the 175-mile route in six or seven days, superseding the twelve days' rationing and implying a rendezvous date of June 16–17, which nicely fits the arrival of Terry and Custer at the rendezvous on June 16 and the forewarning given to Gibbon.

Besides the six companies of cavalry (B, C, E, F, I, L), Reno's force included a squad of 20th Infantry serving one Gatling gun under Lt. Francis X. Kinzie, who was assigned to keep an itinerary but was too busy trying to keep up to do so. Lt. Sturgis, of Company E, had been assigned to keep a journal, but like all but one of the right-wing officers, was killed in the Custer battle. Of Reno's two contract surgeons, Dr. Porter survived but left no information on the mission; Dr. James M. DeWolf did not survive, but his diary did. This terse diary is the sole systematic record of the reconnaissance, although there are other sources of spot information.

The auxiliary personnel included Mitch Boyer as guide and eight enlisted Indian scouts, of whom three left interviews that name all eight.[3] The four Rees were Forked Horn, Young Hawk, One Feather, and William Baker (half-blood Ree), and the four Dakotas were Caroo, Ma-tok-sha, Buffalo Body (Pta-a-te), and White Cloud (Machpeya-ska). Troops served the packtrain of one hundred mules, assisted by five quartermaster packers.

The Reno reconnaissance remained obscure until Luce published Dr. DeWolf's diary and letters[4] and then Stewart and Luce used them to reconstruct a route.[5] They convinced themselves, however, that the mileages were untrustworthy and largely ignored them; and since they drew

---

[3] The three Rees who named four, seven, and eight of Reno's scouts, respectively, were Young Hawk (Libby, 69), Running Wolf (Libby, 139) and Soldier (Camp, 187) (Y).

[4] Luce, ed., "Diary and Letters of Dr. DeWolf" (A). The diary is also listed in Category Y.

[5] Stewart and Luce, "The Reno Scout" (A).

Table 1. Dr. DeWolf's Timed Marches

Date	Start	Stop	Miles	Hours	mph
		Clock-Time			
June 10	3:30 P.M.	(6:30 P.M.)[a]	8.0	3.0	2.67
June 11	(5:00 A.M.)[b]	(1:30 P.M.)[b]	26.0	8.5	3.06
June 12	5:00 A.M.	2:00 P.M.	24.0	9.0	2.67
June 13	5:00 A.M.	1:00 P.M.	24.5	8.0	3.06
June 14	5:00 A.M.	1:00 P.M.	22.5	8.0	2.81
June 15	6:00 A.M.	1:00 P.M.	25.0	7.0	3.57
June 16	5:00 A.M.	2:00 P.M.	27.0	9.0	3.00
" "	8:30 P.M.	11:30 P.M.	8.0	3.0	2.67
June 17	8:00 A.M.	10:00 A.M.	(7.5)[c]	2.0	3.75
" "	4:00 P.M.	8:00 P.M.	(15.0)[c]	4.0	3.75
June 18	5:30 A.M.	12:00 noon	20.0	6.5	3.08
June 19	4:30 A.M.	4:00 P.M.	33.0	11.5	2.87
Totals[d]			240.5	79.5	3.03

[a]This time is an estimate, as the diary omitted it.

[b]This time had to be chosen from duplicate times given in the diary: "5 A.M.–3 P.M." and "5:30 A.M.–1:30 P.M."

[c]This figure had to be chosen from duplicate mileages given in the diary: "6.5 and 7.5" and "14 and 15." DeWolf's letter of June 21 supports the longer mileages.

[d]If we take the first day as $\frac{1}{3}$, the total days become $9\frac{1}{3}$; the average mpd, 25.8; and the average hpd, 8.5.

so little on supplementary sources, they concluded that the reconnaissance revealed nothing not already known to Terry and so was of no consequence to the campaign. A more detailed analysis, now to be presented, supports quite opposite conclusions.

Dr. DeWolf routinely recorded miles marched with start and stop clock-times, which yield speeds. That is important, for as a ratio, speed is very sensitive to errors in either miles or hours. As assembled in Table 1, the totals of $240\frac{1}{2}$ miles and $79\frac{1}{2}$ hours yield a lumped speed of 3.03 mph, the standard marching speed of walking cavalry, especially for days on one-sixth forage. That implies little *systematic* error, that is, measurements that run consistently too high or too low. The speeds of the twelve individual marches range only from 2.67 to 3.75 mph, despite various grades and terrain; that implies small *random* error, with no large "flukes" at all. These figures suggest that the Gatling gun carried an odometer, which explains why Lt. Kinzie was chosen to keep the itinerary.

Thus assured of the reliability of the diary mileages, I traced the route of the reconnaissance on U.S. Geological Survey maps (the 1:250,000 series), using the diary mileages and landmarks and available supplementary material. In only one instance did Dr. DeWolf give an erroneous landmark, but his mileages still defined a clear route. He frequently segmented the daily marches, not always in miles and less often in hours, but the maps identify segments that add up to his totals.

On the maps, marchable routes along the Powder, Tongue, and Rosebud streams were measured, so that locations could be expressed in a simple code, consisting of a letter (the initial of the stream's name) and a number (the miles above its mouth). For example, the location of Terry's camp 24 miles above the mouth of the Powder may be expressed as P-24. The Cheyenne, Wooden Leg, who was with the winter roamers, said their camps extended for 1½ miles along the streams, but for convenience I shall use a single point, leaving this range implicit.

Because of rain on the morning of June 10, Reno's command did not get off until 3:30 P.M. At the start, of course, the trip mileage was zero and the location P-24. That afternoon the column marched 8 miles south up the east bank of the Powder to camp at P-32.

On June 11 Dr. DeWolf divided the day's march of 26 miles into three segments. Moving up the east bank for 6 miles (to P-38), the troops forded to the west bank "without difficulty"; this crossing was the well-known ford just above Mizpah Creek (P-37), which provides a first map check on diary mileages. Proceeding 10 miles up the west bank (to P-48), they crossed a western branch, which the map identifies as Ash Creek (P-49), a second map check. Another 10 miles brought them to the night's bivouac (at P-58), where DeWolf noted "a smoke in the distance" and that the flats they had crossed were very "soft" and made "hard riding."

On June 12 the three-segment march followed up the west bank along an arc bulging to the southeast. When 12 miles out (P-70), they rode opposite the mouth of an eastern branch, named on the map as Dry Creek (P-69). After 8 more miles (P-78) they did the same thing, this time at Crow Creek (P-78), 1 mile above present Powderville (P-77). They bivouacked 4 miles beyond (P-82), and the doctor noted that they had seen a place "where a large body of Indians had moved from, about one week ago, perhaps 30 lodges." These lodges may well have belonged to a party of summer roamers moving out from the agencies to join the winter roamers.

Dr. DeWolf stated that this bivouac was at "the Forks," meaning the junction with Little Powder River (P-101), which was as far as they were ordered to go. Yet the mileages, already confirmed by four map checks, locate this bivouac at P-82, 19 miles short of the Forks and where there is no tributary. Since there is no speed error, the doctor must have made colossal and corresponding errors in both miles and hours or else misidentified the landmark. This problem never recurs, and the next day's march brings the conviction that the landmark is at fault.

On June 13 the march totaled $24\frac{1}{2}$ miles, noted as "S of W," to camp on the south-flowing Mizpah Creek. Segments are lacking, but the description indicates that a last segment was north down Mizpah Creek and a middle segment was west across the little divide, making the first the only one that bore southwest. The map shows Powder River to be flowing from the southwest; in fact, an ascent of $10\frac{1}{2}$ miles up its west bank reaches P-$92\frac{1}{2}$, only $8\frac{1}{2}$ miles short of the forks, and where the Powder runs closest to the upper Mizpah. The scouts could easily have sped ahead to find the forks free of Indians, fulfilling orders without requiring the entire column to plod there and back. That allowed the second segment to bear west 8 miles over the divide to Mizpah Creek, described as a "rough crossing over a very crooked trail." That left 6 miles for a final descent down Mizpah Creek, as ordered, to bivouac at the mouth of a western branch identifiable as Hay Creek. DeWolf implied such a descent by saying that the branches of the Mizpah were "nearly all dry and very little [water] where we camped."

Reno, following his orders, had now completed half his prescribed route and was on his return. He had seen no Indians in the Powder valley and learned nothing useful, with future prospects equally dim. For reasons never disclosed, he now decided to depart from strict orders and veer west to upper Pumpkin Creek, the north-flowing branch of the Tongue. It is a reasonable speculation that he had talked with the knowledgeable Mitch Boyer and learned that the prescribed route would bypass the village that Bradley had seen on the Tongue. The lodges had not been counted, but the deserted lodge sites could still be counted by veering west to the upper Pumpkin and beyond to the upper Tongue and descending it to the campsite. The thought of bringing some useful information must have appealed to Reno, for the next morning he had Mitch lead them in that direction.

June 14 brought another three-segment march of $22\frac{1}{2}$ miles to the upper Pumpkin. The first segment led slightly north of west up Hay Creek for "12 miles to the divide" at a point a little northwest of Coalwood. The second, by difference, led $8\frac{1}{2}$ miles northwest (roughly U.S. 312) down S.L. Creek, an eastern branch of the Pumpkin, to strike the latter a mile below the mouth of Little Pumpkin, a western branch that makes a fork about 4 miles south of present Volborg. The last segment of 2 miles included 1 mile south up to the fork and another mile southwest up the Little Pumpkin. DeWolf's description of this short segment omits a word: "March up Pumpkin from mile [below] to about one mile above its forks, on west fork."

On June 15 the column made another three-segment march of 25 miles. The first segment was "10 miles up a branch of Pumpkin" by a "broad valley to divide," which the map shows was westward up a branch of Little Pumpkin to the divide at a point about 3 miles north of wooded Liscom Butte (4,317 feet elevation). Here they "killed an elk" and the "Gatling gun upset." The second segment was "down a branch of Tongue River," which the map shows was northwest down Lay Creek to its junction with the Tongue at T-44, 15 miles below present Brandenburg. That left a final 3-mile march downstream to camp at T-41.

This day's hard march left its mark in other accounts. Young Hawk told Libby (pp. 69–70) that "they got into the mountains," where he "killed and cut up an elk, which made him lose the rest of the party for some time"; he would not catch up until the next afternoon. Pvt. Peter Thompson narrated (p. 140): "One day we wound through some pine-covered hills, where the narrow trails jammed the horses against one another." Pvt. John McGuire told Camp (n.d., p. 123) that "at some of the ravines we had to unlimber the [Gatling] guns, unhitch the horses and haul them over by hand."

On June 16 the command first marched northeast for "8 miles down the Tongue" to T-33, close to the village first sighted by Bradley at T-30 on May 16, precisely a month earlier. Here the scouts, who had certainly gone ahead to study the site, returned to report to Reno. Dr. DeWolf said nothing of this campsite; in fact, he never mentioned a single one of the five deserted campsites discovered on this mission. An anonymous 7th Infantryman, in a letter of July 4, which covered the preceding two weeks, revealed that Mitch Boyer did examine this site: "Our [Montana column] scout [Mitch Boyer] scouted for Maj. Reno. . . . On the Tongue he came to the old Indian camp he had seen when out on a similar scout with

Bradley [the sole hint that Mitch had seen it then]. . . . He counted the lodge-fires that had been there; they numbered 800 lodges [*sic*, eight hundred warriors, corresponding to four hundred lodges]."[6]

At this moment Reno was only 33 miles from completing his mission and by pushing ahead could report to Terry at the mouth of the Tongue that evening. Instead, he decided to violate his orders drastically by moving to the Rosebud. The reason could only have been Mitch Boyer's report that the month-old Sioux campsite at T-30 numbered about four hundred lodges, representing the majority of winter roamers. Mitch probably added that the same village had been seen a week later on the Rosebud and that so large a village would have to move every few days. By now it could be so far away that Terry's plan to strike it on the lower Rosebud would prove a fiasco. Such news must have given Reno pause. He could obey orders and report promptly—but with only stale facts and tenuous projections; or he could violate orders and secure up-to-date facts that could guide a successful strike. Whatever his reasoning, Reno chose the risky course.

Reno immediately headed the column west for 19 miles and at 2 P.M. of that afternoon of June 16 halted $4\frac{1}{2}$ miles short of the Rosebud to wait while the scouts advanced to examine the valley ahead. Young Hawk, who had just overtaken the command, told Libby (p. 70) that Forked Horn directed the other Rees to ride a little to the right, undoubtedly with Mitch, in search of the deserted campsite at R-19, while Young Hawk diverged slightly upstream. Mitch promptly found what he was seeking, as Lt. Bradley happily recorded on June 18, for it confirmed what his fellow officers had received with such skepticism:

> [Reno found] traces of a large village at the place I discovered it on May 27 [abandoned May 29, nineteen days earlier]. Mitch Boyer, our guide . . . counted 300 lodgefires and estimated there were enough more besides to make the number of lodges about 400. The lodges had been arranged in nine circles within supporting distance of one another, within which the Indians apparently secured their horses at night, showing they considered an attack likely and were prepared for it.

Later, members of the Dakota column also learned about this Rosebud camp. Custer wrote his wife on June 21 that Reno's "scouting party . . .

---

[6] *Helena Herald*, July 20, 1876.

saw the trail and deserted camp of a village of 380 lodges."[7] In his news dispatch of June 22 he wrote: "He [Reno] struck the Rosebud . . . and there . . . discovered signs of a large force of Indians, an abandoned campground on which 380 lodges had been pitched." One of Terry's staff officers (probably Capt. Michaelis, ordnance officer) wrote in one of his regular news dispatches of June 21: "Reno discovered a heavy Indian trail, consisting of nearly 400 lodges, near the Rosebud."[8] Lt. Godfrey's diary for June 20 recorded that "Reno reports a camp about 3 weeks old of about 350 lodges."

In the meantime, Young Hawk (to Libby, p. 70), who was diverging upstream, climbed a hill bordering the Rosebud and spotted another deserted campsite below. This hill was undoubtedly Teat Butte, at about R-25, at the base of which the Sioux village had next camped (abandoned May 30, eighteen days earlier). Riding down to examine it, Young Hawk found proof that it was a "very old" Sioux campsite and ponies had trampled the riverbank at the watering places. Since the command would not reach here until after dark that night, no one recorded its size.

On returning to the nervously waiting command, Mitch could report deserted campsites at R-19 and R-26 and a heavy trail leading up the safe and deserted Rosebud valley. Though it was now 8:30 P.M., Reno ordered a night march, which in $4\frac{1}{2}$ miles struck the Rosebud about midway between the two campsites. From there, the column continued up the Rosebud for $3\frac{1}{2}$ miles to camp at 11:30 P.M. (R-$26\frac{1}{4}$) at the upper end of the Teat Butte campsite, as Young Hawk noted. DeWolf's mileages enable us to pinpoint the place where Reno struck the Rosebud; the troops marched upstream from there 11 miles and then downstream for $33\frac{1}{4}$ miles to its mouth, the difference of $22\frac{3}{4}$ miles identifying R-$22\frac{3}{4}$ as where they had struck the Rosebud and R-$26\frac{1}{4}$ as the Teat Butte campsite.

In confirmation, Pvt. Kennedy told Wheeler (1900) that they struck "the main Indian trail at the Rosebud about 15 or 29 miles above its mouth [the average is R-22]." Custer's June 22 news dispatch says, "Reno struck the Rosebud about 25 miles above its mouth."[9] As for the bivouac at R-$26\frac{1}{4}$, DeWolf mentioned "a large trail" and having to "boil water for camp." Pvt. Thompson (1924, p. 141) also noted the "tepee

---

[7] Custer to Mrs. Custer, June 21, 1876, Elizabeth Custer, *Boots and Saddles*, 311 (B).
[8] Capt. Michaelis news dispatch (unsigned), June 21, *New York Tribune*, July 11, 1876.
[9] See note 7, above.

trails that made it difficult to secure a good camping place, especially so at watering places which were so necessary to us."

Early on June 17 Reno resumed the advance up the Rosebud for another $7\frac{1}{2}$ miles to R-33$\frac{3}{4}$, where the column halted from 10 A.M. to 4 P.M. The Rosebud, here flowing from the southwest, turns north, and at this bend Greenleaf Creek joins it from the southeast. That was the location of the next Sioux campsite (R-34, abandoned June 4, thirteen days earlier). The scouts must have examined it to assure themselves that the heavy trail followed the Rosebud southwest rather than Greenleaf Creek southeast. This campsite drew little attention, but some mentioned signs of a battle here. Young Hawk (Libby, p. 70) recalled that they "found an entrenchment showing evidence that all the white occupants had been killed. Our interpreter [Mitch Boyer] said this was the Bozeman party." A fight between the Bozeman prospecting party and the Sioux had indeed occurred here in the spring of 1874, but as Herendeen could assure Young Hawk, the prospectors had held off the Sioux with little damage to themselves.

During this halt Reno took extra precautions to avoid discovery. Pvt. Thompson recalled (pp. 141–42) that "orders were given that no bugles be blown, nor loud noises made and pickets were posted around camp." Not for weeks, however, would they learn that on this very morning, June 17, the Sioux were vanquishing Gen. Crook's Wyoming column on the head of the Rosebud (R-91). The Sioux village, having already left the Rosebud at its Busby bend, was then camped to the west of the divide. Young warriors had poured out to prevent Crook's large force from approaching any closer to the village of women and children and were succeeding admirably.

While the troops waited at this halt, Mitch Boyer, as the only scout familiar with this country, led the Rees up the Rosebud on the Sioux trail. At $12\frac{1}{4}$ miles out they reached the next Sioux campsite at R-46, Sitting Bull's famous sun-dance camp (abandoned June 8, nine days earlier). No one recorded anything about this camp either, but on June 24, when Custer's column reached it, it drew considerable attention, and Lt. Godfrey noted in his diary that it "was estimated as consisting of three or four hundred lodges." This comment is highly significant, for it means that the village of winter roamers had remained nearly constant in size over the three weeks it spent traveling from the Tongue to this point.

Another 7 miles would bring the scouts to another oblique bend of the Rosebud, where Lame Deer Creek joins from the southeast at R-53. Knowing that, Mitch would certainly want to check it to make sure the Sioux trail did not leave the Rosebud at this point. Advancing this far made a just-feasible round trip for the scouts of $38\frac{1}{2}$ miles in six hours at a steady trot of 6.4 mph. All accounts agree that when last seen the trail was heading southwest up the Rosebud, implying a scout to this oblique bend. Custer (June 22 news dispatch), after saying that Reno struck the Rosebud at R-25, added that "Reno followed the trail about twenty miles up the Rosebud," thus to R-45, near the sun-dance camp, which is too far for the troops; but as the column halted at R-$33\frac{3}{4}$, the additional 20 miles may have referred to the advance of the scouts to R-$53\frac{3}{4}$, or Lame Deer Creek.

Further evidence that the scouts reached Lame Deer Creek appears in two other statements. Custer wrote his wife on June 21 (pp. 311–12) that "the scouts reported that they could overtake the village in a day and a half." Pvt. Thompson related (pp. 141–42) that when the scouts returned to Reno's halt "our scout, Mich Burey, was of the opinion that we could overtake the Indians in a day's march." These overtake claims were based not on a fresher *campsite*, but on fresher overlay *trails*, which joined at Lame Deer Creek and were made by summer roamers coming out to join the winter roamers. I deem it impossible for the scouts to have reached the next winter roamer campsite at R-58 (abandoned five days earlier), as the round trip of $48\frac{1}{2}$ miles in six hours would demand a steady lope of 8.1 mph from ponies overworked for a week.

When the scouts returned to the halted troops, Mitch could report the sun-dance camp no bigger than the others, some fresher overlay trails at Lame Deer Creek, and the heavy lodgepole trail continuing beyond in a southwest direction up the Rosebud. If asked, he could have added that the trail would probably continue to the Busby bend of the Rosebud (R-70), where it could turn south up the Rosebud, west toward the Little Bighorn, or north down Tullock's Fork. Young Hawk (pp. 70–71) then recalled a conversation that followed: "[Reno] called Forked Horn to him and said: 'What do you think of this trail?' He replied: 'If the Dakotas see us, the sun will not move very far before we are all killed. But you are leader and we will go if you say so.' The officer said, 'Custer told us to turn back if we found the trail, and we will return; these are our orders.'"

Pvt. Kennedy told Wheeler (1900) that they were "obliged to turn back . . . not being strong enough to tackle the Indians, although it was pretty hard to persuade Reno to do so." Pvt. McGuire told Camp (p. 123) and Sgt. Kanipe related (1924, p. 247), however, that they turned back for lack of rations; since it was only the eighth day and they were rationed for twelve, they must have meant lack of forage. At 4 P.M. of that June 17 Reno did start back and made 15 miles down the Rosebud before bivouacking at R-18¾, the location of Bradley's Sioux campsite.

On June 18 the weary column plodded the 18¾ miles down to the mouth of the Rosebud and then 1¼ miles down the south bank of the Yellowstone to "near opposite Gibbon's camp" at noon, and "communicated with them," as DeWolf noted. The only other comment came from Pvt. Thompson (p. 142): "We secured a very pretty camping place with plenty of grazing for our horses. . . . They had become quite jaded, for our grain had all been consumed, as the grazing had been poor."

The unexpected appearance of Reno's column nearly opposite Gibbon's camp drew considerable comment from the Montana column. Communication across the river presented difficulties, for Herendeen's boats had been left downriver. Rags tied to sticks were used to spell out messages in army code, but field glasses were needed to read them. When Gibbon decided to send a letter across, scout Bostwick nearly drowned trying to deliver it. So Jack Rabbit Bull tied the letter in a rag around his head, and he and another Crow ran upstream, plunged in, and swam nearly a mile before landing safely. After swimming back with a note from Reno, the Crows earned a drink of whiskey and a nap. [10]

Gibbon's chroniclers, as already quoted, learned a little about the two villages, but none discovered how far Reno, or the scouts, had advanced up the Rosebud, though they freely speculated that the trail was heading "toward" the Little Bighorn, and the village was now "thought" to be there, which was pure guesswork. Gibbon did a little better in his June 18 letter to Terry, which the swimming Crows had brought to Reno:

Col. Reno made his appearance at the mouth of the Rosebud today and I have communicated with him by signal and by scouts swimming the river. He had seen no Indians, but I gather from the conversations which the scouts had with Mitch Bowyer that they found signs of camps on Tongue River and Rosebud, and trails leading up the Rosebud. I

[10] Marquis, *Memoirs* (LeForge), 238–39 (B), tells of Bostwick and Jack Rabbit Bull swimming the river.

presume the only remaining chance of finding Indians now is in the direction of the headwaters of the Rosebud or Little Bighorn. I have been anxiously looking for the boat and shall be glad to meet you or to hear of your future plans.[11]

Obviously, Gibbon had learned enough to realize that Terry's attack plan needed revision, for he expressed interest in Terry's future plans. The letter reveals further that on this June 18 he *presumed* the Indians were then in the *direction* of the *headwaters* of the Rosebud *or* Little Bighorn. That covered a lot of territory, but the *lower* Little Bighorn is conspicuously unmentioned. This omission is significant, for Gibbon would soon join the myth-builders in saying that everyone knew the Sioux were on the lower Little Bighorn all along. He even claimed, giving no date, that his Crows saw "smoke" on the Little Bighorn, but his officers recorded on June 16 that the Crows saw smoke upriver and close to the Yellowstone.

On June 19 Reno headed down the south bank of the Yellowstone to join Terry at the mouth of Tongue River, but the trail proved so rugged that after 33 miles he camped 8 miles short of his destination. The reconnaissance ended here after 240½ miles, for Terry would send Custer's column up to join Reno the next morning. Dr. DeWolf summarized the reconnaissance in a letter to his wife, written on June 21:

> Since my last, we went up to the forks of Powder River, 58 miles [checks diary, and still 19 miles short of forks]; crossed the country to Tongue River, 72 miles [checks diary]; down Tongue R. 8 miles [checks diary]; crossed to Rosebud Cr., about 25 miles [diary gives 23.5]; up Rosebud 12 miles [diary gives 11]; then back and followed it to its mouth; from there down the Yellowstone 33 miles to near Tongue R., where we met Custer and the other six companies of 7th Cavalry.
>
> I and Dr. Porter messed together and had a nice time. We found no Indians, not one; all old trails. They seem to be moving west and are driving the buffalo. I think it is very clear that we shall not see any Indians this summer. It is believed they have scattered and gone back to their reservations. Our battery . . . has hurt three men already by upsetting. We found one buffalo and some elk on the scout.[12]

[11] Gibbon to Terry, June 18, Letters Received, Dept. of Dak., 1876, Box 19 (G-RG98).
[12] DeWolf to wife, June 21, Luce, ed., "Diary and Letters of Dr. DeWolf," 80–81 (A).

As soon as the column bivouacked that afternoon, Reno sped a courier (Mitch was the only one who knew this country) ahead with Gibbon's note and his own report addressed to Gen. Terry:

> I am in camp about eight miles above you. I started this A.M. to reach your camp, but the country from the Rosebud here is simply *awful* and I had given orders to cache the gun, but Kinzie is coming in all right. I am sure you cannot take wagons to Rosebud without going some distance up Tongue River.
>
> I enclose you a note from Gibbon, whom I saw yesterday. I can tell you where the Indians are *not* and much more information when I see you in the morning. I take it the Tongue River is not fordable at the mouth and I will necessarily have to camp on this side. I have had no accident, except breaking the tongue of Kinzie's gun carriage. My command is well. I will be on Tongue River opposite your camp about 8 A.M. My animals are leg weary and need shoeing. We have marched near to 250 miles.[13]

Note that Reno made no effort to predict the Indians' present whereabouts and merely said he knew where they were not, perhaps meaning they are not where Terry expected to trap them. Reno may have thought this was a subtle and diplomatic way of justifying his violation of orders, but it provoked a severe reaction from Terry, already exasperated by Reno's tardiness. His diary that June 19 reads: "In afternoon, received dispatches from Reno, informing me that he had been to mouth of Rosebud. Also note from Gibbon. Sent Hughes [his aide] to meet Reno. Hughes returned at ———. Reno gave him no reason for his disobedience of orders." Terry was less restrained when he wrote his sisters on June 21:

> Here we lay in idleness until Mon. [June 19], where to my great surprise I received a note from Col. Reno, which informed me that he had flagrantly disobeyed my orders and that instead of coming down the Tongue he had been on the Rosebud. . . . It appears that he had done this in defiance of my positive orders not to go to the Rosebud, in the belief that there were Indians on that stream and that he could make a successful attack on them, which would cover up his disobedience. . . . He had not the supplies to enable him to go far and he returned without justification for his conduct, unless wearied horses

[13] Reno to Terry, June 19, Letters Received, Dept. of Dak., 1876, Box 19 (G-RG98).

and broken-down mules could be justification. Of course, this performance made a change in my plans necessary.[14]

Capt. Robert P. Hughes, the aide, recalled his mission and Terry's decision to halt Reno where he was:

> Terry learned through an Indian of the result of Reno's scout in the evening of June 19. That night I rode through to Reno's bivouac with orders for him to remain there and rest the next day, while Custer should bring up the remainder of the 7th, the scouts and Low's battery. After I returned to Terry that night with such information as I had gathered, the maps were got out and the general field gone over.[15]

Custer, in his news dispatch of June 22, heaped more censure on Reno:

> [Reno] returned, having inexcusably and inexplicably disobeyed and violated his orders and thereby embarrassed and marred hopes of future success of the expedition. . . . Had he pursued and overtaken the village, this error would have been forgotten; but instead, he countermarched to the rear . . . to report his blunder to Gen. Terry, who informed him that his disobedience would not bear investigation. A court-martial is strongly hinted at.

There is no doubt whatever that Reno violated his orders, but these hot and hasty charges may well have been designed to direct attention away from more embarrassing facts. Terry's plan to trap the village on the lower Rosebud had been doomed before Reno started, as his disobedience so conclusively proved, and his reconnaissance thereby saved the whole command from a fiasco. Terry recognized this fact the instant he received Reno's cryptic note and Gibbon's more informative one, for, discarding his attack plan, he immediately sent orders for Reno to remain in camp, where Custer would join him the next morning.

The evidence is strong that Reno's reconnaissance could supply no more than a guess as to the location of the Sioux village. Its trail had last been seen on June 17 on the Rosebud no farther up than Lame Deer Creek. On reaching the Busby bend, it could turn south, west, or north, probably depending on game, which the scouts had found to be scarce.

---

[14] Terry to sisters, June 21, 1876. Apparently lost, this letter was quoted in Koury, *Custer Engages the Hostiles*, 29–30 (B).

[15] Hughes, "Campaign against the Sioux," in Graham, *Story of the Little Big Horn*, appendix, 34–35 (B).

This shortage could speed the village's rate of travel anywhere over a wide area. Even Capt. Hughes, who became the most partisan defender of the myth that Terry now knew that the village was on the lower Little Bighorn, admitted that "Reno did not pursue the trail he had found far enough to determine in which direction it finally turned. It was possible, though not probable, that it would turn eastward."[16] Nevertheless, the information Reno secured was enough to cause Terry instantly to discard his original attack plan and devise a new one that incorporated far more flexibility.

The Reno reconnaissance therefore had a profound effect on the campaign, and Mitch Boyer had a profound effect on the Reno reconnaissance.

[16] Ibid., 22.

TERRY SENDS CUSTER UP THE ROSEBUD

Gen. Terry's revised attack plan, though not yet completed in detail, called for moving the entire 7th Cavalry up to the mouth of the Rosebud and Gibbon's column up to the mouth of the Bighorn. Proof of this strategy came early on the morning of June 20 at the mouth of Tongue River, when by Special Field Order No. 14, Terry directed Custer, with the left wing of his 7th Cavalry, Lt. Low's Gatling battery, packtrain, and Ree scouts, to proceed up the Yellowstone to Reno's bivouac, there assume command of both wings, and proceed to the mouth of the Rosebud. Leaving the Tongue at 8 A.M., Custer reached Reno's bivouac at 11:30 A.M. An hour later the supply-laden *Far West* delivered Terry and staff and boat guard to the same point.

Whether Terry and Custer grilled Reno or ignored him, they did extract some information from Mitch Boyer, which may well have reinforced their desire to retain his services; as will emerge, they also enlisted his aid in selecting more of Gibbon's scouts for transfer to Custer. The *Far*

West having resupplied Reno's men, Terry took aboard the entire Gatling battery to spare it the rugged march up to the Rosebud. Mitch was also aboard when the boat pushed off at 3:45 P.M. for Gibbon's camp near the Rosebud. At 4 P.M. Custer's reunited regiment, with Ree scouts and packtrain, resumed its march up the south bank of the Yellowstone.

A Day of Organizing, June 21

At 6 A.M. of June 21 Gen. Gibbon, in camp 4 miles below the mouth of the Rosebud, anticipated the change in Terry's plan by sending Capt. Freeman and three companies of infantry up the north bank of the Yellowstone to do some road work. Then, at 8:35 A.M. (Terry diary), the *Far West* tied up at Gibbon's camp and began unloading supplies for the Montana column. Going ashore, Terry promptly ordered Gibbon to start the remainder of his command on the long march upriver to the mouth of the Bighorn, picking up the road workers on the way. At 9:30 A.M. Lt. Bradley left the camp with his Crows to scout the van for these troops, who all got off by 10 A.M. (English diary, McClernand itinerary), leaving Gibbon's camp deserted.

Also at 9:30 A.M. Terry had taken Gibbon and Brisbin aboard the *Far West* to steam up against the current 4 miles to reach the mouth of the Rosebud at 11:45 A.M. and there await the arrival of Custer's column, still on the march (Terry diary). At 12 noon (DeWolf diary) Custer's troops spotted the best place to camp 2 miles below the mouth of the Rosebud and at 12:30 P.M. (Godfrey diary) had pitched their tents. Without giving clock-times, Terry next entered: "Returned downstream to Custer's camp," a fast 2 miles with the current. That afternoon, between 2 and 4 P.M., Terry held a strategy conference on the *Far West* with Custer, Gibbon, and Brisbin.

This well-defined chronology is of enormous help in interpreting a host of important events of this day. It first reveals that it was before 10 A.M. when Terry penned his report of June 21 to Gen. Sheridan, giving the first outline of his revised attack plan:

> No Indians have been met with yet, but traces of a large and recent camp have been discovered 20 or 30 miles up the Rosebud. Gibbon's column will move this morning [thus this was written before 10 A.M.] on the north side of the Yellowstone for the mouth of the Big Horn,

where it will be ferried across by the supply steamer, and whence it will proceed to the mouth of the Little Big Horn, and so on. Custer will go up the Rosebud tomorrow with his whole regiment and thence to the *headwaters* of the Little Big Horn, thence down the Little Big Horn. I only hope that one of the two columns will find the Indians. I go personally with Gibbon.[1] [Italics added.]

During the twenty-five minutes Terry spent in Gibbon's camp that morning, he negotiated the hiring of George Herendeen by Gibbon's quartermaster, Lt. Jacobs, as scout at one hundred dollars a month for the remainder of the campaign and took him aboard the *Far West* (9:30 A.M.) to be transferred to the service of Custer when the latter arrived. Herendeen related (1878, p. 261): "Gen. Terry told me I could go with Custer on his march up the Rosebud; he told me at Gibbon's tent to go with Custer. . . . I afterward saw Terry on the *Far West*, while she lay at the mouth of the Rosebud [11:45 A.M.] and he asked me about the country along the upper part of the Rosebud and Tullock's Fork."

During that same early interval six Crow scouts were selected to go with Custer: Half Yellow Face (their leader), White Swan, Curley, Goes Ahead, White Man Runs Him, and Hairy Moccasin, all but the first two of whom left interviews. Gibbon narrated (1877, p. 293): "The scouts with Custer's regiment were entirely ignorant of the country he was to pass through. Mitch Bowyer, who knew all about it, was to go with him, and in addition, by direction of Gen. Terry, I assigned to duty with him six of my Crow scouts, who volunteered for the service." Gibbon passed the order on to Bradley, who this day lamented to his diary: "I was directed to detail six of my best scouts to be transferred to Custer, and they joined him at the mouth of the Rosebud. Mitch Bouyer was with him, too. This leaves us without a guide." This transfer had to have been completed before both Gibbon and Bradley left at 9:30 A.M.

What has not previously been recognized is that Boyer, having arrived with Terry on the *Far West* at 8:35 A.M., participated in the selection of the Crows and accompanied them aboard the boat at 9:30 A.M. for later delivery to Custer. This fact is implicit in the timing, but the Crow interviews make it explicit, despite the fact that Dixon, their principal in-

[1]*Army and Navy Journal*, July 15, 1876, 79. The final two sentences of this quotation do not appear in *A & N J*, but Charles Kuhlman, *Did Custer Disobey Orders?*, 12 (B), states: "According to Charles Francis Bates, these words are in every copy of the dispatch on file in the War Dept."

terviewer, routinely mistranslated the Crows' names for the generals and thought the selection had occurred at the mouth of the Bighorn instead of the Rosebud. Curley was most specific:

(Dixon, 1909, pp. 144–45): A steamboat arrived [8:35 A.M.], bringing Bouyer, the scout. . . . Terry [*sic*, Gibbon] and the infantry commander [*sic*, Brisbin, cavalry commander], were on the ambulance and Bouyer was there talking to them. Bouyer then asked me who among the scouts did the most scouting. . . . After they had called these men [names all six], they put us on the steamboat [9:30 A.M.] and sent us down [*sic*, up] the river, sending the other Crows home [*sic*, to march with Bradley]. We were taken down [*sic*, up] to the mouth of the Rosebud on the Yellowstone [11:45 A.M.].

(Same, p. 159): After we landed, we were told to get dinner [noon meal], dress ourselves, paint up, and get ready to scout. Then we heard that Custer wanted to use us. We mounted and rode over [i.e., down] to Custer's camp. He had a big tent and we got off at the door.

Goes Ahead provided confirmation in two separate interviews:

(Dixon, 1909, pp. 164–65): There was a boat at the mouth of the Big Horn [*sic*, below the mouth of the Rosebud]. Soldiers came off the boat and joined Terry [*sic*, Gibbon]. . . . Then he [Gibbon] selected . . . scouts to send to Custer. There were six of us [names all six]. Then they gave us orders to go on the boat [9:30 A.M.]. We sailed down [*sic*, up] to the mouth of the Rosebud [11:45 A.M.], where we got off the boat. Then our interpreter [Boyer] told us there was a man in the camp of the army who wanted to see us, and we went over there. Then we went into Custer's tent.

(Libby, 1912, pp. 157–58): Then a steamboat came up the Yellowstone, opposite [and below] the mouth of the Rosebud [8:35 A.M.]. . . . The roll was called of the Crow scouts on the bank at the boat. Six [names all] were called to go on board [9:30 A.M.]. Their interpreter was Mitch Bouyer (Ka-pesh), a half-breed Dakota. He told them that when they went down below the mouth of the Rosebud, they would see Arikara scouts. When they came to this camp, there was a big tent, with a flag on it, and in it they met Custer.

These Crow interviews lack clock-times, as usual, but everything they say fits the established chronology perfectly. Herendeen (1878, p. 261) does supply one estimated clock-time: "I reported to Custer at noon of June 21, and was sent to Lt. Varnum, who [as Custer's chief of scouts] had charge of some [Ree] scouts. I saw with Varnum Mitch Boyer, the half-breed scout and guide." Noon was probably a little early, but the implication is that all the transferred scouts met Custer before Terry's afternoon strategy conference.

The Crow interviews also reveal that at this first meeting Custer impressed the scouts deeply. Custer did have a better knack for handling Indian scouts than most officers; he treated them decently, made the effort to understand them, and recognized their unique skills and knowledge, all of which inspired their best efforts and loyalty. He was equally impressed by the Crows, for he wrote his wife that evening:

> I now have some Crow scouts with me, as they are familiar with the country. They are magnificent looking men, so much handsomer and more Indian-like than any we have ever seen, and so jolly and sportive; nothing of the gloomy, silent redman about them. They have formally given themselves to me after the usual talk. In their speech they have heard that I never abandon a trail; that when my food gave out, I ate mule. That was the kind of man they wanted to fight under; they were willing to eat mule, too.[2]

Terry's diary never mentions his strategy conference on the *Far West*, which leaves its starting time of about 2 P.M. only an appropriate guess, but there is evidence that it was over by 4 P.M. Low's battery was still aboard, for Terry expected to restore it to Custer, but the latter rejected it at the conference as too unwieldy. Terry's diary ends the day with: "About 4 P.M., put Low's battery across the river; gave him instructions to follow the trail of Gibbon's column and report to Capt. Ball. Sent 13 mules, injured on Reno's march, by Lt. Low." Aide Hughes confirmed that this crossing ended the conference: "After its close, Low's battery was ferried across . . . to overtake and join Gibbon's command." He then added that "half a dozen Crows were carried to the south side."[3] This addition is clearly a memory lapse, for it contradicts all other evidence and makes Terry either thoughtless or prophetic.

At the strategy conference on the *Far West* Terry presented his revised attack plan to Custer, Gibbon, and Brisbin, and together they thrashed out its final details to everyone's satisfaction. Custer's full regiment was to pursue the Sioux trail up the Rosebud, cross to the upper Little Bighorn, and descend it to strike the village from above. Terry, Gibbon, and

---

[2] Custer to his wife, June 21, 1876, Elizabeth Custer, *Boots and Saddles*, 312 (B).

[3] Hughes, "Campaign against the Sioux," in Graham, *Story of the Little Big Horn*, appendix, 35 (B).

Brisbin were to steam up to the mouth of the Bighorn, ferry the Montana column and Low's battery across the river, and march up the Bighorn to the mouth of the Little Bighorn to block any escape of the village downstream. Herendeen (1878, p. 261) was called into the conference and given the duty, when the appropriate time came, of scouting down Tullock's Fork and reporting to Terry at the mouth of the Bighorn. Terry prepared a full letter of instructions to Custer on the morning of June 22, recommending a course for him to follow but allowing him full discretion, should unforeseen circumstances arise, and cautioning him not to allow the Indians to escape to his left, that is, eastward.[4]

Elsewhere I have analyzed the evidence regarding Terry's plan and summarized it as follows:

> It is now apparent that our projections from available Indian intelligence, all our inferences from actions taken and all the statements made at the time of the conference about the new plan converge on the same pattern. Custer's column, stronger, more mobile, better provided with scouts and longer rationed, was expected to overtake the village wherever it might go, the probabilities being judged to favor the upper Little Big Horn. He was to strike the village, probably while still unsupported, and from a direction that would drive it northward. Terry's column, weaker, less mobile, with fewer scouts and shorter rationed, was expected to reach its blocking station at the mouth of the Little Big Horn on June 26, hopefully supported by the supply boat. There it would intercept fleeing refugees, or, if advised of altered circumstances by Custer, would move to a more strategic point. It was a flexible plan that maximized the likelihood of making a strike, wherever the village might be, yet gave promise of bringing the entire force, slow as well as fast units, into the action.[5]

There has probably never been a plan to attack a poorly understood enemy days ahead at a distant and uncertain location which met with no unforeseen conditions. Terry's plan would encounter some major surprises that would bring disaster—and precipitate a century of acrimonious accusations and scapegoating, achieved by warping facts to suit partisan interests.

The 7th Cavalry was far below full strength when it started up the Rosebud the next day, for it had detached many men, including most of its

[4]Terry to Custer, June 22, 1876, in Terry's Ann. Report, Nov. 21, 1876, in Sec. of War, Ann. Report, 1876, 462 (G-CSS).

[5]Gray, Centennial Campaign, 147 (B).

fresh recruits, at the Powder River depot. It numbered only 31 officers and 566 enlisted men. The 13 quartermaster employees included 5 scouts, Boyer, and Herendeen (from Gibbon's column); Charley Reynolds, Bloody Knife (Ree Indian), and Boston Custer (the general's youngest brother); 2 interpreters, Fred F. Gerard (for the Rees) and Isaiah Dorman (a black, for the Dakotas); and 6 packers. The 35 enlisted Indian scouts included the 6 Crows (from Gibbon's column), 25 Rees, and 4 Dakotas. The addition of news correspondent Mark Kellogg and Custer's young nephew, Autie Reed, brought the grand total to 647.

Custer's March up the Rosebud

On the morning of June 22, when last-minute preparations were completed, morale was high in Custer's camp, for the 7th Cavalry had won the honor of finding the enemy and making the main strike. Pvt. Thompson, who had watched Mitch Boyer at work for ten days as guide for the Reno reconnaissance, related (p. 144): "Custer motioned the *Far West* ashore, leaped aboard and lugged Mich Burey ashore amidst the cheers of the command. Mich was very popular, not only for his quiet demeanor, but on account of his knowledge of the country. He always inspired us with confidence." Even the Ree scouts were keyed up, for as the column was preparing to mount, Fred Gerard, their interpreter and veteran trader with their tribe, urged them to put on a show, as Red Star told Libby (p. 177): "Gerard told us he wanted us to sing our death songs. The Dakota trail had been seen and the fight would soon be on. Custer had a heart like an Indian; if we ever left out anything in our ceremonies, he always suggested it to us. We got on our horses and rode around singing our songs." Not to be outdone, Terry, Gibbon, and Custer ceremoniously reviewed the proud 7th Cavalry as it paraded by.

During Custer's two-and-a-half-day march of 72 miles on the trail of the Sioux village to the Busby bend of the Rosebud, the most significant feature is the enemy intelligence his scouts gathered. As before, it is essential to consult good topographical maps to identify landmarks, measure mileages, and calculate speeds as a check on marching distances and durations. This checking enables us to establish a reliable itinerary for the troop column to serve as a framework for concurrent scouting activities, so necessary because Indian accounts neglect the time dimen-

Table 2. Troop Itinerary: Custer Ascends the Rosebud

Events	Clock-Time	dm	dt	mph	Trip Mi.	Rose-bud Mi.
		Increments				
Lv. Yellowstone camp, 2 mi. below Rosebud.	12:00 M.				0	
Up Yellowstone to mo. of Rosebud.	12:40 P.M.	2	0:40	3.0	2	R-0
Up left bank Rosebud to camp.	4:00	10	3:20	3.0	12	R-10
June 22 total		12	4:00	3.0		
Lv. camp.	5:00 A.M.					
Crosses Rosebud; passes Sioux camp #1.	7:40	8	2:40	3.0	20	R-18
Passes Sioux camp #2, right bank.	10:20	8	2:40	3.0	28	R-26
Halts for packtrain.	11:00	2	0:40	3.0	30	R-28
Lv. halt up right bank.	11:30		0:30			
Crosses Greenleaf Cr.; Sioux camp #3.	1:30 P.M.	6	2:00	3.0	36	R-34
Up right bank to camp.	4:30	9	3:00	3.0	45	R-43
June 23 total		33	11:00	3.0		
Lv. camp up right bank.	5:00 A.M.					
Halts 1 mi. above sun-dance camp #4.	6:30	4	1:30	2.67	49	R-47
At halt, 4 Crows report; officers' call.	7:10					
Lv. halt up right bank.	7:30		1:00			
Passes Lame Deer Cr.	10:30	6	3:00	2.0	55	R-53
Herendeen diverges; 4 Crows report.	10:30					
Halts at E. Muddy Cr., Sioux camp # 5.	1:00 P.M.	5	2:30	2.0	60	R-58
Crow courier reports.	4:00					
Lv. halt up Rosebud.	5:00		4:00			
Camps at Busby, right bank.	7:45	12	2:45	4.36	72	R-70
June 24 total		27	9:45	2.77		

sion. Table 2 presents a troop itinerary for this march, segment by segment and in a form that should become familiar.

I also now introduce an illuminating visual aid in the form of a two-dimensional time-motion graph in Figure 1. The scale of its vertical axis is miles from the mouth of the Rosebud, on which landmarks are labeled;

the scale of the horizontal axis is time, on which days and clock-hours are labeled. Cumulative miles and times, taken from the troop itinerary, are plotted as points and joined by continuous lines; the same is done for the scouts' activities (from text data) and joined by dotted lines. Lines with positive slopes are forward movements, and those with negative slopes are retrograde movements; horizontal lines are halts. The steepness of slopes measures speed.

An itinerary table stores number data as a box stores jigsaw puzzle parts, but the time-motion graph displays relationships at a glance in both place and time as an assembled jigsaw puzzle displays a picture. To find a number datum, consult the table, but to visualize what is happening, look at the graph. Both shall be used from now on, and since they will gradually grow more complex, it is worthwhile to take advantage of the simpler one to "get the hang" of them, for the graphs especially will prove a boon.

The *Far West*, with Terry, Gibbon, Brisbin, boat guard, and supplies, would not push off for the mouth of the Bighorn until 3 P.M., but Custer led his column out of the Rosebud camp at 12 noon of June 22. Lt. Wallace's official itinerary of the Custer column (confirmed by other diaries) reveals that the column marched 2 miles up the Yellowstone, crossed the Rosebud (at R-0), and wheeled left to ascend its left bank for 10 miles, bivouacking 12 miles out (at R-10); the pace was 3.0 mph. This two-segment march is posted in Table 2 but is too simple to need plotting in Figure 1.

Since there was no expectation of seeing Sioux signs on this brief march, the scouts were held close to the column. As Herendeen related (1878, p. 261), "Boyer and Bloody Knife" and probably the Crows rode with Custer at the head of the column. Red Star told Libby (p. 77) that the Ree scouts rode on the flanks of the troops, probably because they were less familiar with this country.

Interpreter Gerard told Mrs. Holley (1892, pp. 262–63) that he had been held at the Rosebud camp until 3 P.M. to send off Ree couriers with a mail and did not overtake the command until about suppertime, after it had bivouacked. When he reported to Custer, he found Bloody Knife there "very much under the influence of whiskey": "Bloody Knife told Gerard: 'Tell Gen. Custer that I don't believe he is hunting for Indians; more likely on a pleasure trip. If he should find them, he would not dare

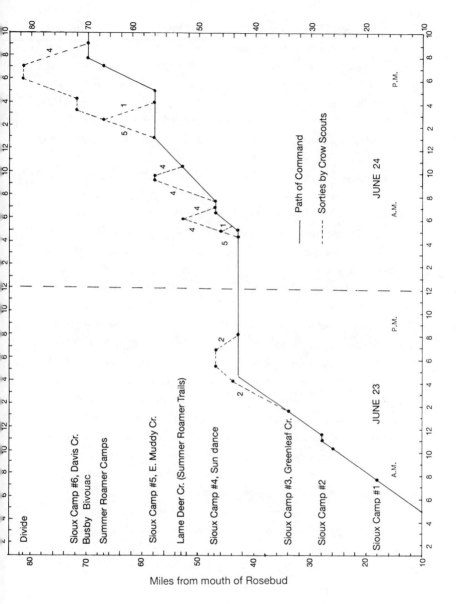

Figure 1. Time-Motion Pattern: Ascent of Rosebud Creek

to attack them.' Custer replied: 'Gerard, tell him that I am on an independent command and shall fight the Indians wherever I find them.' Bloody Knife then seemed satisfied and went to his tent." As a result of prior service together, a mutual regard and respect had developed between Custer and Bloody Knife, although the former was a teetotaler and the latter fond of firewater. So temperate a response reveals that the general was going to great lengths to secure the best possible service on this mission from every member of his command.

Further evidence of this effort surfaced that evening, when Custer held officers' call to give instructions on the conduct of the march and to encourage his officers to cooperate in making the campaign a success. His conciliatory attitude drew comment in nearly every account from those present. At one point Capt. Benteen (1890, p. 177) voiced some testy remarks, but according to Lt. Edgerly (1877, p. 310), Custer quietly smoothed them over, letting nothing distract his officers from the important work ahead.

At this time Custer also presented his information on the strength of the Sioux, as recalled most fully by Lt. Godfrey (1892, p. 134). While in Washington that spring, Custer had taken the pains to inquire at the Indian Office and was told that it estimated the winter roamers at three thousand persons, equivalent to some eight hundred fifty warriors, in agreement with Boyer's count of about four hundred lodges, equivalent to eight hundred warriors. Custer thought there might be as many as one thousand and mentioned the possibility that five hundred more might come out from the agencies that summer, making a maximum of fifteen hundred warriors. This figure was an underestimate, for Gen. Sheridan's attempts to control the agency Indians with heavy garrisons would drive out exceptionally large numbers of summer roamers. That was what Custer did *not* know.[6]

Godfrey related (1892, p. 135) that after the session broke up he made a tour to check the security of his company horses and came on the camp of the Indian scouts:

Mitch Bouyer, Bloody Knife, Half Yellow Face and others were having a "talk." I observed them for a few minutes, when Bouyer

[6]Ibid., chaps. 28 and 29, which analyze the numbers of summer roamers and the strength of the Sioux-Cheyenne village on the Little Bighorn.

turned to me and said, "Have you ever fought against these Sioux?" "Yes," I replied, and then he asked, "Well, how many do you expect to find?" I answered, "It is said we may find between 1000 and 1500." "Well, do you think you can whip that many?" "Oh, yes, I guess so." After he had interpreted our conversation, he said to me with a good deal of emphasis, "Well, I can tell you we are going to have a damned big fight."

We now have three references indicating that Bloody Knife had made the afternoon march, was drunk at suppertime, and attended a talk in the scout camp that evening. These accounts cast doubt on Red Star's claim (to Libby, pp. 77–78) that Bloody Knife was incapacitated all that day and night: "At suppertime Bloody Knife was missing and the scouts waited for him until it was late, but he was drunk somewhere; he got liquor from somebody. Next morning at breakfast, Bloody Knife appeared, leading a horse. He had been out all night." It is more likely that the veteran scout had a good swig before supper, but that Custer kept him at hand all night to make sure it was his last.

On June 23 Lt. Wallace's itinerary says that the day's march began at 5 A.M. and ended 11½ hours later at 4:30 P.M., but it gives no other clock-times nor the total mileage. The Godfrey and DeWolf diaries, a Varnum letter (July 4, p. 232), and Reno's official report (July 5, p. 476) agree that the day's march totaled 33 miles, thus starting at R-10 and ending at R-43. Wallace recorded only one halt, of about half an hour, 18 miles out (R-28). Covering 33 miles in 11 marching hours again yields the standard walking speed of 3.0 mph. The half-hour halt at R-28 thus began at 11 A.M. and ended at 11:30, enabling us to interpolate the time of any event whose mileage is known.

Godfrey (diary) said that this day the column passed three deserted campsites, which have to be the same three that Reno's column had passed. He located the first "8 miles out" (R-18), passed at 7:40 A.M. by interpolation, and both Curley (Dixon, p. 160) and Goes Ahead (Libby, p. 158) identified it as the one Bradley had seen. Wallace did not mention this campsite, but he confirmed its mileage by specifying a segment of 10 miles preceding the halt (R-28 minus 10 yields R-18). The next two deserted campsites drew little comment, but the column passed the Teat Butte camp (R-26) at 10:20 A.M. and after the halt passed the Greenleaf site (R-34) at 1:30 P.M. The night's bivouac (R-43) at 4:30 was near the present junction with the Colstrip Road. These data are posted in itinerary Table 2 and plotted in Figure 1.

This basic troop itinerary may now be used to clarify the more complex activities of the scouts. Curley told Dixon (p. 160) what happened after they had seen the campsite at R-18 and probably that at R-26:

> We followed the Sioux trail and saw that it forked on the Rosebud [probably at Greenleaf Creek, R-34]. Custer ordered Goes Ahead to follow one trail and me to follow the other to see which was the largest camp. We found the trails came together after a while and that the Sioux were all in one camp. When we got to the camp [sun-dance camp, R-46—47, beyond the troop bivouac], we . . . found the scalps and beards of white men [proof of the sun-dance camp]. We went back that night and reported to Custer. It was pretty late, but Custer . . . told his cook to give the boys their meal. . . . We went to Custer's tent . . . [showing him the scalps]. Then Custer asked us if the camp separated or came together, and we told him it came together. Custer said, " . . . Tomorrow I want five of my Crows to go on the trail."

Figure 1 sketches (dotted line) a possible pattern for this scout, by at least Goes Ahead and Curley, ahead of the column to the sun-dance campsite.

Red Star told Libby (pp. 78—79) about the Ree scouts, beginning clearly enough: "[Next morning, June 23] we saddled up, Custer ahead, the scouts following and flanking the army that marched behind. Bob-tailed Bull was in charge, with Strikes Two and others on one side." The implication is that the Rees again scouted the flanks, while the Crows scouted far ahead, a pattern that would prevail for the rest of the march up the Rosebud. On this basis, the Rees would have bivouacked with the troops at 4:30 P.M. But now Red Star becomes confused, for he intertwines events of this day with those of the next: "About nightfall [4—5 hours after the troops bivouacked] they came to an abandoned Dakota camp, where there were signs of a sundance circle. . . . Here they camped, the scouts on the left on the right bank under Bob-tail Bull. They brought in two Dakota horses, which had been discovered by Strikes Two, who brought in one and Little Brave the other." The ellipsis in this quotation described sand pictures at the sun-dance camp that would hardly have been visible after dark. The account then resumes with much more on the sun-dance camp, which imperceptibly merges into events of the next day. I suspect the Rees bivouacked with the troops and first saw the sun-dance camp the next morning.

On June 24 Wallace clocked the start of the day's march at 5 A.M. and the end at 7:45 P.M. His total mileage of "about 28 miles" is confirmed by Godfrey (diary) and Reno's official report (July 5, p. 476), although the map makes it only 27 miles (R-43 to R-70, at Busby). Wallace gave no segmental mileages, but there is general agreement that there were two halts. The first came that morning, which Herendeen estimated at "half an hour," but so much transpired there that I allow a full hour. The second was a long afternoon halt, which Wallace clocked from "1 P.M." to "5 P.M." These halts reduce the marching time to $9\frac{3}{4}$ hours and the lumped marching speed to below 3.0 mph, "so as not to get ahead of the scouts, who seemed to be doing their work thoroughly," according to Godfrey (1892, p. 136). Since the speed was not uniform, the marches must be analyzed segment by segment.

There was reason for caution, as the column was no longer duplicating Reno's route but venturing deep into unknown and hostile country. On the trail of a wily foe that could so easily break up and scatter, discovery could spell disaster. Custer, very attentive to these problems, kept the scouts busy. Lt. Varnum wrote Camp (1909, p. 59) that "with my scouts I acted as advance guard up the Rosebud, and my instructions were, particularly, not to let any trail get away from us without letting Custer know of it." The column had scarcely started when Custer jumped the gun on one scouting detail, as related by Herendeen (1878, pp. 261–62):

> Soon after starting, Custer, who was in advance with Boyer, called me to him to get ready, saying he thought he would send me and Charley Reynolds to the head of Tullock's Fork to take a look. I told the general it was not yet time, as we were then traveling in that direction and I could only follow his trail. I called Boyer, who was a little ahead, and asked him if I was correct . . . and he said, "Yes, further up on the Rosebud we come opposite a gap, and there we could cut across and strike Tullock's in about 15 minutes' ride." Custer said, "All right, you can wait."

The first segment of the June 24 march passed through the sun-dance camp, and there came the hour's halt; as Wooden Leg told Marquis that the sun-dance lodge was at the upstream end of the camp,[7] I fix the halt at R-47. At 2.67 mph, these 4 miles would take $1\frac{1}{2}$ hours, starting the halt at 6:30 and ending it at 7:30 A.M. Wallace estimated this short

[7]Marquis, *Wooden Leg*, 191 (B).

march lasted "about an hour"; Godfrey's diary timed the halt at "7:30," which looks suspiciously like its end. Herendeen's (1876, p. 257) estimates of "5 or 6 miles" and (1878, p. 262) "not far" span our distance of 4 miles. I discard Lt. Varnum's estimate of 10 miles (July 4 letter, p. 342), because that is the map location of Lame Deer Creek, where he related entirely different events.

This sun-dance camp attracted much attention, which helped prolong the halt. Lt. Edgerly (1894, p. 2) recalled that even "Custer examined the area" and that "two white scalps" were found at the sun-dance lodge; Herendeen (1878, p. 262) identified one as that of Pvt. Stoker, killed by the Sioux near Gibbon's camp on May 23. It took time to count scattered lodge sites, and Godfrey's diary says "the camp was estimated as consisting of three or four hundred lodges," signifying that it was the same size as the preceding ones and that the summer roamers had not yet joined the winter roamers. Godfrey later (1892, p. 135) rejected his diary record and introduced hindsight misinformation to support an opposite conclusion.

This sun-dance camp was the sacred place where Sitting Bull, the leading chief of the winter roamers, held the most profoundly religious ceremony of the Sioux as a means of firing the spirit and resolve of his followers to preserve their freedom and last hunting grounds. The Ree scouts, as related by Red Star (Libby, p. 79), sensed the significance of the site and spent much time studying every sign for clues to the mood of their tribal enemies. What they found convinced them that the Sioux had experienced a renewal of faith, hope, and confidence that would bring them victory. The Rees were deeply sobered but no less resolved to serve the troops faithfully.

In response to Custer's request of the night before, five Crow scouts had left the bivouac even before the troops that morning to scout far ahead, leaving Half Yellow Face and Boyer to ride with Custer. They soon sent Curley back while the other four continued, as Curley told Dixon (p. 161):

> We started just before daybreak. When [i.e., after] we started, we saw some of the Rees running around on the top of the hills, and Goes Ahead told me to go back and tell the command . . . to keep them down in the valley, as we might be near the Sioux camp and could be discovered before we knew it. They then ordered the Rees to come

down and stay down. [Curley then probably rode on with the troops to the sun-dance camp.]

The other four Crows continued to the mouth of Lame Deer Creek (R-53), where they found fresh trails of summer roamers joining the main trail, just as Boyer had on Reno's reconnaissance. Turning back, they reported to Custer, still halted at the sun-dance camp, for Wallace recorded their arrival there, reporting "fresh signs of Indians, but in no great number." Godfrey recalled (1892, p. 135) that "the active and efficient Crows discovered fresh signs, the tracks of three or four ponies and of an Indian on foot." Herendeen wrote (1876, p. 257) that "they found fresh pony tracks and said that 10 miles ahead the trail was fresher." If Herendeen meant 10 miles ahead of the morning's bivouac, the discovery was at R-53, or Lame Deer Creek.

These movements of the Crows are feasible, for if they left the bivouac (R-43) at 4:30 A.M. (half an hour before the troops) and trotted 6 mph, they would reach Lame Deer Creek (R-53) at 6:10 A.M.; the same trot would return them to the sun-dance camp (R-47) at 7:10, while the command was halted there. There is leeway at the start and end to allow searching at Lame Deer Creek without impairing feasibility. These movements of the Crows are plotted in Figure 1 as dotted lines, labeled to indicate the number of Crows on each path.

On receiving the report of the four Crows, Custer held an officers' call to relay the news and revise the order of the march. Wallace recorded that "Gen. Custer, with an escort of two companies, moved out in advance, the remainder of the command following at a distance of half a mile." Godfrey recalled (1892, p. 136) that the "troops were required to march on separate trails, so that the dust clouds would not rise so high." Herendeen (1878, p. 262) helpfully added that they now "moved slowly." By the time they were in motion at 7:30 A.M., Custer must have sent the four Crows ahead, but not Curley, for his retention with the column is required to fit future events.

The column moved up the right bank slowly, indeed, for the long halt came at 1 P.M., 5½ hours later, but at R-58, only 11 miles distant, making the speed 2.0 mph. On this slow march Wallace recorded that they "crossed two running tributaries." Dr. DeWolf (diary) specified the first as 6 miles out (R-53), and both Herendeen (1878, p. 262) and Red Star (Libby, p. 30) correctly identified it as present Lame Deer Creek. At

2 mph they would cross it at 10:30 A.M. The second tributary went un-named, but the map identifies it as East Muddy Creek, 5 miles farther at R-58, although Dr. DeWolf estimated it as 6 miles. It was this 5-mile segment that was overestimated to yield 28, instead of 27, miles for this day's march.

On crossing East Muddy Creek at 1 P.M., Custer halted for 4 hours at the next deserted campsite of the winter roamers. It had been occupied June 9–11 and abandoned June 12, twelve days earlier. Only the Crows and Rees mentioned this campsite, and Red Star (Libby, p. 82) noted that "it must have rained at this camp, for the sod was dug up about the lodge circles to carry off water." It may be recalled that it had indeed rained on the 9th and 10th.

Having established the troop itinerary, we may return to Lame Deer Creek, where two notable events had occurred. Herendeen (1878, p. 262) had spotted an Indian trail that diverged up Lame Deer Creek. Knowing Custer's concern about such trails, Herendeen followed it for some dis-tance, and since it was still diverging, he turned back to overtake the column and report the matter to Custer, who "halted the command at once." This discovery was one of two factors that prompted the long after-noon halt at East Muddy Creek.

The second important event at Lame Deer Creek was the return of the four Crows who had gone ahead from the sun-dance camp without Curley and discovered the deserted campsite at East Muddy Creek. Curley met them just as they returned to Lame Deer Creek to report their new finding; they then guided the column on to the new deserted campsite. At least that is the best interpretation I can make of an incoherent story Curley told Dixon (pp. 161–62); in accord with this construal, I insert clari-fications:

> When I started [from Lame Deer Creek to join the four Crows ahead] . . . White Swan, Hairy Moccasin, Goes Ahead and White Man Runs Him were coming in to report. The Sioux had broken camp [of] the day before [sun-dance camp] and had camped [on East Muddy Creek] above where their old camp was on the Rosebud. Custer told us [at Lame Deer Creek] to go ahead [guide the column on] and see which way they went, and we came to where they had broken camp [at East Muddy].

This interpretation conflicts with neither past nor future events and is feasible. By leaving the sun-dance halt (R-47) at 7:30 A.M. (when the column left) and trotting 6 mph, the four Crows would reach East Muddy Creek (R-58) at 9:20 A.M., where they could study the campsite for 20 minutes; leaving at 9:40 A.M., they could trot the 5 miles back to reach Lame Deer Creek (R-53) at 10:30 A.M., just as the column reached that point. Then, by guiding the column on to the afternoon halt, they and Curley would be available to make their next scout even farther ahead.

On the 5-mile march from Lame Deer, everyone noted puzzling changes in the Indian trail they were following. Instead of a single heavy trail with old campsites a day's journey apart, there were now multiple trails in various directions and small scattered campsites, some growing fresher and fresher. These were, in fact, converging trails left by summer roamers coming out to join the winter roamers.

Every officer on the frontier knew only too well that Indians shunned pitched battles and were so mobile and elusive as to be frustratingly difficult to corral. Thus the overriding fear was that the village would break up and scatter, thwarting the whole campaign. Even Terry's instructions had cautioned Custer against allowing the quarry to escape, especially to his left. At the moment this concern was highest, Herendeen reported just such a diverging trail back at Lame Deer. Furthermore, the freshness of the trails gave the impression that the column was overtaking the Indians. It was these two factors that prompted Custer to call the 4-hour halt at East Muddy Creek so that both could be investigated.

While the troops made coffee and prepared a meal, Custer kept the scouts doubly busy. Wallace recorded that "scouts were sent ahead," undoubtedly the Crows, to follow the freshening trails and report whatever they could learn. They probably also delivered Custer's summons to Lt. Varnum and the Rees, scouting the close van, to return to the halted command. Varnum wrote Camp (1909, pp. 59–60) that, when he reported in, Custer ordered him to check out Herendeen's diverging trail. Protesting that his scouts could not have missed such a trail, Varnum left some of his Rees with Lt. Hare, newly assigned to assist him, and dutifully rode back with the rest to Lame Deer Creek. There he picked up the diverging trail and followed it, only to find that it eventually rejoined the main trail, which he then reported to Custer. Herendeen (1878, p. 262) added that Varnum was absent on this mission for "two hours," equivalent to a 12-mile trot.

As the next event at this afternoon halt, Wallace recorded: "The scouts got back about 4 P.M. and reported a fresh camp at the forks of the

Rosebud. Everything indicated the Indians were not more than 30 miles away." Herendeen (1876, p. 257) noted that, "while the officers were eating lunch, the scouts came back and reported that they had found where the village had been quite recently." Only Red Star (Libby, p. 80) identified these scouts: "Six of the Crow scouts, with their interpreter [Boyer] had been out scouting and they returned at this camp [halt]. They reported abandoned camps along the Rosebud. The whole army [had] stopped here and ate dinner."

As will soon appear, Red Star was mistaken in saying that six Crows and Boyer had reported in, but the foregoing accounts do give important clues to what the scouts had, and had not, seen before sending back a courier to report. The "forks of the Rosebud" referred to the junction of Davis Creek and the Rosebud, at R-72, 14 miles from the halt. This creek, heading at the Rosebud-Little Bighorn divide, flows north of west to the west bank of the Rosebud about 2 miles above present Busby (R-70), which lies on the east bank within the Busby bend. Wooden Leg located the next campsite of the winter roamers opposite the mouth of Davis Creek; it was abandoned June 15, nine days earlier, when the village moved up Davis Creek to camp on the divide.

It is clear that the Crows had *not* reached this winter roamer campsite when they sent back a courier, because he reported fresh camps, not an old camp; he would have to complete a round trip of 28 miles in 3 hours at 9.3 mph, which stretches feasibility; and what is most important, he did not report the monumental discovery that the Sioux trail left the Rosebud for the divide and the Little Bighorn. What the Crows must have seen were fresh campsites of summer roamers somewhere *below* Busby.

With this conclusion in mind, let us address the accounts of the Crows. White Man Runs Him told Hugh Scott (1919, p. 15) that, when Custer had sent the Crows ahead that afternoon, "Hairy Moccasin, Goes Ahead and I rode some soldier horses and came to that peak [on the divide]." Curley told Dixon (p. 162) that he was with this party: "We followed the trail until we saw they had camped on the Little Horn [*sic*, Rosebud] and then we noticed that the Sioux had gone toward the Little Horn." Since these four proceeded to the divide, someone else must have been sent back to report before they reached Davis Creek. White Swan is the most likely candidate, for there is no evidence that Custer sent either Half Yellow Face or Boyer from his side that day. I thus propose that five

Crows had started out and that White Swan was sent back as courier to report, and there Mitch interpreted for him. This pattern is feasible, for if the five Crows left the long halt (R-58) promptly at 1 P.M. and trotted 6 mph for 9 miles, they would reach R-67 at 2:30, and White Swan could return at the same speed for the same distance to report to Custer at 4 P.M., as Wallace recorded.

When the courier reported "large camps of Sioux," Red Star (pp. 80–81) recalled that Custer asked the Rees what they thought of the news. Stabbed pantomimed how the Rees dodged and used cover, instead of standing in rows to be shot down as the soldiers did. Custer diplomatically praised the Indian skills and ended up by saying, "My only intention in bringing the Arikara to battle is to have them take away many horses from the Sioux."

Lt. Wallace then described the last segment of the march of June 24: "At 5 P.M. the command moved out; crossed to the left bank of the Rosebud; passed through several large camps. The trail was now fresh and the whole valley scratched up by trailing lodgepoles. At 7:45 P.M. [others confirmed it was nearly sunset] we encamped on the right bank." Godfrey also recalled (1892, p. 136) that "the valley was heavily marked with lodgepole trails and pony tracks," and Dr. DeWolf recorded "new signs and old camps in profusion." Herendeen's account (1878, p. 262) best reveals Custer's frame of mind: "Toward evening the trail became so fresh that Custer ordered flankers to be left far out and a sharp lookout had for lodges leaving to the right or left. He said he wanted to get the whole village and nothing must leave the trail without his knowing it." Under such orders the scouts undoubtedly kept a sharp eye out for diverging trails, and since they reported none, the fresh signs meant converging trails. This fact, however, failed to override the mind-set of the officers that a break-up of the village was the only thing to fear.

The estimates of the day's march of 28 miles (map-corrected to 27) make this final segment one of 12 miles, from East Muddy (R-58) to present Busby (R-70), 2 miles below and opposite the mouth of Davis Creek. Herendeen located the bivouac "2 miles below the forks" and DeWolf "within a few miles of the forks." Goes Ahead told Libby (p. 159) that it was "at the present Busby school," and Benteen (1890, p. 178) recalled "on Muddy Creek," undoubtedly Busby Creek. Varnum wrote (July 4, p. 342) that they bivouacked "in an Indian camp about two days old," implying a summer roamer camp. This march of 12 miles in $2\frac{3}{4}$ hours was made at 4.36 mph, a faster pace that is not surprising, as Custer now knew that the coast was clear and it was getting late in the day.

Up to this point Custer had followed his orders precisely, both in letter and spirit. Making good use of his scouts, he had pursued the trail for 72 miles, 70 along the Rosebud, in $2\frac{1}{2}$ days at a little less than the prescribed 30 miles a day. He was right on schedule, and no hitches had developed in Terry's plan. The test would come at this point, however, and Custer was anxiously awaiting the return of the Crows with an answer to the crucial question: Did the Sioux trail continue south up the Rosebud? Or turn west to the Little Bighorn? Or turn north down Tullock's Fork?

At 9 P.M., as darkness was falling, the unexpected answer came, as Wallace recorded: "Scouts were [sic, had been] sent ahead to see which branch of the stream the Indians had followed. About 9 P.M. the scouts returned and reported that the Indians had crossed the divide to the Little Big Horn." The first sentence contains final proof that on reaching the Busby bivouac Custer did not know the Sioux trail turned west up Davis Creek. The reporting scouts were the four Crows who had left the afternoon halt, for contrary to Wallace's implication, they could not have left Busby and completed a round trip of 22 miles to the divide in $1\frac{1}{4}$ hours.

Three of the four Crows gave some account of their extended ride to the divide. White Man Runs Him told Hugh Scott (1919, p. 15) that he, Goes Ahead, and Hairy Moccasin, "came to that peak [on the divide] and rode back. The soldiers were just below Busby. We were not sure the Sioux were camping there [on the Little Bighorn]; it was late and we could not see so well [through haze into the sun]. We knew the trail and the way the Sioux were moving [on it], but were not sure which way they went [on reaching the Little Bighorn]." Goes Ahead told Dixon (p. 166): "I got to the place where they [the Sioux] had been camping after [sic, before] they fought with Gen. Crook on the Rosebud, and they had moved to the Little Big Horn." Wooden Leg clarified this report by telling Marquis that the winter roamers had left Busby (on June 15) and ascended Davis Creek to camp that single night a mile north of the pass over the divide before proceeding toward the Little Bighorn.

Curley told Dixon (p. 162) a story that confirms the hint that the scouts moved a little north along the divide:

We noticed that the Sioux had gone toward the Little Horn and we waited at the head of Tullock's Fork [north along the ridge] for the command to come up. They did not come up, but camped on the Rosebud, and we went back to the camp. Then the scouts had an argument, and I went by myself and asked Custer what we should do. Custer asked me what I came back for. I told him that the trail of the Sioux had gone to the west toward the Little Horn.

This trip to the divide is feasible only as an extension of the scout from the afternoon halt. Having reached R-67 at 2:30 P.M., the Crows sent back White Swan to report to Custer and then trotted 5 more miles in 50 minutes to reach Davis Creek (R-72) at 3:20. They could spend the next hour there, examining old and fresh campsites and sorting out numerous trails, including those of the warriors who had returned by this route from the fight with Crook, before they could be certain that the main trail turned west up Davis Creek. Leaving at 4:20, they could trot $9\frac{1}{2}$ miles in 1 hour and 35 minutes up Davis Creek to reach the divide at 5:55. They could spend another hour and 10 minutes viewing the valley, moving on the divide, and looking for signs of the approaching command. Starting back at 7:05, they could trot $11\frac{1}{2}$ miles in 2 hours to reach the Busby bivouac and report at 9 P.M., as Wallace recorded. This feasible pattern is sketched in Figure 1.

The unexpected news brought by the Crows that the Sioux were probably on the lower, rather than the upper, reaches of the Little Bighorn posed a serious problem that demanded a weighty decision from Custer.

TO THE CROW'S NEST AND THE DIVIDE

When the Crows reported at 9 P.M. of June 24 that the Sioux had crossed the divide by a trail so fresh as to indicate that they were nearby on the lower Little Bighorn, instead of far distant on that stream's upper reaches, Custer faced a grave decision. This location was not merely unexpected, it was one Terry's plan could least accommodate, flexible though it was. Terry's written instructions had recommended that Custer continue south up the Rosebud before moving west to the upper Little Bighorn; then to move north down that stream so that his strike on the village would drive any refugees north toward Terry's blocking position at the mouth of the Little Bighorn, which he was to reach on June 26. But it was now only June 24, when Terry should be at the mouth of the Bighorn, a good 30 miles from his blocking position.

Custer could follow Terry's recommendation by marching up the Rosebud tomorrow and starting down the Little Bighorn the next day, thus preserving the timing. Even if these marches were made at night, how-ever, he would leave a trail as readable as a poster, and discovery would warn the village to flee and scatter. He would also lose track of the village and at best have to search for it again; at worst it could escape undetected back to the Rosebud and eastward or down the Bighorn and attack Terry's weaker force on the march.

Since Terry's instructions explicitly authorized deviations, should un-foreseen conditions arise, Custer considered an alternative. He could fol-low the Sioux trail tonight, conceal the command the next day in some secluded pocket in the hills near the divide, and that night complete his approach to the village for an attack at dawn of June 26, much closer to Terry's position. This plan would retain the advantage of surprise, and his scouts would have time to pinpoint the village and keep it under surveil-lance. He could still strike from above, while blocking escape to the east, and drive refugees toward Terry.

This alternative was probably running through Custer's mind as he listened to the Crows' story. When questioned further, they said there was a high point near the divide, now known as the Crow's Nest, which they often used to scan the valley of the Little Bighorn. They could easily reach it before daylight and locate the village by its morning smoke and pony herds. Then and there Custer made his decision to send Lt. Varnum and a party of scouts to the Crow's Nest and to march his column that night toward the divide and lie concealed the next day.

Geography and the Time Problem

It should come as no surprise that participant accounts of night marches turn darkly obscure, and recall of events during the next morning, when informants were catching up on sleep, prove less than lucid. For routes and mileages, however, the USGS series of $7\frac{1}{2}$-minute quadrangle maps offer indispensable help. The route from the Busby bivouac up the Rose-bud to the mouth of Davis Creek and up the latter to the pass at the divide measures about $11\frac{1}{2}$ miles. It involves a gradual climb from 2,340 feet elevation to 4,000 feet; the bottom along the creek features occasional patches of timber.

The main troop column followed this route, making two halts on the way. A prolonged Halt 1 terminated the night march about 7 miles out, and a shorter Halt 2 ended a morning march of $3\frac{3}{4}$ miles ($10\frac{3}{4}$ total), $\frac{3}{4}$ mile short of the divide pass. Varnum's party of scouts had already taken the same path as far as Halt 2 and there had turned south for about 1 mile up a tiny branch of Davis Creek to the Crow's Nest ($11\frac{3}{4}$ total). The Crow's Nest, located in the NW $\frac{1}{4}$ of Section 34, T4S, R37E, is a short, double-peaked ridge of 4,400 feet elevation, running north and south. The mile ride to it involves a rugged ascent to a sheltered pocket, leaving a short climb on foot to the viewing points.

As we shall soon learn, Varnum sent Ree couriers from the Crow's Nest back to the column at Halt 1, which prompted Custer to lead a small party from there up to the Crow's Nest. Later the united Custer-Varnum party rejoined the main column, then at Halt 2. It can be foreseen that the movements of all these parties, and sightings from one to the other, will yield a more complex time-motion pattern. These interconnections, however, are an advantage, for they impose powerful constraints that both dictate and test the entire pattern.

For any historical reconstruction, the time dimension is every bit as important as the spatial dimensions. Getting even the sequence of events out of order breeds disaster, especially when one event is the cause of another. Yet time is often neglected because it is so difficult to keep track of, even for participants, for dates and clock-times are the first to flee from the best of human memories. As for the events of June 25, most accounts make no attempt to recall times, and those that do are often off by 3 to 5 hours. Lt. Wallace, as official itinerist, did record some watch readings *at the time*, and they are consistent with themselves and events; but he also tried to recall others that are incompatible. Several other officers recorded rare watch readings that are compatible with Wallace's and recalled others that are hopeless. This inconsistency merely confirms what everyone knows anyhow: that the memory of time is extraordinarily treacherous.

When participants estimated time intervals, the results are appreciably better, especially while marching, for they recognized that distance and duration are associated. It is this association that gives time-motion analysis its power. It not only keeps track of the time dimension, but makes speed explicit, thus providing a feasibility test of a time-motion pattern, which grows more stringent as the number of interconnections increases. Anything that actually happened had to be possible; the corollary is that any pattern that is impossible could not have happened and so must be rejected in favor of another that is possible.

It is advantageous if the time-scale used can be reasonably well anchored. Such a basis requires answers to two questions: (1) Were the officers' watches set to the same time scale, that is, synchronized? (2) To what time-scale were they set? For a century it has been assumed that these questions are eternally unanswerable. This assumption is true if we mean "to the second," but a systematic displacement of the entire scale by even 10 minutes is of no consequence.

Synchronization of watches is a military "must" today and was undoubtedly so in 1876, if coordinated actions were contemplated. Thus the idea could hardly have been unfamiliar. In fact, Lt. Godfrey wrote (1892, p. 235) that at the officers' call on the evening of June 22 Custer announced that there would be no trumpet calls, making even early reveilles "silent," so "we compared watches to get the official time." They must have synchronized their watches on official time, rather than simply making mental notes of discrepancies. This assumption is confirmed by several officers who recorded watch readings at the time, which match so well as to indicate synchronization. Thus we come to the second question: What was the official time to which the watches were set?

Humankind has lived for millennia by local sun time for the simple reason that it is easier to sleep in darkness and work by daylight. After clocks were invented, they all had to be set, and the preference was for local sun time. Long before 1876 everyone knew that, if a watch was carried east or west across 15 degrees longitude, it had to be reset by one hour to read the new local sun time. If 7th Cavalry watches had originally been set to St. Paul sun time, they were now off by more than an hour, and they were also coordinating action with the Montana column, from 5 degrees farther west. It would be convenient for all to operate on the same time, and the most logical choice would be local sun time. But however they were set, there *is* a way to find out. Participant accounts can be searched for instances in which solar phenomena were noted and nearly simultaneously events were officially clocked. Then a comparison of official and local sun times must reveal how the official clock was set.

The *Astronomical Almanac*[1] enables one to calculate the local sun times of solar phenomena on June 24–25 at the Custer battlefield, located

---

[1] *Astronomical Almanac*, 1985 (B).

at 107.3 degrees W Long. and 45.5 degrees N Lat. Even over a century, the largest cyclic variation (precession of the earth's axis) is negligible for our purposes. Besides sunsets and sunrises, two recognized zones of twilight are useful. In the evening, civil twilight begins at sunset and ends (sun reaching 6 degrees below the horizon) when the light becomes insufficient for ordinary activities, such as reading. Nautical twilight ends (sun 12 degrees below the horizon) when a mariner at sea can no longer set a sextant on the horizon, meaning full darkness. Astronomical twilight is so faint as to affect only telescopic observations.

Table 3 presents the calculated local sun times for these phenomena at the Custer battlefield from noon of June 24 to noon of June 25. The sun set at 7:53 P.M. (local sun time), and Lt. Wallace recorded that Custer camped at Busby at 7:45 P.M. (official time); others noted it was "nearly sunset." This instance reveals no evidence of any discrepancy between official and local sun times. We shall soon encounter more examples that confirm that the two times differ by no more than a few minutes.

This result is so obvious as to be embarrassing. The implication is that the numerous major discrepancies in *recalled* times represent perfectly normal memory lapses, not disparate watch settings. We can even draw on observations of solar phenomena to check the timing of occasional events. All this does not make for perfect precision, but it does help to prevent errors in interval estimates from accumulating.

The Night of June 24

Custer, having made his decision at the Busby bivouac, promptly called on Lt. Varnum to form a scouting party and head for the Crow's Nest. Varnum picks up the story in three accounts, the fullest being his letter to Camp (1909, p. 60):

> Custer came over to the scout camp and had a long talk with the Crows. Half Yellow Face was still out to the front somewhere, so there were only five Crows present. After a while, he called me . . . and said that the Crows were going out at once and he wanted an intelligent white man to go with them and take some Rees for messengers, and Boyer as interpreter, and send back word of what we discovered. . . . I said I would take Charley Reynolds with me for some one to talk to.

Table 3. Local Sun Times, June 24–25, Custer Battlefield

12:00 M.	Sun at meridian, June 24.
7:53 P.M.	Sun sets.
8:31 P.M.	Civil twilight ends (too dark to read).
9:22 P.M.	Nautical twilight ends (full darkness begins). Nighttime.
2:44 A.M.	Nautical twilight begins (full darkness ends).
3:34 A.M.	Civil twilight begins (reading still impossible).
4:13 A.M.	Sun rises.
12:00 M.	Sun at meridian, June 25.

He told me to start at 9 [*sic*] and he would move with the command at 11 P.M. [*sic*], and in the morning would be bivouacked under the base of the hill I was on, and he would expect to get word from me there. I left as directed, taking Boyer, Reynolds, five Crows—Half Yellow Face still being away—and eight [*sic*] Rees.

Varnum's Crow's Nest party included Boyer, Reynolds, five Crows, and six Rees, for a total of fourteen. Fred Gerard (testimony, p. 92)[2] and Hairy Moccasin (Camp, 1911, p. 176) confirmed Varnum by saying that Half Yellow Face remained with Custer, but Red Star (Libby, p. 82) caused confusion by naming the Crow leader as "Big Belly," which the Rees applied to both Half Yellow Face and White Man Runs Him; in this case it referred to the latter, which resolves the confusion. As to the Rees, Red Star twice (pp. 82, 86) and Red Bear once (Camp, 1912, p. 194) named all six. I quote Red Star (p. 86):

> We were eating supper at the temporary camp on the Rosebud, when a little after dark, Forked Horn was called to Custer's head-quarters. On coming back, he told Black Fox, Red Foolish Bear, Strikes the Lodge, Red Star and Bull to come with him to report to

[2] Attention is called to a new kind of participant account, testimony given at the Reno Court of Inquiry, held in Chicago, Jan. 1879. Such testimony is cited, but only in the text, bypassing both footnotes and Category Y. The court proceedings were published daily in the *Chicago Times* and have been assembled in *Reno Court of Inquiry* (B). This volume is quoted in the text by the name of the witness, the key words "testimony" or "testified," and the page number, as in the text citation just given. There is also an official transcript of the court proceedings (National Archives), which Wm. A. Graham systematically abstracted as Graham's *Abstract* (B). This volume is cited in the text in the same way, but with the identification, "Graham's *Abstract*."

Custer. . . . In Custer's presence, Gerard gave us our orders: "Long Hair wants you to go tonight without sleep. You are to go on ahead and try to locate the Sioux camp. Do your best to find it. . . . These Crows will be your guides, for they know the country." Then Charley Reynolds, whom the Rees called "Lucky Man," came along, his horse saddled, as he was to be our interpreter.

Since Wallace recorded 9 P.M. as the time of return of the Crows from the divide, we may postpone the departure of Varnum's party to 9:20, allowing him time to assemble his party and complete preparations, which also fits Red Star's mention that it was dark.

Shortly after Varnum left, Custer held an officers' call, which Reno's official report (July 5, p. 476) timed at 9:25 but Godfrey (1892, p. 136) and Edgerly (1894) specified at 9:30, more acceptable because Godfrey and Benteen (1890, p. 179) said they had to grope their way to head-quarters through pitch blackness. Custer announced to his officers that, because the village was so nearby on the Little Bighorn, he had decided to make a night march, then conceal the command near the divide during the next day, and that night approach the village so as to strike it at dawn of June 26. This plan is described in Wallace's itinerary, Reno's official report, Edgerly's letter (July 4, p. 172), and Godfrey's narrative.

Fred Gerard testified (p. 92) as to what was on Custer's mind as the column was assembling to start the unexpected night march:

> Custer ordered me to take Half Yellow Face and Bloody Knife and ride at the head of the column with him. We pulled out at 11:30 P.M. to the head and waited for Custer to come up, when he ordered me to be sure and have the scouts follow any left-hand trails no matter how small, for he wanted no Sioux camp to escape him. He wanted to get them all together and drive them down to the Rosebud [sic, Bighorn]. I told the Indians this and Bloody Knife remarked: "He needn't be so particular about the small camps; we'll get enough when we strike the big camp."
>
> I sat there with Custer while the Indians were finding the trail. We talked and Custer asked me how many Indians I thought we would have to fight; I told him not less than 2,500 [he soon corrected this figure to 1,500 to 2,000 fighting men, which was uncannily accurate]. Custer then asked the two Indians if he could cross the divide before daylight; they replied, "No." He asked if he could cross after daylight without being discovered by the Indians; they said, "No." He asked them if there was timber where they could lie concealed during the

day, where the Indians could not discover them. [Here the questioner changed the subject.]

This exasperating night march postponed sleep and filled the air with expletives and the accounts with exaggerations and discord. Some say they were to march at 11 and assumed they did so, but others say they were to start later and were delayed: estimated distances range from 8 to 12 miles, durations from 2 to 4 hours, and termination times from 1 to 4 A.M. Wallace's itinerary says they were to "be ready at midnight, but we did not get off until near 1 A.M., and owing to delays by the packtrain, we had marched only 8 miles by daylight." He testified (p. 85), however, that on reaching Halt 1 "it was too dark to read my watch," implying it was before 3:34 A.M., when civil twilight began. As this march is not critical and there is no recourse but compromise, I choose a starting time of 12:30 A.M., June 25, a map distance of 7 miles, and a duration of $2\frac{3}{4}$ hours, which yield an overall speed of 2.55 mph and an arrival at Halt 1 at 3:15 A.M. The men promptly napped, without unsaddling, but after sunrise (4:13 A.M.) breakfasted and slept again.

The main column would make two more marches this morning, which Wallace timed accurately and for which the map supplies distances. Wallace dredged three otherwise missing clock-times from his official notes and read them into his testimony (Graham's *Abstract*, p. 200): "8:45 A.M." for leaving Halt 1, "10:07 A.M." for reaching Halt 2, and "12:05 P.M." for Halt 3, "$\frac{1}{4}$ mile over the divide, where division into battalions was made." His official itinerary adds "12 noon" for crossing the divide. Few others ventured to "recall" any of these times, but Lt. Hare made some range estimates that straddle Wallace's notes in his interview with Camp (1912, p. 64): "between 8 and 9 went up nearly to the divide and halted" and marched again "between 10 and noon."

Wallace's clock-times indicate that Halt 1 lasted $5\frac{1}{2}$ hours. The $3\frac{3}{4}$-mile march from there to Halt 2 was thus made at a drowsy speed of 2.74 mph, and this concealment halt lasted 1 hour and 38 minutes. The next march of 1 mile to Halt 3, $\frac{1}{4}$ mile beyond the divide, was made at the standard 3 mph, which precisely fits crossing the divide at 12 noon. These events complete the itinerary of the main column through the morning of June 25, as posted in Table 4 and plotted in Figure 2. The table contains the itineraries for all moving parties for this period; note that they incorporate, in simple chronology form, significant events yet to be

Table 4. Itinerary-Chronology: Busby to the Divide or Crow's Nest

Unit / Events	Clock- Time	dm	dt	mph	Cum. Mi.
		Increments			
MAIN COLUMN (June 25 A.M.)					
Lv. Busby camp on night march under Custer.	12:30				0
Arr. Halt 1 on Davis Cr., still dark.	3:15	7	2:45	2.55	7
Breakfast smoke seen (by Varnum party).	5:00				
Ree couriers arr. from Crow's Nest.	7:20				
Custer reads Varnum's note.	7:30				
Sgt. Curtis lv. on back trail for lost pack.	7:45				
Custer party lv. for Crow's Nest.	8:00				
Lv. Halt 1 under Reno.	8:45		5:30		
Arr. Halt 2 on Davis Cr. for concealment.	10:07	3¾	1:22	2.74	10¾
Sgt. Curtis arr., reporting Cheyennes.	10:20				
Custer-Varnum party arr., Cheyennes spying.	10:35				
Officers' call: Custer will attack.	10:50				
Lv. Halt 2 under Custer.	11:45		1:38		
Crosses divide at noon.	12:00	¾	0:15	3.0	11½
Halt 3, Custer assigns battalions (P.M.)	12:05	¼	0:05	3.0	11¾
CUSTER'S CROW'S NEST PARTY (June 25 A.M.)					
Lv. Halt 1 for Crow's Nest.	8:00				7
Spotted by 2 Sioux, as seen from Crow's Nest.	8:05				
Arr. Crow's Nest.	9:00	4¾	1:00	4.75	11¾
Lv. Crow's Nest with Varnum party.	10:20		1:20		
Meets Tom Custer with Sgt. Curtis's news.	10:30				
Arr. Halt 2.	10:35	−1	0:15	4.0	10¾
VARNUM'S CROW'S NEST PARTY					
Lv. Busby camp in dark (June 24 P.M.).	9:20				0
Arr. pocket below Crow's Nest (June 25 A.M.).	2:50	11¾	5:30	2.14	11¾
2 Crows first sight Sioux village at Little Bighorn.	3:40				
Varnum awakened for climb to peak.	3:50				
Varnum, scouts study Sioux village.	4:00				
Scouts sight breakfast smoke at Halt 1.	5:00				

Table 4. (*continued*)

Unit Events	Clock-Time	dm	dt	mph	Cum. Mi.
		Increments			
Varnum sends 2 Rees to Custer at Halt 1.	5:20				
Crows sight 2 Sioux west of divide.	5:40				
Varnum leads sortie against 2 Sioux.	6:20				
Varnum returns, unsuccessful.	6:40				
Scouts sight 2 Sioux crossing divide.	7:10				
Varnum sights 2 Sioux meeting Custer's party.	8:05				
Custer party arr. Crow's Nest.	9:00				
Custer studies valley and discusses findings.					
Custer, scouts watch column arr. Halt 2.	10:07				
Custer-Varnum party lv. Crow's Nest.	10:20		7:30		
Custer-Varnum arr. Halt 2.	10:35	−1	0:15	4.0	10¾
REE COURIERS (June 25 A.M.)					
Lv. Crow's Nest with note to Custer.	5:20				11¼
Arr. scouts' camp at Halt 1.	7:20	−4¾	2:00	2.38	7
SGT. CURTIS'S PARTY (June 25 A.M.)					
Lv. Halt 1 on back trail for lost pack.	7:45				7
Finds Cheyennes rifling lost pack.	8:25	−2	0:40	3.0	5
Arr. Halt 2 and reports Cheyennes.	10:20	5¾	1:55	3.0	10

described. The main troop itinerary may now be used to untangle the sleepy confusion in the accounts of these events.

In the meantime, Lt. Varnum's party, far ahead of the main column, had also marched by night up Davis Creek as far as Halt 2, where it turned south and had already reached the Crow's Nest. Varnum's letter to Camp (1909, p. 60) described this march: "Except that we stopped two or three times in the dense undergrowth along the stream to let the Crows smoke cigarettes, we were on the go till about 2:30 or 3:00 A.M. of the 25th, and [later] as day broke, I found myself in a peculiar hollow . . . near the summit of a high ridge on the divide. . . . A timbered tributary led down to the Rosebud, up which we had evidently come during the night." White Man Runs Him told Hugh Scott (1919, p. 14), while both were at the Crow's Nest: "We reached here about 2 A.M. The officer

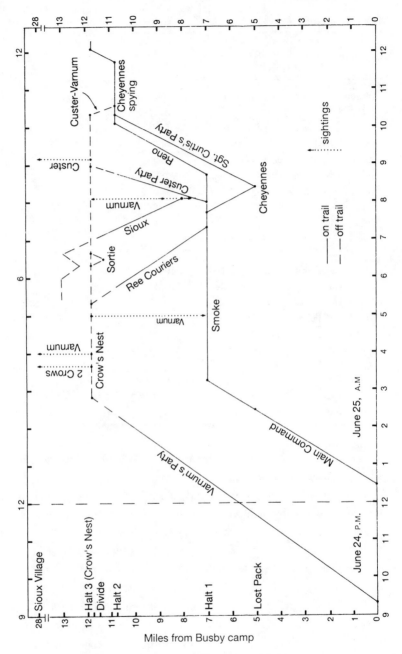

Figure 2. Time-Motion Pattern: Busby to the Divide

[Varnum], Boyer and I led the horses into the pocket. I was guide, as I had been here many times before with Crow expeditions." Red Star (Libby, p. 87) recalled that they stopped twice to smoke; at the end they climbed a mountain, dismounted near its top on the side facing the Rosebud, and smoked again. Most then slept while waiting for daylight.

While most of Varnum's men were napping, two Crows climbed to the peaks before dawn, for Red Star continued (pp. 87–88): "I saw two Crows climb up on the highest peak. . . . The scouts were all sitting together, when the two Crows came down from the highest point. . . . One then told Forked Horn by signs that they had seen Sioux tepees ahead. Then all the scouts climbed to the peak to look for Sioux signs." One of the two Crows was Hairy Moccasin, who told Dixon (p. 139): "Leaving the others asleep, Hairy Moccasin went to the summit of the Crow's Nest, and as dawn broke, saw the white tents, the brown hills covered with horses, and the smoke from hundreds of tepees." The other Crow may have been White Man Runs Him, who told Scott (1919, pp. 14–15): "When it became light, we could see the smoke from the Sioux camp . . . and white horses across the Little Big Horn." Curley told Dixon (p. 162) that he "was lying down at daybreak, half asleep, when the boys said they saw the Sioux camp." I post this first sighting at about 3:40 A.M.

Lt. Varnum wrote Hughes (1896, p. 29) that he was also one of the sleepers: "I threw myself down and fell asleep, but in about ¾ hour or an hour, I was waked up. It was then just daylight. The Crows wanted me on the bluff. I scrambled up." If Varnum slept an hour, he was awakened about 3:50, by which time the two Crows had spotted the village. This timing is feasible, as civil twilight began at 3:34 A.M., and probably by 4:00 all were on the peaks to look for themselves; 13 minutes later the sun rose.

The practiced eyes of the scouts soon confirmed the sighting of the village, as Red Star continued (p. 88):

> The first two Crows pointed out the Sioux camp. . . . Red Star looked and saw a dark object and above it light smoke rising up from the Sioux tepees. It was at the upper [south] end of the village, whose tepees were hidden by the high ridge, but the smoke was drawing out and up. Beyond the smoke were black specks he thought were horses. Charley Reynolds looked a long time, then took out his field glasses and looked a long time. Then he put them down and nodded his head.

It was Lt. Varnum who had trouble seeing the signs, for he continued (p. 60):

> I crawled up the hill and watched the valley until the sun rose [4:13]. . . . The Crows tried to make me see a smoke from the village behind the bluff on the Little Bighorn and gave me a cheap spy-glass, but I could see nothing. They said there was an immense pony herd out grazing and told me to look for worms crawling on the grass and I would make out the herd, but I could not see worms, or ponies either. My eyes were somewhat inflamed from loss of sleep and hard riding in dust.

The scouts continued to study the country for some time, hoping the improving light would reveal more. In fact, Varnum continued (p. 60) that later they drew his attention to another smoke in the opposite direction arising from the breakfast fires of the main column at Halt 1 on Davis Creek. He noted that "the Crows were angry at Custer for allowing fires" that broadcast his presence so openly. Nevertheless, the sight assured Varnum that Custer had halted his night march and was awaiting news of the scouts' findings. He penned a note to the general but could only recall the gist: "tremendous village on the Little Big Horn." He claimed that he sent the note back by Ree scouts at "5 A.M." and that Custer received it at "8 A.M." (in his July 4 letter), but this timing flashes a warning light, for couriers should travel $4\frac{3}{4}$ miles in less than 3 hours. In fact, I suspect that it was the first sighting of breakfast smoke that came at 5 A.M. and that Varnum presumed, from other things he saw at 8 A.M., that the note reached Custer at that time.

Red Star, who was one of the two couriers, shed light on this matter (pp. 88–89):

> [Varnum] sat down and wrote a note and handed it to Forked Horn, who said to Red Star, "You and Bull saddle up your ponies." When they had saddled up, Forked Horn told them, "Look, you can see the smoke of our [Custer's] camp." Red Star saw a cloud of smoke rising up, which he and Bull could follow to find their way back. They started down the hill and after they were down, Red Star urged his horse on, for he had the note, and he paid no attention to Bull, except to look back and see where he was, as Bull's horse was bad. . . . When he got into [the scouts'] camp, the sun was just coming up [*sic*, he had started long after sunrise]. . . . Stabbed . . . [greeted Red Star and awakened the sleeping Rees, while Red Star unsaddled and then re-

ported to Bloody Knife]. Then Red Star saw Gerard coming up with Custer.

Red Star thus revealed a delay in starting and another in making final delivery. His account suggests the following reconstruction: the first sighting of breakfast smoke came at 5 A.M.; the couriers did not get off until 5:20; Red Star then rode slowly, in order to keep Bull's slow horse in sight, at 2.38 mph for 2 hours, reporting to Bloody Knife at 7:20; while awaiting Bull's safe arrival, Red Star handed the note to Custer at 7:30 A.M. This itinerary, as posted and plotted, fits the evidence and ensuing events at Halt 1.

The Morning of June 25

The somnolent troops at Halt 1 noticed little and thoroughly confused what they did see or hear about. As an example, Lt. Wallace exhausted his record of this entire halt with: "While waiting here, a scout came back from Lt. Varnum, who had been sent out the night before. In a note to Gen. Custer, Lt. Varnum stated that he [sic] could see the smoke of the village about 20 miles [sic] away on the Little Big Horn. The scout pointed out the butte from which the village could be seen . . . about 8 miles [sic] ahead."

Let us therefore resume with Red Star's interview (pp. 89–90), which is far more informative:

> Custer sat down . . . near Red Star, who was squatted down with a cup of coffee. Custer signed, asking if Red Star had seen the Sioux; Red Star signaled yes, and handed Custer the note. . . . Custer read it at once and nodded his head. . . . Custer then told Red Star, through Gerard, to saddle up at once, as we are going to where your party is on the hill. Red Star was not through with his breakfast, but he left his coffee, saddled up and joined Custer. In the party were Gen. Custer, his bugler [sic], Tom Custer [sic], Red Star, Bob-tailed Bull, Little Brave, Bloody Knife and Gerard.

Fred Gerard's four accounts agree that he was asleep at Halt 1 when Custer awakened him; his account to Mrs. Holley (1890, p. 263) is the fullest: "About 4 A.M. [sic] Custer awoke Gerard and said, 'Here is a

Ree scout sent from Lt. Varnum with a note saying he has discovered the Indian village. Ask the scout if he saw the camp and how far away it was.' Then Custer told him to lead off to where he had left Varnum. Custer then took two or three scouts [and Bloody Knife] and started to find Varnum."

These accounts from two members of Custer's party make it abundantly clear that, in response to Varnum's note, Custer soon left Halt 1 for the Crow's Nest, taking only Gerard, Bloody Knife, and the three Rees: Red Star, Bob-tailed Bull, and Little Brave. The sole officer, of those left behind at Halt 1, who would recall Custer's departure was Lt. Hare, who told Camp (1910, p. 64) that "before" the main column pulled out, "between 8 and 9 [actually 8:45], Custer had been ahead with scouts viewing the valley of the Little Big Horn." The others probably did not see him leave, but all must have learned of his absence, though they still failed to mention it.

There are obvious reasons why a commander as energetic and alert as Custer would feel compelled to make a personal trip to the Crow's Nest at this time. The day was still young, with only a short march to be made, which could be left to Maj. Reno. Custer would be anxious to see the village and its location for himself, especially if the note from Varnum had disclosed that he could not verify it. It was even more important that Custer seize this perfect opportunity to study the lay of the land, over which he planned to approach the village that night in darkness. Before leaving his sleeping command, he must have left orders for Reno to move the column to a place of concealment near the divide, for that is precisely what it did at 8:45 A.M.

Lt. Godfrey, in his diary, gave a wrong clock-time and repeated a sentence, which disturbed his sequences, but years later corrected both. His diary reads:

> About 8 [sic] a scout came with news that they had discovered a village and could see ponies and smoke, although Varnum said [or wrote?] he could not distinguish anything. We continued our march [sic, out of sequence]. Genl. Custer came around personally and informed us that the Sioux village was in view . . . [but as he missed me] I went up to hqrs. to hear the news. Bloody Knife was talking to the Genl. and said we would find enough Sioux to keep us fighting two or three days. Genl. remarked laughingly that he thought we could get through in one day. We took up our line of march. . . . [This sequence is correct.]

This conversation, of course, must have occurred before Custer and Bloody Knife left for the Crow's Nest. In his narrative (1892, p. 136) Godfrey not only verified this sequence, but indicated that the courier had arrived *before* 8 A.M., to which he attached another important event that no one else mentioned: "Some time before 8 o'clock, Gen. Custer rode horseback to the several troops and gave orders to be ready to march at 8 o'clock." This is one reason I posted Custer's receipt of Varnum's note at 7:30, early enough to allow him to make the company rounds to spread the news and give orders to prepare to march at 8 A.M. Godfrey and several others claimed the column did march at 8 A.M., but we know it left at 8:45. That is strong evidence that Custer was absent during this delay.

Otherwise cryptic statements from both Red Star and Gerard imply that it was Custer's small party that left Halt 1 at 8 A.M., as future interconnections in the time-motion pattern require. It may be recalled that Red Star thought Capt. Tom Custer and a bugler had joined the party, but they were merely seeing it off; he then added that he "heard a bugle as he left camp, blown by Custer's bugler, who turned back on his horse to do so." If Custer was leaving at 8 A.M., and found the column unready to march as ordered, it is more than likely that he ordered the bugler to arouse the entire regiment. Gerard, without knowing it, added confirmation by testifying (p. 121) that, as they were leaving, Tom Custer or Adjt. Cooke asked whether the column should follow, to which Custer replied, "No. You will remain here until I return and then we shall go into camp." Since Gerard was not privy to the earlier marching order, he did not understand the context of this exchange; Custer probably told the officers to move out as soon as possible; he would not wait but rejoin them where they would halt. Recall also that Varnum, from the Crow's Nest, saw something that made him think Custer received his note at 8 A.M. and started for the Crow's Nest.

Gerard's testimony (p. 149) appears to describe Custer's route to the Crow's Nest: "The country the command moved over from where Custer left it [Halt 1] to where he returned [Halt 2], was smooth-level and a little rising." This distance was given as "about 3 miles" (p. 143). The description corresponds to the map route up Davis Creek of $3\frac{3}{4}$ miles to Halt 2, where Custer turned south for another mile to the Crow's Nest. I allow 1 hour to cover these $4\frac{3}{4}$ miles at 4.75 mph, thus timing the party's arrival at the Crow's Nest at 9 A.M., as posted and plotted.

Not until 45 minutes after Custer had left did the main column pull out for Halt 2. Reno, who had command in Custer's absence, and Benteen, next in command, were remarkably silent, even evasive, about their activities this morning. Officially, Reno reported merely that "the march was renewed and the divide crossed [sic]," but he testified (p. 400) that at Halt 1 "Benteen came over and I discovered that the column was moving and I followed; I had not been consulted," and at Halt 2 "I was informed that Custer had gone to the mountain top." In testimony Benteen evaded the issue by pretending to confuse the two halts, but his 1890 narrative (p. 179) says that after breakfast at Halt 1 "the column moved on, without orders [sic], but I followed the procession." Others agreed, however, that the column halted short of the divide and went into concealment.

We must return now to Varnum's party at the Crow's Nest, where events had been unfolding that led to the discovery of the troops by enemy Indians even before Custer's party arrived. White Man Runs Him told Hugh Scott (1919, pp. 14–15): "We saw two Sioux out there by the lone tree, due west 1½ miles. . . . [Later] the Sioux had gone down Davis Creek toward the soldiers' camp [Halt 1]. The soldiers and Sioux met. . . . We also saw six Sioux to the northeast, over on the other side of Tullock's Fork . . . hunting buffalo." Red Star told Libby (p. 91) that when he arrived with Custer the Crows related to him: "Two Sioux had gone over the ridge [divide] and down the dry coulee. . . . The Crows thought the two were planning to ambush the couriers [Red Star and Bull] and they wanted to kill them first. They did not do so because they were afraid Custer would not like it."

Varnum gave a detailed story of these events in his letter to Camp (1909, pp. 60–61).

> After sending off the Rees [at 5:20], we saw one Indian riding a pony and leading another, and some distance behind an Indian boy on a pony. They were . . . perhaps a mile off toward the Little Big Horn, riding parallel to the ridge we were on. There was a gap in the ridge [pass over the divide] to our right [north], and the Crows thought they would cross there and soon discover Custer [by the breakfast smoke]. . . . Boyer said that White Swan, who seemed to be a sort of leader, wanted us to try and cut them off and kill them where they crossed the range, so they could not discover the troops. Boyer, Reynolds and I, with the Crows, started off, dismounted, to do so.

After a half-mile of hard work through very broken country where we could see nothing, I heard a call like a crow cawing from the hill, and we halted. Our two Crows repeated the imitation, but you could see they were talking or signaling, and we started back. I asked Boyer what was the matter, but he did not know.

On our return, we learned that the Sioux had changed their course away from the pass, but soon after our return, they changed again and crossed the ridge [divide]. We could see them as they went down the trail toward the command [at Halt 1], and could see a long trail of dust, showing Custer [his small party] was moving, but we could not see the column [still at Halt 1]. Before it came in sight, the Sioux stopped suddenly, got together and then as suddenly disappeared, one to the right and one to the left, so we knew the Sioux had discovered our [Custer's] approach.

About this time seven Sioux rode in single file eastward along the crest of a [spur ridge]. That they would soon discover Custer's command we knew and watched them. . . . The seven Sioux rode leisurely, but soon, all of a sudden, they disappeared and soon afterward one black spot took their place. They had apparently run off to alarm their camp, leaving one man to watch the column.

Black Bear, an Oglala from the enemy village, shed helpful light on these Sioux "spies." He had left the Red Cloud agency with six other Oglalas in search of stolen ponies and tracked them to the village on the Little Bighorn. On the morning of June 25 they left that camp to return to their agency, taking the trail over the divide. They did see the breakfast smoke at Halt 1 and, on approaching, saw a marching party, obviously Custer's, which they watched from concealment and then resumed their journey home.[3] Thus all the Sioux seen from the Crow's Nest probably belonged to this Oglala party, which would carry no alarm to the village. But soon this party met some Cheyennes coming out from the agency, who were also trailing and watching the troops, as we shall learn.

Varnum's story provides time clues to the events and sightings at the Crow's Nest, which are posted in his itinerary. In Figure 2 Varnum's little sortie is plotted, and key sightings are plotted as vertical (instantaneous) dotted lines. The movement of the Sioux down Davis Creek to where they encountered Custer's small party is also plotted as a dotted line. It is clear that, even though the Sioux had earlier spotted the breakfast smoke, they

[3] Camp, "Interview with Black Bear, 1911," Hammer, *Custer in '76*, 203 (B).

had to meet Custer coming up the trail while the main column was still at Halt 1. And Varnum never did realize that Custer had moved out first.

When Custer's party reached the Crow's Nest (9:00 A.M.), Varnum's letter of July 4 (p. 342) covered what happened in one sentence: "When Custer came up, we informed him of the state of affairs and he concluded, as we had been discovered, to hurry up and strike them as soon as possible." His letter to Camp (1909, p. 61) adds more but sandwiches the arrival between out-of-sequence events, which I reorder:

> [Ellipsis 1, shifted to end.] I rode down toward the column [Custer's party] and soon met the general. . . . [Ellipsis 2, postponed until later.] I told the general all I had seen, as we rode toward Crow's Nest hill, which we climbed together. Custer listened to Boyer, while he gazed long and hard at the valley. He then said, "I've got about as good eyes as anybody, and I can't see any village, Indians, or anything else," or words to that effect. Boyer said, "Well, general, if you don't find more Indians in that valley than you ever saw together, you can hang me." Custer sprang to his feet, saying, "It would do a damned sight of good to hang you, wouldn't it?" He and I went down the hill together. [Ellipsis 1 is here inserted:] The command came in vision about this time and we watched it approach the gap where it halted [Halt 2, 10:07 A.M.].

White Man Runs Him told Scott (1919, p. 15) that "Custer came up Davis Creek and stopped opposite the point. We went down and told him about the smoke [of the Sioux village], and Custer came up part way, far enough to see the smoke." Gerard's four accounts agree that the Crow's Nest afforded a good view of the valley, for it was some hours after daylight and the air was clear; Gerard saw no tepees but a large black mass from which dust was rising, indicating an enormous pony herd.

Red Star's story resumes (pp. 90–93) as the most revealing of all:

> Charley Reynolds and Custer went ahead, leaving the others behind. Reynolds pointed where Custer was to look; they looked for some time and then Gerard joined them. Gerard called back to the scouts, "Custer thinks it is no camp." Custer thought Reynolds had merely seen the white buttes that concealed the lone tepee. So Reynolds pointed again, explaining Custer's mistake, and after another look, Custer nodded that he saw signs of the camp. Next, Reynolds pulled out his field glasses and Custer used them and nodded his head again. . . .

Forked Horn now told Gerard to ask Custer how he would have felt if he had found two dead Sioux on the hill. Custer replied it would have been all right—he would have been pleased. Then the scouts sat down and one of the Crows, Big Belly [White Man Runs Him], got up and asked Custer, through the Crow interpreter [Mitch Boyer], what he thought of the Sioux camp. Custer said, "This camp has not seen our army; none of these scouts have seen us." The Crow replied, ". . . These Sioux we have seen at the foot of the hill, two going one way and four the other, are good scouts. They have seen the smoke of our [the command's] camp." Custer said angrily, "I say again, we have not been seen. That camp has not seen us. I am going ahead to carry out what I think. I want to wait until it is dark, and then we will march; we will place our army around the Sioux camp." The Crow replied, "That plan is bad; it should not be carried out." Custer said, "I have said what I propose to do; I will wait until dark and then go ahead with my plan."

Red Star, as he sat listening, first thought Custer's plan was good. The Crows insisted that the Sioux scouts had already seen the army and would report its coming, and that they would attack Custer's army. They wanted them to attack at once, that day, and capture the horses of the Sioux and have them unable to move rapidly. Custer replied, "Yes, it shall be done as you say." The army now came up to the foot of the hill [Halt 2, 10:07] and Custer's party rode down and joined the troops.

Since Custer was still at the Crow's Nest when the main column made its concealment halt at 10:07, he had spent more than an hour there. Whether or not he had seen the village for himself, he certainly accepted the unanimous conviction of his scouts. He listened as the scouts told of the discovery of the troops. It was unwelcome news indeed, which he first resisted but then accepted reluctantly, for it meant he would have to attack that afternoon under circumstances less favorable than expected. Though no one mentioned it, he must also have devoted time to studying the country and the approaches to the village, while he had the knowledgeable Boyer and Crows at hand for questions.

The combined Custer-Varnum parties then left the Crow's Nest to join the main column at Halt 2, 1 mile north. Since no one clocked either their departure or arrival, the strongest constraint stems from distance and speed. Half the distance consisted of a steep, slow descent, suggesting an overall speed of 4 mph, which would cover the mile in 15 minutes.

As the departure came not long after the column was seen to halt at 10:07, I choose 10:20, making the arrival at 10:35, which encounters no difficulties with events at Halt 2. These data are posted and plotted.

Let us now focus on events at Halt 2 during the hour and 38 minutes it lasted. It began quietly enough, for Godfrey recalled (1892, p. 137) that "our officers collected in groups to discuss the situation, while some sought solitude in sleep." Edgerly wrote (July 4, p. 172) that "while Custer was away, trying to find some trace of the village, Cooke, Tom Custer, Calhoun, Moylan and myself went down in a ravine and smoked a cigarette together." Shortly before Custer returned, however, the quietude was broken by a local report that hostile Indians had discovered the trail left by the troops, as recorded in numerous accounts.

There is excellent agreement on the highlights of this incident: that sometime during the night march to Halt 1 Capt. Yates's Company F had lost a load of hardtack from a mule; that Yates sent his Sgt. William A. Curtis and squad back to retrieve the load; that on approaching it they saw and fired on a few Indians rifling the load, who fled in the direction of the village; that on returning to Halt 2 Curtis reported the facts to Yates and other officers; that Capt. Tom Custer and Lt. Calhoun rode out to report the discovery to Custer, whom they met coming down from the Crow's Nest.

No one gave the point from which Sgt. Curtis had been sent back, but the only sensible place was Halt 1. Pvt. Brinkerhoff recalled[4] that Custer was present, which identifies both the location—Halt 1—and the time—before Custer left at 8 A.M., say at 7:45. Since Curtis reached Halt 2 before Custer did, say at 10:20, the sergeant was absent 2 hours and 35 minutes, which at a pace of 3 mph would cover $7\frac{3}{4}$ miles. From these figures and the locations of the two halts, it can be calculated that he backtracked 2 miles to the lost pack and encountered the Indians at 8:25 A.M., and then reversed for $5\frac{3}{4}$ miles to overtake the command at Halt 2. This trip, as posted and plotted, is perfectly feasible and wholly compatible with the conjectured return of the Custer-Varnum party.

Varnum (in the postponed Ellipsis 2) mentioned meeting Tom Custer, which could only have been on his descent to Halt 2: "Tom Custer and

[4]Brinkerhoff, Pvt. Henry M. (Co. G), "Story of the Little Big Horn," unidentified newspaper clipping (1928), in Billings, Montana, Public Library.

Calhoun came up to us and Gen. Custer was angry at their leaving the column and ordered them back." Custer's reaction was probably to his brother's news of a second discovery by the Sioux. Gerard testified (p. 121) that the command had "come toward us, from where we left them in the morning." He also told Libby (1912, p. 172) that when they met Tom Custer the general asked him, "Tom, who in the devil moved these troops forward? My orders were to remain in camp all day and make a night attack on the Indians, but they have discovered us, and are on the run." Neither Varnum nor Gerard apparently caught Tom Custer's news, and Gerard was still misled by not knowing of Custer's earlier march order.

The Indians on whom Sgt. Curtis had fired on the back trail were part of Little Wolf's party of seven lodges of Cheyennes, who had left the Red Cloud agency to join the hostile camp. Wooden Leg[5] said they had been following the trail of the troops for some time and some of the young men had found the lost hardtack; they continued to keep track of the main column and crept up to spy on the troops, "concealed" at Halt 2. They then circled a little northward, however, and did not reach the hostile camp until just after Custer's battalion had been annihilated. The result was that these Cheyennes would not deliver an advance warning either.

When George Herendeen had reached Halt 2 with the main column, he had found a secluded ravine, where he slept until the scouts from the Crow's Nest rode in at the van of the Custer-Varnum party. His three accounts and testimony reveal that he first saw Mitch Boyer, who told him that he had just spotted some Indians (undoubtedly Little Wolf's Cheyennes) lurking around the camp; one had come within 150 yards of Herendeen before running for the divide in great haste. Herendeen admitted to seeing something but had not known what it was. On searching the ravine, the two scouts found fresh pony tracks. Then Custer rode in, saying he had been unable to see the Sioux village, but Mitch assured Herendeen that the scouts had seen it 15 miles distant.

Before long Custer held an officers' call to announce a change in plan. Wallace recorded, with never a hint that Custer had been absent: "Lt. Varnum joined us and reported that the Indians had discovered the command and that he had seen couriers go in the direction of the village.

[5]Marquis, *Wooden Leg*, 349–51 (B).

Custer assembled the officers, told them what he had heard and said he would move ahead and attack the village without further delay." Elaborating on his diary, Godfrey wrote (1892, p. 138):

At officers' call Custer recounted Capt. Keogh's report [from Sgt. Curtis] and also said the scouts had seen several Indians moving along the divide overlooking the valley we had marched over, as if observing our movements: he thought these Indians must have seen the command's dust. In any case our presence had been discovered and further concealment was unnecessary; that we would move at once to attack the village; that he had not intended to attack until next morning, June 26, but our discovery forced us to attack at once, as delay would allow the village to scatter and escape.

Lt. Edgerly made the same points in his 1881 account (p. 219) and confirmed some technical items that Godfrey recorded in his diary: "Company commanders were authorized to have six men and one NCO with the packs, and that companies would move out in the order of reporting they were ready." Benteen (July 4, p. 298) added that companies were to be inspected, especially for arms and ammunition, but bragged that he reported without doing so. Reno was utterly silent on the change in plan and orders. It is relevant that Reno (p. 400) and Benteen (p. 320) testified under oath that Custer *did not believe there was any village to be seen*, which appears to insinuate that a Don Quixote was ordering them to attack a windmill.

The head of Tullock's Fork lay just north of this halt, and Custer had planned to send Herendeen down it and report his findings to Terry at the mouth of the Bighorn. Herendeen was available, but Custer, now with the command, did not send him out. Both Herendeen (1911, pp. 221–22) and Gerard (1909, p. 231) told Camp that the question came up at Halt 2, and the two agreed on the reasons Custer did not act. Herendeen's statement reads:

Early on June 25, I told Custer that Tullock's Fork was just over the divide, but he replied rather impatiently that there was no occasion to send me through, as the Indians were known to be in his front and that his command had been discovered by them [thus at Halt 2]. He said the only thing he could do was to charge their village as soon as possible. . . . It appeared to me at the time that Custer was right and there really was no use in scouting Tullock's Fork.

While the officers were inspecting and detailing 84 troopers to service the packtrain, Custer talked with the scouts. Lt. Hare told Camp (1910, p. 64) that he heard Mitch Boyer say to Custer, "General, I have been with these Indians for thirty years, and this is the largest village I have ever heard of." The Indian scouts had repeatedly warned Custer of this fact, but size was not what worried Custer; his overriding concern was that the Sioux would break up and scatter. If the scouts also tried to tell him that, if the village was surprised, the warriors would fight desperately to protect their women and children, it failed to register in any troop accounts.

As for Custer's talk with the Rees, Young Hawk told Libby (pp. 93–94):

> Custer gave his instructions to the scouts through Gerard, who said, "Boys, I want you to take the horses away from the Sioux camp." Then Stabbed told the scouts to obey Custer's instructions and take away as many horses as possible. Custer continued: "Make up your minds to go straight to their camp and capture their horses. Boys, you are going to have a hard day; you must keep up your courage. You will get experience today."

Red Star also recalled (p. 84) these instructions and added that Stabbed not only gave the younger scouts a pep talk, but ceremoniously rubbed their chests with sacred clay he had brought all the way from their home village.

When the whole command was ready at 11:45 A.M., it began its 15-mile approach to the Sioux village. Crossing the divide at 12 noon, it proceeded another $\frac{1}{4}$ mile, when Custer called a halt to make battalion assignments at 12:05 P.M. of that hot and sunny Sunday, June 25, 1876.

Since leaving the Busby bivouac just after midnight, the command had marched $11\frac{3}{4}$ miles, the larger portion in the dark of night, but most had caught up on sleep during the morning halts. The scouts, however, had been working continuously and effectively. The energetic Custer had advanced cautiously, only to learn that discovery compelled him to improvise an attack that afternoon in full daylight.

18

THE DESCENT TO THE LONE TEPEE

Unforeseen circumstances had forced Custer to make two independent decisions that had brought his regiment just over the divide at 12:05 P.M. of June 25, fully committed to a daylight attack on the hostile village some 15 miles distant on the Little Bighorn. In the light of what he knew at the time, neither decision can be faulted, but there were relevant circumstances that he did not know.

In the past few days a horde of summer roamers had expanded the Sioux and Cheyenne village from the four hundred lodges of the winter roamers which had been counted along the trail to one thousand lodges, equivalent to two thousand fighting men, over three times Custer's force. Furthermore, Crook's two earlier attacks had fully warned the Indians that the army had marked them and their way of life for destruction; to them, the issue was nothing less than survival, and when it came to defending their women and children, the warriors would fight as skillfully and courageously as any white man. That is not speculation; only a week before, the winter roamers alone had sent out their young warriors to fend off Crook's army, considerably stronger than Custer's regiment, and had succeeded so well as to cow it for seven weeks.

When Custer halted ¼ mile over the divide, it was for only 7 minutes, just long enough to make battalion assignments, for which he had several reasons. The 15-mile approach offered the last chance to gather information on which to base an attack plan. He needed assurance that the village was not moving upstream and that there were no satellite villages to his left, for he was ordered to drive all refugees downstream. He promptly decided to send a battalion to the left to seek a viewing point of the upstream valley and report back to him. Also, if the village, on receiving the alarm, tried to scatter, as he so feared, he should have battalions ready to pursue as needed; and depending on the terrain near the village, it might prove advantageous to strike from more than one direction. Finally, since he would have to approach at a faster pace than a walk, he must detail an escort to protect the lagging packtrain and its spare ammunition from disastrous capture.

Custer retained for himself five right-wing companies (C, E, F, I, L), and to Maj. Reno he assigned three left-wing companies (A, G, M); both battalions would start down Reno Creek at once. To Capt. Benteen he assigned the other three companies of the left wing (D, H, K), which would also leave at once, but on the left oblique to view the upper valley and then report to the main column. The last right-wing company (B), under Capt. McDougall, was assigned to escort the slow packtrain, which was in the charge of Lt. Mathey and served by 84 trooper-packers, drawn from all twelve companies; it would not start down Reno Creek until 20 minutes after the others had left.

This chapter conducts all these units down Reno Creek for only two-thirds of the distance to the Little Bighorn, by which time Benteen's battalion will have returned to the Reno Creek trail the others were on. For each unit, itineraries are constructed and the resulting time-motion patterns plotted, but first some map geography and mileages are needed.

Terrain Features and the Lone Tepee

The trail down Reno Creek from the divide halt to its mouth on the Little Bighorn measures about 12 miles, the country consisting of sagebrush hills divided by deep ravines. The route promptly strikes a short header of Reno Creek and runs northwest for several miles before curving to a westward course; for most of its length Reno Creek runs in a deep gulch with a narrow bottom. Along its upper 8 miles several branches, flowing from the southeast, join its left bank. The first of these of significance to us, which I dub "*No-Name* Creek," joins Reno Creek 7 miles below the divide halt, or 5 miles above the Little Bighorn. One mile farther downstream, and thus 8 miles from the halt and 4 miles from the river, the major *South Fork* enters the left bank from the southeast, forming the upper, or main, forks of Reno Creek. At this point the bottom widens somewhat, and the north side of the canyon features a high *bluff* that affords a view of the river valley. Also at this point a present dirt road, descending the right bank of Reno Creek, crosses to the left bank.

The troopers, never having seen this country, called Reno Creek "the creek," and most never noted any branches. They usually located events by estimated mileages from either the divide halt or the river. Some also located events by an ephemeral landmark, the *lone tepee*, whose image stuck in their memories, but for some its location emphatically did not. Because of the resulting contradictions, the first task is properly to locate the lone tepee. Fortunately, some winter roamers who occupied the camp of which the lone tepee was a residue, as well as the Crow scouts, who knew this country well, remembered very specifically where it was, and so did many of the troopers.

The lone tepee (some noted two, one standing and one collapsed) contained the body of a Sioux warrior mortally wounded on June 17 in the fight with Crook's column; it was left standing on the campsite on the morning of June 18, when the winter roamers moved on down to the Little Bighorn. Our first witness is Wooden Leg, the reliable Cheyenne chronicler, who was in the camp as a winter roamer:

> The next morning [June 16], we went over the divide and down Reno Cr. We stopped where the main forks of the creek come together. Our camps were formed along the valley and on the bank, the Cheyennes at the west end and the Hunkpapas at the east end. From our camp to theirs was about two miles. The camp centered about where the present road crosses a bridge at the forks of the creek. As darkness came on . . . many bands of Cheyennes and Sioux young men, with some older ones, rode out and up the South Fork toward the head of Rosebud Creek . . . [to attack Crook, June 17]. I believe that all

the Sioux were left in burial tepees on the campsite when we left there . . . early the next morning [June 18] after the Rosebud battle.[1]

Kate Bighead, an intelligent Cheyenne woman, was also present in this camp, which she also located "at the forks of Reno Creek," from which that night "our young men rode out" to attack Crook.[2]

Custer's Crow scouts also knew this country intimately, and they confirmed the Cheyenne accounts; they called Reno Creek "Ash Creek," but I freely substitute Reno Creek in their accounts. Walter Camp interviewed Curley at the site of the lone tepee (1908, pp. 155–56):

> He [Curley] directed me to the site of the big camp, which had moved before Custer's arrival, except for the lone tepee covering a dead warrior. This was located on the north side of Reno Creek, about 4 miles from the Little Big Horn [thus the upper forks], on a wide and smooth piece of ground gently sloping toward the creek. When we arrived on this ground, Curley drew my attention to rotten pieces of wood, buffalo heads and joint bones . . . [which he] said were still good evidence of an Indian camp, which evidently extended about a $\frac{1}{2}$ mile. The site of the tepee he could not locate exactly, but said it was on one side or the other of a gulch running through the campground. . . . He identified the locality by a high rocky bluff. . . . Curley said the tepee stood just opposite the bluff, and as the troops came along, the tepee was set on fire by the soldiers.

Hugh Scott also interviewed both Curley and White Man Runs Him on Reno Creek in 1919. Curley (p. 13) again located the lone tepee as "4 miles" above the Little Bighorn, and White Man Runs Him (p. 17) took Scott to the site, "9 miles down Reno Creek from the Crow's Nest," on a flat near the junction with the "South Fork," and he, too, remarked that "the soldiers, not the scouts, burned the tepee." This comment is undoubtedly true, for the scouts knew better than to broadcast their presence by smoke signals.

The accounts of these two enemy Indians and two friendly Crows, the participants most able to recognize the familiar site, agree perfectly, both by mileages and landmarks, that the lone tepee had stood on the north bank of Reno Creek opposite the mouth of its South Fork. As will appear in due course, the majority of the troopers gave the same location by

[1] Marquis, *Wooden Leg*, 197–99, 203 (B).
[2] Marquis, *She Watched Custer's Last Battle*, 2 (B).

estimated mileages. Though this confirmation is enough, it is possible to dispel all confusion by showing how and why a minority of accounts, which I call "paradoxical," *appeared* to locate the lone tepee about a mile from the Little Bighorn. Such paradoxical accounts are marked by a unique pattern; they locate an *event* about a mile from the river and then add "at the lone tepee," this tag being a memory lapse—in short, a phantom tepee. The mileages are reasonable estimates for the location of the events but are incompatible with that of the lone tepee. Attaching these mileages to the events and disregarding the phantom tepee resolves the contradiction and brings agreement among all accounts, as will be shown.

The Custer-Reno Battalions

The Custer and Reno battalions left the divide halt at 12:12 P.M., as Lt. Wallace read into his testimony from his official notes (Graham's *Abstract*, p. 200). The scouts, however, had already been sent ahead in the charge of Lts. Varnum and Hare. Interpreter Gerard, Charley Reynolds, and probably Bloody Knife stayed at Custer's side, but Mitch Boyer and George Herendeen rode with the scouts. All accounts agree that Custer's battalion started down the right bank of Reno Creek and Reno's battalion the left bank, during which time the ride was uneventful. We still need an itinerary, however, as a framework for the scouting operations and events when they begin to happen.

The first event in the troop itinerary came when Custer called Reno's battalion over to join him on the right bank. Reno alluded to this move in his official report (p. 477): "As we approached a deserted village, in which one tepee was standing, about 11 A.M. [*sic*, hours too early], Custer motioned me to cross to him, which I did and moved nearer to his column." Wallace's official itinerary is also brief: "When within 3 miles of the Little Big Horn [*sic*], Reno was ordered across to the right bank, and the two columns moved together for some distance, when Reno was ordered ahead."

Fortunately, Reno divulged more in his testimony (p. 401):

> [When] we got down within sight of the Indian tepee . . . Custer beckoned to me with his hat to cross over to the bank on which he was. When I got on that side, the battalion was somewhat scattered. I

was [had been?] slightly in advance and it threw me opposite the rear of Custer's column. I therefore received the order from Adjt. Cooke to move my column to the front. When I got there, there was a tumult among the Indian scouts; they were stripping to fight, but I understood afterward that they would not go on, and that Custer had ordered them to give up their guns.

There is conclusive evidence that this "tumult" among the Rees occurred at the lone tepee, so Reno remembered that the call-over order came *above* it. There is still ambiguity about a second order brought by Adjt. Cooke; was it merely a verbal reiteration of the call-over gesture or a second order given at the lone tepee?

Lt. Wallace's paradoxical testimony also divulges a little more:

> (p. 48): After 10−12 miles [*sic*] Reno was called to the side of the stream Custer was on, and the two columns moved along some distance. We passed a tepee . . . and Reno was ordered to go on.
> (p. 65): After 9−12 miles [*sic*] . . . Reno was called to Custer's side. . . . Custer motioned him over first and afterward an order came, I think. They continued along for almost or quite a mile, I should say.
> (Graham's *Abstract*, p. 201): I saw Custer beckon Reno to come to the opposite side . . . and it is my impression that an orderly came about the same time and asked him to the other bank.

Wallace is even more ambiguous than Reno about a possible second order, but he agrees that the call-over order came above the lone tepee, and even specifies a mile above, which implies 5 miles above the river and 7 miles below the divide halt.

The nonparadoxical testimony of two other officers supports this conclusion. Lt. Hare testified (p. 248): "Reno's battalion went ahead of Custer's about 5 miles from the Little Big Horn . . . by Custer's order." Lt. DeRudio also testified (p. 268): "Reno and Custer, on opposite sides, followed down the creek for several miles. I think Reno marched ahead of Custer some 4 or 5 miles from the Little Big Horn."

There are reasons why Custer would order Reno to join him a mile above the lone tepee. No-Name Creek joins Reno Creek on Reno's side a mile above the lone tepee; Custer may have figured that, if Reno must cross this branch, he might as well cross the main creek. Furthermore, at this point Custer may have heard or glimpsed the Rees milling around the lone tepee or seen the Crows on the high bluff just north of it. The possibility that these were signs of hostile presence or action would prompt him to unite his force. These reasons reinforce this point as the location of the call-over order.

The 8-mile descent to the lone tepee began at 12:12 P.M., but to complete the troop itinerary we need clock-times and speed checks. The fact that Custer's objective was to attack and destroy a village 15 miles distant brackets his pace between 3 and 6 mph, for the following reasons. A 3-mph walk would delay the attack until 5:12 P.M., leaving little time for destruction and pursuit of refugees before twilight. A faster 6-mph trot would tire the horses before the action started, and worse yet, Benteen would have to gallop to catch up, or be left behind, reducing the strike force.

Lt. Wallace, despite his evident disorientation, managed to supply an observed watch-time and an estimated one that fall nicely within these limits. He testified (Graham's *Abstract*, p. 33): "I had looked at my watch when Custer called Reno to his side of the creek; it was then about two o'clock; taking the distance we passed over [1 mile], I estimate it was 2:15 when Reno received the charge [*sic*] order." We shall soon learn that the next order after the call-over order was not a charge order, but a lead-out order that Custer gave on reaching the lone tepee. Thus Wallace is saying that the call-over order came at 2:00 and the lone tepee was reached at 2:15. The first 7 miles were thus covered in 1.8 hours at 3.9 mph, and the last mile to the lone tepee in $\frac{1}{4}$ hour at 4.0 mph, both representing somewhat more walking on rough terrain than trotting on level ground, which makes perfect sense. These data complete the troop itinerary as posted in Table 5 and plotted in Figure 3, which can now be used to clarify the important activities of the scouts.

Lt. Hare gave valuable information about the scouts during this march, but what Camp obtained from him (pp. 64–65) contains a sequence error, for which I leave an ellipsis to pick up later: "After leaving the divide, Varnum pulled out with the Rees and Hare took the Crows. [Postponed ellipsis.] Before they got to the lone tepee, Varnum's scouts [Rees] had come over to Hare, and Varnum and his orderly [Pvt. Elijah T. Strode] had gone on ahead toward the river." To fit much evidence to come, the two officers must have switched scouts, for the Rees were slowed by worn-out ponies; Varnum, as chief of scouts, appropriately took the lead with the better-mounted Boyer, Herendeen, and the Crows.

Table 5. Itineraries: Descent to the Lone Tepee

Unit Events	Clock- Time	dm	dt	mph	Cum. Mi.
CUSTER-RENO BATTALIONS					
Lv. divide halt to descend Reno Cr.	12:12				0
Pass No-Name Cr.; Reno called to right bank.	2:00	7	1:48	3.9	7
Pass lone tepee; scouts report Sioux, Little Bighorn valley.	2:15	1	0:15	4.0	8
Custer orders Reno to lead out at a trot.	2:15				
BENTEEN'S BATTALION					
Lv. divide halt on off-trail scout to left.	12:12				0
Arr. upper No-Name Cr. and turns down it.	1:20	$3\frac{3}{4}$	1:08	3.32	$3\frac{3}{4}$
On high ridge ahead, Gibson finds Little Bighorn valley empty.	1:20				
Arr. Reno Cr., $\frac{1}{4}$ mi. above mouth of No-Name Cr.	2:32	4	1:12	3.32	$7\frac{3}{4}$
Sights packtrain $\frac{3}{4}$ mi. above; B. Custer joins.	2:32				
(Shift cum. mi. from off-trail to Custer trail.)	2:32				$6\frac{3}{4}$
Halts at morass to water; B. Custer trots on.	2:37	$\frac{1}{2}$	0:05	6.0	$7\frac{1}{4}$
Lv. morass as packtrain arr.	2:57		0:20		
Walk to pass lone tepee.	3:12	$\frac{3}{4}$	0:15	3.0	8
PACKTRAIN					
Lv. divide halt on Custer's trail.	12:32				0
B. Custer trots ahead to overtake Gen. Custer.	2:17	$5\frac{1}{4}$	1:45	3.0	$5\frac{1}{4}$
Sighted by Benteen.	2:32	$\frac{3}{4}$	0:15	3.0	6
Arr. morass; halts to water and close up.	2:57	$1\frac{1}{4}$	0:25	3.0	$7\frac{1}{4}$
Lv. morass.	3:17		0:20		
Passes lone tepee.	3:32	$\frac{3}{4}$	0:15	3.0	8
BOSTON CUSTER					
Lv. packtrain to overtake Gen. Custer.	2:17	$5\frac{1}{4}$	1:45	3.0	$5\frac{1}{4}$
Overtakes Benteen, $\frac{1}{4}$ mi. above No-Name Cr.	2:32	$1\frac{1}{2}$	0:15	6.0	$6\frac{3}{4}$
Arr. morass; trots on as Benteen waters.	2:37	$\frac{1}{2}$	0:05	6.0	$7\frac{1}{4}$
Passes lone tepee.	2:45	$\frac{3}{4}$	0:08	5.6	8

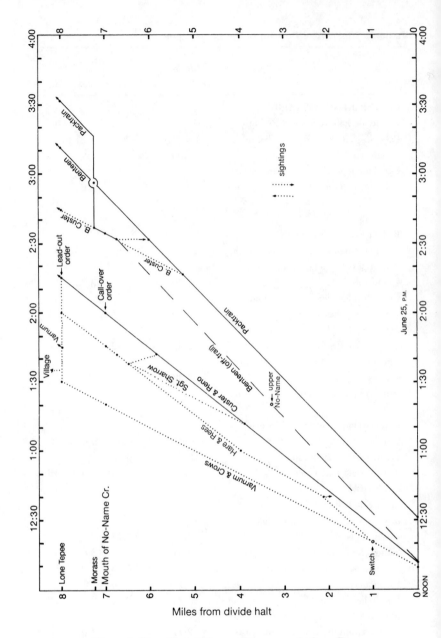

Figure 3. Time-Motion Pattern: Descent to the Lone Tepee

Custer was eagerly awaiting useful news of the Indians, not only from Benteen, but from these scouts he had sent ahead. Just how eager is revealed in the ellipsis postponed above:

> Custer had told Hare to keep a lookout and send back a report as soon as he should discover any Indians. After going some distance, Hare looked back and saw Custer coming right behind with the command, so he increased his gait [thus Hare was already in the rear with the Rees]. Before Hare got to the lone tepee, he was overtaken by Sgt. Maj. [William H.] Sharrow in a great rush . . . and said Custer had not yet heard anything from Hare. Hare . . . said he would report Indians as soon as he could get sight of any.

Custer would hear nothing from Benteen but on reaching the lone tepee would hear much from the scouts and act on their news. It is significant that he would there find Lt. Hare and the Rees, as well as Boyer, Herendeen, and the Crows, but not a soul would mention Lt. Varnum (or his orderly).

Lt. Varnum's accounts are rather confusing, but Camp (p. 61) also understood him to say that "Varnum and his orderly, Strode," had gone ahead as if alone and "had passed the lone tepee, some distance over to the left, and had gone on over to the southwest to a point on high ground from which he could overlook the valley of the Little Big Horn," with no hint that he saw anything. That is another case of faulty sequencing, as Varnum's paradoxical testimony reveals. He testified (p. 168) that "I did not stop to look at it [the lone tepee]," and (p. 153) "I did not go down to look at it, as I was out of the column at the time."

If Varnum passed the lone tepee on his "left" and did not stop to go down to it, he must have seen it from "high ground" to the north of it, which can only refer to the high bluff opposite the lone tepee, from which he could indeed "overlook the valley of the Little Big Horn," just as his scouts did, as we shall learn. Then, before Custer arrived, Varnum left his scouts on the high bluff and moved "southwest" with his orderly to pick up the Reno Creek trail and follow it "toward the river," as Hare said. This testimony merely corrects Camp's sequence. Varnum's independent scout ended a long time later, when Custer overtook him, for he testified (p. 148) that "I reported to Gen. Custer . . . about a mile from the ford [of the Little Bighorn]," where he then located a phantom tepee.

To help visualize the sequence of these movements of the scouts, feasible time-motion paths have been sketched in Figure 3, starting at 12:10 (2 minutes before Custer) but soon followed by the switching of the scouts. Varnum, Boyer, Herendeen, and the Crows moved at 6 mph to reach the high bluff opposite the lone tepee at 1:30, when they all halted and studied the river valley; before long (1:45?), Varnum and his orderly proceeded ahead, leaving the others there. After the switch, Hare and the slower Rees fell behind, then speeded up when they spotted Custer behind them. Later Sgt. Maj. Sharrow overtook them and turned back, while they proceeded to reach the lone tepee at 2:00, where Varnum's scouts joined them just before Custer arrived at 2:15. This pattern satisfies hard evidence that Varnum and his scouts had time to study the valley before Custer arrived.

Varnum testified that he made significant observations from the high bluff opposite the lone tepee; I italicize the words that specify this location and the early timing:

> (p. 148): I had seen a large force of Indians on the bottom an *hour* or more *before* reporting to Custer [a mile from the river].
>
> (p. 169): When I first saw the Indian ponies I was away back from the river, *5 or 6 miles* or more. I saw them from the high bluff there; at that time they [the Sioux] were driving the ponies in to the village, evidently getting the horses to saddle up.

This testimony does not preclude the possibility that Varnum may have seen the Indians again after nearing the river.

Varnum's scouts, who remained longer on the high bluff, made similar observations. Curley told Camp (p. 186), while both were at the site of the lone tepee: "Just opposite the lone tepee was a high rocky bluff, from which he, with Mitch Boyer and three other Crow scouts had been watching the Sioux with field glasses all that forenoon [*sic*, early afternoon] before the arrival of Custer's command." It was Herendeen, however, who gave the most detailed story; I quote his 1878 account (p. 263) and, for reasons that will become apparent, insert corrections from his earlier account of July 1, 1876 (p. 258):

> [From the divide] the scouts under Varnum and Hare pushed on at a lope and the command followed at a trot. I was with the scouts and we kept down a creek that led to the Little Big Horn. When we got near the mouth [1876: "after going about 6 miles"], we rode up on a hill so as to flank and overlook the lodge and soon saw it was deserted.

From the top of the hill we looked ahead down the Little Big Horn and saw a heavy cloud of dust and some stock, apparently running [1876: "about 5 miles distant"]. We could see beyond the stream a few Indians on the hills, riding very fast, seemingly running away. I said the Indians are running and we would have to hurry up, or we would not catch them. Lt. Hare wrote a note to Custer . . . and I presume he thought, as the rest of us did, that the Indians were getting away. Custer was near at hand [i.e., approaching] and was riding at a trot. The scouts charged down on the abandoned lodge, cut it open and found a dead Indian.

Custer came up while we were at the lodge, Reno having the advance. I heard Custer tell Reno, "Take the scouts, lead out and I will be with you." [1876: "Custer sent word to Reno, who was ahead with his battalion, to push on the scouts rapidly and head for the dust."]

Varnum, Curley, and Herendeen thus agree that before Custer arrived, and from the high bluff opposite the lone tepee, they saw many Sioux, 5 miles distant, apparently ready to run away. When Lt. Hare arrived after Varnum had left, the scouts passed this grave news on to him. Herendeen added another significant event in his last paragraph, which gives the first clear version of Custer's second order, the lead-out order delivered to Reno at the lone tepee. This order does not use the word *charge* nor in any way imply a charge; perhaps it is the order both Reno and Wallace alluded to so ambiguously at this time. The significance of the scouts' findings and the lead-out order will be addressed below when all the evidence is in.

Another instructive feature of Herendeen's interdigitated accounts is that they expose the role of memory failure in the evolution of paradoxical accounts. Between 1876 and 1878 Herendeen's memory shifted the lone tepee from 6 miles below the divide to "near" the mouth of Reno Creek. His 1879 testimony carries the evolution to the final paradoxical stage:

(p. 237): I heard Custer tell Reno to lead out and he would be with him [lead-out order]; that was probably ¾ mile [*sic*] from the Little Big Horn. Reno led out and I went with him; directly after Custer gave that order, he said, "Take the scouts with you." I supposed that meant me, and I started with Reno.

(p. 243): When Custer ordered Reno to charge the Indians and he would support him [charge order], I was standing right beside this lodge [*sic*]. I had helped to cut it open and see what was in it. The column was in motion; Custer was within 15 feet of me and Reno was right there with his officers.

Not only has the phantom tepee reached $\frac{3}{4}$ mile from the river, but the lead-out order has merged with a later charge order. If fading memory, exposure to other witnesses, and cross-examination could trick as honest and impartial a witness as Herendeen, it is not surprising that others suffered the same affliction.

The Ree scouts had much to say about Reno's "tumult" at the lone tepee, but nothing of Sioux sightings, as they had fallen behind. Young Hawk told Libby (p. 94) of his arrival:

> Young Hawk saw a group of scouts at the lower ridge peering over to the lone tepee. The scouts he was with slowed up as the others came toward them. Then from behind, they heard a call from Gerard, who said, "The chief says for you to run [i.e., hurry on]." At this, Strikes Two gave the war whoop and called back, "What are we doing?" and rode on. . . . Strikes Two reached the tepee first and struck it with his whip. Then Young Hawk . . . took a knife . . . and slit the tepee to the ground. Inside he saw a scaffold with a dead body wrapped in a buffalo robe.

Red Bear elaborated on Custer's reaction to overtaking the scouts (pp. 121–22):

> All the scouts stopped at the lodge. . . . Then Custer rode up with Gerard, who called out: "You were supposed to go right on to the Sioux village [and run off horses]." While the scouts were examining the tepee, Custer, who was ahead of his troops, overtook them and said by words and signs: "I told you to dash on and stop for nothing. You have disobeyed me. Move aside and let the soldiers charge past you. If any man of you is not brave, I will take away his weapons and make a woman of him." One of the scouts replied: "Tell him, if he does the same to all his soldiers who are not as brave as we are, it will take him a long time." The scouts all laughed at this, and by signs said they were all hungry for battle. They then rode on ahead. . . . Gerard rode on with the scouts here.

Strikes Two gave Camp (p. 183) a briefer version: "At the lone tepee Custer became impatient and said that we were slow, and if he had to urge us again to go forward, he would take our guns and put us afoot."

Lt. Hare's nonparadoxical testimony (pp. 248–49) now helps to tie all the events near the lone tepee together:

> My attention had been called to some Indians ahead [seen by Varnum, Herendeen, and Crows] and I spoke to Custer about it. He

told me to take the Indian scouts and he would follow. The [Ree] Indians refused to go and he ordered them dismounted, and turned to
Adjt. Cooke and told him that as the Indians would not go ahead, to
order Reno with his battalion ahead [confirming the lead-out order].
This was within 100 yds. of this tepee and about 5 miles from the
Little Big Horn. Reno's battalion started ahead immediately at an in-
creased rate, a fast trot. [Thus no troop halt at the lone tepee.]

Lt. Hare repeated the lead-out order and tied up one loose end regarding the Rees and Gerard for Camp (p. 65): "At the lone tepee, Hare heard
Cooke tell Reno to go on in pursuit of the Indians and Custer would follow
right behind. . . . But [shortly] before this, Custer had ordered the scouts
ahead, but they refused to go and Custer ordered them dismounted and
their horses taken away from them. Gerard explained matters to the Rees,
so they rode out ahead of Reno."

Note that Gerard reached the lone tepee with Custer, there interpreted
for him, and then smoothed over Custer's contretemps with the Rees, with
whom he left the scene without halting. This sequence is enough to establish that Gerard had no opportunity to climb a high bluff and sight Indians
running like devils in the river valley and shout this news to Custer. As
shown in the next chapter, Gerard's paradoxical testimony relates such
events far down Reno Creek by mileage but "near" a phantom tepee.

Nonparadoxical accounts from two more of Reno's officers locate the
lone tepee far from the river and also confirm the lead-out order. Capt.
Moylan testified (pp. 207–8) that "the two battalions travelled several
miles . . . and reached the lone tepee, where, as I afterward understood,
Reno was sent for by Custer and received orders to move forward with his
battalion, as the Indians were supposed to be a few miles ahead and
retreating." Lt. DeRudio, in a July 5 newspaper dispatch (p. 253), wrote
that "after marching 2 or 3 miles, Reno's command was ordered to trot
and hold the gait until we reached the river, 6 or 7 miles distant."

All the available evidence thus points to the same clear picture. It was
Varnum's scouts who told Lt. Hare of spotting the Sioux and their pony
herds in the valley, apparently running away. Lt. Hare then reported this
dreaded news to Custer the moment the latter arrived. Though Custer had
been growing more anxious every minute over Benteen's failure to rejoin
him, he could not simply ignore such evidence of fleeing Indians. Hoping
that Benteen was near and would catch up, he promptly ordered Reno to

take the scouts and lead out at a trot, while he followed right behind. This simple lead-out order, given at the lone tepee, has long escaped notice.

Benteen's Battalion, the Packtrain, and Boston Custer

Benteen's battalion left the divide halt at 12:12 P.M., the same time as Custer's and Reno's, but diverged to the left to make a reconnaissance. Lt. Mathey's packtrain, escorted by Capt. McDougall's Company B and accompanied by Boston Custer (a nominal quartermaster scout), did not get off until 12:32 P.M., "20 minutes" later, as McDougall testified (p. 376), but took the Reno Creek trail. Benteen, after completing his off-trail scout, picked up Custer's trail a little above the lone tepee, at which time he sighted the packtrain a little above him. At this same moment, Boston Custer, who had left the packtrain to overtake the general, also overtook Benteen. These several interconnections will prove valuable in timing the progress of these parties, for the packtrain followed a known trail at a uniform speed.

With draft mules and novice soldier-packers, the train moved slowly, the escort bringing up the rear. Incessant loosening of loads gradually strung out the train, requiring the van to halt to allow the rear to catch up. Two of the citizen-packers who testified (John Frett, p. 266, and Benjamin F. Churchill, p. 348) insisted they did not even "trot" until the end. This testimony guarantees that the van moved at a 3-mph walk, taking 2 hours and 40 minutes to cover the 8 miles to the lone tepee; adding a 20-minute halt to water at a morass makes the total time 3 hours. The van thus passed the lone tepee at 3:22 P.M. This itinerary and those of the other parties are included in Table 5 and Figure 3.

Benteen's off-trail scout presents a problem, for his officers' accounts are vague and faulty, and Benteen himself resorted to flagrant falsehoods. Under cross-examination at the Reno Inquiry, he turned utterly irrational regarding the orders Custer gave him. He branded them "senseless," mere "valley hunting ad infinitum," and claimed he was "to pitch into anything I came across." He even bragged that his return to Custer's trail was "in violation of orders" that would have taken him "to Fort Benton." In short, he charged Custer with sending him on a stupid and endless combat mission.

Custer gave Benteen his initial orders at the divide halt, orally and with no witnesses present, and Benteen did not relay them to Capt. Weir or Lts. Godfrey and Edgerly. He was forced, however, to give instructions to his company subaltern, Lt. Gibson, whom he was ordered to send ahead to examine the valley. Gibson, in a personal letter of July 4, 1876 (p. 268), annihilated Benteen's ravings in one lucid sentence: "Benteen's battalion was sent to the left about 5 miles to see if the Indians were trying to escape up the valley of the Little Big Horn, after which we were to hurry and rejoin the command as soon as possible."

This sensible, limited, rapid, and information-gathering version of Benteen's orders was confirmed by Benteen himself. He wrote in his official report, also dated July 4, 1876 (p. 479):

> The directions I received from Gen. Custer were to move with my command to the left, to send well-mounted officers with about 6 men, who would ride rapidly to a line of bluffs about 5 miles to our left and front with instructions to report to me, if anything of Indians could be seen from that point. I was to follow the movements of this detachment as rapidly as possible. Lt. Gibson was the officer selected.

In early August 1876 Benteen gave the same version to a news reporter (p. 227): "I was sent to the left to a line of bluffs about 5 miles off with instructions to look for Indians and see what was to be seen. . . . Custer also instructed me to send an officer and six men in advance of the battalion and ride rapidly." Benteen repeated this version in his testimony (p. 320), adding that he was to "send back word to Custer at once." But this time he replaced "look for Indians" with the misleading "pitch into anything I came across."

The foregoing references to a line of bluffs 5 miles off are misleading, for the first line of bluffs was only about 1 mile from the divide halt. Custer's *initial* orders directed Benteen to move to this nearby ridge and send the advance detail to the top to examine the distant upper valley for Indians, either moving upstream or camped there; he was to move rapidly and rejoin Custer as quickly as possible. Clearly, Custer intended Benteen's absence to be brief. Within minutes, however, Custer had advanced far enough to see that this first ridge would give Benteen no view of the valley, for he sent a courier with permission to proceed to the next ridge; soon Custer saw the next ridge was no better and sent a second courier with similar orders. These *follow-up* orders reveal how anxious

Custer was to know about Indians in the upper valley, for this information would affect his mode of approach to the village.

Benteen's official report resumes with an incoherent account of his off-trail scout, with no hint of these follow-up orders:

> I followed [Gibson] closely with the battalion, at times getting in advance of the detachment [*sic*, they diverged]. The bluffs designated [the first ridge] were gained, but nothing could be seen but other bluffs quite as large and precipitous as were before me. I kept on to those and the country was the same, there being no valley of any kind that I could see on any side [*sic*, between each ridge, he crossed small valleys of branches of Reno Creek]. I had gone about fully ten miles [*sic!*]; the ground was terribly hard on horses, so I determined to carry out the other instructions, which were that if in my judgement there was nothing to be seen of Indians, valleys, etc., in the direction I was going, to return with the battalion to the trail the command was following. I accordingly did so. . . .

Benteen did tell the news reporter (p. 227) the next August about the two couriers from Custer, but to correct the sequence, I reverse the order of the two sentences:

> Before I proceeded a mile in the direction of the bluffs, I was overtaken by the chief trumpeter [Henry Voss] and the sergeant major [William H. Sharrow] with instructions from Gen. Custer to use my own discretion, and in case I should find any traces of Indians, at once to notify Custer. If I found nothing there, to go on and when I had satisfied myself it was useless to go farther in that direction, to join the main trail.

Benteen testified (p. 320) that the couriers came separately, but he remained evasive about the orders they brought:

> I had gone about a mile, when I received instructions, through the Chief Trumpeter, that if I did not find anything before [?] reaching the first line of bluffs, I should go on to the second. I had gone a little farther when I received orders, through the Sergeant Major, that if I saw nothing from the second line of bluffs, to go on to the valley, and if I saw nothing there, to go on to the next valley. . . .

In his 1890 narrative (pp. 179–80) Benteen repeated this version, adding that the couriers arrived "15 or 20 minutes" apart and both brought orders "to pitch in and notify Custer at once."

That these follow-up orders permitted Benteen to go beyond the first and second ridges seems certain. It is equally certain that they did not countermand the initial order to hurry and rejoin the main command as quickly as possible. If he was to be absent longer than originally expected, it was appropriate for Custer to urge him to report by courier and caution him to use discretion, so as *not* to be left behind. But Benteen's claim that he was given discretion to return *only* if he found no Indians seems absurd.

As it turned out, Benteen was in fact left behind. He ignored repeated orders to hurry and never reported by courier, two omissions that add up to indiscretion. When it later developed that Custer's battalion was wiped out, Benteen must have realized that his indiscretion had spared his battalion the same fate as Custer's. This recognition apparently drove him to an indefensible cover-up, so simplistic as to be transparent and which scarred his conscience for the rest of his life. Such painful prying into Benteen's psyche offers a speculative explanation of his deceptive accounts of his off-trail scout.

Using a few clues from Benteen's men, we may follow his off-trail route closely enough on good maps. Leaving the divide halt at 12:12 P.M., Benteen headed nearly west into country that was neither cliffs nor badlands, but easier sagebrush hills. He climbed several ridges that separated minor branches of Reno Creek, but Lt. Gibson obtained no view of the upper Little Bighorn valley. The entire battalion then descended into the next valley, that of upper No-Name Creek, which courses northwest to join Reno Creek. This little valley was broader on its right bank where Reno struck it, but from its left bank arose a promising higher divide that does yield a view of the upper valley. The off-trail march had now covered about 3¾ miles to reach No-Name Creek at this point, about 4 miles above its mouth. Here the battalion turned downstream along the easier right bank, but Gibson's detail, having crossed the creek, climbed to a high viewpoint on the next promising ridge, going an extra distance of at least ½ mile. [3]

[3] In *Centennial Campaign* I proposed troop itineraries for the descent from the divide halt to the Little Bighorn, but no farther. The present time-motion analysis, more systematic and detailed and based on better maps and more extensive sources, continues all the way to 6 P.M. of June 25. This extension revealed that the earlier itineraries were unacceptable, for they led to later impossibilities. The main problem was Benteen's off-trail scout; better

Here Gibson picks up the story in a letter to Godfrey, August 8, 1908 (p. 131):

> As to my little scout to the left to find the Little Big Horn valley, I can state definitely that I did find and see it. . . . Benteen sent me with a small detail . . . and gave me his field glasses to take with me. I got some distance in advance. . . . I crossed one insignificant stream [No-Name Creek] running through a narrow valley, which I knew was not the Little Big Horn valley, so I kept on to the high divide on the other side of it, and from the top of it I could see plainly up the Little Big Horn Valley for a long distance with the aid of the glasses, but in the direction of the village I could not see far on account of a sharp turn in it, . . . which obstructed the view. I saw not a living thing on it and I hurried back and reported so to Benteen, who then altered his course so as to pick up the main trail.

Gibson had thus secured the intelligence that Custer was anxiously awaiting, negative in that no Indians were seen, but positive in that it would allay Custer's concern about Indians escaping or attacking from that direction. It is incredible that Benteen never revealed that he had accomplished his mission; he officially reported that after "10 miles" he simply returned to Custer's trail. It is now apparent that the 10 miles was an invention, for he and the battalion went only $3\frac{3}{4}$ miles, although Gibson went about $4\frac{1}{2}$. This finding, in turn, reveals another ambiguity: the distance of "4 or 5 miles to a line of bluffs," quoted so often earlier, applied not to the first but to the last and successful ridge. This was the moment for Benteen to send a report of his findings to Custer and to press on to join him "as quickly as possible." He did neither.

Benteen moved down the widening right side of No-Name Creek for 4 miles to reach and cross Reno Creek, where he picked up Custer's trail about $\frac{1}{4}$ mile above the mouth of No-Name Creek, thus completing his off-

---

maps showed that Lt. Gibson had to continue to the higher ridge between No-Name Creek and the South Fork before he could view the valley of the Little Bighorn. I therefore had to revise the old itinerary for Benteen's off-trail scout to eliminate impossibilities.

Soon thereafter providence supplied an independent confirmation of the revision. A publisher sent me a manuscript to review for possible publication. I was delighted to find that this author had come to the identical conclusion I had, using the same quadrangle maps, but had verified the off-trail route by extensive, detailed, and careful fieldwork on the ground and from the air. This excellent work has now been published: Darling, *Benteen's Scout-to-the-Left* (B). The differences between his itinerary and mine are minute, and the reader is referred to his book for further details.

trail scout in a total of $7\frac{3}{4}$ miles. The distance to this point by Custer's trail was $6\frac{3}{4}$ miles, revealing that Benteen had traveled only 1 extra mile. Some account estimates come very close to $7\frac{3}{4}$ miles, and duration estimates correspond; a few cite much longer mileages, which demand impossible speeds.

From here on Benteen became less deceptive, signifying that he wanted most to conceal the off-trail scout. He officially reported that he struck the main trail "just in advance of the packtrain" and testified (p. 321), "I struck the trail I suppose a mile or less than a mile ahead of the packtrain." If we take this sighting distance as $\frac{3}{4}$ mile, at that moment Benteen was $6\frac{3}{4}$ miles and the packtrain 6 miles below the divide halt, both by Custer's trail. Here we have a providential time check on Benteen's progress, for the packtrain at its uniform speed of 3 mph covered its 6 miles in 2 hours and was thus sighted at 2:32 P.M., and that was the moment Benteen's column picked up Custer's trail.

Thus the duration of Benteen's off-trail scout was 2 hours and 20 minutes, and since his off-trail distance was $7\frac{3}{4}$ miles, his overall pace was only 3.32 mph, slower than Custer's 4 mph, although the general had moderated his pace to allow Benteen to catch up. By interpolation, Benteen reached upper No-Name Creek at 1:20 P.M., only an approximation, because terrain features probably made his speed nonuniform. This interpolated point and the anchor points supplied by the sighting are posted in the itineraries for both Benteen and the packtrain (Table 5) and plotted (Figure 3); note that in the figure Benteen's off-trail scout is plotted as a dashed line, to which the mileage scale applies only at its start and finish.

Benteen now turned left down the right bank of Reno Creek, passing opposite the mouth of No-Name Creek in $\frac{1}{4}$ mile and passing the lone tepee in another mile. For this interval he officially reported (pp. 479–80) significant details:

> I pushed rapidly on, soon getting out of sight of the advance of the train, until reaching a morass, I halted to water the animals, who had been without water since about 8 P.M. of the day before. This watering did not occasion the loss of 15 minutes, and when I was moving out, the advance of the train commenced watering from that morass. I went at a slow trot until I came to a burning tepee. . . . We did not halt.

Since Benteen's testimony is identical to the foregoing account, I accept the $\frac{1}{2}$-mile trot to the morass to outdistance the train. Others confirmed the watering at the morass and the arrival of the train there just as they left it, but Godfrey (1892, p. 139) wrote that the officers became impatient at the watering, which he testified (p. 357) lasted "20 or 30 minutes." This testimony prompts me to choose 20 minutes, and since none then claimed even a slow trot, I let the column walk the next $\frac{3}{4}$ mile to the lone tepee. The exact location of the morass has never been certain, for it was seasonal and there are many potential sites along Reno Creek. All accounts agree only that the morass was above the lone tepee. Benteen's route and the packtrain interconnection provide the best evidence for its approximate location.

Benteen's 6-mph trot to get ahead of the train brought him to the morass at 2:37, and the 20-minute watering held him there until 2:57. The train, at its uniform speed, reached the morass at 2:57, and as McDougall testified (p. 376) that it also halted there "20 minutes" to water and close up, it left at 3:17. Then, walking in tandem, Benteen passed the lone tepee at 3:12 and the train at 3:32, as posted and plotted. Regardless of the location of the morass, the two columns left it 20 minutes and 1 mile apart and so must retain this interval as long as they maintain that speed.

Lt. Edgerly recalled (1894, p. 5) another event when Benteen's battalion reached Custer's trail (2:32 P.M.): "About this time, Mr. Boston Custer, the general's youngest brother, rode by on his pony. He had stayed back with the packtrain and was now hurrying up to join the general's immediate command. He gave me a cheery salutation as he passed, and then with a smile on his face, rode to his death."

Boston Custer had undoubtedly taken a steady trot in order to overtake Custer, far ahead. He probably met Benteen at 2:32, when the latter reached Custer's trail and trotted to outdistance the packtrain. Then, when Benteen halted to water $\frac{1}{2}$ mile later, Boston trotted on alone. On the basis of a 6-mph trot, we can extrapolate back to when Boston left the packtrain at 2:17, $5\frac{1}{4}$ miles below the divide halt, and ahead to when he passed the lone tepee at 2:45. These data for Boston's itinerary are posted and plotted also.

Having now conducted all parties as far as the lone tepee, we can make some interesting comparisons. The train, as expected, brought up the rear, but note that Benteen passed the lone tepee 57 minutes behind Custer. It was there that the sighting of running Indians compelled Custer to order a trot, so that when Benteen passed that point Custer and Reno were already 4 miles ahead. There was simply no way that Benteen's battalion could now participate in attacking the village.

These itineraries raise a pertinent question: Simply by following orders to move rapidly, could Benteen have completed his mission and still cut 57 minutes from his time so as to overtake Custer at the lone tepee? He could have saved 20 minutes by watering below the lone tepee, as Custer and Reno did. Then, moving at 5.73 mph over the last $5\frac{1}{4}$ miles from upper No-Name Creek to the lone tepee would save the remaining 37 minutes. To conclude that this timing was feasible would be rash, however, for the calculation is based on his interpolated time of arrival at No-Name Creek and the assumption that neither terrain nor waiting for Gibson to report enforced delay thereafter. But surely a fast courier could have overtaken Custer at the lone tepee.

THE APPROACH TO THE LITTLE BIGHORN

The 7th Cavalry had left the divide halt in three separate units, but by the time all had reached the Little Bighorn they had become four units, separated in time and space, forming a complex time-motion pattern. In order to follow these units, it is necessary to identify key landmarks and mileages from good maps.

Reno Creek features a lower, and minor, fork where its *North Fork* enters its right bank, only $\frac{3}{4}$ mile from the Little Bighorn and thus $3\frac{1}{4}$ miles below the lone tepee. Half a mile above this junction lies another landmark, which may be called the *flat*, $1\frac{1}{4}$ miles above the river and $2\frac{3}{4}$ miles below the lone tepee. This flat consists of a tongue of level bottomland between the gradually approaching North Fork and Reno Creek, which terminates at its upper end in a little *butte*, or knoll. At the mouth of Reno Creek on its left bank was a natural ford across the Little Bighorn, called *Ford A* at the Reno Court of Inquiry. The Indian trail the command had been following crossed to the left bank of Reno Creek just above the North Fork and descended for $\frac{3}{4}$ mile to Ford A.

To help fix these landmarks in mind, it may be pointed out, in advance of the evidence, that at the flat Custer gave Reno his charge order and Reno sped ahead, while Custer followed slowly, making a *speed* separation of the two battalions. Then, at the mouth of the North Fork, Reno crossed to the left bank of Reno Creek and descended to Ford A; Custer, lagging behind, crossed the North Fork and turned right down the right bank of the river, making a *trail* separation.

From Ford A the Little Bighorn River flows northwest in meandering fashion for some miles. Its left (west) bank consists of a broad and level bottom, on which stood the large *Sioux village*, beginning about 3 miles below Ford A and extending another 3 miles downstream. The right (east) bank of the river features high, steep *bluffs* that tend to crowd the eastward loops of the river. A long, steadily rising *ridge* on the right bank of the river extends from the mouth of the North Fork of Reno Creek directly to *Reno Hill*, $1\frac{1}{2}$ miles distant, which lies on the edge of the steep bluffs overlooking the river valley.

Reno's battalion crossed the Little Bighorn at Ford A and halted to reform before charging down the bottom toward the village. Custer's battalion halted to water its horses in the North Fork before advancing down the long ridge toward Reno Hill. When Benteen's battalion later, and the packtrain still later, came to the diverging trails, both followed Custer's trail to Reno Hill. This chapter conducts Reno to Ford A and Custer to the North Fork, but Benteen and the packtrain all the way to Reno Hill.

Custer and Reno Trot to the Flat

At the lone tepee the scouts had relayed to Custer their news of Indians in the valley some 5 beeline miles distant and apparently running away. This report was certainly an adequate reason for Custer to order Reno to lead out at a trot, taking the scouts, but no reason whatever to order a charge on the village. The village was 7 trail-miles distant, and a 7-mile charge is a contradiction in terms. Furthermore, Custer still lacked information on which to base an attack plan, and Benteen's battalion was still missing, but presumably bringing part of the needed information. Com-

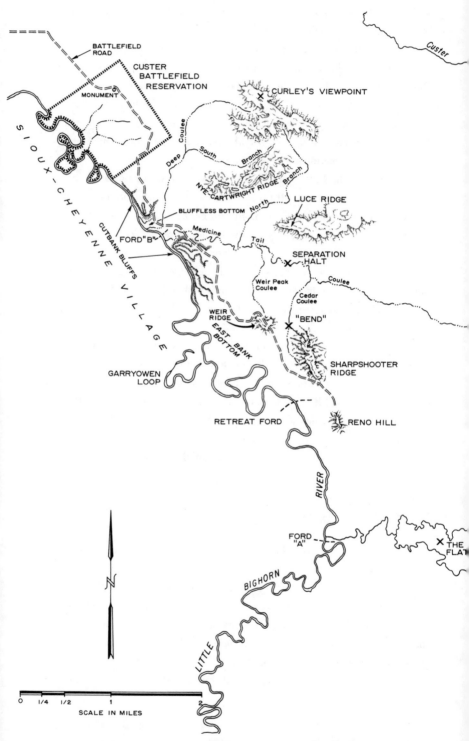

The Custer Battlefield Country. Map by Bob Bolin.

mon sense demanded that Custer trot right behind Reno to keep his force together, as all accounts agree.

Participant accounts also agree that the descent of the two battalions from the lone tepee was uneventful until they reached the flat, $2\frac{3}{4}$ miles distant, where three major incidents occurred: fresh discoveries were made, Custer ordered Reno to charge, and the battalions separated. These events are inseparable, for the first promptly caused the second, and the second caused the third, albeit in two stages. Only paradoxical accounts introduce a contradiction by associating an image of the ephemeral lone tepee with the mileage location of these events at the flat, thereby obliterating a march of $2\frac{3}{4}$ miles and 28 minutes, which no feasible time-motion pattern can accommodate.

For this uneventful march the Crow scouts gave specific mileages that agree with the map; they also mentioned fresh discoveries, new orders, and separations of the battalions, although their interviewers missed the distinction between speed and trail separations. Postponing the fresh discoveries for the moment, we find that White Man Runs Him told Scott (p. 18): "Custer came down the north side of Reno Creek to a little flat between the north and south forks . . . about $1\frac{1}{4}$ miles from the Little Big Horn." Curley confirmed and amplified this statement in four interviews, here assembled:

> (Roe, 1881): The scouts came to a butte between two streams, Custer Creek [North Fork] and Reno Creek, a mile and a half from the Little Horn. . . . About a mile from the Little Horn, the command separated. [Reno's] part went down Reno Creek to its mouth and forded the Little Horn.
> (Dixon, 1909, p. 163): We [Crows] all stopped at the fork of Little Reno Creek [North Fork]. Custer split up his command here, and told Reno to follow down Reno Creek.
> (Scott, 1919, p. 13): We came to the flat over there ($1\frac{1}{4}$ miles from the river).
> (Russell White Bear, pp. 18–19): Mitch Bouyer remained with Custer's men when Reno separated to go to the valley. We rode to the North Fork of Reno Creek and crossed it.

Only Reno, in his official report (p. 477), ventured to estimate the duration of the trot to the flat. He wrote that the call-over order (at our 5 miles from the river) came at "12:30 A.M." a sure "typo" for "11:30" A.M. These times are far too early, but if the "typo" is corrected, the duration of Reno's 3-mile march becomes 30 minutes and the speed

6 mph, the standard cavalry trot. At this pace the map distance of $2\frac{3}{4}$ miles would take 28 minutes, and since the column left the lone tepee at 2:15, it reached the flat at 2:43 P.M., as posted (Table 6) and plotted (Figure 4) for both Reno and Custer. The important thing is that this march fills a segment in both itineraries left disastrously vacant in paradoxical accounts.

We can now turn to the first event at the flat: fresh sightings of Indians that evoked the charge order and initiated the speed separation. It was the Crow scouts in the lead who made the first sighting of Sioux when they reached the little butte at the upper end of the flat, as Curley related to Roe (1881): "From there [the little butte], we saw two mounted Indians coming from toward the village; they came up pretty close, saw us and saw big dust of the command coming down Reno Creek; when the Indians ran back, they got on the ridge [leading toward Reno Hill] just above [i.e., overlooking] the Little Big Horn, and commenced to circle [as an alarm to the village]."

The version that White Man Runs Him gave Scott (p. 13) implies that Custer, on reaching the flat, also glimpsed these two Sioux:

Custer looked down the creek and saw dust rising near its mouth, and called Half Yellow Face, the leader of the Crows, to him and asked what the dust was. Half Yellow Face said, "The Sioux must be running away." Custer then said, "I am through with the scouts; you have brought me to the Sioux. I will throw Reno's battalion [to attack from the] south, in case the Sioux should go south. Then Reno started south [*sic*, ahead].

This sighting was confirmed by several Sioux then in the village. Feather Ear-ring, a Miniconjou, gave Hugh Scott the most detailed account:

Reno's men came down Reno Creek; they were seen by two Sans Arc young men, who went up Reno Creek to get a horse that had been wounded in the Rosebud fight. Two Bear was killed by Reno's scouts; Lone Dog, the other, went back and gave the alarm, riding from side to side. Feather Ear-ring saw him signalling that soldiers were coming, calling, "One of us got killed; they are right behind me." He had no sooner arrived at the village than Reno's command began firing at the tepees.[1]

[1] Scott, "Interview with Feather Ear-ring, at Poplar R., Mont., Sept. 9, 1919," Graham, *Custer Myth*, 299 (B).

Table 6. Itineraries: The Lone Tepee to the Little Bighorn

Unit Events	Clock-Time	Increments dm	dt	mph	Cum. Mi.
CUSTER'S BATTALION					
Lv. lone tepee down right bank Reno Cr.	2:15				0
Trots to flat right behind Reno.	2:43	2¾	:28	6.0	2¾
Scouts report Sioux alarming village.	2:43				
Reno ordered to charge, taking Adjt. Cooke.	2:43				
Custer sends 2 Crows to bluff who join Reno.	2:43				
Fast walk to No. Fork; halt to water.	2:51	½	:08	3.75	3¼
Adjt. Cooke reports Sioux attacking Reno.	3:01	(¾	:06	7.5)	
Starts down right bank Little Bighorn (trail separation).	3:01		:10		
RENO'S BATTALION					
Lv. lone tepee, in lead.	2:15				0
Trots to flat, Custer right behind.	2:43	2¾	:28	6.0	2¾
Receives charge order (speed separation).	2:43				
At No. Fork, crosses to left bank Reno Cr.	2:47	½	:04	7.5	3¼
At Ford A, crosses to left bank Little Bighorn.	2:53	¾	:06	7.5	4
Halts to water and reform.	2:53				
Troops and scouts see Sioux attacking.	2:53				
Adjt. Cooke lv. to report to Custer.	2:55				
Starts charge down left bank Little Bighorn.	3:03		:10		
BENTEEN'S BATTALION					
Lv. lone tepee on Custer's trail.	3:12				0
Meets Rees driving Sioux ponies.	3:40½	1.42	:28½	3.0	1.42
Meets Sgt. Kanipe with Custer's message.	3:42	.08	:01½	3.0	1½
Meets Tptr. Martin at flat; hears firing.	3:58	1¼	:16	4.7	2¾
At No. Fork, takes Custer's trail.	4:02	½	:04	7.5	3¼
At knoll, sights Reno's retreat and halt.	4:06	½	:04	7.5	3¾
Meets 3 Crows and 1 Ree; lv. halt.	4:10		:04		
Reaches Reno Hill and joins Reno battalion.	4:20	1	:10	6.0	4¾

Table 6. (*continued*)

Unit Events	Clock- Time	Increments dm	dt	mph	Cum. Mi.
PACKTRAIN					
Lv. lone tepee on Custer's trail.	3:32				0
Meets Rees driving Sioux ponies.	3:45	.65	:13	3.0	.65
Meets Sgt. Kanipe, with Custer's message.	3:48	.15	:03	3.0	.8
Overtaken by Rees returning to Reno Hill.	4:04½	.83	:16½	3.0	1.63
Halts at flat to close up; Mathey sees smoke.	4:27	1.12	:22½	3.0	2¾
Lv. flat, sighting troops on Reno Hill.	4:47		:20		
At No. Fork, takes Custer's trail.	4:57	½	:10	3.0	3¼
Meets Lt. Hare with orders for ammo. packs.	5:02	¼	:05	3.0	3½
(Ammo. packs reach Reno Hill.)	(5:19	1¼	:17	4.5	4¾)
Reaches Reno Hill.	5:25	1¼	:23	3.25	4¾

The view has long prevailed that it was Fred Gerard who sighted running Indians in the valley and that this sighting evoked the charge order, *both* at the *lone tepee*. I have already established, however, that Gerard had no opportunity to make such a sighting at the lone tepee. The misunderstanding stemmed from the paradoxical nature of Gerard's testimony, which located the sighting at the flat, by mileage, but added "at the lone tepee." I quote his testimony, including a reference to the phantom tepee, but italicizing the other locators:

> (pp. 91–93): A few minutes before Reno received his [charge] order, I rode up a little knoll . . . and from it I could see the village, Indian tepees and ponies. I turned my horse, took off my hat, waved it and hallooed to Custer: "Here are your Indians running like devils." I rode down from that knoll and joined Custer, who was still marching on. This knoll was probably 40–50 yds. to the right . . . not on the Little Big Horn, but on Reno Creek, *1 or 1¼ miles above* the Little Big Horn. . . . Custer hallooed over to Reno, beckoning him with his fingers, and told him, "You will take your battalion and try and bring them to battle and I will support you." As Reno was going off, Custer said, "and take the scouts with you." This occurred about a *mile* from the Little Big Horn.

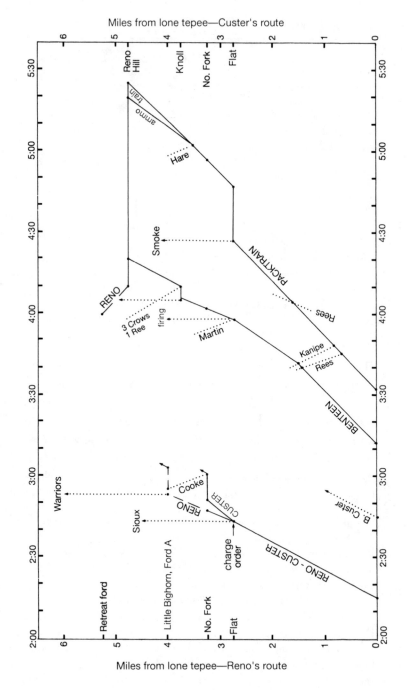

Figure 4. Time-Motion Pattern: Descent to the Little Bighorn

(pp. 124–26): The [above] knoll . . . was a small hillock, 20 to 25 feet higher than where the lone tepee stood [*sic*]. That is where I first saw the Indians to know they were Indians. From this first knoll, I saw them down in the bottom of the valley on the left bank; I estimate they were over *3 miles* from me. This knoll was about a *mile* from the ford. I did not report to Custer, but merely waved my hat to attract general attention and hollered, "Here are your Indians running like devils." At that time I saw Reno and Cooke and some officers with Custer. I rode down and heard Custer call Reno over and order . . . [repeats charge order]. Reno started on and I told the scouts, "We are going to go with this [Reno's] party; fall in."

The evidence, now clearly consistent, is overwhelming that, when the two battalions reached the flat, the Crows had spotted Sioux downstream and were watching them flee to the ridge overlooking the valley, from which they signaled the alarm of approaching troops to the village; even Custer glimpsed their dust. Then Gerard saw Indians and ponies down in the valley, "running like devils," and saw the village. This information was not only fresh but solid: there *was* a village, not only near but alarmed and running away. It was a case of attack now or never, and Custer promptly gave Reno the charge order.

Various versions of the charge order generally follow the pattern given by Reno in his official report (p. 477): "Adjt. Cooke came to me and said the village was only 3 miles above [?] and running away; to move forward at as rapid a pace as prudent and to charge afterward, and that the whole outfit would support me. I think those were his exact words." Reno's testimony is identical, except for the introductory phrase, "Adjt Cooke came to me for the second time, and said. . . . " Some versions replace "charge afterward" with "charge after crossing the river," which is more reasonable. Most versions locate the village $2\frac{1}{2}$ to 3 miles ahead, but it should be noted that such distances identify the flat, not the true lone tepee.

Adjt. Cooke did more than relay Custer's charge order, for Lt. Wallace testified (p. 67): "Adjt. Cook and Capt. Keogh started down to the ford with us; I saw them and heard them talking as they rode along. They went with us when we started to obey that order of Custer." Sgts. Davern and Culbertson, and Gerard, confirmed that Cooke reached the ford. Custer must have detached his adjutant at this time for the purpose of assessing the actions of the enemy and the outlook for Reno's charge and then speeding back to report his findings.

Custer and Reno Separate

The troop itinerary for Reno's rapid descent of $1\frac{1}{4}$ miles from the flat to Ford A is fairly simple. Lt. Wallace (p. 49) testified to the route: on approaching the mouth of the North Fork, the troops crossed to the left bank, as the Indian trail did, and proceeded $\frac{3}{4}$ mile to the ford. Many accounts give mileage estimates that vary only modestly from the map distance, and some duration estimates center on a pace of 7.5 mph, an accelerated trot that would require some horses to lope occasionally. This pace would take 10 minutes to cover $1\frac{1}{4}$ miles, to reach the ford at 2:53 P.M. While fording, the troopers watered their horses, and Reno officially reported (p. 477) that he then "halted about ten minutes or less to gather the battalion." If we accept 10 minutes for the total halt, Reno launched his charge down the left bank bottom at 3:03 P.M. These events complete Reno's itinerary, as posted and plotted.

The fact that Lt. Wallace's paradoxical testimony (p. 73) had lost all track of the trot to the flat is revealed by his *estimate* of the time Reno reached Ford A, "2:20 P.M." This time is 33 minutes too early and throws everything out of kilter; itineraries violate evidence, interconnections become impossible, and "error" lights flash every step of the way.

As Reno's battalion neared the ford, a spate of Indian sightings began. Sgt. Davern testified (p. 279) that he "saw 30 to 40 Indians away down on the bottom, apparently riding in a circle." Sgt. Culbertson similarly testified (p. 308) to seeing "a very large cloud of dust, such as Indians driving ponies might make." Pvt. O'Neill told Brinninstool (p. 129) that when he reached the left bank (Reno Creek), overlooking the river, "he saw the Indian camp across the river and a mile [or more] downstream . . . with a great number of Indians at the edge of camp, mounted and running in great excitement." He also told Camp (p. 106) that the Indian "trail split and went around a little rise of ground, on which some of the Rees were sitting, discussing the numbers of Sioux. One was picking up handsfull of grass and dropping it and pointing to the Sioux, indicating they were as thick as the grass."

Herendeen recalled (1878, p. 263) that as he was fording, he "heard the [two] Crow scouts call to one another, 'The Sioux are coming up to meet us.' As I understood the language, I called this to Reno." Reno, who was already across the river, did not describe the scene but revealed his response by officially reporting (p. 477) that he promptly sent "word to Custer that I had everything before me and that they [the Indians] were strong." He testified (p. 401) further: "I first sent my striker, [Pvt. Archibald] McIlhargey [Co. I], to Custer to say that the Indians were in front of me and in strong force. Some minutes after, I sent my cook, [Pvt. John] Mitchell [Co. I]." McIlhargey was sent promptly indeed, for Sgts. Davern (p. 294) and Culbertson (p. 307) testified that before they crossed they met him as he emerged from recrossing the ford on his way to Custer.

Gerard also learned from the scouts at the ford that the Sioux were not fleeing, but riding up the valley to attack. He testified (pp. 96, 127–28) that he primed Adjt. Cooke with this news to carry back to Custer:

> We came to a second knoll in a little valley right on the right bank of the Little Big Horn; it was 12 feet or more higher than the bench on the left bank of Reno Creek. Just before crossing the river, the scouts were to my left and called my attention to the fact that all the Indians were coming up the valley. I called this to the attention of Reno, who only paused and ordered "Forward," to ford the river. As I thought it important that Custer know this, I started back toward his command, but at this little knoll, I met Adjt. Cooke and told him. He said, "All right, I'll go back and report." I knew Custer was under the impression that the Indians were running away and [he] was probably behind us, and it was important for him to know the Indians were not running away.

It thus appears that Adjt. Cooke started back at about 2:55 for Custer's column, followed by McIlhargey. As no one mentioned Capt. Keogh at this time, he may well have been the first to turn back, with what news is uncertain. Pvt. Mitchell must have been last, though Reno must have sent him off during the halt. Clearly, a small parade of couriers was rushing back to deliver news of a kind that Custer was not expecting.

Meanwhile, Custer, having committed Reno's battalion to an attack on the village from the south, had left the flat on Reno's trail, but at a reduced pace. He was anxiously scanning his back trail for Benteen, whose missing battalion was now needed more than ever, and anticipating Adjt. Cooke's return with news on how Reno was faring. Sticking to Reno's trail at a reduced speed was the best he could do at the moment.

That Custer reduced speed is revealed by Lt. Varnum, who had just reported to the general. He testified (p. 149) that, when he left to overtake

Reno, "Custer was moving at a walk, and Reno [had] pulled out at a trot." Two of Custer's own troopers verify the ½-mile route to the North Fork. Sgt. Kanipe recalled (1903, p. 280) that "Custer followed the same route Reno did, for a short distance, and then turned squarely right," and wrote Camp (1908, p. 92) the same, adding that the turn came "about ½ a mile from the ford"; in 1924 (p. 249) he reduced this distance to ¼ mile, both being too short. Tptr. John Martin's testimony (p. 312) corrected this error and added another important item: "We did not go near the river at all. We stopped at the little creek [North Fork] and watered the horses. . . . Here Custer gave the order: 'Do not let the horses drink too much, because they have to travel a good deal today.' I judge we halted ten minutes there altogether."

We are now able to complete Custer's itinerary. At a reduced speed of 3.75 mph, the battalion would advance the ½ mile in 8 minutes to reach the North Fork at 2:51. If we accept the 10-minute halt to water the horses there, Custer was ready to start up the long ridge on the east bank that led to Reno Hill at 3:01 P.M., as posted and plotted. During these 18 minutes events had transpired that explain Custer's decision to descend the right bank of the Little Bighorn.

When Custer left the flat, he ordered Half Yellow Face and White Swan to scout ahead to the rising ridge that led to Reno Hill and afforded a view of the valley. Through some misunderstanding, the pair ended up with Reno's battalion, as both Curley and White Man Runs Him related to Scott (p. 13):

> (Curley): On reaching the flat, Mitch Boyer told us that Custer wanted Half Yellow Face and White Swan to go over on the hill to the ridge and look over at the [Sioux] camp. The two scouts were almost to the foot of the hill, when the trumpeter sounded a call and Reno started moving. The scouts turned to the left and joined Reno.
> (White Man Runs Him): Reno started and crossed [Reno] creek just below the flat. Custer called Half Yellow Face and White Swan and told them to go over to the ridge and see if the Sioux were there. They started, but instead of going over to the ridge, they followed Reno and that was the last we saw of them.

Since these two Crows fought bravely with Reno that afternoon, evening, and the next day, this disregard for Custer's order must have been a mishap, which may have happened in the following way. Varnum testified (p. 149) that, on leaving Custer, he overtook Reno as he was about to cross Reno Creek, but the column forced him aside: "There were 8 or 10 Indians with me at the time, and as soon as the column passed, I was joined by Lt. Hare." All the Rees were supposed to be with Reno, but some had lagged behind, even behind Custer. Varnum may have been rounding up such stragglers, and he or Hare may have gathered up the two Crows by mistake.

This mishap abruptly reduced Custer's complement of scouts to Mitch Boyer, Curley, Goes Ahead, White Man Runs Him, and Hairy Moccasin. It was the alert Mitch who noted that the other two Crows had joined Reno and so led the remaining four to the ridge to carry out Custer's assignment, as two Crows told Scott (p. 13):

> (Curley): Mitch Boyer said, "Come on, we will go up on the hill and look over." So Mitch and we four Crows started up the hill on a gallop.
> (White Man Runs Him): Mitch Boyer noticed the scouts Custer had sent to look over the ridge had followed Reno, so he called [the four Crows] and said, "Let us go over to the ridge and look at the lodges."

The implication is that all Custer's scouts started for the ridge before the battalion reached the North Fork to water the horses.

Sgt. Kanipe told Camp (p. 92 n. 6) that when near the North Fork he spotted a sizable group of Indians up on the ridge, apparently near Reno Hill ($1\frac{1}{2}$ miles distant) and relayed the news to Custer; he even suspected this was the reason Custer turned right. It is more probable that the major reason was the return of Adjt. Cooke with Reno's news. This explanation is feasible, for if Cooke left the ford at 2:55 and traveled $\frac{3}{4}$ mile in 6 minutes at 7.5 mph, he could report to Custer at 3:01 P.M.

Custer responded immediately to this wholly unexpected news. He could delay no longer waiting for Benteen, for if the village was of a mind to fight, Reno's small force would need support quickly. Custer had already sent all his scouts ahead to the long ridge on his side of the river to catch a view of the village and valley. By following, he could see the terrain and action for himself and find a route by which to make a flank attack that might support Reno sooner and more effectively than by following around in Reno's rear.

We now leave Reno and Custer at their respective halts, $\frac{3}{4}$ mile apart, poised to move against the village by separate routes.

Benteen's Battalion to Reno Hill

Although Mitch Boyer and the scouts were with Custer and Reno, it is still necessary to complete itineraries for Benteen's battalion and the packtrain. The reason is that, the farther we proceed with Custer, the more his participant accounts dwindle, requiring supplementation from peripheral participants. As the total time-motion pattern grows into an intricate network, each part supports the others by interconnections, whether meetings, couriers, cross-sightings, or cross-hearings. As an analogy, the pattern without interconnections looks like a scaffold about to collapse, but feasible (and only feasible) interconnections supply braces that make it stabile. The plan of procedure is to construct time-motion patterns for all the other units to form a "surround" of Custer's path and use the interconnections to impose constraints on his progress, both in time and space. This process will take two more chapters before we are ready to tackle Custer's advance beyond the North Fork.

Benteen's battalion, having passed the lone tepee at 3:12, followed Custer's trail to Reno Hill, a distance of $4\frac{3}{4}$ miles, with only a 4-minute halt. Lt. Godfrey recorded (1892, p. 142n) a watch-time of 4:20 P.M., which he later decided was the time the battalion reached Reno Hill. Subtracting the halt time makes the marching time 1 hour and 4 minutes and the overall speed 4.5 mph, indicating that Benteen walked a portion of the time, despite orders to hurry. This march is productive of valuable interconnections.

As the first interconnection, Benteen met Sgt. Kanipe, the first courier Custer sent back to the rear with messages. Kanipe recalled (1903, p. 280) his instructions: "Go to Capt. McDougall. Tell him to bring the packtrain straight across country. If any packs come loose, cut them [off] and come on quick—a big Indian camp. If you see Capt. Benteen, tell him to come quick—a big Indian camp." Some of Benteen's men heard Kanipe shout as he rode on to the packtrain, "We've got them, boys."

In his official report (p. 480) and testimony (p. 321) Benteen located this meeting "about one mile below the lone tepee." He told the news reporter (August, p. 227) that it was "3 miles" above the river, and as he located the lone tepee $4\frac{1}{2}$ miles above the river, the meeting was $1\frac{1}{2}$ miles below the tepee. In 1890 (p. 180) he located the meeting "one or two miles" below the tepee. I accept an average of $1\frac{1}{2}$ miles, and as he walked this distance, it took 30 minutes, timing the meeting at 3:42. This time anchors the termination of Kanipe's important interconnection from Custer. These data are posted in Benteen's itinerary (Table 6) and plotted (Figure 4). This meeting must also satisfy Kanipe's itinerary, not to be completed until Chapter 22.

Only a minute or two before meeting Kanipe, Benteen had also been passed by a party of Reno's Ree scouts driving a herd of Sioux ponies, captured from the village area, back to the packtrain, though neither party mentioned the other. The Rees had just overtaken and passed Kanipe, as both parties noted. The itinerary of the Ree pony captors is completed in the next chapter, but all these meetings must satisfy all three itineraries. In Benteen's itinerary I have posted and plotted this meeting with the Rees in *final* form that satisfies all these constraints.

Prodded by Kanipe's message, Benteen picked up his pace a little and next met Tptr. Martin, of Benteen's own Company H. Martin was the second courier Custer sent back, this time with a written message addressed to Benteen: "Come on. Big Village. Be quick. Bring pacs. P.S. Bring [ammunition] pacs. W. W. Cooke."[2] In his haste Adjt. Cooke omitted, even from the postscript, the key word I have inserted. This note carries a subtle implication; as Custer addressed it to Benteen, he must have figured Benteen had joined the train and was there to speed it up. Benteen ignored this subtlety in his official report (p. 480): "I inquired of the trumpeter what had been done, and he informed me that the Indians had 'skedaddled,' abandoning the village." He repeated this statement in his testimony (p. 321) but added: "Therefore there was less necessity for my going back for the packs," which he claimed were "7 miles" behind him! His sole response to this direct order was to *retain* Martin and "take a trot."

Benteen made five estimates of the distance between the meetings with Kanipe and Martin, ranging from "about one" to a "couple of miles," but they average mighty close to $1\frac{1}{4}$ miles, which falls on the flat, $\frac{1}{2}$ mile above the North Fork. Martin confirmed this distance to Graham (1922, p. 290), saying that he followed Custer's trail back to the watering place at the North Fork, then began looking for Benteen, and "pretty soon" saw the battalion and met it in "a few hundred yards." If this search totaled

---

[2] A photograph of the original message appears in Graham, *Custer Myth*, 299 (B).

$\frac{1}{2}$ mile, it again locates the meeting at the flat, which I accept. To meet future requirements, I adopt a pace of 4.7 mph for Benteen's $1\frac{1}{4}$-mile march, which would take 16 minutes and fix the meeting with Martin at 3:58, as posted and plotted. This timing anchors the termination of another interconnection with Custer, which must satisfy Martin's future itinerary.

In response to Custer's message and spurred by the "sound of firing ahead," as noted by Godfrey (1892, p. 141), Benteen's column took a fast pace (7.5 mph) for the next $\frac{1}{2}$ mile (4 minutes) and, on reaching the North Fork at 4:02, found that the trail of shod horses they were following suddenly split in two. Camp learned from Godfrey and Gibson:

> (Godfrey, p. 75): When they came to point where Custer's trail separated from Reno's, there was some discussion as to which should be followed. The debate was settled by Capt. Weir starting off on the left hand trail, while the other two companies followed the right hand trail. Benteen with his orderly took a mid-position between the two trails and went ahead.
>
> (Gibson, pp. 80–81): Where Custer's trail parted from Reno's, Benteen said, "Here we have the horns of a dilemma." Gibson advised taking the right hand trail and says his Company H took it. Does not remember [about the others].

Benteen did not mention the dividing trails but repeatedly said that he rode ahead of the battalion. That it turned right on Custer's trail is confirmed by Tptr. Martin, who had twice ridden it and was now with Benteen. He told Camp (p. 104 and n. 9) that, "as Benteen approached the river, we turned north along the bluffs above [overlooking] the river" and also that "we marched on Custer's trail . . . and got on the ridge."

Godfrey (1892, p. 141) described what happened next: "The firing became more pronounced and appeared to be coming toward us. The column took the gallop with pistols drawn. We were forming in line . . . when we came in full view of the valley and saw it full of horsemen in dust and smoke." Benteen, still ahead and to the left, saw the tail of Reno's headlong retreat from his fight in the valley; he usually said he saw this from Ford A but described it more feasibly in a letter to his wife (July 4, p. 298): "When getting to top of hill so that the valley could be seen, I saw an immense number of Indians on the plain, mounted and charging some dismounted men of Reno's; the balance of his command was mounted and flying to the bluffs on the same side of the river I was." Godfrey, skeptical that Benteen could see this action from Ford A, said, as related to Camp (p. 76), that "he does not think Benteen got to Ford A and thinks he could not have seen Reno's retreat until he got to the ridge; he must have been ahead of the command."

The map shows that about $\frac{1}{2}$ mile from the mouth of the North Fork lies the first little knoll on this ridge that commands a view of the valley. Continuing at 7.5 mph for this additional $\frac{1}{2}$ mile would deliver the column to this viewpoint at 4:06, and Benteen even earlier. The van of Reno's retreat recrossed the river at the "retreat" ford, about $\frac{1}{2}$ mile below Reno Hill (including a steep bluff climb); Lt. Wallace testified (p. 51) that his watch read "4:00" when he splashed over the river on this retreat. Although Reno's van reached Reno Hill at 4:10, it was followed by a long comet's tail, and some men, set afoot, had to scramble back to the timber whence they had come. Thus this 4:06 sighting corresponds to the tail of Reno's retreat and is posted and plotted as a visual interconnection by Benteen's column.

Godfrey's diary now picks up the story: "Some Crow scouts came up over the hills, driving a herd of ponies, and soon came to us. I asked by signs which way to go; he motioned to go to the right and I told Benteen, so we went that way." In 1892 (p. 141) he wrote that this was "a small herd of ponies." Benteen testified (p. 321) that "I noticed 3 or 4 Indians 4–500 yds [$\frac{1}{2}$ mile] to my right and saw they were Crows. They told me Reno was in battle and that the men had gone up on the hills." In 1890 (p. 181) he added: "From where I saw the 3 or 4 Crows, I first saw Reno's battalion, who had retreated from the bottom, recrossed the river a couple miles below [me] and were showing up on the bluffs."

These statements leave the impression that Benteen's column paused at this viewing point to identify the troops in trouble, to allow Benteen to rejoin and help decide which way to move, and to hear what the Crows could tell them. Because it fits so nicely, I allow 4 minutes for this pause, which thus ended at 4:10; I also adopt 4:10 as the meeting time with the Crows. There were three Crows—Goes Ahead, White Man Runs Him, and Hairy Moccasin—whom Custer had released to seek safety in the rear; Benteen was correct in thinking there were four men, but the fourth was the Ree scout, Black Fox. This pause terminates another interconnection from Custer, as posted and plotted in final form, although the itineraries for the three Crows and for Black Fox will not be completed until later.

The four scouts joined Benteen's battalion for its remaining 1-mile trot to unite with Reno's defeated remnants on Reno Hill at 4:20 P.M., according to Godfrey's watch-time and estimates by Reno's men. Benteen's itinerary is now complete.

The Packtrain to Reno Hill

The packtrain, having passed the lone tepee at 3:32, also followed Custer's trail for its 4¾-mile march to Reno Hill. At its uniform speed of 3 mph, the van covered the first 2¾ miles in 55 minutes, to reach the flat at 4:27 P.M., by which time Reno and Benteen had united on Reno Hill. During this first segmental march the train made three interconnections, which are posted in its itinerary (Table 6) and plotted (Figure 4) as finalized by future itineraries.

The first interconnection was with the Ree pony captors, who recalled meeting the packtrain "near the lone tepee" and then halting to exchange their worn-out mounts for fresh Sioux ponies before turning back for Reno Hill. A Company C soldier-packer, Pvt. John McGuire, told Camp (p. 124) that he "saw the Rees go back with a herd of Sioux ponies, and no officer with the packtrain tried to stop them." Capt. McDougall wrote Camp (p. 69) that, "shortly after passing the burning tepee, 8 or 10 Indians passed with about 15 ponies." I post and plot this meeting 0.65 miles below the lone tepee at 3:45 P.M.

The second interconnection was with Sgt. Kanipe, who related that on meeting the packtrain he joined it for his return to Reno Hill. Two citizen packers, John Frett (p. 366) and Ben Churchill (p. 348), testified to the arrival of a "sergeant" or "orders" from Custer. Lt. Mathey testified (p. 370) that "no sergeant reported to me with a message from Custer," which is not surprising, as Kanipe was to report to McDougall at the rear. McDougall testified (p. 377), strangely enough, that he "thought Mathey got that order and informed me." I post and plot this meeting 0.8 miles below the lone tepee at 3:48 P.M.

The Ree pony captors, who made a fast return to Reno Hill, soon overtook and passed the slower packtrain. Since neither party mentioned this event, it has been calculated and posted as the intersection of the packtrain itinerary with that of the pony captors, yet to come.

The next important event was a halt to allow the mules straggling in the rear to close up, because signs of fighting ahead were seen. Lt. Mathey testified (pp. 369–70):

> Probably 3 or 4 miles below the lone tepee . . . I could see a great deal of smoke and stopped the packtrain at a little knoll and sent word back to Capt. McDougall that there had been fighting and I would wait for him to come up. I halted there 10 or 15 minutes, about 2 or 3 miles from Reno Hill. I saw smoke and thought I saw men on top of a hill, who turned out to be Reno's men.

Capt. McDougall, in the rear, testified (p. 376) that he "told Mathey to halt so they could close up," and on reaching the halted van "about 3 miles below the lone tepee" and "2 miles" from Reno Hill, he "saw a black mass; thought they were Indians, but found they were Reno's men." Both officers thus locate the halt 2 miles from Reno Hill, which falls on the flat, the most convenient place and close to the little butte that affords a glimpse of Reno Hill. Both also specified it was 3 miles below the lone tepee, only $\frac{1}{4}$ mile in excess of the map distance. John Frett, who thought Kanipe had joined them at the morass above the lone tepee, testified (p. 366) that they "went $2\frac{1}{2}$ to 3 miles and halted for a while to get the packtrain together." His average of $2\frac{3}{4}$ miles happens to be the distance from the lone tepee to the flat.

The uniform pace of the packtrain would bring it to the halt at the flat at 4:27 P.M. Mathey estimated that the halt lasted 10 to 15 minutes, but if McDougall was a mile in the rear, it would take 20 minutes to close up. I settle on a 20-minute halt, which makes the march resume at 4:47, as posted and plotted. The closed-up train proceeded another $\frac{1}{2}$ mile in 10 minutes to reach the North Fork at 4:57, when it diverged on the heavier Custer-Benteen trail.

The next event was a meeting with Lt. Hare, whom Reno had sent back from Reno Hill to have ammunition mules forwarded at once. This interconnection is especially useful in checking events at both ends. Mathey testified (p. 370) that "shortly after I went on from the halt, I met Lt. Hare, who said they wanted ammunition, and I sent on two mules with two boxes each, and instructed the drivers to hurry." Churchill's testimony (p. 348) provides confirmation: "This order came to send the ammunition mules ahead. . . . [Frank C.] Mann and I took one mule, but I don't know who took the other."

As indicated by the testimony of Lt. Hare (p. 258) in Chapter 21, he made a fast round trip in "20 minutes," which at 7.5 mph translates to $2\frac{1}{2}$ miles and so locates the meeting $1\frac{1}{4}$ miles from Reno Hill, or $\frac{1}{4}$ mile short of the North Fork. Hare also told Camp (p. 66) specifically that he did not go back as far as the North Fork. McDougall (to Camp, p. 69), Mathey (testimony, p. 370), and Churchill (testimony, p. 348), all estimated the remaining distance to Reno Hill, and the average of all is $1\frac{1}{4}$ miles, the same as Hare's. The train thus walked $\frac{1}{4}$ mile beyond the North Fork in 5 minutes to meet Lt. Hare at 5:02 P.M.

Although Lt. Hare sped ahead to Reno Hill, the two heavily laden ammunition mules probably lumbered along at 4.5 mph to cover the remaining $1\frac{1}{4}$ miles in 17 minutes, thus reaching Reno Hill at 5:19. I allow the rest of the train 23 minutes (3.25 mph) to reach Reno Hill at 5:25 P.M. The next chapter reveals how well these arrival times mesh with the chronology of events there.

RENO'S FIGHT AND RETREAT

Reno's charge down the valley ended in a halt to battle with a formidable force of Indians, which soon compelled a retreat back across the river to Reno Hill. There is no need to dwell on the minutiae of Reno's fight, but a troop itinerary is needed as a time framework to elucidate the activities of the scouts and to establish interconnections with other units and thereby extend the "surround" of Custer's movements. Again, we must begin with mileages and landmarks taken from the "Crow Agency" 7½-minute quadrangle map.

Reno charged down the valley from Ford A, but before actually reaching the village, he halted to form a dismounted skirmish line, which required each fourth trooper to hold four horses in safety while the other three troopers deployed in line. Although the precise location of this halt and the initial open skirmish line is uncertain, I compromise on a position about ¼ mile upstream from the long, westward-projecting Garryowen loop of the Little Bighorn, which is no longer connected with the main stream. This point measures about 2 miles from Ford A, making this distance the length of Reno's charge. The skirmish line was anchored at its right on the edge of some timber skirting the river; it extended to the left across the bottomland toward a line of low bluffs.

When the Indians circled around the open end of the line, it had to be withdrawn into the edge of the timber for better defense. Soon it became apparent that even this position could be held only so long as ammunition lasted. Reno then mounted and reformed the column in a clearing within the timber and led it out by climbing a bench through brush and timber to reach the open bottomland upstream, over which they had charged. During the total halt period there had been some maneuvering, but to keep things simple, I shall disregard this motion, while incorporating its time into the total halt.

On breaking into the clear, the retreating column dashed upstream, with a horde of triumphant Indians crowding its right flank and pushing it toward the river, exacting a heavy toll of casualties. In about 1 mile they found not a good ford, but a crossable place, which may be called the "retreat" ford, at the foot of the high bluff on the east bank. After plunging across, the troops struggled up this steep bluff, obliquely upstream, to reach Reno Hill, this additional distance measuring $\frac{1}{2}$ mile. The itinerary distances are thus simple: a 2-mile charge down the valley, a 1-mile retreat to the crossing, and a $\frac{1}{2}$-mile climb to Reno Hill.

With these mileages, an itinerary for Reno's troops can easily be blocked out. The charge started from Ford A at 3:05 P.M. A controlled charge of 2 miles at an overall 8 mph would take 15 minutes, making the halt begin at 3:18. A later retreat of 1 mile at 9 mph would take 7 minutes to reach the retreat ford at 4:00, as read by Lt. Wallace from his watch. The retreat, therefore, had started at 3:53, which makes the total duration of the halt 35 minutes, including maneuvering time. Using numerous participant estimates, I assign 15 minutes of this time to skirmishing in the open and the remaining 20 minutes to skirmishing from the timber. This timing makes the withdrawal into the timber come at about 3:33. The final $\frac{1}{2}$-mile climb to Reno Hill, at 3 mph, would take another 10 minutes, fixing the arrival there at 4:10 P.M.

The retreat times apply only to the column's van, for the disorganized movement spread out the column and there were many late starters. Some of these stragglers were dismounted by falling, wounded, or killed horses, leaving the riders to scramble back to the timber for safety. All but the dead, however, would eventually escape to Reno Hill. Benteen saw these late unfortunates in the valley by 4:06, which supports the Reno itinerary; so does his sighting of troopers on Reno Hill at 4:10. Godfrey's watch-reading of 4:20 for the arrival of Benteen's battalion provides another check, for Reno's men estimated that Benteen arrived about 10 minutes after Reno's van.

These data for Reno's itinerary are posted in Table 7, including the timing of sighting interconnections to be described in the next section. The time-motion pattern is plotted in Figure 5, as an addition to Figure 4 (previous chapter). Figure 5 is complex because it includes material to be developed step by step in the rest of this chapter as well as the next, until it completes the Custer "surround." It furnishes the terminal nodes of all interconnections that help dictate Custer's whereabouts in time and place.

Figure 5 shows interconnections as dotted lines; vertical dotted lines are instantaneous sightings or hearings, with points to indicate direction (from observer to observed). Motion of troop columns on Custer's trail are shown as continuous lines; those on Reno's trail by interrupted lines. This time a mileage scale for Reno's trail appears on the left margin, and one for Custer's trail on the right margin. Reno's scale is broken by a $\frac{1}{4}$-mile gap, and mile "4" appears at both its ends; this displacement avoids superimposing a future Custer halt on Reno's skirmish halt, without altering mileages read on the Reno scale nor time read on the mutual time scale. The $\frac{1}{4}$-mile gap was chosen because it allows Reno's retreat to strike Reno Hill at the correct mileage by both scales.

Reno's abrupt halt short of the village was clearly well-advised. At that moment he had no support at all, and there was no way his 140 soldiers could expect to survive a charge through a village of 1,000 lodges and 2,000 fighting men. Even the minority of warriors who poured out to attack him made bad enough odds. The Indians soon began to turn the left flank of the open skirmish line, forcing it to take a better defensive position just within the timber. The men were safe there for a time, but the perimeter of the timber was so long as to spread them quite thinly. Worse yet, the ammunition the troopers carried on their persons and saddlebags was fast diminishing, spelling imminent disaster. Reno's officers and men

Table 7. Itinerary: Reno's Charge, Fight, and Retreat

Unit Events	Clock-Time	Increments dm	dt	mph	Cum. Mi.
RENO'S BATTALION (Reno's trail)					
Lv. Ford A; charges down left bank Little Bighorn	3:03				4
Sights Custer or scouts on right bank bluff.	3:05	$\frac{1}{4}$	:02	8.0	$4\frac{1}{4}$
Sights Custer battalion at Reno Hill.	3:13	1	:08	8.0	$5\frac{1}{4}$
Halts to deploy open skirmish line.	3:18	$\frac{3}{4}$	:05	8.0	6
Sights Custer battalion on bluffs, disappearing.	3:18				
DeRudio sights Custer et al. at Weir Peak.	3:30				
Open skirmish line withdraws into timber.	3:33		:15		
Retreat upstream begins.	3:53		:20		
Crosses Little Bighorn at retreat ford.	4:00	−1	:07	9.0	5
Climbs bluff obliquely to Reno Hill.	4:10	$-\frac{1}{2}$	:10	3.0	$4\frac{1}{2}$
(Mileage to Reno Hill by Custer's trail					$4\frac{3}{4}$)

fully accepted the necessity of the retreat, but much criticism was leveled at its management. All the men were not formed before it began; nothing was done to cover the running retreat, the jammed-up river crossing, or the exposed climb up the bluff. The casualties were indeed heavy, and missing men numerous. The only thing that saved them was the failure of the Indians immediately to pursue the disorganized men across the river.

Sightings of Custer's Column on the Bluff

During Reno's charge and skirmish halt some of his men made sighting interconnections with Custer's column on the bluff across the river at successive and identifiable intervals and locations, which reveal much

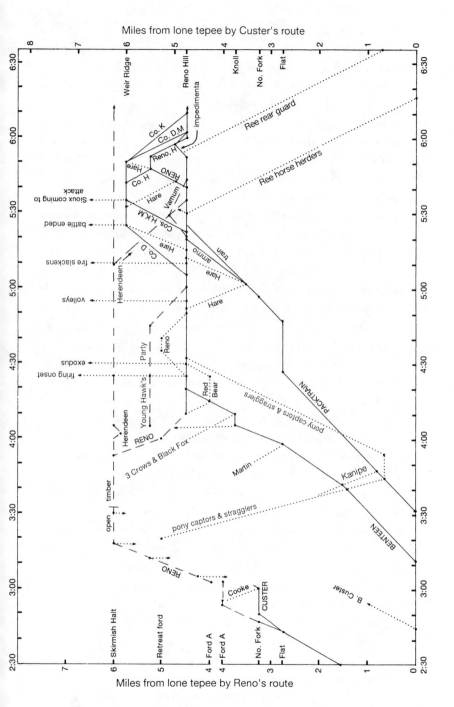

Figure 5. Time-Motion Pattern: The Complete Custer "Surround"

about Custer's progress. I now identify the Reno ends of these sightings (as interpolated in Reno's itinerary) in final form, having coordinated them with Custer's itinerary, which appears in Chapter 22.

The earliest sighting of Custer's men was recalled by two of Reno's enlisted men. Pvt. Stanislaus Roy (Co. A) told Camp (p. 112): "After passing Ford A, we formed in line, and while forming I heard some of the men say, 'There goes Custer.' He could be seen over on the hills to our right and across the river." Since Reno started his charge at 3:03, this sighting came near that time. Pvt. Daniel Newell (Co. M) told J. P. Everitt (p. 4): "As we galloped down the bottom . . . I remember seeing Custer's command on the bluff on the opposite side of the river, marching along to the north, possibly a mile or so from the point where we left them." If this separation point refers to the North Fork, Reno's charge had covered only $\frac{1}{4}$ mile and the time was 3:05. These similar sightings were early and nonspecific as to just whom they saw; I merge them into one at 3:05, only 4 minutes after Custer had left the North Fork.

The second sighting was made a little later by three men during Reno's charge. Pvt. Henry Petring (Co. G) told Camp (p. 133): "While in the bottom going toward the skirmish line, I saw Custer over across the river on the bluffs, waving his hat. Some of the men said, 'There goes Custer. He is up to something, for he is waving his hat.'" Camp also interviewed Pvt. Thomas O'Neill (Co. G) (p. 106): "When about halfway down to where the skirmish line was formed, O'Neill saw Custer and his whole command on the bluffs across the river over to the east, at a point which he thinks was about where Reno fortified later [Reno Hill], or perhaps a little south of there . . . going at a trot." This may be the sighting Red Star described to Libby (p. 119): "When Custer stood on the bluff where Hodgson's stone stands [Reno Hill], Curley and Black Fox [*sic*, an error] were with him." These three accounts reveal that Custer's column was seen at Reno Hill, moving at a trot, the general waving his hat, but only O'Neill gives a clue to the time. I convert his "about half way" (1 mile) to $\frac{5}{8}$ way ($1\frac{1}{4}$ miles), which times the sighting at 3:13.

Since Custer did not halt at Reno Hill, later sightings must locate him farther downstream, where more landmarks and mileages must be identified from the map. About $1\frac{1}{4}$ miles downstream from Reno Hill lies a major landmark, the short east-west *Weir Ridge*, with two high *peaks* at its west end very close to the bluff edge. But only $\frac{1}{2}$ mile below Reno Hill lies the midpoint of narrow, north-south *Sharpshooter Ridge*, set back a little from the bluff edge, but with peaks almost as high as Weir Peaks. At this same midpoint, but between the ridge and the bluff edge, begins a depression that gradually deepens to form *Cedar Coulee*, which runs $\frac{1}{2}$ mile north to the eastern base of Weir Ridge, where the coulee bends northeast. Less than $\frac{1}{2}$ mile downstream from Reno Hill, the bluff edge makes a little jog to the west, and the river, which has been crowding the base of the bluffs, moves away from them as much as a mile in meandering fashion, leaving a wide, flat bottom that extends for a mile down the east bank, which may be called the *East Bank Bottom*. Reno's valley fight took place west of this side bottom.

Three of Reno's men made the third sighting of Custer's column 5 minutes later, at 3:18, just as they halted to deploy the skirmish line. Pvt. O'Neill told Brinninstool (p. 130): "[As the line was being formed] Custer's command was on the opposite side of the river, the space between the columns becoming greater as we advanced; when the fighting commenced, I judge Custer and Reno were about $1\frac{1}{2}$ miles apart. Custer and his five companies now disappeared behind a high bluff, going . . . [downstream] and that was the last we saw of them." Both the distance across the East Bank Bottom and the disappearance behind the bluff edge indicate that Custer was $\frac{1}{2}$ mile below Reno Hill and disappearing into the very head of Cedar Coulee.

At this same moment Lt. Varnum also sighted Custer's column, as he testified (p. 159): "At the time the skirmish line was being deployed [3:18] . . . I saw the gray horse troop [Co. E] moving along the bluffs. . . . It was back from the edge of the bluff . . . and the head of the column was behind the bluff, so I caught only the gray horse company. . . . It was traveling at a not very fast trot." The map used at the Reno Inquiry was a crude and faulty sketch made by Lt. Maguire, Terry's engineering officer, two days after the battle, and baffled all witnesses; Lt. Varnum gave up trying to locate Custer's position on this map and resorted to verbal descriptions, which included (p. 160) "probably $\frac{3}{4}$ mile" and (p. 176) "$\frac{1}{4}$ mile" below Reno Hill. His average thus matches Pvt. O'Neill's $\frac{1}{2}$ mile.

Fred Gerard both testified and told other interviewers that at 3:18, "just as the skirmish line was forming," he saw "Custer's column . . . going at a fast trot . . . and raising dust." His efforts to locate this position on the Maguire map spread from above Reno Hill to below Weir Ridge, but he verbally testified (p. 133) to "$1\frac{1}{2}$ or 2 miles from Ford A"; the average of $1\frac{3}{4}$ beeline miles below Ford A strikes the bluff $\frac{1}{2}$ mile below Reno Hill, in agreement with O'Neill and Varnum. Gerard's later interviews specified "Reno Hill," but this location is eliminated by the timing. Thus three witnesses sighted Custer at 3:18, trotting, about $\frac{1}{2}$ mile below Reno Hill, and two reinforce this location by noting that the column was disappearing from view.

The fourth sighting was made by Lt. DeRudio only, who testified (pp. 269, 285) that he led a few troopers into the timber to head off an attack by Indians on the right end of the skirmish line a few minutes before the entire line withdrew into the timber, and then he saw Custer. I estimate that his sighting came at about 3:30, or 3 minutes before the command entered the timber. It is significant that this sighting was 12 minutes *after* the preceding sighting at 3:18, during which time Custer's column could have trotted another 1.2 miles down Cedar Coulee, far beyond its bend at the eastern base of Weir Ridge, unless it had halted.

DeRudio's sighting was not only much later, but what he saw was unique, for he testified:

> (p. 284): I saw Gen. Custer, Lt. Cooke and another man I could not recognize come on the highest point of the bluff and wave their hats and motion as if cheering; but they soon disappeared, from which I judge that probably his column was behind the bluff.
> (pp. 287–88): Custer could take a nice birdseye view of our position and could have seen the largest portion of the village, but not all of it. . . . Custer and Cooke were dressed in blue shirts and buckskin pants . . . and Cooke had an enormous black beard. . . . Custer [then] went down a narrow deep ravine, from which he could see little.

The highest peak in the area was Weir Peak, on the bluff edge, but DeRudio's attempts to identify it proved confusing indeed. Half his attempts fit Weir Peak, and the timing makes this location essentially certain, for Custer had earlier passed Sharpshooter Ridge and disappeared down Cedar Coulee. As DeRudio obviously learned later, when Custer's party left the peak, it joined the troops somewhere out of sight and proceeded down Cedar Coulee, still out of sight. The implication is that the troops had trotted only $\frac{1}{2}$ mile down the coulee to its bend and halted, while Custer's party climbed Weir Peak and returned, which took additional time. We shall find later, from Custer's own men, that this is precisely what they did.

All four of the successive sightings of Custer on the east bank by Reno's men are interpolated in Reno's itinerary (Table 7) and plotted in Figure 5 as vertical dotted lines, which make important contributions to the "surround" of Custer's advance.

The Actions of Reno's Scouts

Attention is now directed to the thirty-six scouts who served in various ways with Reno's battalion. Their participation in the valley fight deserves recognition, and in addition, their itineraries of the interconnections they made with other units provide valuable support for the entire time-motion pattern.

As a quick reference aid, Table 8 names all these scouts. They are divided into four main categories according to their activities: valley fighters with the troops, valley fighters with the scouts, pony captors, and stragglers.[1]

Quartermaster employees were presumably answerable to Reno, although he ignored them. Varnum, assisted by Hare, had charge of the Indian scouts, but these officers, too, relinquished control before the engagement opened. How did the 21 unsupervised valley fighters perform? A comparison of their casualties with those of Reno's troops provides one kind of answer. Of the 140 officers and men, 35 were killed and 11 wounded, for a casualty rate of 33 percent. Of the 21 scouts, 5 were killed and 2 wounded, for the same casualty rate. Left behind in the timber were an officer and 13 enlisted men, and 3 scouts out of 8 who fought with them. Ten of the surviving scouts remained with the troops until rescued by the Terry-Gibbon column. The rest were listed as "missing in action," until it was learned that all had reported for duty to Maj. Moore at the Powder River base camp.

Lt. Hare gave Camp (p. 65) his general observations on the Indian scouts:

---

[1] The names of the Ree and Sioux scouts used here are those most commonly used in Libby, *Arikara Narrative* (B). For alternate names and those used on muster rolls, ages, and previous enlistments, etc., see Gray, "Arikara Scouts with Custer" (A). The present analysis of their actions is a considerable revision of this early article.

Table 8. The 36 Scouts Who Served with Reno

		June 25		June 28
Category and Name	Status	Action[a]	Code[b]	
VALLEY FIGHTERS WITH TROOPS (8)				
Bloody Knife (Ree)	QM	KIA at Reno's side, 2:51		
Chas. A. Reynolds	QM	KIA at timber's edge, 2:55		
Isaiah Dorman (black)	QM	" " " "		
Geo. B. Herendeen[c]	QM	Left in timber; Reno Hill, 5:35	WA	Reno
Fred F. Gerard[c]	QM	Left in timber; Reno Hill, 26h	Absent	Reno
Wm. Jackson[c] (¼ Blackfoot)	Ree	" "	Absent	Reno
Wm. Baker (½ Ree)	Ree	Reno Hill, 4:10	WA	Reno
Wm. Cross[c] (½ Sioux)	Ree	" "	WA/RG	Moore
VALLEY FIGHTERS WITH SCOUTS (13)				
Black Fox[c]	Ree	Bluffs, 3:52; Reno Hill, 4:30	WA/RG	Moore
Bob-tail Bull	Ree	KIA on E bank, by 4:00		
Little Brave	Ree	" "		
Red Bear[c]	Ree	Reno Hill, 4:10 & 4:30	HH	Moore
White Cloud	Sioux	" " " "	WA/RG	Moore
Ma-tok-sha	Sioux	Reno Hill, 4:10	WA/RG	Moore
Caroo	Sioux	" "	WA/RG	Moore

Name	Tribe	Notes	Status	Source
White Swan	Crow	" " " " WIA"	WA	Reno
Goose	Ree	WIA"	WA	Reno
PONY CAPTORS (7)				
Little Sioux[c]	Ree	(All 7 diverged from Reno's	WA/RG	Moore
Strikes Two[c]	Ree	charge; drove captured Sioux	WA/RG	Moore
Red Star[c]	Ree	ponies up bluff; there met 7	HH	Moore
Boy Chief[c]	Ree	stragglers, 3:20; 14 drove herd	WA/RG	Moore
One Feather	Ree	back to packtrain and halted,	HH	Moore
Bull Stands in Water	Ree	3:45; Pretty Face joined and 15	HH	Moore
Whole Buffalo	Sioux	returned to Reno Hill, 4:32.)	HH	Moore
STRAGGLERS (8)				
Soldier[c]	Ree	(None crossed Little Bighorn; 7 lagged	WA/RG	Moore
Stabbed	Ree	behind on Custer's trail; met	WA/RG	Moore
Bull	Ree	7 pony captors on bluff, 3:20;	HH	Moore
White Eagle	Ree	14 drove pony herd back to	HH	Moore
Red Wolf	Ree	packtrain and halted, 3:45;	HH	Moore
Strikes the Lodge	Ree	Pretty Face joined and 15	WA/RG	Moore
Charging Bull	Ree	returned to Reno Hill, 4:32.)	HH	Moore
Pretty Face	Ree	With packs to 3:45.	HH	Moore

[a] KIA = killed in action; WIA = wounded in action.

[b] WA = Weir advance; RG = rear guard; HH = horse herder.

[c] Left accounts.

While Reno was watering, Hare went on down the valley with the scouts and about halfway to the skirmish line, some of the Rees [7 pony captors] took off after a herd of Sioux ponies. A Sioux with these ponies turned and fired on these Rees, but they chased him and captured some of the ponies and ran them off. The remainder of the Rees went on down [to skirmish] and went into the timber after Reno and his men did; they forded the river . . . about halfway between the timber and where Reno retreated across. Hare remembered seeing the Rees after he got to the top of [Reno] hill on the retreat. He says they were up there while Reno was advancing downstream [the Weir advance].

Let us begin with the story of the pony captors, for they were the first to escape the valley. First, however, the inclusion of Bull Stands in Water as a pony captor rather than a straggler needs justification. All accounts agree that he was with these two categories after they united but disagree on whether he crossed the Little Bighorn. Red Star (pony captor) listed him as a noncrosser, and Red Bear (valley fighter) omitted him from his list of crossers; but Soldier (straggler) never mentioned him as a straggler. Strikes Two (pony captor) specifically (Camp, p. 184) saw Bull Stands in Water in the valley on Reno's charge, and he, Red Star, and Boy Chief (Libby, p. 118) mention him as helping to drive the captured ponies up the bluff *before* they met the stragglers. The weight of evidence thus indicates that he was a pony captor.

As may be summarized from the accounts of the pony captors, they diverged to the right, about in the middle of the charge they were leading (3:10?) in pursuit of some Sioux boys and women across the river. On charging through the timber, they spotted a tempting herd of two hundred Sioux ponies on the East Bank Bottom. Plunging across the river, they had to dash some distance downstream before they could turn the herd back. They saw the village pouring out frantic warriors to rescue the ponies, but the scouts drove their booty fast back upstream, the Sioux gaining on them and opening fire. Just ahead, the river on their right was converging on the bluffs to their left, which forced them to drive the herd up the steep bluff to the top. They made it under hot fire, but at the top their haul had dwindled to thirty-eight ponies.

The scouts' description of the terrain identifies the place where they reached the bluff top as about ½ mile below Reno Hill, where Custer had just passed, for Little Sioux and Strikes Two told Camp (p. 184) that while they were driving the herd up the bluff, some troopers fired down on them. Little Sioux (Camp, p. 180) added that Stabbed (foremost of the stragglers) was among those troopers and signaled them to cease firing; he said they were "the rear of a body of soldiers going downstream," but they may have been a few troopers whose horses had given out. Since the pony captors had diverged from the charge at about 3:10 and had ridden fast for under 2 miles, taking 10 minutes, I post their arrival at the bluff top, now on Custer's route, at 3:20, in their itinerary (Table 9), as the beginning of their interconnection with the rear.

Here the pony captors met six of the stragglers coming on Custer's trail, who joined them to help drive the captured herd back to a safe place. Soldier recalled (Camp, p. 188; Libby, p. 116) that Stabbed had been in the lead, followed by himself, Bull, and White Eagle, with Red Wolf and Strikes the Lodge not far behind. Together, all thirteen drove the herd back on Custer's trail at a fast clip. They overtook and passed Kanipe *before* the latter met Benteen at 3:42, $1\frac{1}{2}$ miles below the lone tepee.

Kanipe recalled (1924, p. 249) seeing these Rees: "As I went back to Benteen, I saw some Indians running along. I thought they were hostile . . . but they were scouts from Reno's command making their getaway from the big battle that was going on." Kanipe told Camp (p. 92 n. 10) that he could not have been mistaken, as there were half a dozen or more and he was within 500 yards of them; he then added: "They passed to my right and went ahead. . . . They had the herd down to a dead gallop and were certainly losing no time. They were raising a tremendous cloud of dust and giving voice to more kinds of yells, yips and ki-yis than I had heard in many a day. Soon after this, I saw Benteen coming."

Strikes Two (pony captor) confirmed to Camp (p. 184) this passing and told of the scouts' meeting with the packtrain, which McDougall located "a little below the lone tepee": "A soldier with stripes on his arm asked, 'How goes it?' While we were going back, we saw the packtrain going along. Bull [Charging Bull, last of the stragglers] and Pretty Face [assigned to the packtrain] were each leading a pack mule."

We now have a fixed starting point and four constraints: the pony captors rode very fast; they passed Kanipe more than $1\frac{1}{2}$ miles below the lone tepee, passed Benteen less than $1\frac{1}{2}$ miles below the tepee, and met the packtrain a little below the lone tepee. A fast pace of about 11 mph meets

Table 9. Itineraries: Interconnections by Reno's Scouts

Unit Events	Clock- Time	dm	dt	mph	Cum. Mi.[a]
PONY CAPTORS AND STRAGGLERS (Custer trail)					
Pony captors lv. Reno charge to capture Sioux herd.	3:10				
Reach bluff; joined by 7 stragglers.	3:20				$5\frac{1}{4}$
Overtake and pass Sgt. Kanipe.	3:36	−3	:16	11.3	$2\frac{1}{4}$
Meet Benteen (unnoted by either).	$3:40\frac{1}{2}$	−.83	$:04\frac{1}{2}$	11.1	1.42
Meet packtrain and halt; Pretty Face joins.	3:45	−.77	$:04\frac{1}{2}$	10.3	.65
Change to fresh Sioux ponies.					
Start back for Reno Hill.	3:55		:10		
Overtake packtrain (unnoted by either).	4:04	.98	:09	6.6	1.63
Arr. Reno Hill; greeted by Red Bear.	4:32	3.12	:28	6.6	$4\frac{3}{4}$
RED BEAR AND WHITE CLOUD (Custer trail)					
Arr. Reno Hill and lv. to join pony captors.	4:10				$4\frac{3}{4}$
Meet 3 Crows and Black Fox; halt to await return.	4:15	$-\frac{1}{2}$	:05	6.0	$4\frac{1}{4}$
Lv. for Reno Hill, as Crows fail to return.	4:25		:10		
Arr. Reno Hill.	4:30	$\frac{1}{2}$	:05	6.0	$4\frac{3}{4}$
Greet pony captors and stragglers at Reno Hill	4:32		:02		
YOUNG HAWK'S PARTY (Reno trail)					
Trapped on E Bank Bottom by Sioux and fight.	4:05				$(5\frac{1}{4})$

Table 9. (*continued*)

Unit Events	Clock-Time	Increments dm	Increments dt	Increments mph	Cum. Mi.ᵃ
Hears heavy Custer firing.	4:25				
Sioux leave upper valley.	4:30				
Lv. for Reno Hill.	4:45		:45		
Arr. Reno Hill.	5:00	$(-\frac{3}{4})$	:15	3.0	$4\frac{3}{4}$
HERENDEEN'S PARTY (Reno trail)					
Scrambles back to timber from retreat.	4:05				(6)
Meets 12 troopers left in timber.	4:10		:05		
Hears onset of heavy Custer firing downstream.	4:25		:15		
Sees Sioux clear upper valley.	4:30		:05		
Heavy firing diminishes; lv. with 12 troopers.	5:10		:40		
Meets Varnum's burial party.	5:29				
Meets Ree rear guard on Weir advance.	5:32				
Arr. Reno Hill.	5:35	$(-1\frac{1}{2})$	:25	3.6	$4\frac{3}{4}$
Interprets for Half Yellow Face and Reno.	5:35+				

ᵃ Miles from lone tepee by Custer's trail; Reno trail miles in parentheses.

all these constraints. The resulting data have been posted in the itinerary for this ride back (Table 9) and plotted in Figure 5.

The pony captor accounts reveal that, on meeting the packtrain and picking up Charging Bull and Pretty Face, the party, now fifteen, halted to allow some laggards to catch up and to exchange worn-out ponies for fresh Sioux mounts from the captured herd. I estimate this halt lasted 10 minutes. Then, satisfied that the troops would rendezvous somewhere on the Little Bighorn, they reversed direction to rejoin them, as it turned out, at Reno Hill. Red Bear (valley fighter), whose movements will soon be narrated, was there to greet the pony captors and stragglers at about

4:32. This return leg of the trip was made at a moderate pace of 6.6 mph, with the scouts thus overtaking and passing the slow packtrain at a calculated 4:04½, 1.63 miles below the lone tepee. These additional data for the pony captor itinerary are posted and plotted, strengthening the general time-motion pattern.

The next of Reno's scouts to escape from the bottom was Black Fox, a Ree valley fighter with the scouts, whose peregrinations have long been a puzzle. The Crows vehemently denied Red Star's hearsay allegation that Black Fox had never crossed the river because he was seen on the bluff with Custer. Two other Rees also deny this allegation: Red Bear (valley fighter) told Libby (p. 22) that Black Fox did cross and diverged from Reno's charge, and Little Sioux (pony captor) told Libby (p. 180) that he saw Black Fox ahead of Reno's skirmish line. Since no one ever mentioned Black Fox among the pony captors and stragglers on their long trip, I have classified him as a valley fighter with the scouts.

There is strong evidence that Black Fox was the first of the valley fighters to escape from the bottom. The story of the three Crows whom Custer released to seek safety in the rear (told in Chapter 22) reveals that they picked up some Sioux ponies and then met Black Fox on the bluff a little below Reno Hill, giving him one of the Sioux ponies; this encounter was *before* Reno's retreat started at 3:53. Then, at 4:10, as already related, Benteen, when a mile above Reno Hill, met "four" Crows driving a few Sioux ponies and took them on to Reno Hill. I said then that Benteen's "fourth" Crow was the Ree scout Black Fox; this conclusion was based on the story of the three Crows, which establishes that after Custer released them no four Crows were together anywhere, for two were with Reno and Curley was still with Custer. Another item can now be added to verify Black Fox's presence.

Red Bear and White Cloud were two valley fighters with the scouts who escaped to Reno Hill at the same time as Maj. Reno. Red Bear told Libby (pp. 124–30) that he had retreated from the scouts' skirmish line with Little Brave but fell behind because of a series of mishaps and had to cross the river separately. He last glimpsed Little Brave on the right bank, dismounted and wounded, a fatality in the making. Red Bear then joined Maj. Reno and some troops halfway up the bluff. As Red Bear reached Reno Hill (4:10), White Cloud, who had been scrambling up behind, joined him. White Cloud proposed to Red Bear that they ride upstream and join the pony captors, who were to come back but had not yet appeared. The pair started out and soon "came to a little hill, from which they saw four riders approaching." Red Bear and White Cloud took them for hostiles at first, but they proved to be "four" Crows, who said, "Two of their number [necessarily Half Yellow Face and White Swan, who had gone with Reno] had been killed [*sic*] . . . and they were going back there [Reno Hill] and then would come back [to join Red Bear and White Cloud]." The two valley fighters waited "a long time," but as the Crows failed to return, they, too, decided to go back to Reno Hill. There they "found Reno with his soldiers still there."

To make the timing specific, an itinerary is constructed for this little excursion. If the scout pair left Reno Hill at 4:10 to trot upstream, they would meet Benteen and his "four" Crows with Sioux ponies $\frac{1}{2}$ mile above Reno Hill at 4:15; the latter, including Black Fox, then rode on to reach Reno Hill at 4:20, but Red Bear and White Cloud, having waited, say for 10 minutes, would reach Reno Hill at 4:30, all as posted in Table 9 and plotted in Figure 5. Thus, when Red Bear and White Cloud met the three Crows, Black Fox was again the fourth scout. Red Bear probably failed to recognize Black Fox because he was now riding a strange pony and, perhaps at a distance, was holding the extra mounts.

It may be recalled that I also used Red Bear to complete the itinerary of the pony captors and stragglers. Having reached Reno Hill (4:30), Red Bear continued (p. 130) that "just then" these scouts began returning to Reno Hill. He correctly named all fourteen Ree scouts but omitted the Sioux scout Whole Buffalo. This first group to arrive were nine who had taken fresh mounts. "After a while" came five more, including Pretty Face, who had "joined them from the packtrain." They were driving a "herd of about 40 horses." I translated "just then" as 4:32, 2 minutes after Red Bear had arrived, in completing the itinerary for the van of these scouts.

Besides Red Bear and White Cloud, two other valley fighters with the scouts escaped to Reno Hill about the same time as Reno (4:10). These were the Sioux scouts Ma-tok-sha and Caroo. None of the four Sioux scouts left accounts, and the Ree narrators were not as systematic in accounting for the Sioux as for their fellow Rees. Since these two were seen on the scouts' skirmish line with White Cloud, as Strikes Two told Camp (p. 183), all three probably retreated at the same time. Two other valley fighters with troops had retreated with the troops. One was Billy Cross, half-blood Sioux, whose own account verifies his presence; the other was William Baker, half-blood Ree, who left no account and was not mentioned at this time by others. Since he spoke English, as did all the others who fought with the troops, and was still with them throughout the fighting on Reno Hill, I surmise that he retreated with the troops.

The next valley fighters on the scouts' extended skirmish line were long delayed in reaching Reno Hill. These were Young Hawk's party of four Rees and two Crows, whose story Young Hawk gave Libby (pp. 92–103). The encircling Sioux forced this line to curl back, and Bob-tail Bull, farthest out on the whip end of the line, had to move mighty nimbly. As the scouts were retreating toward the river, they made a stand to cover the escape of Bob-tail Bull from pursuing Sioux; he managed to reach and cross the river below where Reno was crossing but became another fatality. Young Hawk's party of six also recrossed lower down but was forced to take cover in a grove of timber and underbrush on the East Bank Bottom, near where the converging river and bluffs pinch it off. This event I estimate at about 4:05, and for a considerable time the party was hotly engaged. Goose and White Swan were soon disabled by wounds, but the other four more than evened the score by killing a number of Sioux who held them surrounded.

During this action the party heard some Sioux women exhorting their warriors to kill the scouts. Eventually, Young Hawk noted that the Sioux attack was slackening and the warriors were beginning to ride off downstream, which made him think that Custer had attacked in that direction. He saw many Sioux cross the river and run down past his place of concealment. The troops on Reno Hill, as shown in the next chapter, also noted this exodus of Sioux downstream from 4:25 to 4:30. Young Hawk's party was still trapped after this time, however, for three pony captors, who reached Reno Hill at 4:32, told Libby (p. 9) that, soon after, "they could see downriver much firing around the grove where Young Hawk's party was hiding."

After it had been quiet for some time, Young Hawk ventured to crawl out and look around. Not only was the coast clear of Sioux, but he could see a soldier flag flying on the bluff upstream at Reno Hill. On Forked Horn's suggestion that they join these troops, the scouts placed their two wounded on horses and started in that direction. Young Hawk tied a white cloth to one end of a stick and waved it so the party would not be mistaken for hostiles, as Custer had instructed. On reaching Reno Hill, they saw Lt. Varnum and then Maj. Reno and learned that the horses of Bob-tail Bull and Little Brave had come in alone. Strikes Two (pony captor) told Camp (p. 185) that at some vague time after reaching Reno Hill he and other scouts "went to where they could see the timber, and Young Hawk, Forked Horn, Red Foolish Bear, Goose, White Swan and Half Yellow Face came out of the timber in the valley."

On this evidence I post and plot an itinerary for Young Hawk and his companions, starting at their hole-up position on the East Bank Bottom at 4:05. They witnessed the Sioux exodus downstream at 4:25–4:30 and were reported dead by the three Crows at 4:40 (see Chapter 22). I estimate that they left their hideout at 4:45 and walked with their two wounded for $\frac{3}{4}$ mile to reach Reno Hill at 5:00, which makes a proper sequence in the chronology of Reno Hill.

Six of the valley fighters with the troops remain to be accounted for. Three were fatalities: Bloody Knife was at Reno's side while the companies were forming for the retreat from the timber, when a shot through the head killed him instantly; Charley Reynolds and Isaiah Dorman tried to join the rear of the retreat but were quickly shot down. George Herendeen made 150 yards before his horse stumbled and threw him, forcing him to scramble back to the timber for safety. Fred Gerard and Billy Jackson were simply left behind in the timber, as were Lt. DeRudio and at least thirteen troopers. All these unfortunates were soon gathered in two groups that holed up separately. One group of four remained together until evening, when they got separated into pairs; Gerard and Jackson reached Reno Hill at 11 P.M., June 26, and Lt. DeRudio and Pvt. O'Neill not until 2 A.M., June 27.

When Herendeen returned to the timber (4:05), he found a dozen frightened and dismayed troopers, only half with horses and two or three wounded, though ambulatory. A cool and competent frontiersman, he told them he had survived many a worse scrape with Indians and could get them out of this one, but they would have to abandon the horses and work together under his orders. With the stout backing of Sgt. Charles White (Co. M), he soon had them organized, well concealed, and prepared for defense.

Herendeen's party was not molested by Indians, but he soon heard the onset of heavy firing downstream and noted the exodus of Sioux warriors in that direction. He recalled:

(1876, p. 259): I could hear heavy firing below on the river about two miles distant . . . and learned later it was Custer's command. Nearly all the Indians in the upper valley drew off down the river.

(1878, p. 264): Just as we got settled down, firing below us opened up and we knew Custer was engaged. The Indians had been leaving Reno and going down the valley in considerable numbers at full speed.

(Testimony, pp. 240, 244): I heard firing begin in volleys down the river in Custer's direction, not over half an hour after I got back in the timber. . . . I heard this firing about 20 minutes after Reno's column had left the timber.

Lt. DeRudio, concealed elsewhere in the timber, testified (p. 274) that the onsets of these two events were nearly simultaneous: "The Indians that had engaged Reno did not move down before the firing began, but as soon as they heard the firing." He timed the onsets (p. 272) at "two minutes after Reno arrived on the hill" but later changed this interval (p. 287) to "ten minutes." Gerard also heard firing, but his testimony as to its onset and direction corresponds to the earlier skirmishing of Young Hawk's party, rather than Custer's command.

Herendeen and DeRudio provide only ambiguous intervals, but they can be adjusted to correspond to the more extensive and consistent observations made from Reno Hill and cited in the next chapter. Starting DeRudio's interval at 4:15, when most of Reno's men had reached Reno Hill, and adding his 10-minute interval yields an onset time of 4:25. Starting Herendeen's interval at 4:05, when he probably scrambled back to the timber, and adding his 20-minute interval yields the same onset time, 4:25.

Herendeen best described the character and duration of firing, because he escaped before the later firing of the Weir advance began, which confused the others still in the timber:

(1876, p. 259): The fight with Custer lasted about an hour, when the heavy firing ceased and began to die away.

(1878, p. 264): The firing was very heavy; there were about nine volleys at intervals, and the firing between was quite rapid. The heavy firing lasted three-fourths to one hour, and then died away.

(Testimony, p. 240): The firing began in volleys. A great many volleys were fired, but not very fast, with scattering fire between. After the volleys ceased, there were many scattering shots. It may have lasted an hour, but not over an hour.

If the firing began at 4:25, the 45 minutes of volleys lasted until 5:10 and then died away during 15 minutes to end at 5:25. These auditory interconnections provide the first clues to the timing of Custer's engagement.

When the firing began to diminish (5:10), Herendeen anticipated that the Sioux would vanquish Custer's battalion and then throng back to clean out Reno's men, and he therefore began to lead his dozen soldiers back to safety. Heading straight for the river on foot, they forded it, half at a time, while the other half provided cover. On the East Bank Bottom they encountered five Sioux warriors, whom Herendeen dispersed with a single shot. Seeing troopers on Reno Hill, they turned upstream, covering the $1\frac{1}{2}$ miles at a good walk (3.6 mph), to reach Reno Hill at 5:35.

Herendeen told Camp (p. 226), "When I got up to Reno Hill, White Swan and Half Yellow Face were already there." These two Crows had arrived at 5:00, 35 minutes before Herendeen. On his climb up the bluff, Herendeen noted other events (amplified in the next chapter) that help pinpoint his arrival time and elucidate the actions of others. He also testified (pp. 241–42):

> I met Lt. Varnum with four or five men coming down the hill to meet me [5:29, to bury Lt. Hodgson]. . . . [At 5:32 he also met the Ree rear guard, joining the Weir advance.] The command was not engaged. . . . The packtrain was nearly opposite me, but I don't know when it arrived [5:25, 10 minutes before Herendeen].
>
> Directly after I got on the hill, I had a conversation with Reno. He called me to interpret for the Crow, Half Yellow Face. He asked the Crow's opinion as to what the Indian village was doing. He replied he did not know and went away. But directly afterward he came down and said the Indians were all back again, putting up their lodges in the same place.

These events are interpolated in Herendeen's itinerary (Table 9) and may be visualized in Figure 5 in completed form.

DISORDER ON RENO HILL

When the chastened survivors of Reno's headlong retreat began assembling on Reno Hill at 4:10, they had learned the hard way that their Indian foe was present in overwhelming numbers and primed to fight desperately. And having seen Custer's battalion advancing down the right bank of the river, they would understand, when they recovered their wits, what a hornet's nest it would encounter.

Reno testified (p. 405) that, just before Benteen's arrival at Reno Hill (4:20), he had ridden out to welcome his rescuer. Benteen testified (p. 322) that at that moment he showed Reno the urgent note from Custer calling for quick delivery of the ammunition packs, a direct order not subject to override by Reno or anyone else. Yet Benteen again failed to take action. Five minutes later (4:25) Reno absented himself from his command for nearly half an hour; at that same moment, others on Reno Hill began to hear heavy firing, often repeated, downstream in Custer's direction. Not until 5:05, however, did Capt. Weir move downstream with his Company D toward these sounds of battle, the rest following at intervals over nearly an hour. This was the disorganized movement known as the Weir advance. For Custer, it proved too little, too late.

It would be charitable to skip these unpleasant events, which the officers tried to smother in silence, misinformation, and incoherence. These barriers, however, must be penetrated, not as an exposé, but as necessary to retrieve crucial evidence that completes the Custer "surround." The key to this penetration is the time dimension. I shall therefore focus on timeable events throughout the delay period and the Weir advance and use them to time the onset and end of Custer's engagement. As we proceed, Table 10 will accumulate a full chronology of events at Reno Hill from 4:10 to 6:00. These data are plotted in the time-motion pattern for the Custer "surround" in Figure 5 (last chapter). This chapter closes with a section on the later activities of Reno's scouts which clarifies long-standing confusion regarding Custer's own scouts.

The Long Delay

Reno was clearly upset by the loss of his friend and battalion adjutant, Lt. Benjamin Hodgson (Co. B), killed while climbing the bluff. Hoping his friend might still be alive, he testified (p. 405) that he "went down to the river after him . . . on foot. I suppose I was gone half an hour, leaving Benteen in command." Godfrey's testimony (p. 358) provides confirmation: "Soon after we came up [4:20], I saw Reno talk to Benteen. I understood he was arranging to go down after Hodgson's body." Sgt. Culbertson (Co. A), a member of the party, testified (p. 300) that soldiers joined with canteens to fetch water, that at the river they found two other bodies, and that on starting back they did find Hodgson's body and retrieved some personal belongings; he also confirmed that this mission took about "half an hour."

This testimony suggests that Reno absented himself soon after Benteen arrived, say at 4:25. His 1-mile trip down to the river and back would take 20 minutes; adding 5 more to examine bodies makes a total of 25 minutes, timing Reno's return at 4:50. These data are posted in Table 10, but the simple itinerary is merely plotted in Figure 5 (Chapter 20).

Table 10. Chronology: Events on Reno Hill

4:10	Van of Reno's retreat arr.
"	Red Bear and White Cloud lv. upstream.
4:20	Benteen's battalion, 3 Crows, and Black Fox arr.
"	3 Crows lv. downstream to find Reno's 2 Crows.
4:25	Onset of heavy firing heard in Custer's direction.
"	Reno lv. in search of Hodgson's body.
4:30	Red Bear and White Cloud return to Reno Hill.
"	Sioux warriors seen to have cleared upper valley.
4:32	Pony captors and stragglers arr. with pony herd from lone tepee.
4:40	3 Crows return, reporting 2 Crows killed to Red Star.
4:45	3 Crows lv. for home village.
4:50	Reno returns from search for Hodgson; talks with Varnum.
4:52	Hare lv. with Reno's order to speed up ammo. mules.
4:55	Sound of Custer volleys prompts Weir to ask to move downstream.
5:00	Young Hawk party arr. from bottom; meets Varnum and Reno.
5:02	Reno orders Varnum to bury Hodgson but awaits tools.
5:05	Weir's Co. D lv. downriver to find Custer.
5:10–12	Custer's last heavy firing heard on Reno Hill.
5:12	Hare returns in advance of ammo. mules.
5:15	Hare leaves with Reno's order for Weir to contact Custer.
5:19	2 ammo. mules arr. with tools.
5:21	Varnum lv. to bury Hodgson.
5:22½	Benteen lv. with Cos. H, K, M to join Weir.
5:25	McDougall, Co. B, and Mathey arr. with packtrain.
5:30	Ree horse herders lv. for Powder R.
"	Ree rear guard lv. to join Weir advance.
5:35	Herendeen party arr. from timber; talks with Reno and 2 Crows.
5:40	Reno and orderly lv. to join Weir advance.
5:43	Varnum returns from his burial mission; joins Co. A.
5:52½	Cos. A, B, G, packtrain (impedimenta) lv. to join Weir advance.
5:55	Rear guard, chased by Sioux, passes Reno Hill for Powder R.
6:00	Reno, Benteen, and Co. H return to Reno Hill.
6:02½	Cos. D, M, A, B, G and packtrain return to Reno Hill.
6:10	Godfrey, Hare, and Co. K, covering retreat, arr. Reno Hill.
9:00	Evening battle on Reno Hill ends at dark.

Varnum's testimony (pp. 151–52) reveals that nothing had been done to speed up the ammunition during Reno's long absence:

> Reno came up from the river [4:50] and spoke of finding Hodgson's body. . . . McDougall and the packtrain were not in sight, for Lt. Hare started out soon afterward to go hurry them up. We waited there 5 or

10 minutes, when Reno told me to take a detachment and go down and bury Hodgson's body. I told him I would have to wait for the packs to come up for something to bury him with.

On the assumption that during his absence Reno realized he had erred in not sending for the train before he had left, I post Hare's departure at 4:52, 2 minutes after Reno's return. Accepting that Reno and Varnum remained together for another 10 minutes, I also post at 5:02 the order for Varnum to bury Hodgson, which allows Young Hawk's party to have met Reno and Varnum at 5:00. The chronology in Table 10 posts all arrivals and departures of the scouts during Reno's absence, taken from the last and next chapters.

Lt. Hare confirmed his packtrain mission, although both his accounts begin with misleading time clauses, incompatible with Reno's long absence:

> (Testimony, pp. 257–58): As soon as Benteen joined us [*sic*], Reno told me to go and bring the packtrain up as soon as possible. I went back about a mile and a half and told the captain to move up as quick as possible and get the ammunition. I reported back to Reno. . . . I was gone twenty minutes and got back before it got up.
> (Camp, p. 66): About ten minutes after Benteen came up [*sic*], Reno sent Hare to the packs. Hare's horse had been shot in the jaw . . . and he traded horses with Godfrey [his Co. commander] and started for the packs. He met them north of the North Fork, a mile or not much more from Reno, and returned right away—he was gone about 20 minutes.

Reno, having testified to his long absence, suddenly inserted sentences in a jumbled time sequence that conceals the timing of Hare's departure; from this melange I extract (p. 405): "I told Lt. Hare to act as my adjutant. I sent him to go down to the packtrain, pick out some ammunition mules and get up with them as quick as he could." Benteen, who had ignored Custer's urgent note, never even mentioned Hare's mission.

If Hare left at 4:52 and was gone 20 minutes, he returned at 5:12, as posted in the chronology. Riding $1\frac{1}{2}$ miles back at a good speed of 7.5 mph, he met the packtrain at 5:02, as earlier posted in the packtrain itinerary. Hare's mission, as plotted in Figure 5, strengthens both the packtrain itinerary and the chronology of Table 10.

During Hare's absence came the first abrupt move of the Weir advance. Capt. Weir's Company D, of Benteen's battalion, which had expended no ammunition and so had no need to await the packtrain, started marching alone downstream along the bluff in Custer's direction. As for the time, Camp's interview with Hare (p. 66) indicates that "just as Hare got back [from the packtrain, 5:12], he saw Co. D advancing toward Custer; they were some distance out, but still in sight." Sgt. Culbertson testified (p. 301) that Weir moved out "about 15 or 20 minutes after I returned [from the Hodgson search, 4:50]," which translates to 5:05–5:10. Weir's subaltern, Lt. Edgerly, testified (p. 342) that the move came "about 45 minutes" after his arrival with Benteen (4:20), which translates to 5:05. On this evidence, I post the departure of Weir's company at 5:05.

Reno testified (p. 405) that he promptly sent Hare out again on another mission as his acting adjutant: "After Hare returned from the packtrain, I told him to go to Capt. Weir, who had gone out with a company, and tell Weir to communicate with Custer, if he could, and to tell him where we were." In confirmation, Hare testified (pp. 257–58): "I reported to Reno and he told me to go and tell Weir, who had left while I was gone with the train, to open communications with Custer and that Reno would follow as soon as the packtrain came up." Allowing 3 minutes for Hare to report and leave again, I post his second departure at 5:15.

The next event was the arrival of the two lumbering pack mules at 5:19, bringing two spades, which equipped Varnum to execute Reno's earlier order to bury bodies. Varnum testified (p. 152): "We remained until the [ammo] packs came up. . . . I then got two spades and started with about six men to go down to the river to bury the bodies." I post Varnum's departure on this mission 2 minutes later, at 5:21. His testimony resumes: "About two-thirds of the way down [⅓ mile], I saw a lot of men coming out of the woods and I stopped them to see what was up. There was a citizen [Herendeen] and quite a number of dismounted soldiers, who came from the woods and were climbing the bluffs from the bottom." As noted earlier, Herendeen had mentioned meeting Varnum while approaching Reno Hill. As it would take Varnum 7 minutes to descend ⅓ mile and at least another to stop and talk with Herendeen, I time this encounter at 5:29, which falls on Herendeen's path and thereby supports both itineraries, as sketched in Figure 5.

Varnum's testimony continues: "As I started to bury the bodies, Lt.

Wallace, I believe it was, called me back and I started up the hill immediately, but it was very slow, hard work" (p. 152); "Possibly 20 or 25 minutes from when the packtrain [*sic*, ammo] arrived, I had got up on the hill again" (p. 181). Since the ammunition mules arrived at 5:19, Varnum's return 20 or 25 minutes later came at 5:39−44. I choose 5:43, as posted, making his absence last 22 minutes and leaving 14 minutes for the slow climb back, as sketched in Figure 5.

The packtrain and McDougall's Company B had arrived (5:25) before Varnum had gotten back at 5:43, but the scene had also changed in other ways, as Varnum testified:

> (p. 152): When I got up there most of the command had started to move on down the river along the bluffs, except Capt. Moylan's company [A, to which Varnum belonged], and possibly some of the others. Moylan had most of the wounded . . . and I stayed with him.
> (p. 181): When I got back, the command was on the move . . . and it seems to me that some other companies [had] started about the time I went down the hill [5:21] . . . and just about the time the packtrain [*sic*, ammo] came up [5:19].

Varnum is consistent in saying that other unidentified companies had left near the time he had started his mission; note that he did not report to Reno (nor even mention him in this testimony) but instead helped his captain with the wounded.

Other officers were equally reluctant to identify the three companies that left to join the Weir advance, until Godfrey disclosed the information to Camp (p. 76): "Co. D [Weir's] went out first, then H [Benteen's], K [Godfrey's], and M [French's]." Since M had to replace its expended ammunition from the two ammo mules, it left *after* 5:10, as Varnum hinted. Pvt. Charles Windolph (Co. H) made this fact quite clear to Everitt (p. 8): "Just as soon as the ammunition came up, we all started forth, following the same course as Weir." Benteen's testimony (pp. 322−23) reveals that he left without orders, still ignoring Custer's urgent call for ammunition: "No movement was ordered, but I went in the same direction Weir had gone. . . . When I started, I don't know whether Reno had started [sent Varnum] to Hodgson's body or not. They had next to bury the dead and pick up the wounded. After I left, Reno then brought up the remounts [remnants?], because it was the only thing he could do." On this consistent evidence I post in Table 10 that Companies H, K, and M left Reno Hill to join Weir at $5:22\frac{1}{2}$, only $1\frac{1}{2}$ minutes after Varnum had left to bury bodies.

These separate departures of one and three companies in Custer's direction left at Reno Hill only Maj. Reno in charge of what may be called the impedimenta. For mere minutes, the impedimenta consisted of Company A, now burdened with all Reno's wounded, and the decimated Company G, now in the command of Lt. Wallace, replacing Lt. McIntosh, killed. Then, at 5:25, more impedimenta arrived in the form of Lt. Mathey's slow-moving packtrain, escorted by McDougall's intact Company B, as posted in Table 10.

At this point a heavy fog of incoherence, even disinformation, clouds the accounts, growing denser the higher the rank of the source. I quote only a brief, but illustrative, sample from Reno's testimony (p. 405), on how he took charge of the impedimenta: "After I got the packtrain up, I formed with three companies on the left, the packtrain in the middle, and started downstream. I went 1 or $1\frac{1}{2}$ miles downstream. I was at the head of the column. I regarded Capt. Weir and his Company D as an advance guard." Reno thus conceals the identity of his three companies (A, B, and G); adopts Company D but disowns H, K, and M; has a left and a middle but no right; and rides boldly at the head of the crippled impedimenta beyond Weir Ridge.

This confusion calls for a double-barreled defogger, and one is at hand. As the first barrel, both McDougall (p. 378) and Mathey (p. 370) testified that the impedimenta did not start downstream until "about half an hour" after they had arrived, that is, at 5:55. For reasons that will come clear, I post the departure of all the impedimenta at $5:22\frac{1}{2}$ in Table 10. Reno himself, as confirmed by others, supplies the second barrel in his testimony (p. 412). Admitting that his clock-times were merely hearsay, he insisted that one was absolutely correct: it was 6:00 P.M. when he arrived at Reno Hill on his *return* from Weir Ridge. If we accept this time, the implication must be rejected that Reno and the impedimenta steeple-chased $2\frac{1}{2}$ miles to Weir Ridge and back in 5 minutes at 30 mph. The conclusion is that Reno did not leave with the impedimenta and may not have reached Weir Ridge. That is the key that unlocks the enigma of the Weir advance.

Recognition of this impossibility exposes evidence that Reno did leave *ahead* of the impedimenta and with only his orderly and perhaps a few troopers, as a very small party. There is even evidence as to when he left. It was *after* 5:35, when Herendeen arrived from the timber, for he interpreted while Reno talked with Half Yellow Face. It was also *before* 5:43, when Varnum returned from his burial mission, for he neither reported to nor mentioned Reno, but did help Moylan prepare the wounded for transport. This information alone suggests that Reno left about 5:40, and later interconnecting evidence supports this timing. The departure and return of Reno are also added to the chronology table.

The Reno Hill chronology, as thus far established, can now be used to time other events that throw light on Custer's progress.

The Sounds of Custer's Firing

Shortly after Benteen's battalion arrived at 4:20, the troops on Reno Hill began to hear heavy firing far downstream and also witnessed the exodus of Sioux warriors in the same direction, as did Herendeen and DeRudio, then in the timber. Since all knew that Custer had taken this direction, they realized he was battling Indians. It was these sounds of firing that generated the Weir advance; they also provide auditory interconnections with Custer.

The first object is to pinpoint the onset of Custer's firing, as heard at Reno Hill. Both Godfrey (1892, p. 141) and Edgerly (1894, p. 8) recalled that when they reached Reno Hill (4:20) there was only scattered Indian fire, and even that quickly died down when Benteen's companies dismounted to form a skirmish line along the bluff edge overlooking the river. There a number of men collected and were in a good position to see and hear what followed. About the time Reno's party started down to search for Hodgson's body (4:25), three witnesses testified to hearing the first heavy firing, which they attributed to Custer's battalion and called to the attention of others:

> (Culbertson, pp. 301–2): I heard the firing when Lt. Varnum called to me for some water. We were sitting on the edge of the bank [bluff] and could hear the firing. At first it was a couple of very heavy volleys, and afterward lighter and appeared more distant. Lt. Varnum remarked, "Custer is hotly engaged." A few minutes later, Reno came and I went down to the river with him [4:25]. Reno was on top of the

hill and came right over to us while the firing was going on. He was looking down the river and Varnum was sitting facing downriver.

(Varnum, p. 162): I heard firing away downstream and spoke of it to Lt. Wallace, having borrowed his rifle to fire a couple rounds at the bottom. I was handing it back, when I heard the firing and said, "Jesus Christ, what does that mean?" This was very soon after Benteen came up. It was heavy firing, crack, crack, but not exactly a volley. It lasted only a few minutes. It was from Custer's field and I thought he was having a pretty warm time down there.

(Hare, p. 258): Just after Benteen came up, I heard firing. Godfrey called my attention to it, asking if I heard it and I said yes.

On this evidence, which is compatible with that of Herendeen and De-Rudio, I post in the chronology of Table 10 that the onset of Custer's heavy firing was heard at Reno Hill at about 4:25. Is it mere coincidence that Reno and Wallace, as well as Benteen, claimed never to have heard any heavy firing?

The second objective is to pinpoint the time when the Sioux warriors had cleared out of the upper valley by running downstream toward Custer, a movement that DeRudio earlier testified began right after the onset of Custer's firing at 4:25. On this point Godfrey testified (p. 358), a little ambiguously, that "on reaching Reno Hill [4:20], there were 6–700 Indians in the bottom. They went downstream afterward, about 10 minutes after we arrived [thus at 4:30]." This 1892 description of this event (p. 141) suggests that the time of 4:30 referred to when the warriors had cleared the valley:

At this time ["officers collected on the bluff edge"] there were a large number of mounted Indians in the valley. Heavy firing was heard down the river. Suddenly they all started down the valley [4:25], and in a few minutes scarcely a horseman was to be seen [4:30]. During this time the questions were being asked: "What's the matter with Custer that he don't send word about what we should do?", "Wonder what we are staying here for," etc.

Apparently, a lull followed the initial firing, but it then resumed with more volleys. Many accounts give no clues to the timing, but a few do indicate that it was the sound of repeated firing that precipitated the abrupt departure of Weir's Company D at 5:05. Godfrey (1892, p. 142) implied such a connection:

During a long time . . . we heard firing down the river . . . and were satisfied that Custer was fighting the Indians somewhere. The conviction was that "our command ought to be doing something, or Custer would be after Reno with a sharp stick." We heard two distinct volleys, which brought the remark that "Custer was giving it to them for all he was worth." I have little doubt now that these volleys were . . . *signals of distress* to indicate where he was. Weir and Edgerly . . . heard the firing, became impatient at the delay and thought they would move down that way. [Godfrey's italics.]

Tptr. Martin, who had arrived with Benteen at 4:20, made the connection even stronger when he told Graham (p. 291):

> We heard a lot of firing down the river; it kept up for half an hour [to 4:55]. It sounded like a big fight was going on and the men thought it was Custer whipping the Indians. We all wanted to hurry and join them, but they would not let us go. Capt. Weir had some words with Reno [who had returned to the hill at 4:50], and I could tell . . . he was excited and angry. He waved his arms and gestured and pointed down the river. Then we heard some volleys and Weir jumped on his horse and started down the river all alone, but his troop followed right away.

Lt. Edgerly, Weir's subaltern, clinched the cause-and-effect relationship in his testimony (p. 341):

> We heard firing from down the creek where we supposed Custer was. . . . Capt. Weir and I talked about it. We thought Custer was engaging the Indians. . . . He said we ought to go over there . . . and I told him I was ready to go. . . . He started off . . . [to ask permission] and shortly after came back, mounted his horse, and we started out in the direction of firing [5:05].

I post in the chronology at 4:55 the two volleys that prompted Weir to find and consult with Reno.

It is unlikely that Reno granted Weir permission to move out with only one company, but did Weir act without, or against, orders? Tptr. Martin's reference to vehement words suggests it was against orders, and Pvt. Windolph recalled (p. 8) that "it was known that Weir had a heated argument with Reno and started out alone." Lt. Edgerly dodged the issue until 1883 (p. 179), when he revealed what Weir told him before the latter died in December 1876: "Weir told me he hadn't spoken to Reno or Benteen, but rode out on the bluffs, hoping to glimpse Custer's command. . . . Without orders, but presuming Weir had permission, I mounted the troop and followed him." Benteen, who bragged of leaving later on his own hook, testified (p. 322) that "Weir sailed out in a fit of bravado, I think, without orders." Reno testified lamely that he considered Weir his advance guard. Thus it is a case of "reader's choice."

As quoted earlier, Herendeen, while still in the timber, heard numerous volleys up to 5:10, when the sound died down to scattered fire. Several officers at Reno Hill also heard the last volleys at about this same time. According to Camp's interview with Hare (p. 66), "just as Hare got back from the packtrain [5:12], he heard firing in Custer's direction." Godfrey testified (p. 358) that "soon after Hare came up with [sic, from] the packtrain [5:12], I heard two distinct volleys that seemed a long way off. After that there was scattering fire." McDougall also testified (p. 376) that "about 15 minutes" before reaching Reno Hill, which translates to 5:10, "I heard firing to my right, or north—just two distinct volleys." Moylan testified (p. 224), "I heard firing in the direction of the Custer field about an hour after I reached Reno Hill," which also translates to 5:10. Moylan, however, added an apparent contradiction: "McDougall had come up with the packtrain [5:25] and was deploying his men as skirmishers. I asked him [about the firing] and he said it was Custer." The temporal contradiction vanishes if both Moylan and McDougall had heard the firing at 5:10 but discussed it at 5:25.

Camp claimed in his interview with McDougall (p. 70) that firing was heard as late as 5:25, but this account is so riddled with contradictions that I dismiss it as a misunderstanding and insert corrections:

> As soon as McDougall reached Reno Hill, he reported to Reno [correct]. . . . He says Reno's and Benteen's [sic] men were all quiet [only Reno and Cos. A and G were still there]. As no skirmish line had been formed [it had but withdrew when H, K, and M left at 5:22½], McDougall immediately threw one out [correct]. . . . Right away he heard heavy firing [earlier at 5:10] and asked Godfrey [absent] about it [it must have been Moylan]. McDougall then said, "I think we ought to go down there with him [Custer]," and went up to Reno [present] and Benteen [absent] and expressed the same opinion.

I conclude that the last heavy firing in Custer's direction was heard at Reno Hill at 5:10–5:12, as posted in Table 10's chronology. Note that it was only about 10 minutes before Benteen pulled out on Weir's trail with three more companies, apparently delayed by the need of Company M to replenish ammunition, which arrived at 5:19. The implication is that all four of the advance companies of the Weir advance had responded to repeated heavy firing.

The Weir Advance and the End of Custer's Fight

Table 10 reveals that the uncoordinated Weir advance evacuated Reno Hill in stages from 5:05 to 5:52½. Despite the widespread reluctance of officers to disclose the embarrassing facts, it is possible to reconstruct itineraries for all units throughout the Weir advance, which will be accumulated in Table 11 and plotted in Figure 5 (last chapter) as we proceed. Interconnections between advance and rear units will serve to check the complex time-motion pattern. All these data are necessary because the advance units made observations from Weir Ridge that signal Custer's fate. As usual, more map geography is needed as background.

The north slope of Weir Ridge descends to the rim of *Medicine Tail Coulee*, which drains a little north of west to strike the Little Bighorn where there is a sizable gap in the high bluffs that gives access to *Ford B*, lying opposite the center of the Sioux village. Beyond Medicine Tail Coulee the land slopes up away from the river, but more ravines and coulees carve it into grassy ridges and hills. Among them is *Custer Ridge*, running rather parallel with the river but about a mile back from it; at its northerly end lies *Custer Hill*, the site of the "last stand," nearly 3 miles from high Weir Peak, which gives a clear view of the lower country beyond, including the village and the Custer battlefield.

The significance of this geography is that, when the advance companies reached Weir Peak, they could make visual and auditory observations of the Custer battle area. We already know when they left Reno Hill and that the distance to Weir Peak along the bluff edge is 1¼ miles. With clues to speeds, we can calculate the times at which they made their observations.

When Capt. Weir left Reno Hill at 5:05, alone and without support, to advance toward an invisible Indian battle, audibly in progress, it is reasonable to expect that he proceeded cautiously. At 3.75 mph it would take 20 minutes to march 1¼ miles, timing his arrival at Weir Peak at 5:25. Then, when Lt. Hare started after him at 5:15, bearing Reno's orders to make contact with Custer, he would travel faster; at 7.5 mph,

Table 11. Itinerary-Chronology: The Weir Advance

Unit and Its Events	Clock-Time	dm	dt	mph	Mi. from Lone Tepee
Weir's Co. D: lv. Reno Hill.	5:05				$4\frac{3}{4}$
Hare: lv. Reno Hill.	5:15				$4\frac{3}{4}$
Benteen, Cos. H, K, M: lv. Reno Hill.	5:22$\frac{1}{2}$				$4\frac{3}{4}$
Weir's Co. D: arr. Weir Ridge and halts.	5:25	$1\frac{1}{4}$	:20	3.75	6
Hare: arr. Weir Ridge and halts.	5:25	$1\frac{1}{4}$	:10	7.5	6
Both of above see Custer fight has ended.	5:25				
Hare: lv. Weir Ridge to report to Reno.	5:32$\frac{1}{2}$				6
Benteen, Cos. H, K, M: arr. Weir Ridge and halt.	5:35	$1\frac{1}{4}$	:12$\frac{1}{2}$	6.0	6
All see Sioux coming to attack.	5:35				
Reno party: lv. Reno Hill.	5:40				$4\frac{3}{4}$
Benteen, Co. H: lv. Weir Ridge to find Reno.	5:42$\frac{1}{2}$				6
Hare: meets and joins Reno party.	5:42$\frac{1}{2}$	-1	:10	6.0	5
Benteen, Co. H: meet Reno party; halt 10 min.	5:47$\frac{1}{2}$	$-\frac{1}{2}$	:05	6.0	5$\frac{1}{2}$
Reno party: meets Benteen, Co. H; confers 10 min.	5:47$\frac{1}{2}$	$\frac{1}{2}$	:05	6.0	5$\frac{1}{2}$
Hare: lv. halt for van with Reno's retreat order.	5:47$\frac{1}{2}$				5$\frac{1}{2}$
Hare: arr. Weir Ridge; joins Co. K.	5:50	$\frac{1}{2}$	:02$\frac{1}{2}$	9.0	6
Cos. D, K, M: lv. Weir Ridge for Reno Hill.	5:50				6
Reno, Benteen, Co. H: lv. halt for Reno Hill.	5:52$\frac{1}{2}$				5$\frac{1}{2}$
Impedimenta: lv. Reno Hill for Weir advance.	5:52$\frac{1}{2}$				$4\frac{3}{4}$
Reno, Benteen, Co. H: meet imped.; order it back.	5:57$\frac{1}{2}$				5

Table 11. (*continued*)

Unit and Its Events	Clock-Time	Increments			Mi. from Lone Tepee
		dm	*dt*	*mph*	
Reno, Benteen, Co. H: arr. Reno Hill.	6:00	$-\frac{3}{4}$	:07$\frac{1}{2}$	6.0	4$\frac{3}{4}$
Cos. D, M: arr. Reno Hill.	6:02$\frac{1}{2}$	$-1\frac{1}{4}$	:12$\frac{1}{2}$	6.0	4$\frac{3}{4}$
Impedimenta: arr. Reno Hill.	6:02$\frac{1}{2}$	$-\frac{1}{4}$	:05	3.0	4$\frac{3}{4}$
Godfrey, Hare, Co. K: arr. Reno Hill; covered rear.	6:10	$-1\frac{1}{4}$	:20	3.75	4$\frac{3}{4}$

he would make it in 10 minutes, thus reaching Weir Peak at 5:25, the same as Weir. Lt. Edgerly implied to Camp (p. 56) that Hare arrived very promptly, and Lt. Hare also told Camp (p. 66) that he found Weir on the high peak, but Edgerly and the company to the right, just over onto the north slope.

The question now is, What observations did Company D and Hare make at 5:25, as the first troops to reach Weir Ridge? Cpl. George W. Wylie (Co. D) was with Capt. Weir on the peak, and told Camp (p. 129): "Seeing many horsemen over on the distant ridge with guidons flying, Capt. Weir said, 'That is Custer over there,' and he mounted to go over. When Sgt. [James] Flannagan said, 'Here, captain, you had better take a look through these glasses; I think those are Indians,' Weir did so and changed his mind about going over."

Lt. Hare never testified to what he saw at this time, but what Camp learned from him (p. 67) is worded as a first impression, as mistaken as Weir's: "While out in the advance with Company D, the Indians were thick over on Custer Ridge, and at that moment, Hare thought Custer was firing at them." Lt. Edgerly, however, gave three unambiguous descriptions of the scene:

(Testimony, p. 341): When we got on top of a ridge, we saw a good many Indians galloping up and down and firing at objects on the ground. . . . The firing was loud enough to be heard by the command. . . . I know the men [Custer's] must have all been killed from the scattering fire and firing down at the ground.

(1883, p. 179): I saw no Indians on the bluff during our advance, until nearest the lowest [farthest downstream] point, where we could see the bodies of Custer's men and horses, with swarms of Indians.

(Camp, p. 56): When Edgerly looked over toward Custer field, he saw Indians shooting as though at objects on the ground, and one part of a hill on Custer field was black with Indians and squaws standing there.

These accounts describe not a battle in progress, but a battle's end; many warriors, yes, and even women, but standing around; some shooting, but at bodies on the ground. The time, 5:25, corresponds to Herendeen's statement that the firing lasted no more than an hour, and this kind of firing would scarcely be audible at Reno Hill. I accordingly post in the chronology table that the Custer battle had ended by 5:25, as observed from Weir Ridge.

Benteen's three companies (H, K, and M) were the next to pull out from Reno Hill, at 5:22½. Since Benteen had been chafing at the delay and there was a company well ahead of him, he probably took a 6-mph trot, requiring 12½ minutes to reach Weir Ridge at 5:35, only 10 minutes behind Weir. There is evidence to support this timing and that all three companies arrived together.

Edgerly had led Company D over onto the north slope, but Weir, from the high peak, saw that Indians had spotted the company and signaled Edgerly to circle back to a less exposed position behind the ridge. Edgerly testified (p. 341) that "I did so, and shortly after met Benteen." In 1881 (p. 220) he added that "when I reached Weir, I saw Benteen, Godfrey and French coming toward us with their companies." Hare also told Camp (p. 66) that "Edgerly did not hold his advance position for more than ten minutes." Finally, Pvt. Windolph (Co. H) tied it all together when he told Everitt (p. 8) that "when we came up to Capt. Weir . . . [his company] had run into a large band of Indians and was backing up in our direction."

When Benteen's three companies had their opportunity to observe the Custer field at 5:35, they found the scene had changed materially during the preceding 10 minutes, as best revealed by Godfrey's several accounts:

(Diary): We got on some high bluffs and large numbers of Indians were seen on some bluffs [ridges], about two miles away, but the firing had ceased, except for an occasional shot. Upon our appearance, the

Indians directed their attention toward us and large numbers almost immediately ran toward us. They approached, apparently meaning business.

(Testimony, p. 359): While I was viewing the country, the Indians turned back toward us. We were ordered to dismount and Co. K was placed on the skirmish line above [upstream, or back from] the high point.

(1892, p. 142): Although the air was full of dust, we could see stationary groups and individual horsemen moving about and could tell they were Indians. . . . On the Custer field and a hill two miles away, we saw a large assemblage. At first they appeared not to notice us, although some closer to us did. We heard occasional shots, most a great distance off and beyond the large group on the hill. We concluded Custer had been repulsed and that the firing was parting shots of the rear guard. The firing ceased. The group dispersed, clouds of dust appeared and the horsemen converged toward our position. The command now dismounted to fight on foot.

Benteen provided confirmation, making much of his planting a guidon on the highest peak so that Custer might see them; the rest reveals Benteen's aberrations:

(July 4 letter, p. 300): We could see nothing of Custer, could not hear much firing, but could see numerous bodies of Indians coming to attack us from both sides of the river.

(Testimony, p. 323): When I reached the high point, I first saw the village . . . but no signs of a fight, or men [troops]. In a few minutes the gorge was filled with Indians, and we fell back.

(Testimony, pp. 329–30): Some officers say the battlefield was in sight, but I knew positively that it was not [sic]. I saw no evidence, nor did I hear any firing. . . . I thought the command was still alive. [He had already testified that Custer's men were all dead, 1½ hours earlier.]

These observations, made at 5:35, amply confirm that Custer's engagement had terminated earlier. Only an occasional shot was heard, and no fighting was seen; instead, the mounted warriors were deserting the area en masse and riding toward Weir Ridge with the evident intention of attacking the four advance companies, who dismounted to fight on foot.

Reno's small party was the next to ride out from Reno Hill, at 5:40, a time that is further supported by two interconnections; on his way down, Reno first met Lt. Hare returning to report and then Benteen and Company H returning for a conference. There is evidence that Hare started back from Weir Ridge shortly before Benteen arrived there (5:35), for Edgerly told Camp (p. 56) that "Hare returned to Reno, and then H, K and M came out," and Hare testified (p. 263) that he "reported to Reno what Weir's company was doing when it began to stand at bay and then retired [on Weir's signal]." Thus for Hare's departure from Weir Ridge, I choose 5:32½, 2½ minutes before Benteen reached there. Hare further testified (p. 258) to meeting "the command coming downstream" but soon admitted (p. 263) that "I met Reno when I came back from Weir's line." In confirmation Reno testified (pp. 405–6) that after leaving Reno Hill he "soon received a report from Lt. Hare, who said he had authorized the return of Company D to the main command." When Camp quoted Reno's last phrase to Hare, the latter denied it vehemently (and correctly).

It can now be calculated that if Reno left Reno Hill at 5:40, and Hare left Weir Ridge at 5:32½, both trotting at 6 mph, the two would meet ¼ mile from Reno Hill at 5:42½. This interconnection fits the evidence and is perfectly feasible, thus strengthening the time-motion pattern for the entire Weir advance.

Benteen's similar interconnection with Reno soon followed, but both Reno and Benteen remained forever silent about it; only others let the cat out of the bag. Benteen retreated from Weir Ridge with his whole company, leaving the other three to fend for themselves, an unhappy fact that Godfrey confided to his diary, in code form, though easily cracked: "The Indians, evidently meaning business, Benteen suggested that we go back . . . [to Reno Hill], so as to throw ourselves in position to receive them and protect our stock [horses]. All companies were moved except Weir's [D], French's [M] and mine [K]. [Thus only H moved back.]"

In his brief testimony (p. 359) Godfrey inserted a blatant red herring to help conceal Benteen: "Soon after we were ordered to dismount, I saw the packtrain [sic!] and a part of the command moving to the rear." In his narrative (1892, pp. 142–43) Godfrey resorted again to his code but revealed still more:

> The command now dismounted to fight on foot . . . and Weir's and French's companies were posted to the front of my company next to the river. The rest of the command [Benteen & Co.] moved to the rear, as I supposed, to occupy other points in the vicinity to make this our defensive position. Busying myself with posting and instructing my men, I was startled by the remark that the command [Benteen & Co.]

was out of sight. At this time Weir's and French's companies were being attacked.

Years later Godfrey admitted to Camp (p. 76) that "Benteen did not remain long, but went back and joined Reno." Lt. Gibson, Benteen's subaltern, confirmed this retreat to Camp (p. 81): "When Benteen . . . saw that the Indians were coming over from Custer Ridge to meet them, he said, 'This is a hell of a place to fight Indians. I am going back to see Reno and propose that we go back . . . to [Reno Hill] where we lay before starting here.'" Pvt. George W. Glenn (Co. H) related the same to Camp (p. 136) and then, after an undisclosed jump in time and space, quoted what Benteen told Reno on meeting him: "We looked down and saw the country thick with Indians, and some of the men said, 'Captain, the Indians are getting around us.' [The abrupt jump occurs here.] Benteen said, 'Maj. Reno, we cannot fight from here; we had better fall back and make a stand somewhere.' On our way back the Indians did not press us [Co. H] closely."

It must be emphasized that there can be no quarrel with Benteen's judgment that Weir Peak was no place to make a stand and that they should fall back to Reno Hill. The reasons, however, applied to all four companies, compelling a prompt and strategic retreat by all. Yet Benteen turned back with only his own company and without warning or instructions to the other three.

It can now be calculated that if Benteen and his company left Weir Ridge at 5:42½ (7½ minutes after reaching there) and trotted back, they would meet Reno's party and Hare ¾ mile below Reno Hill, thus ½ mile short of Weir Ridge, at 5:47½. This interconnection provides a further check on the time-motion pattern for the Weir advance.

Two others who were present at this meeting revealed what the principals so assiduously tried to obscure: that it brought a halt (probably of 5 minutes, from 5:47½ to 5:52½) for a conference, which produced orders for a general retreat to Reno Hill. Lt. Hare's two accounts suggest that he was also reluctant to reveal all:

> (Testimony, pp. 258–59): Reno said that position [Weir Peak] would not do, and that we should take the position . . . [at Reno Hill]. He ordered [Hare carried the order] Capts. Weir and French to cover the retreat back. . . . I could see the Indians coming up from down-

stream, and heard Reno say that it was not a good position . . . and that we would go there [Reno Hill] and make a stand. It was very evident that we had to fight. . . . I heard Benteen remark to Reno that he thought it [Reno Hill] was the best place to make a stand and Reno answered that it was.

(Camp, p. 67): Benteen and Reno were discussing matters, and Benteen suggested to Reno that they fall back, as they were in a poor place for defense. Benteen remarked that Indians could pass around them on the east and by the river flat to the west, and would soon be in our rear, if we did not fall back.

Pvt. Davern, Reno's orderly, was the other who testified (p. 293) about this conference:

When the command [Reno's party] started down to where Weir was, I was with Reno, and he at the head [*sic*] of his three companies. After moving down, the column halted and Reno sent after Capt. Weir [sent Hare with retreat orders to Weir]. I heard no orders; I saw Reno and Benteen talking together, but heard nothing. We did not go far [$\frac{3}{4}$ mile], 15 minutes perhaps [including the halt], when the command [Reno, Benteen & Co.] came back. Reno went back and threw out a skirmish line [at Reno Hill].

Benteen kept mum about the retreat, and Reno resorted to incredible incoherence in his official report and testimony, but we are now so near 6:00 that no leeway remains. Reno, Benteen, and Company H trotted back to Reno Hill, where they set up a defense perimeter at 6:00. Meanwhile, Lt. Hare delivered the retreat order to the three advance companies; D and K trotted back to reach Reno Hill a couple of minutes after Reno, but Godfrey, assisted by Lt. Hare, deployed Company K as foot skirmishers to cover the retreat of the others and so were the last to reach Reno Hill. The impedimenta had gotten into motion at $5:22\frac{1}{2}$ but, after struggling a mere $\frac{1}{4}$ mile, met Reno and Benteen and struggled back. All these events are posted in the itineraries of Table 11 and plotted in Figure 5.

One final comment is in order. The moment Capt. Benteen reached Reno Hill, he underwent a remarkable transformation from a recalcitrant and contemptuous subordinate to a conspicuous and inspiring leader, for it was primarily he who held the command together during the ensuing siege of Reno Hill.

The Later Activities of Reno's Scouts

The preceding chapter covered the activities of Reno's scouts on the afternoon of June 25 while all but the five fatalities and the two left in the timber were gathering on Reno Hill. Late in the afternoon these twenty-nine scouts broke up into three groups and one individual (Black Fox, as a special case). One group of eight remained with the troops on Reno Hill to fight throughout the siege of that evening and the next day; they were joined by the two who eventually escaped from the timber, and all ten were at Reno Hill on June 28, after Terry's column had arrived. The other twenty-one had left to reach Maj. Moore's Powder River base camp on June 28. The final column of Table 8 (previous chapter) identifies the ten still with Reno and the twenty-one with Maj. Moore on June 28.

Let us begin with the eight scouts who fought with the troops throughout the siege of Reno Hill. Black Fox, the special case, was apparently with them until the morning of June 26, when he left, alone, for Powder River. All nine probably joined the Weir advance as part of the impedimenta. They included Herendeen, Baker, and the six members of Young Hawk's party, who had two of their own wounded to care for.

Only two of this group left accounts implying their brief participation in the Weir advance. Herendeen recalled (1876, p. 259) that he had been on Reno Hill "not more than 15 minutes," which translates to 5:50, $2\frac{1}{2}$ minutes before the delayed impedimenta joined the rear of the Weir advance, when he "saw the Indians coming up the valley from Custer's fight." In 1878 (p. 264) he wrote that "Reno [*sic*, impedimenta] did not go more than a third of a mile before the Indians met him and drove him back to his old stand on the hill." Young Hawk's story to Libby intertwines his escape from the bottom with the Weir advance but does include (p. 102) that "they rode downstream" and "saw Dakotas riding back," revealing that "the Custer fight was over."

Of more significance is the departure for Powder River of the other scouts, who had gathered early enough on Reno Hill to grow appalled at the confusion, indecision, and inaction of the troops. These scouts had full faith in Custer, but the only sign of him was the sound of distant battle. They were in the charge of no one, for Reno not only ignored them, but had assigned their two officers to other duties. Even their interpreters were dead or missing, severing communications, which helped to precipitate a breakup. The Rees were in unfamiliar country, swarming with enemy Sioux from the largest village they had ever seen. They decided to take charge of themselves, as Red Bear told Libby (pp. 130–31):

> Stabbed was riding around on horseback, making a speech. He said, "What are we doing now, we scouts? We ought to do what Custer told us to do if we were defeated. He told us to fall back to the Powder River, where the rest of the scouts are and the wagons and provisions." . . . Stabbed told them that part of the scouts were to take the herd of horses on, while the rest were to stay behind and keep the Dakotas off. So some of the scouts got ready to go on with the horses.

These scouts thus organized themselves into two parties of ten each, which I dub "horse herders" and "rear guard." Their names are repeatedly given in accounts (see Table 8). The horse herders soon left Reno Hill, taking the back trail to Powder River, but the rear guard was delayed because they decided to join the Weir advance, as Soldier (rear guard) told Camp (p. 189):

> Stab proposed that we [rear guard] follow the ridge toward where Custer had gone. We did so. Sioux were coming and getting around us before we got to the end of the ridge. A group of soldiers stood on the ridge behind us. [Names all ten rear guard.] The Sioux now attacked us and drove us and the soldiers, and we went back beyond the lone tepee. . . . A band of Sioux pressed us hard.

There is evidence that the two groups left Reno Hill at about the same time, but in opposite directions. Red Star (horse herder) told Libby (p. 120) that he "saw the pack mules unharnessed by their drivers," which means that his party started back *after* 5:25. As for the scouts in the rear guard, Herendeen told Camp (p. 225) that he had met them as they started to join the Weir advance while he was nearing Reno Hill with his squad of troopers from the timber: "As we neared the top of the bluff, I met Cross [rear guard] coming down. . . . He had Rees with him and they were all mounted. They went on down [downstream], and I did not see them again on the Little Big Horn. Cross afterward told me that when the Sioux charged Reno that evening, they were cut off and had to cut around and went back to Powder River."

In Herendeen's itinerary (Table 11) this meeting is posted as occurring at 5:32, whereas the departure of the horse herders was after 5:25. This timing prompts the estimate that the two groups left Reno Hill, in opposite directions, at 5:30, 5 minutes after the packtrain arrived and $7\frac{1}{2}$ minutes after Benteen's three companies joined the Weir advance. To reduce clutter in Figure 5, the path of the rear guard on the Weir advance is not plotted; I estimate, however, that when driven back by the Sioux, the rear guard passed Reno Hill at about 5:55. The 5:30 and 5:55 times are added to the chronology in Table 10.

After a three-day ride the horse herders and rear guard arrived at Maj. Moore's Powder River base camp, as recorded there by a sergeant of 6th Infantry: "Billy Cross, with Custer's Indian scouts, came to this camp in two different parties. Cross and one party [eleven rear guard] came at about 2 P.M., June 28, and another party of ten more [horse herders], leading surplus ponies, about 5 hours later [7 P.M.]."[1] Note that the horse herders had started back first but arrived second, and thus they had been overtaken and passed by the rear guard. Note also that the rear guard numbered eleven, for it included Black Fox, as will be shown.

Using the estimated starting times, the arrival times, and map mileages, as well as locations and sun times from Ree accounts, I have constructed itineraries for both parties (Table 12). They reveal that the point of passing came shortly before reaching the divide, 13 miles out, when it was growing dark on the evening of June 25. At about this time both parties had encounters with pursuing Sioux, though neither party was aware of the other's proximity.

When these scouts brought the first news of the Custer battle to Maj. Moore on June 28, Billy Cross, as the only one fluent in English, was subjected to a lengthy debriefing, a verbatim transcript of which was submitted to the *New York Times* (July 13, 1876) in an anonymous letter dated July 4, probably by Lt. Byrne. The questions came in helter-skelter fashion but can be ordered chronologically to yield an account of Cross's participation in Reno's valley fight, retreat, and the Weir advance. The debriefing also solves a long-standing puzzle about Black Fox, to whom we now turn.

Despite their usual confusion regarding Black Fox, Ree accounts agree that he overtook and joined the rear guard, already ahead of the horse herders, at the mouth of the Rosebud on the morning of June 27. Little

---

[1] *New York Herald*, Aug. 1, 1876. This letter by a sergeant of 6th Inf., dated "Yellowstone Depot, July 15," is reprinted by Graham, *Custer Myth*, 356–57 (B).

Table 12. Itineraries: Ree Scouts to Powder River

Date	Unit Events	Clock-Time	dm	dt	mph	Trip Mi.
	HORSE HERDERS					
6/25	Lv. Reno Hill for Powder R.	5:30 P.M.				0
	Pass lone tepee and slow down.	6:17	4¾	:35	6.0	4¾
	In 6 mi., "sun touches hills."	7:47	6	1:30	4.0	10¾
	Shots ahead, pursuit behind; lose trail.	8:30?				
6/26	Halt to water; cross divide "in dark."	9:17	2¼	1:30	1.5	13
	Pass Rosebud (Busby) "at midnight."	12:04 A.M.	12½	2:47	4.5	25½
	Arr. Lame Deer Cr. "at daylight"; camp.	4:19	17	4:15	4.0	42½
	Lv. camp "at sundown."	8:00 P.M.		15:41		
6/27	"Noon," mouth of Rosebud; see rear guard trail.	11:35 A.M.	53	15:35	3.4	95½
	Camp for night short of Tongue R.	7:05 P.M.	30	7:30	4.0	125½
6/28	Arr. Powder R. base camp.	7:00 P.M.	36	9:00	4.0	161½
	REAR GUARD					
6/25	Driven past Reno Hill for Powder R.	5:55 P.M.				0
	Passes lone tepee and slows down.	6:43	4¾	:48	6.0	4¾
	6 mi. beyond lone tepee.	8:13	6	1:30	4.0	10¾
	Final attack by pursuing Sioux.	8:30?				
	Passes divide "before dark."	8:47	2¼	:34	4.0	13
	Passes Rosebud (Busby).	11:45	12½	3:08	4.0	25½
6/26	Passes Lame Deer Cr. "at daylight."	4:00 A.M.	17	4:15	4.0	42½
	Arr. mouth of Rosebud "in evening"; camp.	5:15 P.M.	53	13:15	4.0	95½
6/27	Black Fox overtakes, "8 A.M. breakfast."	8:00 A.M.				
	Camp for night at Tongue R.	5:30 P.M.	38	9:30	4.0	133½
6/28	Arr. Powder R. base camp.	2:00 P.M.	28	7:00	4.0	161½

Sioux (rear guard) gave Libby (p. 155) the most detailed account of this event:

> They were cooking breakfast when Black Fox came in sight a long way off, at about 8 o'clock. Little Sioux was sent back to meet him and called to him that he was an Arikara, but Black Fox could not hear him, as the wind was wrong, and thought it was a party of Dakotas. Black Fox got off the Dakota horse he was riding, leaving it saddled, and mounted his own bareback. He . . . [finally recognized Little Sioux] and rode out, glad to see Little Sioux.

Note first that Black Fox had two horses, one his own and the other a Sioux pony (given him earlier by the three Crows). Note also that no other scout is left unaccounted for, so that Black Fox was the sole scout who could have joined the others on the back trail.

This fact positively identifies Black Fox as the unnamed scout whom Billy Cross referred to in his debriefing as an overtaking Ree: "One of the Ree scouts overtook us yesterday [June 27] and told me the fight [at Reno Hill] was going on yet. . . . This other scout told me that . . . [more men] had been killed on Monday [June 26]." Cross was thus saying that this other scout, who could only have been Black Fox, did not leave Reno Hill until June 26 but overtook the rear guard on June 27. An addendum to the debriefing confirms this:

> Another scout [Black Fox], just arrived, was interpreted to say: "I left Monday [June 26] about 10 [A.M.]. They were fighting Sunday night and early Monday morning. They commenced about sunrise; the Indians began the attack. I 'skinned out' because it was getting too hot. The troops were out of water and didn't try to get down to water [but did after he left]. Bloody Knife was killed in the first day's fight."

Not only is every detail given by Black Fox correct, but his overtaking ride is reasonable and feasible. He had 22 hours to cover 96 miles at an overall speed of 4.36 mph; with two horses to ride alternately at 6 mph, he could even have slept for 6 hours of darkness.

This revelation of Black Fox's late departure yields a bonus, for the misinformation about this Ree scout has always entangled the three Crows and Curley. Red Star provides a last glaring example; although a horse herder, he ventured to tell Libby (p. 120) what Black Fox told the rear guard on overtaking them: "In answer to their queries, Black Fox said he and Curley got together near Reno ford. Curley told Black Fox he would take him back to show him where the soldiers left some hardtack. So Curley took Black Fox to the flat below the hills overlooking the present Busby, north side. Curley told Black Fox that for his part he was going home."

This nonsense apparently gave birth to the fable that Curley went home by way of Busby and the mouth of the Rosebud. To begin with, Curley headed for Gibbon's base camp at the mouth of the Bighorn and insisted he met no one. Since he knew the country intimately, it is absurd to think he would take so roundabout a route, every inch over enemy Sioux country. That Black Fox would be seeking hardtack, when it was freely available at Reno Hill, is equally absurd. What makes the tale impossible is that when Black Fox left Reno Hill at 10 A.M., June 26, Curley was far down Tullock's Fork, and when Black Fox met the three Crows on the bluff before 4:00 P.M. on June 25, Curley was still with Custer.

We are finally ready to return to Custer's battalion and his scouts.

CUSTER MOVES DOWN THE RIGHT BANK

Two chapters ago we left Custer's battalion at the North Fork of Reno Creek, where Adjt. Cooke brought the unexpected news that the Sioux village was not fleeing, but pouring out warriors to attack Reno's three companies. Unable to wait longer for Benteen, Custer led his five companies at 3:01 downstream along the ridge toward the bluffs in order to assess Reno's situation, see the village for himself, and find a route by which to launch a supporting flank attack.

Since, from this point on, Custer's route has usually been considered unknown, two chapters were devoted to constructing a "surround" of interconnections that impose hard constraints on his movements, both in time and space, and from which heavy dividends may now be drawn.

The March to Reno Hill

Reno's men in the valley first spotted Custer's men on the bluff on the east bank of the river at about 3:05, only 4 minutes after Custer had left the North Fork. Then, while charging down the bottom, Reno's men again saw Custer's column on Reno Hill at about 3:13, 8 minutes later. This timing implies that Custer took the direct route along the rising ridge to Reno Hill, a distance of $1\frac{1}{2}$ miles, in 12 minutes, at a lively pace of 7.5 mph. Accounts from Custer's men confirm both the route and the speed, and reveal that from Reno Hill they saw Reno's men charging down the bottom, making this a mutual cross-sighting.

The accounts of Sgt. Daniel Kanipe, of Capt. Tom Custer's Company C, are presented first, for the special reason that as the first courier Custer sent back, Kanipe had no opportunity to confuse events of this first segment of Custer's march with subsequent ones. His three consistent accounts are quoted in chronological order:

(1903, p. 280): Custer . . . charged up the bluffs on the bank of the Little Big Horn. . . . When we reached the top . . . we were in plain view of the Indian camp, . . . we were charging at full speed. Reno and his troops were seen to our left, moving at full speed down the valley. At sight of the camp, the boys began to cheer. Some horses became so excited that some riders were unable to hold them in ranks, and the last words I heard Custer say were, "Hold your horses in, boys; there are plenty of them down there for all of us." Custer and troops were within half a mile [*sic*] of the Indian camp, when I received the message from Capt. Custer . . . [quotes message to McDougall and Benteen]. [Then, on my return,] the packtrain went directly to the bluff, where I had left Custer. When we reached there, we found Reno . . . and Benteen [thus Reno Hill].

(1908, p. 92) [At North Fork] Custer turned square right, increasing our speed; he never left his companies or halted. When the command got up on the bluff . . . we could see across the valley . . . see Reno, his three companies and about 35 Indian scouts going right to the Indian camp, which we could plainly see. . . . (p. 137): Nathan Short was with the company [C], when I left it at Reno Hill.

(1924, p. 249): We headed for the range of bluffs . . . riding hard . . . and reached the top. . . . We could see the tepees for miles. . . . When the troops saw the Indian camp in the valley, they began to holler and yell and we galloped along to the far end of the bluffs. . . . Just then Capt. Custer told me to go back and find McDougall [again quotes message]. I went back . . . and the others went on. . . . I remember Custer's last words; the men were on the hill and we all gave three cheers, riding at a full gallop; some could not hold their horses and galloped by Custer who shouted, "[repeats this quote]."

Kanipe's accounts agree on the following salient features: (1) Custer moved rapidly downstream directly toward Reno Hill; (2) from Reno Hill the command saw the Indian village and Reno's battalion charging down the valley, which evoked cheering; (3) some horses, having got out of control, were checked, and the column proceeded on without a halt; (4) Kanipe was very soon sent back with oral messages for McDougall and Benteen, telling of a big village and calling for the packtrain.

Pvt. Peter Thompson (Co. C) confirmed these salient points but identified Reno Hill only indirectly by soon meeting the Ree pony captors. His verbose pages (153–57) are condensed to the following paragraph:

After Reno left us we travelled parallel to the river, leaving the valley [of Reno Creek], and began to climb the bluffs overlooking the river, our horses in a trot. We soon gained the top of the bluffs and viewed the surrounding country. We came in sight of the village on the left bank, the tepees stretching for three miles, and beyond was a black mass of grazing ponies. On sighting the village, the companies gave the charging yell and urged their horses into a gallop. From this point I was gradually left behind. The Indian village was in commotion, because Reno's three companies, a mile distant from it, were galloping toward it. . . . I saw a party of Rees driving a bunch of horses captured from the Sioux.

Nine interviews from four of Custer's Crow scouts paint the same picture of seeing Reno's charge and the Sioux village from Reno Hill, where Custer waved his hat. Curley made it especially clear that Mitch Boyer had led them up along the ridge, ahead of the troops, and on reaching an early knoll, they saw that Reno's column had crossed the river and that Custer's was in motion. It is thus possible that the first sighting by Reno's men at 3:05 was of these scouts rather than the troop column.

All this concordant evidence was presented first because it provides the key to the confusing testimony of Tptr. John Martin, who was the sole person with Custer at this time who testified at the Reno Inquiry. He was the second courier sent back by Custer, but some time later than Kanipe. Inept questioning made his testimony *appear* to mention only one courier and one sighting of the valley by Custer. But now that we know the events that preceded Kanipe's departure, they can be recognized in Martin's testimony, *before* a bombshell order forced him to skip far ahead.

Because Martin's testimony (pp. 312–13) was elicited in such disorderly fashion, I place his answers in more coherent sequence:

> From the watering place [North Fork] to the top of the ridge was about an hour and a half [*sic*, he was asked the distance, and 1½ *miles* is correct for Reno Hill]. We went down the right bank of the river. We did not travel very fast, but at a regular trot up [climbing]. The horses began galloping again on the level. From on top of the ridge, we could see the river below [downstream]; the river was right at the foot of the bluff [true at Reno Hill]. There we looked down [downstream] on the bottom and saw the Indian village and the ponies, dogs and children around the village. We did not see any warrior Indians at all. Custer thought they were sleeping in their tepees. We could see nothing of Reno's column at all [see below]. We could not hear any firing [Reno was still charging]. After seeing the village and no Indians around, Custer pulled off his hat and waved it: "Courage, boys, we have got them. As soon as we get through, we will go back to our station." Some fast horses wanted to go ahead and it was hard to hold them back. . . . [ellipsis postponed]. We went about 300 yards farther and Custer called his adjutant [*sic*, Tom Custer] and sent an orderly [Kanipe] back to Benteen [and McDougall].

All the events that Martin relates had also been mentioned by Kanipe and therefore can only pertain to this first segmental march to Reno Hill. Martin, however, saw neither Reno's charge nor warriors in the bottom; he must not have looked or was in a poor position to see over the bluff edge to the near bottom, but he did see the river and village downstream. At that moment, unmounted Indians were herding the women and children to the north end of the village, running west to the pony herds, or running upstream through the timber to check Reno's charge.

In the postponed ellipsis Martin told of events that followed Kanipe's departure (to be quoted later). He apparently realized this mistake and tried to correct himself in the last quoted sentence by speaking of an orderly (not a trumpeter) in the third person (not as himself) being sent back, as we know Kanipe was. But before Martin, a recent Italian emigrant with poor English, could make that clear, the interrogator interrupted with a bombshell order: "Tell about the order *you* got *there*." Martin, of course, had got no order there but, as an obedient witness, jumped far ahead of his story. The ellipsis only partially filled the gap, but the witness later gave a red-flag clue to the hiatus by saying that on his ride back to Benteen he went $\frac{3}{4}$ mile before reaching the point where "Custer saw the village the first time." This phrase also implies that he knew Custer saw the village more than once.

It was earlier established that both Benteen and the packtrain followed Custer's route to Reno Hill, and so did the Ree stragglers. Soldier told Libby (p. 116) that "at the ridge, they began to see signs of Custer's march . . . trails through the grass," and soon overtook two of Custer's troopers whose horses had given out. Before meeting the pony captors, $\frac{1}{2}$ mile beyond Reno Hill, Soldier "saw the whole Dakota camp and . . . Bob-tailed Bull far out on the end of the [scouts' skirmish] line." Even Reno testified (p. 417) that just after 4:50 that afternoon he had "seen Custer's trail . . . of shod horses" close to Reno Hill.

With this wealth of concordant evidence, there is no hesitation in posting the itinerary for Custer's march from the North Fork to Reno Hill, with sighting interconnections, in itinerary Table 13. The data are also plotted in the final time-motion pattern of Figure 6, which serves this chapter as well as the next. A further critical check on this march is provided by Kanipe's courier ride, which made an interconnection with the rear units.

As already quoted, Martin estimated that the first courier was sent back from a point "about 300 yards" or $\frac{1}{8}$ mile beyond Reno Hill, far enough to have pulled the excited horses down to a trot and given Kanipe his instructions. Thus Kanipe turned back at about 3:15 from a point $4\frac{7}{8}$ miles from the lone tepee, and since we already know that Benteen met him at 3:42, $1\frac{1}{2}$ miles below the lone tepee, Kanipe rode $3\frac{3}{8}$ miles back in 27 minutes at 7.5 mph, which is perfectly satisfactory for a courier. His time-motion path and that for the pony captors and stragglers intersect at 3:36, $2\frac{1}{4}$ miles below the lone tepee, and by extrapolation at 7 mph, he met and joined the packtrain 0.8 miles below the lone tepee at 3:48. These data are posted in Kanipe's itinerary in Table 13 and plotted in Figure 6. Kanipe's interconnection thus strengthens the paths of Custer, Benteen, the packtrain, and the pony captors, as another dividend from the "surround" technique.

Table 13. Itineraries: Custer and All Interconnections

Unit Events	Clock-Time	dm	dt	mph	Mi. from Lone Tepee
CUSTER'S BATTALION					
Lv. No. Fork of Reno Cr.	3:01				$3\frac{1}{4}$
(Sighted on bluff by Reno's men.)	3:05	$\frac{1}{2}$	:04	7.5	$3\frac{3}{4}$
Passes Reno Hill; sees Reno charge and village.	3:13	1	:08	7.5	$4\frac{3}{4}$
Kanipe lv. for Benteen and packtrain.	3:15	$(\frac{1}{8})$			$(4\frac{7}{8})$
Passes Sharpshooter Ridge; enters Cedar Coulee.	3:18	$\frac{1}{2}$	:05	6.0	$5\frac{1}{4}$
Sees Reno halt to skirmish.	3:18				
Arr. bend of Cedar Coulee and halts.	3:23	$\frac{1}{2}$	:05	6.0	$5\frac{3}{4}$
Custer lv. on sidetrip to Weir Peak.	3:24				
Three Crows lv. halted command.	3:26				
Custer returns from Weir Peak.	3:34		:11		
Martin lv. for Benteen.	3:34				
Custer starts down Cedar Coulee.	3:34				
Halts at mouth of Cedar Coulee.	$3:46\frac{1}{2}$	$\frac{5}{8}$	:$12\frac{1}{2}$	3.0	$6\frac{3}{8}$
Boston Custer overtakes with news.	3:49				
Sees signals by Boyer and Curley on Weir Ridge.	3:55				
Starts down Medicine Tail Coulee.	$3:56\frac{1}{2}$		:10		
Halts in Med. T. Coulee; Boyer, Curley join.	4:04	$\frac{3}{8}$	:$07\frac{1}{2}$	3.0	$6\frac{3}{4}$
CUSTER'S SIDETRIP TO WEIR PEAK					
Custer, officers, Boyer, Curley lv. bend.	3:24				$5\frac{3}{4}$
Arr. Weir Peak; see village and Reno skirmishing.	3:28	$\frac{1}{4}$	:04	3.75	6

Table 13. (*continued*)

Unit Events	Clock-Time	Increments			Mi. from Lone Tepee
		dm	*dt*	*mph*	
Find concealed route to ford B and village.	3:30				
Custer and officers lv. peak for command.	3:31		:03		
Arr. at halt in bend.	3:34	$-\frac{1}{4}$	:03	5.0	$5\frac{3}{4}$
KANIPE'S COURIER RIDE					
Lv. Custer for Benteen and packtrain.	3:15				$4\frac{7}{8}$
Overtaken and passed by Ree pony captors and stragglers.	3:36	$-2\frac{5}{8}$	:21	7.5	$2\frac{1}{4}$
Meets Benteen's battalion.	3:42	$-\frac{3}{4}$	:06	7.5	$1\frac{1}{2}$
Meets and joins packtrain.	3:48	$-.7$	:06	7.0	.8
MARTIN'S COURIER RIDE					
Lv. Custer, bend of Cedar Coulee, for Benteen.	3:34				$5\frac{3}{4}$
Meets Boston Custer, head of Cedar Coulee.	3:38	$-\frac{1}{2}$	:04	7.5	$5\frac{1}{4}$
Sees Reno fighting in timber.	3:40	$-\frac{1}{4}$	:02	7.5	5
Meets and joins Benteen's battalion.	3:58	$-2\frac{1}{4}$	:18	7.5	$2\frac{3}{4}$
BOSTON CUSTER OVERTAKES CUSTER					
Passes lone tepee.	2:45				0
Passes Reno Hill; Reno fight visible next 5 min.	$3:32\frac{1}{2}$	$4\frac{3}{4}$	$:47\frac{1}{2}$	6.0	$4\frac{3}{4}$
Meets Tptr. Martin.	$3:37\frac{1}{2}$	$\frac{1}{2}$	:05	6.0	$5\frac{1}{4}$
Joins Custer, halted at mouth of Cedar Coulee.	3:49	$1\frac{1}{8}$	$:11\frac{1}{2}$	6.0	$6\frac{3}{8}$
THREE CROWS RIDE BACK					
Lv. Custer, bend of Cedar Coulee (off-trail).	3:26				$5\frac{3}{4}$
Halt on bluff above Weir Peak.	$3:28\frac{1}{2}$	$\frac{1}{4}$	$:02\frac{1}{2}$	6.0	6
See Reno skirmish, fire at Sioux, then lv.	3:33		$:04\frac{1}{2}$		
Halt (drink in Little Bighorn, capture 5 ponies).	3:39	$-\frac{1}{2}$	:06	5.0	$5\frac{1}{2}$
Continue upriver.	3:49		:10		

Table 13. (*continued*)

Unit Events	Clock-Time	Increments			Mi. from Lone Tepee
		dm	dt	mph	
Black Fox joins, given Sioux pony (Custer trail).	3:52	$-\frac{1}{4}$	:03	5.0	$5\frac{1}{4}$
Pass Reno Hill; see Reno's retreat.	3:58	$-\frac{1}{2}$	:06	5.0	$4\frac{3}{4}$
Meet and join Benteen's battalion.	4:10	-1	:12	5.0	$3\frac{3}{4}$
Meet Red Bear and White Cloud.	4:15	$\frac{1}{2}$	:05	6.0	$4\frac{1}{4}$
Pass Reno Hill, seeking Reno's 2 Crows.	4:20	$\frac{1}{2}$	:05	6.0	$4\frac{3}{4}$
Arr. Sharpshooter Hill; hear Custer firing.	4:30	$\frac{1}{2}$	:10	3.0	$5\frac{1}{4}$
Arr. Reno Hill; Crows dead; will go home.	4:40	$-\frac{1}{2}$	:10	3.0	$4\frac{3}{4}$
Lv. Reno Hill for home.	4:45		:05		

On to Weir Peak

Having caught his first glimpse of the Sioux village at 3:13 from Reno Hill, Custer saw that it was impressively large, and its still-standing lodges gave convincing evidence that it would fight. Though Reno's three companies, charging down the valley, were clearly headed for trouble, a supporting flank attack was not yet feasible, for the steep bluff, several hundred feet high, blocked Custer's access to the river. He could only reduce speed to a controlled trot and continue to seek a suitable crossing place.

A little ahead loomed the north-running Sharpshooter Ridge, which Custer would have to pass; the trail on the left was direct and level, whereas that on the right was roundabout and hilly. Taking the trail on the left, between the ridge and the bluff edge, Custer trotted $\frac{1}{2}$ mile beyond Reno Hill in 5 minutes to reach a point opposite the center of this ridge, where he entered the shallow head of Cedar Coulee at 3:18. At this same moment, Reno halted his charge to deploy his open skirmish

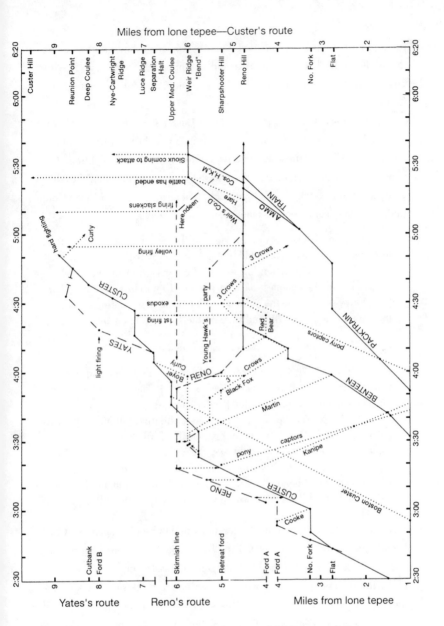

Figure 6. Time-Motion Pattern: Custer and All Interconnections

line, and three of his men spotted a part of Custer's column trotting along the bluff ½ mile below Reno Hill and disappearing from view, leaving no doubt as to the time and Custer's speed, route, and entrance into Cedar Coulee.

The Crow scouts amply confirmed that Custer's column passed Sharpshooter Ridge, saw Reno's men halt and deploy a skirmish line, and entered Cedar Coulee, thus making this another mutual cross-sighting. The Crows did not use our landmark names, but some hinted that they lingered a little to watch Reno's fight begin before they followed Custer into Cedar Coulee. Two accounts came from Goes Ahead:

(Dixon, p. 167): We were in sight of the Sioux camp. As we stood looking, we saw Reno take his battle position [3:18].

(Libby, p. 154): When [*sic*, after] they arrived at the point where Lt. Hodgson's headstone was later placed [Reno Hill], the three [*sic*, four] Crow scouts saw the soldiers under Reno dismounting in front of the Dakota camp [3:18], and thought the Dakotas too many.

Hairy Moccasin also gave two relevant accounts:

(Camp, p. 177): Custer's command, as well as Boyer and the four Crows, saw Reno's fight in the valley [3:18+]. Then Custer and command turned down south coulee [Cedar Coulee].

(Coffeen, p. 67): Custer told us to go to the high hill ahead [Sharpshooter Ridge], the high point just north of where Reno later entrenched. From here we could see the village and could see Reno fighting [3:18+]. . . . We four scouts turned and charged north to where Custer was headed. . . . We went with the command down into a dry gulch [Cedar Coulee], where we could not see the village.

Curley, in his near-deathbed interview with his English-speaking Crow friend, Russell White Bear (1923, p. 13), said: "The troops kept marching on the east side of Reno Hill and going downstream on the west side of the [Sharpshooter] ridge down a ravine running northward [Cedar Coulee]." Tptr. Martin also confirms this sequence in the ellipsis postponed from his previous testimony: "We passed high bluffs [Sharpshooter Ridge], where the Indians were after the fight [siege of Reno Hill]. After that we went a little more to the right and Custer found a ravine [Cedar Coulee] and went down it." If Martin saw anything in the valley from here, the bombshell order silenced him. All this evidence from Custer's men, as well as Reno's, establishes Custer's route, and the mutual cross-sighting helps fix the time, as posted and plotted.

It can now be said with some confidence that from the bluff in front of Sharpshooter Ridge Custer learned that Reno, unable to push his charge into the village itself, was halting to deploy a skirmish line. Reno should thus be able to hold out for a time, which Custer now needed, for he could see that the high, steep bluffs extended for at least another $\frac{3}{4}$ mile to Weir Ridge, which blocked his view beyond. In fact, its high peak on the bluff edge was the very point he needed to head for in order to examine the country beyond and find a place to cross the river for an attack. To march there along the bluff edge, however, would parade his entire force in full view of the enemy. It would be better to take a concealed route down Cedar Coulee leading north, but back from the bluff edge, to the eastern base of Weir Ridge. That is undoubtedly the reason he entered the head of Cedar Coulee.

Custer's movement down Cedar Coulee needs a little more geography. As a tributary of Medicine Tail Coulee, Cedar Coulee drains northward for only $\frac{1}{2}$ mile, where a "*bend*" directs it northeast (away from the river) for $\frac{5}{8}$ mile before joining Medicine Tail Coulee. At its "bend" the coulee comes closest to Weir Peak, only $\frac{1}{4}$ mile to the northwest. From the mouth of Cedar Coulee, Medicine Tail Coulee descends a little north of west to join the Little Bighorn where there is a gap $\frac{1}{2}$ mile wide in the steep river bluff, giving easy access to Ford B and the Sioux village. Medicine Tail Coulee has another south branch, which may be called *Weir Peak Coulee*, for it heads on the north slope of Weir Peak and drains northward for $\frac{5}{8}$ mile to join the main coulee $\frac{1}{2}$ mile below the mouth of Cedar Coulee and 1 mile above Ford B. Interviewers had some trouble deciding whether their informants were referring to Weir Peak Coulee or Cedar Coulee.

At about 3:30, when Reno was preparing to withdraw his open skirmish line into the timber, Lt. DeRudio saw Custer, Adjt. Cooke, and one other on Weir Peak, but not the troop column, as related earlier. That was still another mutual cross-sighting, but before I present the considerable evidence supporting it, its feasibility can be demonstrated by an itinerary for the march and halt of the troops and for Custer's sidetrip to Weir Peak.

Entering the head of Cedar Coulee at 3:18, the column descended it for $\frac{1}{2}$ mile in 5 minutes (6 mph) to halt at its "bend" at 3:23. Custer's small party then left a minute later, at 3:24, to climb $\frac{1}{4}$ mile northwest in 4 minutes (3.75 mph) and reach Weir Peak at 3:28. Making observations from there for 3 minutes, they were seen by DeRudio at about 3:30. Leaving at 3:31, Custer descended $\frac{1}{4}$ mile in 3 minutes (5 mph) to rejoin the halted column at 3:31, thus making the troop halt last 11 minutes. The data of this feasible pattern are also posted and plotted.

Before Custer's party left the halted column at 3:24, the general had ordered the release of all five of his scouts to seek safety in the rear. Boyer and Curley rejected this offer, but the other three Crows did turn back, as Curley specifically told Camp (1913, p. 172): "The four Crows remained with Custer until we got to the base of the ridge south of Medicine Tail Coulee [thus Weir Ridge]. Here Hairy Moccasin, White Man Runs Him and Goes Ahead left us, and Mitch and I went on." By eliminating out-of-sequence events that recognizably came later, we can extract the same story from Hairy Moccasin, who told Coffeen (p. 67) that the four Crows followed Custer down Cedar Coulee, and "when we met [overtook?] Custer he asked, 'How goes it?' I said, 'Reno's men are fighting hard.' Custer told Mitch Boyer to tell us to go back to[ward] the packtrain, which we did. We saw no more of Curley after that." Hairy Moccasin also told Camp (p. 177) where this separation occurred: "Mitch Bouyer told us to go. Curley left us at Weir Ridge [base thereof?]." The fact that none of the three Crows claimed to have gone to Weir Peak or to have seen anything from there, with or without Custer, implies that they turned back from the halt at the "bend" and probably right after being dismissed. Their accounts of their trip back to meet Benteen make this early departure necessary, as will soon be demonstrated.

Curley told Russell White Bear (p. 19) about Custer's sidetrip to Weir Peak:

> At this point ["bend" of Cedar Coulee], Custer, two officers, Boyer and I rode over to a high point [Weir Peak] that overlooks the Little Big Horn Valley to see what was going on. We could see dust rising everywhere down the valley. Reno's men were riding toward the Indians [sic]. None of us dismounted. Custer made a brief survey of the situation and rode back to his command. He did not ask Boyer or me about the country.

The sole item here that does not fit is Reno's charge; Curley and Custer had seen it earlier at Reno Hill, but when they reached Weir Peak, Reno was about to withdraw into the timber. Curley did specify Custer and two officers in the party, just as DeRudio did; the two scouts may have moved around to become invisible when DeRudio looked. Curley also said that the officers returned to the column, but note that he did *not* say that he and Boyer returned with them.

Having already exposed the gap in Martin's story, we can now find some confirmation in his testimony that came after the bombshell order, tangled though it may be:

> (p. 313): Custer called the adjutant, who said, "I want you to take this dispatch to Benteen and go as fast as you can." He told me . . . if there was danger, I should remain with my company [H] and [then] report to him when the company got here. (p. 314): The command was still going on. The adjutant stopped to write the message. (p. 316): I waited not more than ten minutes with Adjt. Cooke before I turned back with the message.
>
> (Graham's *Abstract*, p. 133): Only the Indian scouts went to the top of the hill. Custer did not go himself. His brothers [Tom and Boston] and his nephew [Autie Reed] were with him there on the hill.

That Martin missequenced the halt is obvious; Adjt. Cooke may well have gone to the peak, but even if he did not, he wrote the urgent note the moment Custer got back, and *hastily*. The halt had to be concurrent with Custer's absence, and Martin departed *immediately* as the column started on. As for who went to the peak, Martin twice contradicted himself; he said only some scouts went and Custer did not, but took all his relatives there. This confusion and the fact that he waited during the halt and never saw anything is evidence enough that Martin did not go to the peak.

When Camp and then Graham later interviewed Martin, they ignored all other accounts that expose the gap in his testimony and were so influenced by it that they merely solidified the confusion. Camp's first interview (1908, p. 100) located Custer's sole sighting and 10-minute halt at Reno Hill, and Martin's turnback $\frac{1}{2}$ mile beyond (which corresponds to Sharpshooter Ridge); his second interview (1910, p. 103) located Custer's first sighting and halt *on* Weir Peak, and Martin's turnback at a second sighting and halt halfway down Medicine Tail Coulee (which is impossible). Graham's interview (1922, pp. 289–90) located a sole sighting and 10-minute halt at Reno Hill, and Martin's turnback, without a halt, a mile beyond (which corresponds to the "bend" of Cedar Coulee). None of these patterns is compatible with the "surround" evidence.

In support of participant accounts, there are compelling reasons why

Custer would make a sidetrip to Weir Peak. To assume that he would march this close to where he could easily learn what he so desperately needed to know and then merely rest for 10 minutes is simply absurd. Furthermore, only what he could have learned there can explain his actions when he returned.

From Weir Peak between 3:28 and 3:30 Custer could have seen that the Sioux village was even larger than previous glimpses had revealed and that the Indians were already outflanking Reno's skirmish line, forcing it to withdraw into the timber, where it could hold out, but only so long as ammunition lasted. Both findings meant that the regiment was facing a hard fight and would need Benteen's support and all the ammunition available. These were reasons enough to send, as soon as Custer returned to his command, a courier with urgent orders for Benteen to come quickly and bring ammunition.

Before Custer could attack and destroy this village, as he was ordered to do, he also had to find a suitable place to cross the river. While surveying the terrain from Weir Peak, he must have noted that the branch coulee in which his battalion was then halted afforded a roundabout but concealed passage to the main coulee that led directly to the center of the village, where there was no bluff to hinder a crossing. An approach by this route, while Reno held the Indians' attention, might preserve the advantage of surprise for his heavier attack, which could then free Reno's battalion to resume the offensive. As we shall see, Custer did take this concealed route as soon as he rejoined his column.

Tptr. Martin's Courier Ride

Since Martin's interconnection provides another test of Custer's itinerary, it must be checked out before we proceed further. If Martin left the halt in the "bend" of Cedar Coulee, $5\frac{3}{4}$ miles from the lone tepee at 3:34, and then met Benteen $2\frac{1}{4}$ miles below the lone tepee at 3:58, he rode 3 miles back in 24 minutes at a speed of 7.5 mph. That being the same pace as Kanipe's ride, it is equally acceptable and is posted and plotted. This gratifying result affords more support for both Custer's and Benteen's itineraries. But there is more.

Martin testified to his route and gait and estimated the distance and duration, all but the last fitting our itinerary:

(p. 313): The adjutant told me to follow the same trail we came down on and I did so. My horse was kind of tired, but I ran him as fast as I could. I put spurs to him and made him gallop on the level. (p. 314): It took about ¾ or 1 hour [*sic*], but I had no watch. I made no halt. After I left Custer it was mostly up hill, then I took the level and then I took it down again. (p. 130): From where I was sent back to where I saw Benteen, it was 3 or 4 miles. I think it took me 1¼ to 1½ hours [*sic*], but had no watch.

Martin also testified that on his way back he saw Reno fighting in the valley and gave the distance from his starting point:

(p. 313): After I started back from Custer, I followed the trail perhaps ¾ mile and then I got on the same ridge from which Custer saw the village the first time, and on looking down on the bottom, I saw Reno's command engaged already, but I paid no attention to that. (p. 316): I went back ¾ mile from where I left Custer and saw Reno fighting in the valley. Yes, his line was deployed as skirmishers.

Martin could have seen the valley as soon as he emerged from Cedar Coulee, ½ mile from his starting point, and then during the next ½ mile to Reno Hill. His ¾ mile falls in the center of this range. By interpolation, he looked down at 3:40, when Reno's men were skirmishing in the timber, not in the open; Martin had answered yes only to the question's wording. This sighting interconnection furnishes another check on Martin's time and place of departure.

Martin made still another interconnection when he met Boston Custer coming to overtake the general, for he told Camp (1910, p. 104) that "I kept up the north-south coulee [Cedar Coulee] . . . and met Boston Custer." A footnote adds that, when Martin warned him about the Indians, Boston said, "I am going to join the command anyhow." Martin also told Graham (p. 290) that, "just before I got to the hill [Sharpshooter Ridge], I met Boston Custer. He asked, 'Where's the general?' I answered, 'Right behind the next ridge [Weir Ridge].'" Both accounts imply that this meeting occurred near the head of Cedar Coulee.

When last mentioned, Boston Custer had passed the lone tepee at 2:45. If we extrapolate his path at his steady 6 mph, it is found to intersect Martin's path at 3:38, 5¼ miles below the lone tepee, which marks the head of Cedar Coulee. This rewarding result reinforces not only Boston's steady trot, but also the time and place of Martin's departure. Note in addition that Boston's path (Figure 6) also crosses those of Kanipe and the pony captors, although the other parties failed to mention it, but they may have taken slightly different paths through the hills and ravines.

It is now clear that Martin's interconnection satisfies all constraints if he turned back from the "bend" of Cedar Coulee at 3:34. He could not have left at the start of the halt, for Custer had sent Kanipe back only 8 minutes before and had learned little in this interval. He did have significant new information at 3:34 which demanded action. If Martin's turn back had been delayed 10 minutes while the command advanced another $\frac{1}{2}$ mile, he would have had to ride $3\frac{1}{2}$ miles in 14 minutes at a dead run of 15 mph! That he could have turned back from halfway down Medicine Tail Coulee is utterly impossible; so is another claim that on the ride back he saw Custer's retreat from Ford B. I rejected the impossible *statements*, not Martin or his interviewers, and found that the residue was consistent with other accounts and perfectly feasible.

The Story of the Three Crows

The three Crows made the final personal interconnection from Custer when they joined Benteen's battalion 1 mile upstream from Reno Hill at 4:10, 15 minutes before the onset of Custer's heavy firing. For this reason the claims made in some of their accounts that they remained long with Custer and from nearby witnessed the opening of his engagement at Ford B must be rejected, just as in the case of Tptr. Martin.

Goes Ahead's interview with Camp (1909, p. 175) is notable for its direct and forcible denial of the impossible claim, but it also hints that the Crows turned back from Cedar Coulee and gives the first clue to their route and timing:

> We three Crows did not see Custer after he turned down [Cedar] coulee to the right [beyond its "bend"]. We saw Reno's battle and went back south along bluff and met Benteen's command. Did not see Custer's fight. Did not see beginning of it or any part of it. Do not know whether Custer went to river. We turned back too early to see where Custer went north of Dry Creek [Medicine Tail Coulee].

Goes Ahead's account to Libby (p. 160) amplifies these clues; note that his description identifies Weir Ridge:

Custer had told the Crows to stay out of the fight, and they went to the left along the [Weir] ridge overlooking the river, while Custer took his command to the right [beyond the "bend"]. (Goes Ahead is sure that Curley was not with them.) . . . The three Crows rode along [the south base of] the high [Weir] ridge, keeping back from view of the Dakotas, until they came to the end of the [Weir] ridge and to the bluff just above the lower ford [it was farther above Ford B]. There they dismounted and fired across into the Dakota camp; they could see the circle of tents over the tree-tops below them. They heard two volleys fired and saw the soldiers' horses standing back of the line in groups [Reno's open skirmish line].

Clearly, the three Crows did not start back up Cedar Coulee on Custer's back trail but rode west along the south base of Weir Ridge to the edge of the bluff. This off-trail route and the sighting of Reno's open skirmish line support an itinerary for the first segment of the ride to the rear. The departure of Custer's party for the peak at 3:24 released the three Crows to turn back, but I post their departure 2 minutes later, at 3:26 (primarily to avoid superimposing their path on that of Custer's party in Figure 6). But note that they left *before* Martin. They rode out of Cedar Coulee to the west for $\frac{1}{4}$ mile along the south base of Weir Ridge and in $2\frac{1}{2}$ minutes (6 mph) reached the bluff edge just upstream from Weir Peak at $3:28\frac{1}{2}$, when they halted for $4\frac{1}{2}$ minutes, until 3:33. During this halt they saw Reno's open skirmish line in action, as it was about to retire into the timber, and also fired a few defiant shots in the direction of the visible Sioux tepees.

By continuing another $\frac{3}{4}$ mile upstream along the bluff, the trio would strike Custer's back trail opposite the center of Sharpshooter Ridge, but this move was slowed by a significant sidetrip. Goes Ahead told Coffeen (p. 70) that "we took a drink of water . . . and made haste for our lives." Having ridden the first $\frac{1}{2}$ mile, they could see that the river was approaching the foot of the bluff and that during the remaining $\frac{1}{4}$ mile they could descend for a drink and climb back up. It could only have been during this sidetrip that they also picked up five loose Sioux ponies, as will soon appear; they were probably ponies missed or lost earlier by the Ree pony captors when the Sioux drove them up the bluff in this area. It is simpler to treat this sidetrip as a "halt" that interrupted the ride $\frac{1}{2}$ mile out. This first $\frac{1}{2}$ mile took 6 minutes (5 mph), thus starting the "halt" at 3:39; allowing 10 minutes extra time, it ended at 3:49. The final $\frac{1}{4}$ mile would take another 3 minutes to pick up Custer's trail at 3:52, as posted and plotted. Another consideration guided this reconstruction: since there is no indication of any meeting with Tptr. Martin or Boston Custer, the three Crows must have been slowed while they were still off-trail (see Figure 6).

Having picked up Custer's trail $\frac{1}{2}$ mile short of Reno Hill at 3:52, the three Crows met Black Fox, the early escapee from the valley fight. As the first clue to this meeting, Goes Ahead told Libby (p. 160) that "they rode back along the bluff and met the Arikara scouts." The plural must be a slip, for the pony captors were far up Reno Creek. Hairy Moccasin gave Camp (p. 177) the second clue and a location: "As we came along the bluff a short distance north of the DeWolf marker [nearly $\frac{1}{2}$ mile below Reno Hill], we met a dismounted soldier, who had come up the bluff, and he went along with us until we met the packtrain [sic, Benteen]. We supposed this soldier had been in Reno's fight in the valley." This single "soldier" must have been an enlisted Indian scout, for no one with Benteen remarked on meeting a lost trooper. The suspicion is strong that the "Arikaras" and the "soldier" both referred to Black Fox.

Fortunately, Goes Ahead, on or after July 14, 1876, told Young Hawk that the Ree the three Crows met was Black Fox, and years later Young Hawk relayed this statement to Camp (p. 192): "The Ree who wore the rabbit ears (Black Fox) was the one whom we [the three Crows] picked up. . . . We saw a man going away off and we chased him and found out he was a Ree. I told the Ree that I had captured five head of horses and I gave a black one to Black Fox." This statement does not locate the meeting, and the ellipsis in the middle times it as "after the Custer Fight" and "when we left the Little Big Horn," but it had to be *before* the battle. The account does reveal, however, that the three Crows had already captured five Sioux ponies and had given one to Black Fox, undoubtedly the one he had when he later overtook the rear guard at the mouth of the Rosebud.

Having picked up Black Fox, the party proceeded another $\frac{1}{2}$ mile upstream in 6 minutes (5 mph) to pass Reno Hill at 3:58. By this time the scouts were aware of the firing and yelling of Reno's retreat in their rear, which provides another time check, for this retreat started at 3:53 and reached the retreat ford at 4:00. This timing identifies the context of the following statement that Goes Ahead gave Dixon (p. 167): "There was so much dust that I could scarcely tell, but Reno was driven back by the Indians toward the bluffs." Covering the next mile in 12 minutes (5 mph), the quartet met Benteen's battalion at 4:10. Benteen thought he had met "four Crows," but one must have been Black Fox, and Godfrey noted that they had a little band of horses, all of which now fits.

Hairy Moccasin gave Coffeen (p. 67) the best description of this meeting:

> We met Benteen's command just [1 mile] south of where they afterward entrenched [Reno Hill]. We said to Benteen, "Do you hear that shooting back where we came from? They're fighting Custer [*sic*, Reno] there now." We started to leave Benteen to join the Ree scouts, who were quite a way back up the creek [pony captors were $1\frac{3}{8}$ miles back, en route to Reno Hill], but Benteen told us to stay, and we did. We went with him and helped dig entrenchments.

As previously related, it was while the three Crows and Black Fox were en route to Reno Hill with Benteen's battalion that Red Bear and White Cloud met "four" Crows, one the obviously unrecognized Black Fox, who were planning to search for their missing comrades, Half Yellow Face and White Swan. On reaching Reno Hill at 4:20, the three Crows must have made such a search, for after Red Star had come back with the pony captors to Reno Hill at 4:32, he witnessed the Crows dejected return (Libby, p. 120):

> There, one ridge to the north [Sharpshooter Ridge], came three scouts, Goes Ahead, Hairy Moccasin and White Man Runs Him. They came to the Arikara scouts and told them to go back because the army was beaten, "the Dakotas kill the soldiers easy," and White Swan, Half Yellow Face and Curley were killed. The [three] Crows were intending to circle west and go home where they lived.

If the three Crows started their search downstream at 4:20 and returned 20 minutes later, at 4:40, they could have gone at least $\frac{1}{2}$ mile to Sharpshooter Ridge and back. If so, they must have heard Custer's heavy firing and seen the exodus of the Sioux (4:25–30), and if they climbed to a peak of that ridge, they may also have seen signs of the action (which was not at Ford B, but on the north rim of Medicine Tail Coulee, as we shall learn). This sequence of events may be what, by misunderstanding, gave rise to the notion that they had seen action at Ford B. They had not found Half Yellow Face and White Swan, for these two were still holed up in the brush on the East Side Bottom; and now knowing what Custer must be facing, the Crows concluded that Curley was, or would be, killed.

The three Crows frequently implied that they remained at Reno Hill until "near sunset" (7:45), or even "at dark" (9:00), but not a soul mentioned them, and after 6:00 a cordon of Sioux warriors kept Reno Hill surrounded under merciless fire. Again, it is Goes Ahead who set the record straight, for he told Camp (p. 175): "Half Yellow Face and White Swan went into the valley with Reno and had not got out when we left." Since these two Crows reached Reno Hill at 5:00, the other three must have left *before* that time. I post their departure for home at 4:45, 5 minutes after they told Red Star they intended to leave, as posted in chronology Table 10 and itinerary Table 13 and plotted in Figure 6.

This itinerary for the returning Crows is reasonable and possible, based on their own accounts and supported by numerous interconnections with other parts of the total time-motion pattern, thus strengthening them all. As in the case of other informants, some of their statements were rejected because they are impossible, but the residue proved invaluable.

The three Crows then returned to their home village, as revealed in their accounts. They said they took the back trail to Reno Creek before circling north and then west around the battle area and Sioux village. Knowing the country, they undoubtedly ascended the North Fork, which curves northward into high and rugged country. On circling west, they said they cut across headers of Tullock's Fork and struck the Bighorn River several miles below the mouth of the Little Bighorn. This route of at least 30 miles was rough and broken, and they admitted that, having had little sleep, they and their horses were exhausted. It only sprinkled that night on the troops, but the Crows contended with a heavy rain that turned the trail muddy and slippery. Even at 3 mph this ride would consume 10 hours; having left at 4:45 P.M., they would reach the Bighorn at about 2:45 A.M. of June 26, which fits their claims that it was still dark.

The scouts probably napped for an hour or two before good daylight enabled them to swim across the river to its west bank. They then spotted Indians riding up the east bank, who proved to be Bradley's eighteen Crows, scouting the van for the Terry-Gibbon column. The trio shouted their dismaying news across the river: "The Sioux have killed Custer and all his command." Claiming that Gibbon had given them permission to go home, they left and took all of Bradley's Crow scouts with them. "Two sleeps" later they all reached the Crow village on Pryor Creek, where they announced that Half Yellow Face, White Swan, and Curley were all killed. The relatives started mourning for the dead.

From the standpoint of army discipline these Crow scouts had all deserted, but on July 14, and long before the troops were ready to resume the frustrating campaign, they all returned to duty, with reinforcements.

Custer Advances into Medicine Tail Coulee

Having rejoined his halted troops in the "bend" of Cedar Coulee at 3:34, Custer was now fully aware of the formidable strength and temper of the Sioux village, and of Reno's necessity for taking a defensive position in the timber, but he had also found a concealed route by which to make a supporting attack. He promptly started down Cedar Coulee, confident that Reno could hold out for a time and expecting that his orders would soon bring Benteen and the ammunition.

From here on, Curley is the sole participant to leave accounts. They have often been rejected *in toto* because of blatant contradictions that make him turn back with the three Crows yet remain to see a portion of Custer's fight. We now know that the three Crows have already turned back, leaving Boyer and Curley with Custer. Thus in Curley's accounts we must reject an early turnback and see what the residue has to say; it will prove consistent, reasonable, and extraordinarily illuminating. Of the "surround" technique, there now remains only Boston Custer trotting to overtake the general and the onset of Custer's firing, first heard at 4:25, still 50 minutes in the future.

When Custer descended Weir Peak to rejoin his troops, he left Mitch Boyer and Curley there, perhaps under orders to keep an eye on events and later report anything of significance, for that is what they did. Among other things, they watched Custer lead his column down Cedar Coulee to its mouth on upper Medicine Tail Coulee and halt again. The results of Curley's 1923 interview with Russell White Bear were conveyed by the latter in letters to Graham (1926) and Fred Dustin (1938). The 1926 version (p. 18) reads: "Custer . . . on reaching upper Medicine Tail Coulee, halted his command and the men rearranged their saddles." The 1938 version (p. 19) needs correction of ambiguous pronouns to conform to the 1926 statement: "We [Custer] rode following the creek, as you know; we were [Custer was] all the time going away from the valley [thus Cedar Coulee]. We [Custer] finally came out at Medicine Tail Coulee, and seeing we were [he was] a long way from the valley, Custer turned left and rode down Medicine Tail Coulee."

There are good reasons why Custer would slow to a walk for this descent of Cedar Coulee and then halt at its mouth. The slowed pace would minimize a betraying dust cloud, and both pace and halt would give Benteen more time to come up; the first firing is still a long time in the future. The halt may also have been prompted and extended by the sight of a courier—perhaps, it was hoped, from Benteen—coming at a trot on the back trail, but he proved to be Boston Custer. On this evidence I add to Custer's itinerary a march of $\frac{5}{8}$ mile from the "bend" to the mouth of Cedar Coulee, at 3 mph in $12\frac{1}{2}$ minutes, which starts this halt at $3:46\frac{1}{2}$. I also complete Boston Custer's itinerary by extrapolating his 6-mph trot for $1\frac{1}{8}$ miles from where he met Tptr. Martin to the mouth of Cedar Coulee, and thus find, to my satisfaction, that he arrived at $3:49$, while the troops were still halted. These new data are posted and plotted.

On being questioned for news from the rear, Boston could have given the general only excessively reassuring news. He could report that he had passed Benteen above the lone tepee, from which Custer could figure that, if Boston had overtaken at a trot, then Benteen, so often ordered to hurry, ought not be far behind. As to Reno, Boston could only report seeing him still fighting in the timber (see Figure 6) and thus holding out. Both items may have encouraged Custer to wait for reinforcements and ammunition.

In the meantime, Boyer and Curley were keeping vigil from Weir Ridge, for they next witnessed the three Crows moving to the rear and the retreat of Reno's battalion, and they signaled to Custer's halted column. After the impossible is rejected from Lt. Roe's interview with Curley (1881), the residue contains the following:

> The Sioux got after the [three] Crows and ran them back to the packtrain [Benteen] this side of Reno Creek. . . . Reno's command moved out of the timber [$3:53$] and was running back [until $4:00$]; at same time, the [three] Crows were running back, driven by the Sioux

[3:49 to 3:58]. I could see them (Reno's men) running, while the Crows were running. . . . Reno's men ran from timber about same time Custer's command turned from mouth of deep coulee [Cedar Coulee], and same time [three] Crows ran back.

To Camp (1910, p. 166), Curley gave his viewing point and added the signaling incident: "Custer did not see [all of] Reno's fight. Mitch Boyer and myself did. When Reno was fighting [after Custer left], only Boyer was with me. . . . Saw Reno fighting from Weir Peak. . . . I saw Reno's retreat [3:53 to 4:00], and Boyer then gave a signal to Custer [at mouth of Cedar Coulee]. Custer and Tom Custer returned signal by waving hats and men cheering."

These sighted events were indeed concurrent and thus provide a time check on Curley's observations; they also reveal that Mitch and Curley lingered in the vicinity of Weir Ridge for a considerable time after Custer left them there. Furthermore, the signal to Custer at the mouth of Cedar Coulee after Reno's retreat started means that Custer's halt was not a fleeting one.

Mitch and Curley next saw Custer's column marching down Medicine Tail Coulee and hastened, via the east rim of Weir Peak Coulee, to intercept it and report their grave news:

(1910, p. 166): Bouyer probably told Custer that Reno had been defeated, for he did a whole lot of talking to Custer when he joined him.

(1913, p. 172): We joined Custer in Medicine Tail Coulee, as he was advancing toward the village. . . . I had seen Reno defeated in the bottom and discussed it with Mitch. I saw Mitch say something to Custer when we met him and presumed Mitch must have informed him about Reno's situation.

In early interviews with Curley, Camp was confused in the first about the coulees and in the second thought that all five scouts went down the bluff nearly to Ford B (impossible). Inserting corrections salvages the following:

(1908, p. 150): Taking Curley with him, Bouyer passed on and over Weir Peak and then [after lingering], on a course directly north [along Weir Peak Coulee], parrallel [sic] to Custer, until they came down in the bed of Reno Creek [sic, Medicine Tail Coulee], where they met Custer about half a mile [over a mile] from the river.

(1909, p. 162): While we [Boyer and Curley only] were here [Weir

Ridge, not bluff near Ford B], Custer's command hove in sight, galloping right down [Medicine Tail] coulee toward the river. Boyer now said
he would cut across and meet it, and he started off the east slope of
the bluff [north slope of Weir Ridge], and I with him.

These accounts provide clear evidence that the two scouts intercepted
Custer's column coming down Medicine Tail Coulee and that Mitch reported to Custer that Reno had retreated headlong upriver, with triumphant Sioux taking a heavy toll. If the arrival of the scouts was not enough
to prompt another halt, this grave and startling news certainly was. As
will be shown soon, this meeting and short halt came about $\frac{3}{8}$ mile below
the mouth of Cedar Coulee.

If the halt at the mouth of Cedar Coulee lasted 10 minutes, to $3:56\frac{1}{2}$,
Custer's concealed march of $\frac{3}{8}$ mile down Medicine Tail Coulee at a dust-
controlling 3 mph would bring him to the short halt in $7\frac{1}{2}$ minutes, or
4:04. If the two scouts lingered at Weir Ridge for 31 minutes, until 3:58,
and then rode at 6.25 mph for $\frac{5}{8}$ mile down the east rim of Weir Peak
Coulee in 6 minutes, they would intercept Custer at the same 4:04. These
data for Custer are posted and plotted, but not those for Boyer and Curley,
for this area of Figure 6 is too crowded to accommodate this off-trail path
and the numerous verifying sightings.

It is now 21 minutes before the onset of Custer's firing.

CUSTER'S MANEUVERING AND SKIRMISHING

The grave news that Mitch Boyer and Curley brought Custer in upper Medicine Tail Coulee at 4:04 must have come as a severe shock. Only a few minutes earlier Boston Custer had reported that Reno was still holding out and Benteen ought to be up soon. But there was still no sign of the latter, and the headlong retreat of Reno's men placed them in danger, more in need of help than able to give help. The warriors who had accomplished this feat were now free to counter any second attack. The only force at hand was Custer's battalion, which numbered only 13 officers, 193 enlisted men, 3 scouts, and 2 noncombatants, for a sobering total of 211, without reserve ammunition. Under these circumstances, did Custer attack immediately with what little he had or play for a little time to allow support to come up?

Until relatively recently, everyone *knew* the answer: Custer rashly made a wild dash down Medicine Tail Coulee to Ford B, bent on destroying the village, only to meet thousands of warriors, who threw his troops back in utter disorder to the distant Custer battlefield, where the last remnants were themselves destroyed. This scenario violates the evidence gathered two days after the battle, that nearly all the bodies of Custer's dead were found on the distant Custer field, with no trail of carnage from Ford B. Thus there is a mysterious gap in events between 4:04 at upper Medicine Tail Coulee and the time when the disastrous fighting began. It is the purpose of this chapter to fill this long-missing phase, preliminary to the actual battle.

Custer Divides His Force

Curley, still the only surviving participant with Custer, fortunately revealed to Russell White Bear the unexpected decision Custer made on receiving Boyer's report, which is the key to the whole preliminary phase. The 1938 version (p. 19) picks up from the preceding halt at the mouth of Cedar Coulee:

> Custer, turning left, rode down Medicine Tail Coulee. After riding a while, he halted the command [to hear Boyer's report]. Then the gray horse troop [Co. E] left us and started down the creek, when we turned north, crossing Medicine Tail Creek, going on the hills north of the creek. Here the command halted again; Custer wrote a message and handed it to a young man on a sorrel-roan horse, who galloped away.

Curley thus confirmed the second halt (4:04) in upper Medicine Tail Coulee, which may now be called the *separation halt*, for Custer here divided his command, sending a part on down the coulee and leading the remainder up and out of the coulee to its north rim, where he halted again and sent off a courier.

The 1926 version of this same interview (p. 18) tells of the same events but reverses their sequence. I divide it into two paragraphs but re-reverse them to match the 1938 version and identify the clauses that had reversed the sequence:

> After Custer sent his message away [a reversing clause], he rode to an officer [Lt. A. E. Smith] who seemed to be in command of one of the troops, which had gray horses [Co. E], and gave an order. Immediately, the troop turned [*sic*, continued] its direction toward the

Little Horn. Custer, with the remainder of his command, continued [*sic*, turned], going northward. His trail was about 1½ miles from the river.

At this point [the antecedent was "the halt on reaching Medicine Tail Coulee"], Custer gave a trooper a paper, and after a brief conversation, the trooper rode away *north*. This trooper rode a *sorrel-roan horse*. [Russell White Bear's italics.]

One reason (more will emerge) for choosing the 1938 sequence is that it seems unlikely that Custer would send a courier north when he was about to take that direction himself. The courier's sorrel-roan horse suggests he was from Company C; he was certainly *not* Tptr. Martin, who was about to meet Benteen miles to the rear at 4:10. It was Russell White Bear who italicized his direction as "*north*" rather than by the safer back trail. His destination may have been the Terry-Gibbon column, due the next day at the mouth of the Little Bighorn, but if so, he never arrived.

Curley's most significant revelation is that at the separation halt Custer divided his small force, sending a detachment down the coulee toward Ford B, while he led the remainder, with Boyer and Curley, up and out of the coulee to its north rim and halted again, sending off a courier. There can be no doubt that the grave news brought by Boyer triggered this division and sending a courier. The next section presents more recent evidence of a firm kind that solidly confirms the separation, its location, and the directions taken by the two parties, but already we can explore the implications of Custer's unexpected decision.

Five companies are easily divided in only two patterns, both *unequal*: one and four, or two and three. In either case, Custer would certainly retain the larger and detach the smaller, just as Curley remembered. This simple fact leads to an eye-opening conclusion. If, as everything thus far indicates, Custer had planned to attack and destroy this village quickly, with his full force and via Ford B, he now drastically modified that plan. He would certainly *not* send one or even two companies down to attack and destroy so enormous a village via Ford B, while he and the remainder merely watched from the high rim over a mile away. He must, therefore, have had a different and temporary objective in mind that would delay a full attack but improve its chances for success.

This conclusion follows whether the detachment was one or two companies, but it would be helpful to know its composition. So far, Curley has identified only Lt. Smith's gray-horse Company E, to which he made more references, and on two occasions he hinted at two companies. Some village Cheyennes told Grinnell[1] that "two troops, the gray horse troop in the lead," approached Ford B. Besides confirming Company E, this report more strongly suggests there were two.

A different approach may identify the second company and thereby the remaining three. Capt. Moylan testified (p. 206) that back at the divide halt Custer had assigned a battalion of three companies to his senior captain, Keogh, including his Company I, and a battalion of two companies to his next senior captain, Yates, including his Company F; Lt. Edgerly, in four of his accounts, said the very same thing, but neither officer could name the other companies so assigned. Only Sgt. Kanipe told Camp that his Company C was in Keogh's battalion.[2] *If* Custer, at the separation halt, divided his five companies according to these earlier assignments, then Yates's battalion consisted of E and F, and Keogh's of C, I, and L. The *if*, however, robs this full identification of certainty.

Still, there are other hints that Companies C and L actually remained with Custer *after* the separation halt. *If* the courier who left the north rim on a sorrel-roan horse was indeed from Company C, it had remained with Custer. Two infantry buttons were found north of this rim; *if* they had been lost on June 25, they could only have belonged to Lt. Crittenden, Company L, for he was the sole infantry officer attached to the 7th Cavalry.[3] That again leaves Company F as detached, but the *ifs* remain. For convenience, but with full admission of the uncertainty, I refer to the detachment as Yates's battalion (E and F) and to the remainder (C, I, and L) as Custer's battalion, or the main force.

Since Custer could not have detached Yates's battalion to destroy the village via Ford B, why did he detach it at all? There is an obvious alternative mission: to *pretend* to attack, as a *feint* or threat, for even a semblance of an attack on the Indian women and children should draw the warriors from Reno's endangered battalion, allowing it to regroup in safety; it might then join Benteen and/or the packtrain and provide backup for a stronger Custer attack. Any firing by Yates should attract all the rear units like a magnet, and his presence should block the use by

[1] Grinnell, *Fighting Chéyennes*, 338 (B).

[2] Transcripts of Camp Manuscripts, as quoted by Hardorff, *Markers, Artifacts and Indian Testimony*, 41 (B).

[3] Greene, "Evidence and the Custer Enigma," 22 (A).

Indians of Medicine Tail Coulee as a route by which to cut off approaching reinforcements and ammunition. A feint by a weak force against a strong enemy, of course, entails risk, but it can be reduced by a skillful disengagement and reunion with the main force.

Meanwhile, Custer's main force could seize a holding position on the north rim of upper Medicine Tail Coulee, where it could wait a little longer for reinforcements and ammunition via Cedar Coulee and cover their approach. This high rim also overlooked the valley, enabling Custer to keep an eye on Yates's feint and the Indians' reaction to it; he could watch the disengagement and know when and where to effect a reunion, with reinforcements, if they arrived. Both the feint and the holding position could only be temporary measures, however, for victory demanded an aggressive attack. Custer may have figured that it could best be made by crossing the river farther downstream, below the village and with less opposition, and then charging back up the wide and flat west bottom. If so, the reunion should also take place downriver.

We shall find strong evidence to support a scenario of this kind, which implies that Custer was trying to buy time that would enable his full regiment to deliver a decisive attack.

Geography and Newer Physical Evidence

More geography and landmarks are needed for the sizable area that lies between Medicine Tail Coulee and the present fenced-in Custer battlefield reservation. From the separation halt the main coulee runs about $1\frac{1}{4}$ miles a little north of west to join the river across a narrow strip of bottomland, which forms a gap in the steep river bluff. Across this strip another large coulee joins the river, a little farther downstream, with Ford B between the two mouths; now called *Deep Coulee* (formerly North Medicine Tail Coulee), it runs down from a little east of north, passing near the southeast corner of the reservation, about a mile above its mouth. These two coulees thus form a right-angled V, with a blunted apex at the river. Medicine Tail has a *north branch* and Deep Coulee a *south branch*, both invading the V, cutting it into ridges. The crest of the narrow divide between Medicine Tail and its north branch is called *Luce Ridge* and lies right opposite the separation halt, as the north rim. Near the center of the

V and between the two branches lies *Nye-Cartwright* (or Blummer) *Ridge*; its crest comes down from the northeast but curves northwest toward the southeast corner of the reservation, terminating at the east rim of Deep Coulee, just below its south branch. It is about $1\frac{7}{8}$ miles, on nearly a straight line, from the separation halt to the northeast corner of the reservation.

The battlefield *reservation* is about 1 mile square, rotated to parallel the river, which there flows northwest, forming one meandering border. Within its southeast corner, about 0.2 mile from that corner post, lies *Calhoun Hill*, which is a knoll on *Calhoun Ridge*, which extends down a little south of west toward the southwest fence line. Within the northeast corner, about 0.3 mile from that corner post, lies *Custer Hill* at the termination of *Custer Ridge*, which extends from Calhoun Hill. Yates's and Custer's battalions rendezvoused (as I suggest) on the southeast border of the reservation about $\frac{1}{4}$ mile from the southeast corner post; I call this place the *reunion point*.

Since the 1930s the lack of participants to interview has stimulated relic hunting on the field. Gradually, private parties began to discover battle artifacts in wholly unexpected places, outside the reservation but within the area just described. This accumulating evidence, though primarily locational, has made it possible to spot matching clues in previously puzzling participant accounts, especially Curley's. These new findings have established that a preliminary phase of maneuvering and skirmishing preceded Custer's hard fighting.

Beginning in 1928, Joseph A. Blummer, a local storekeeper at Garryowen, followed by R. G. Cartwright, a South Dakota schoolteacher, and Col. Elwood L. Nye, an army veterinarian, found .45/.55 carbine shell cases, of the kind used in 1876 by the 7th Cavalry, scattered along Nye-Cartwright Ridge. Now totaling hundreds, many were found at intervals corresponding to mounted cavalry in motion. They were supplemented by several human skeletons and those of saddled horses, as well as equipment items. Such findings continued across upper Deep Coulee to the reservation border.[4]

In 1943 Col. Edward S. Luce, then superintendent of the Custer

[4]Blummer to Cartwright, Sept. 13, 1928 (M); Cartwright to Leland Case, Nov. 1944, in *Chicago Westerners Brandbook*, 1 (Nov. 1944): 9 (mimeograph edition, not in book edition); Cartwright to W. Boyes, Jan. 1, 1961, as quoted by Weibert, *66 Years in Custer's Shadow*, 150 (B).

Battlefield National Monument, began finding similar shell cases on Luce Ridge. Again, totaling hundreds, many were only nine or ten feet apart, corresponding to the intervals taken by dismounted cavalry. These, too, were supplemented by human and horse skeletons and items of equipment, and some extended north to Nye-Cartwright Ridge. This long trail of cavalry artifacts, starting right opposite the separation halt and continuing to the reunion point, clearly marks the route taken by Custer's battalion and reveals heavy firing during a halt on Luce Ridge and further firing while in motion along Nye-Cartright Ridge.[5]

In 1956 these findings prompted Don Rickey, Jr., of the National Park Service, and Jesse W. Vaughn, a lawyer of Windsor, Colorado, to scour the area around the mouth of Medicine Tail Coulee with metal detectors. The results were rather meager, only a dozen or so carbine shell cases and a few equipment items, but enough to show that troops had been there and fired very lightly. Similar scattered findings extended along the bottom strip and up along Deep Coulee. Clearly, these are clues to the route of Yates's battalion to the reunion point.[6]

These two very different routes confirm the separation in upper Medicine Tail Coulee, just as Curley remembered. Furthermore, the artifact findings indicate heavy firing by Custer's men but only light firing by Yates's men, in conformity with my deduction that Yates made only a sham attack. We now return to Curley's accounts, which describe Yates's action in considerable detail.

Yates's Battalion

Although Curley told Russell White Bear that he and Boyer remained with Custer, he gave detailed accounts of Yates's action, which he could only have witnessed from afar. His interviewers, having never dreamed of a separation, simply assumed that everything Curley said pertained to the united command. They used only Custer's name and corresponding pro-

---

[5] Luce to Robert Ellison, Sept. 7, 1943; Luce to E. A. Brinninstool, Oct. 3, 1943; and Luce to Nye, Oct. 11, 1943 (M); Luce, "Custer Battlefield and Some New Discoveries," 7–10 (A).

[6] Greene, "Evidence and the Custer Enigma," 16–18 (A). This article tabulates all relic findings (filed at CBNM) up to 1973, discusses them, and plots them on the 1891 battlefield map. It should thus be added to footnotes 4 and 5, above.

nouns; to call attention to these misidentifications, I have inserted question marks.

Lt. Bradley's news article, based on his debriefing of Curley, July 3, 1876, is the only one to claim that Yates's men dismounted at Ford B, but it certainly does not describe a Custer-style charge of five companies to destroy an Indian village:

> When they [?] reached the river, the Indians concealed in the underbrush on the opposite bank, opened fire on the troops. Here a part of the command was dismounted and thrown forward toward the river and returned the Indian fire. During this, warriors were seen riding out of the village by hundreds, deploying across his [?] front to the left, as if intending to cross the stream . . . while the women and children were seen hastening from the village in the opposite direction. During the fight at this point, Curley saw two of Custer's [?] men killed, who fell into the stream. After fighting a few moments, Custer [?] seemed convinced it was impracticable to cross. . . . He [?] ordered the column to the right and bore diagonally into the hills downstream.

The firing was thus light, only an answer to Indian fire, and neither troops nor Indians attempted to cross the river. It was a feint, and Curley's next interview with Roe (1881) brings the same picture into sharper focus, with final sentences hinting at the separation of two companies and a move to rendezvous:

> They [?] came down ravine to its mouth and one man with stripes on his arm on a gray horse rode into the river very fast, right into the Indians; acted like a man who wanted to die [or whose horse ran away]. The Sioux could be seen mounting and coming toward Custer [?] and commenced to fire . . . and the troops fired back, remaining mounted; only the front part of the column fired. The column was stretched up a deep coulee [Medicine Tail] and away back on the side of the ridge [Luce Ridge?]. The troops then turned from the mouth of the coulee, the men in the lead motioning with their hands to go northeast, when the companies [note the plural] broke from the main column, as if to meet again on the main ridge.

Curley told Camp (1908, p. 159) the same story, clarifying a few points:

> After Boyer and Curley joined Custer [at the separation halt], the command [?] passed rapidly down to Ford B. As soon as the soldiers came in sight of the village, the Sioux gave a "heap big yell," and

when the soldiers got closer, there was "heap shoot." The troops did not dismount here and some rode into the river before stopping and turning back. Curley saw one soldier gallop across the river just below the ford at great speed, pass up the bank through the Sioux posted along it and come into full view on the open ground beyond. The Sioux defending the ford he observed to be all unmounted. He afterward learned that they did not have time to get their ponies, which were grazing back on the hills west of the village.

Thus, according to Curley, the two troopers, first described as killed in the river, had in fact turned back to safety. Confirmation came from Lt. DeRudio, who studied the area on June 27 and later told Camp (p. 86) that "two shod horses had gone quite to the river bank and the tracks indicated that they had shied around quickly in some blue clay, as if suddenly turned by their riders." The Company E noncom, however, who was carried across the river, still remains a presumed casualty. He could have been any of seven noncom casualties of this troop, except 1st Sgt. Hohmeyer, whose body was recognized by Capt. McDougall (to Camp, p. 72) on the distant Custer field. Only Sgt. Kanipe wrote Camp (p. 157) of seeing a body on the west bank: "A sergeant of I troop was lying across the ford in the Indian village. He was not mutilated; his horse was 20 or 30 steps from him." Camp apparently thought this was the body of Sgt. James Bustard, although Lt. Edgerly (p. 58) told him that Bustard and the only other sergeant fatality of I Troop were found lying next to their captain (Keogh) on the Custer field.

Curley's consistent accounts indicate that the village had little forewarning of this second threat, for only a few warriors had run on foot to defend the river from the underbrush on its west bank. Neither they nor the first of the mounted warriors to arrive from the village dared cross the river against cavalry fire. They were merely making a show of resistance while awaiting reinforcements, and with both sides shamming, the firing was light and brief. Without halting, the troops moved downriver, which characterizes this action as a feint.

Curley next described a disengagement by choice, rather than a forced and disorderly retreat. Lt. Roe's account breaks down entirely, as Roe thought Curley turned back here with the three Crows, but Lt. Bradley and Camp continue with consistent and revealing stories:

(Bradley, 1876): In the meantime the Indians had crossed the river below in immense numbers and began to appear on his [?] right flank and rear; he [?] had proceeded but a few hundred yards in this direction [diagonally into the hills], when it became necessary to renew the fight with Indians who had crossed the river.

(Camp, 1908, p. 157): When Custer [?] withdrew from the ford, he proceeded downriver for some distance and then struck out for higher ground in columns of fours [another hint of two companies], going directly to the . . . southeast point of the battlefield. Before they got to this point . . . the Indians were in front and in the ravines on both sides, and a strong force of Indians was coming up in the rear.

These recollections describe a bold show and withdrawal downstream in columns of fours, followed by a right oblique away from the river toward high ground for some distance, all without opposition. During this interval the Indians were crossing the river both above and below, intending to strike on both flanks.

In 1909 (p. 162) Camp had Curley focus more closely on the route in the strip of bottomland:

Custer [?] left coulee of Medicine Tail Creek 900 ft. east of its mouth and struck the river 1000 ft. below its mouth. It is about 900 ft. farther to the first high cutbank. It appeared to Curley here that Custer [?] would charge across into the village, but the west bank was thick with dismounted Sioux, and back in the village hundreds of mounted ones were coming up. . . . Curley thought it would be necessary for Custer [?] to retreat, and he did so, going downstream and quartering back upon the high ridge.

Note that the entire distance from where the battalion diverged from the creek to the riverbank and on down to the first cutbank lies within the strip of bottomland along the east bank. While moving along this bottom, Yates had to cross the creek of Deep Coulee near its mouth, and then when he turned away from the river at the cutbank, he ascended the *west* rim of Deep Coulee. He undoubtedly chose this route to reach high ground quickly and to avoid a dangerous crossing of Deep Coulee higher up.

Yates ascended along the west rim for some distance without opposition, and Curley in this same interview (p. 162) described in his own words what happened next:

While Custer's [?] firing at the cutbank was in progress, I saw no large body of Indians fording, but as soon as we [?] began to retreat, they must have swarmed across, both above and below us, for we [?] had not proceeded one-third of the way to the ridge [Calhoun Ridge?] before the Sioux were thick on our right and left flanks, firing into us heavily. I do not know whether anyone was killed on the way to the ridge, but the firing was so heavy, I do not see how the command made it without some loss. Going up from the river, Sioux on all sides except front. . . . Did not stop, but did some firing.

It was the movement downstream from Ford B that enabled mounted warriors from the village to cross there without opposition. Some who crossed there rode up Deep Coulee and then turned left up its branch ravines to appear on Yates's right flank. Others crossed at suitable places farther downstream and turned right up ravines to emerge on Yates's left flank. He had to deploy dismounted skirmishers to parry these thrusts, but the column forged ahead to meet Custer's battalion at the reunion point.

On the basis of Curley's accounts, the map, and artifact evidence, an itinerary is proposed for Yates's battalion. Allowing 4 minutes at the separation halt for Custer to digest Boyer's grave news, reach a decision, and brief Yates, I post the latter's departure at 4:08. At 7.5 mph the $1\frac{1}{4}$-mile descent of the coulee in 10 minutes would bring Yates to Ford B at 4:18, when the exchange of light firing began with unmounted Indians across the river. Slowing to 3 mph for show, Yates rode $\frac{1}{4}$ mile down the right bank in 5 minutes, reaching the first cutbank at 4:23. Making a right oblique, he ascended the west rim of Deep Coulee for $\frac{1}{2}$ mile in 10 minutes, when at 4:53 the mounted Indians appeared on his right and left flanks. Deploying skirmishers on foot, Yates covered another $\frac{1}{4}$ mile in 13 minutes (1.9 mph) to join Custer's battalion at the reunion point, on the southeast line of the reservation, about $\frac{1}{4}$ mile from the southeast corner post at 4:46. These data are posted in Table 14 (this chapter) and plotted in Figure 6 (preceding chapter).

This itinerary reflects a feint, not an attack; a disengagement by design, not a rout by an overwhelming Indian attack; and a planned reunion downstream on high ground, all in accord with the evidence. It also furnishes an all-important time element: the 38-minute interval from 4:08 to 4:46 was a preliminary phase of maneuvering and skirmishing, which preceded the heavy fighting within the battlefield reservation.

Note also that the itinerary times the onset of Yates's light firing near

Table 14. Itineraries: Preliminary Phase of the Battle

Unit Events	Clock- Time	Increments			Mi. from Lone Tepee
		dm	dt	mph	
Boyer, Curley meet Custer's 5 Cos. at separation halt, Med. T. Coulee.	4:04				6¾
YATES'S BATTALION (Cos. F, E, off-trail)					
Lv. separation halt down Med. T. Coulee.	4:08		:04		6¾
Arr. Ford B; light firing over Little Bighorn begins.	4:18	1¼	:10	7.5	8
Crosses Deep Coulee, arr. cutbank unopposed.	4:23	¼	:05	3.0	8¼
Ascends W rim Deep Coulee; Sioux attack flanks.	4:33	½	:10	3.0	8¾
Fights on foot to reunion point.	4:46	¼	:13	1.9	9
CUSTER'S BATTALION (Cos. C, I, L)					
Lv. separation halt N out of Med. T. Coulee.	4:08		:04		6¾
Arr. Luce Ridge; halts on defensive position.	4:16	0.4	:08	3.0	7.15
Sees and hears light firing at Ford B by Yates.	4:18				
Sees Sioux coming up Med. T. Coulee to attack.	4:20				
Sees Yates start up W rim Deep Coulee.	4:23				
Pins down Sioux with heavy firing.	4:25				
Lv. Luce Ridge to meet Yates downstream.	4:27		:11		
Arr. Nye-Cartwright Ridge.	4:32	½	:05	6.0	7.65
Fires at Sioux on left flank to upper Deep Coulee.	4:38	0.6	:06	6.0	8¼
Joins Yates at reunion point.	4:46	⅜	:08	4.9	8⅝
Curley lv. for mouth of Bighorn.	4:50		:04		

Ford B at 4:18, 7 minutes *before* heavy firing was heard on Reno Hill at 4:25. This timing makes no problem, for this light firing was concurrent with diminishing firing in the upper valley, some to and from Reno Hill, some by warriors celebrating their victory, and some from the skirmishing with Young Hawk's party. It would be difficult to distinguish the various locations of such sporadic firing. It can now be foreseen that it must have been Custer's much heavier firing at Luce Ridge that was heard so distinctly at Reno Hill.

Custer's Battalion

Curley's late statements to Russell White Bear have indicated that, when Yates's battalion left the separation halt, Mitch and Curley went with Custer to Luce Ridge, where another halt was made. It must have been from this high ridge that Curley had such a good view of Yates's feint and orderly withdrawal. His early interviewers failed to perceive this aspect of his story, for they had no suspicion that Custer had divided his force. For the same reason, it never occurred to them to ask Curley about the movements of a separated Custer battalion. If Curley volunteered such information, it fell on uncomprehending ears, for nothing of the kind appears in their interviews.

Nevertheless, knowing that the separation had occurred, we can find evidence in Curley's accounts that a reunion followed. While telling about Yates, Curley had not mentioned himself, Mitch, or other Custer personnel; only Custer's name is used, because his interviewers thought it to be correct. Once the reservation was reached, however, Curley mentioned the gray horse troop among the others and abruptly reintroduced himself, Mitch, Tom Custer, and the general, an unmistakable signal that the two battalions had reunited.

These indications of a reunion have one feature in common: the location is always near the "southeast corner" of the reservation, or near the "Calhoun marker" on Calhoun Hill, or the "Finley marker." Markers for enlisted men bear no names, but judging from Camp's cryptic references, the one for Sgt. Jeremiah Finley (Co. C) was on lower Calhoun Ridge, near the southeast border of the reservation. Some of Curley's clues to the reunion are assembled from Camp's interviews:

(1908, pp. 158–59): Before they [?] got to this point ["southeast point of the battlefield (Finley marker)"], Mitch Bouyer lost his horse. . . . In ascending toward the Calhoun marker, an attempt was made to cover the retreat until some kind of stand could be made. Men were left at the Finley marker, and some troops dismounted just beyond this, Curley staking his horse with the rest. The dismounted men then tried to drive the Indians from the gulch ahead, but the men left in the rear were quickly killed and the advance of the Indians was hardly checked at all.

Custer stopped at this point briefly. . . . There was a hurried conference of officers and Bouyer told Curley . . . [that they decided] that if the command could make a stand somewhere, the remainder of the regiment would probably soon come up and relieve them. Personally, Bouyer did not expect relief would come, as he thought the other commands had been scared out. Bouyer thought the orders would be to charge straight ahead, drive the Indians from the ravine and try to find more favorable ground . . . [but] the scheme had to be given up. There was then "heap shoot" . . . and Custer struck out westward [northwest?], it being understood some soldiers would try to hold the ground at this corner. Curley says, however, that the men went for their horses, or ran in the direction of the retreat toward the Custer monument [Custer Hill] . . . the men with gray horses keeping well together.

(1909, pp. 162–63): Mitch Bouyer told me to keep out of the skirmish as much as possible, as they might wish to send me with a dispatch to the other troops. After we made the ridge just west of . . . ["Calhoun marker"], we were twice ordered to load and fire together. It occurred to me at the time that this must be some kind of signal.

(1910, p. 167): When the whole command was at Finley marker, the volleys were fired at the Sioux who were closing in.

With knowledge of when and where the separation and reunion occurred, and the trail of artifacts connecting them, a feasible itinerary can be constructed for Custer's battalion. It can also be fleshed out with Custer's probable thoughts and actions in response to what he observed. Since there was no reason to linger at the separation halt, I post Custer's departure at 4:08, the same as Yates's, making this halt last 4 minutes for both. A steep climb of 0.4 mile to Luce Ridge on the north rim suggests a 3-mph walk, taking 8 minutes to reach the top at 4:16. Halting at this holding position, Custer posted his three companies on a defensive perimeter, while keeping an eye on Yates as well as on his own back trail, hoping for signs of reinforcements.

Custer, Mitch, and Curley could see Yates approaching the river and at 4:18 saw and heard light firing near Ford B. They watched him move leisurely downstream toward the first cutbank without opposition; he was making a bold show, and the village was reacting by rushing mounted warriors out toward the river. Soon after Yates had moved down from the ford, these warriors began crossing there, while others were diverging downstream to cross the river far below. When, at 4:23, Yates turned to ascend the far rim of Deep Coulee toward higher ground, still unopposed, Custer could lay out his own path to join him.

But something else had been happening. Some of those Indians crossing at Ford B were coming up Medicine Tail Coulee and its north branch directly toward Custer's holding position. He waited to give these brash warriors a good dose of lead. At about 4:25 his alerted men pinned them down in ravines and gullies with heavy gunfire. That was the heavy gunfire heard at Reno Hill at this time, which furnishes a check on Custer's itinerary. These warriors were not numerous, and most probably came from the village. Only those who had left the Reno fight *early* could have participated, for the full exodus, from the upper valley, of the warriors who had treed Reno did not begin until they heard this firing downstream at 4:25. It was then that Custer's effort to relieve Reno's men took effect.

Custer's messages to speed up Benteen and the ammunition and his delays to permit being overtaken had still brought no response of any kind. We know why, but there is no way he could have known; he may have suspected that somehow the Indians had immobilized all the units somewhere in his rear. But if he delayed longer, he would lose Yates's battalion, too. Quickly mounting, while the Indians he had fired on were still scrambling for cover, Custer pulled out at 4:27, thus ending this halt on Luce Ridge after 11 minutes.

With little opposition he trotted $\frac{1}{2}$ mile in 5 minutes across the shallow north branch to reach the crest of Nye-Cartright Ridge at 4:32. Trotting the next 0.6 miles in 6 minutes along this ridge, he came to the east rim of Deep Coulee at 4:38; for this distance he had to fire repeatedly to hold at a respectful distance the gathering Indians moving parallel along his left flank (toward the river). He then negotiated a crossing of upper Deep Coulee, suffering a few casualties, but effected a junction with Yates at the reunion point. This final $\frac{3}{8}$ mile in 8 minutes (4.9 mph) also times the reunion at 4:46, as posted in Table 14 and plotted in Figure 6.

These two feasible itineraries for this preliminary phase may not be hard and firm, but they are compatible with one another and with the available evidence. Their principal utility (as well as vulnerability) is that they are specific regarding both time and place. The numerous accounts of village Indians, vague in both respects, have remained more confusing than enlightening, but note that they, too, were obtained before the interviewers knew that Custer had divided his command.

Now that we know that Yates's firing at Ford B was light and obscured by concurrent firing, it is not surprising to find that only a few villagers saw, or even heard about, unmounted Indians on the west bank firing at troops; nevertheless, those that did, correctly diagnosed it as a fleeting threat or alarm. Many witnessed heavier action by mounted Indians and troops *east* of the river, which means that they looked or arrived some time later. The majority, including those who fought Reno, did not reach the scene until 4:30, after Custer's firing and while Yates was ascending toward high ground. Other Indians, still in the village, saw troop formations far back from the river (Luce Ridge) and some moving along the high ridges (Nye-Cartwright); these observers had to be late, too, for the approach of the five companies via Cedar Coulee had been concealed and their descent to the separation halt was inconspicuous. It thus becomes apparent that these Indian informants were not giving misinformation, but exemplifying the truism that different persons at different times and places see different things.

Custer's five companies are now, at 4:46, reunited on the reservation, all under engagement and facing death within the next 39 minutes.

CURLEY'S ESCAPE

The oft-maligned Curley has proved so reliable an informant that justice demands narrating his successful escape to deliver his news of disaster to the *Far West* several days later. The story also deserves telling because it has been subjected to flagrant distortion.

Shortly after Custer's two battalions reunited on the reservation border at 4:46, Mitch Boyer induced Curley to make an escape and carry the news of imminent disaster to Terry at the mouth of the Bighorn. Curley described the circumstances in several interviews, here assembled:

> (Camp, 1908, p. 159): Mitch Bouyer now turned to Curley, saying that Tom Custer had suggested that the scouts had better save themselves if they could. Bouyer advised Curley to try it, and Curley told Bouyer he would do so, if Bouyer also would try it. Bouyer declined by saying he was too badly wounded, and he would have to stay and fight it out, although he believed they would all be killed. Curley now decided to stay no longer.

(Camp, 1910, pp. 168–69): Mitch Bouyer said, "You had better leave now, for we will all be cleaned out." Bouyer had just been talking with Custer and his brother, Tom, and then he came and told me . . . to ride out through the coulee over to the east.

(Camp, 1913, p. 172): On the battlefield, near Calhoun marker, I saw Mitch talking with the general. Mitch said that Custer had told him the command would likely all be wiped out and that he wanted the scouts to get out if they could. I was riding my own horse.

(Russell White Bear, p. 18): Mitch Boyer told Curley to leave the command and go to Terry: "Curley, you are very young and do not know very much about fighting. I advise you to leave us, and if you can get away by detouring and keeping out of the way of the Sioux, do so, and go to the other soldiers," meaning Terry's men, "and tell them that all are killed. That man," pointing to Custer, "will stop at nothing. He is going to take us right into the village, where there are many more warriors than we are. We have no chance at all." The two men shook hands and Curley departed.

(Russell White Bear, p. 19): Boyer called to me and said: "Curley, you better leave us here. You ride back over the trail a ways and then go to one of the high points," pointing eastward to the high ridge east of Custer Hill, "and watch a while and see if the Sioux are besting us, and you make your way back to Terry and tell him we are all killed." Curley immediately turned back and did as instructed.

Curley had earlier stated that Mitch had lost his horse and now said he was wounded, but apparently not disabled. Mitch had often escaped from Indians before, notably in 1865, on foot and wounded in the leg, and in 1867, on foot and half frozen. Now his battle prognosis was directly on target, yet he declined Custer's second offer to save himself, saying he would "stay and fight it out," a decision that brought the very fate he knew was in store. That was an uncommonly loyal and courageous act by Michel Boyer. *He* studied the options; *he* made the choice; *he* accepted the consequences, all in accordance with the character *he* developed, no matter how it may have been influenced by his Indian, half-blood, and white heritages.

What about Curley? He, too, had declined Custer's first offer and was reluctant to accept the second, until Mitch, in fatherly fashion, gave the youngster the mission of reporting the disaster to Terry. Curley agreed to try, and what is more, he succeeded. He rode out from a point in the southeast corner of the reservation, not far from Calhoun Hill, only a few minutes after the reunion of battalions. I choose 4 minutes, yielding a time of 4:50, which, it may be noted, was 5 minutes after the three Crows had left Reno Hill for home.

The oft-told fable of Curley's escape goes like this: on that blazing hot afternoon Curley wound his body and head in a blanket and spurred his horse at breakneck speed through a cordon of thousands of naked Sioux warriors, miraculously unnoticed! Usually branded an "Indian lie," this tale bears the earmarks of white sensationalism. Curley was skilled in the use of cover, and hills and ravines abounded for that purpose. At this early stage of the battle there was no cordon at all, only small and scattered bunches of warriors, trying to harass the troops until more could come up; most were still between the troops and the river to hold them away from the village. That is why Mitch told him to ride out through the coulee to the east, keeping out of the way of the Sioux, and then go to a high point east of Custer Hill and watch a while before making his way to Terry.

And Curley said that is precisely what he did:

(Camp, 1908, p. 159): Curley was soon in a ravine out of sight. He went up a right-hand ravine, to the right of Godfrey's Spring, and stopped to look back. He estimated that this must have been $\frac{1}{2}$ an hour after leaving, and the soldiers were still fighting, although he could not discern formation.

(Camp, 1909, p. 163): I escaped by riding to the right and front. . . . I went straight east or south of east.

(Camp, 1910, p. 168): (The bearing to the coulee up which Curley rode was 9 degrees north of east.) When I rode out, there were no Sioux in front. . . . I rode up the coulee to the head of it and over the distant ridge.

(Russell White Bear, p. 18): Curley rode back [?] to the creek and followed its meandering up until a tributary took him in a northerly direction. He followed it until he reached the high ridge east of the battlefield, about $1\frac{1}{2}$ miles. From this place Curley could see the battle with field glasses. He saw the Indians circled Custer's men. After being satisfied that what Mitch Boyer said was true, he rode away to the pine hills.

Almost any ravine Curley took in an easterly direction would lead him into upper Deep Coulee, where at this time there were no Sioux, as he said. Riding northward up this coulee provided excellent cover, and on a small branch to the left there was in fact a spring, known as Godfrey's Spring. Curley rode up the main coulee, which makes a wide bend to the east and heads on the side of a high ridge with a knoll, bench-marked at 3,420 feet elevation, from which he viewed the end of the Custer battle through field glasses. Just as he said, this knoll is about 1½ miles east of Custer Hill and easily reached in 30 minutes (5:20), when the fighting was indeed ending. What Curley said fits the map and timing so precisely as to leave no doubt of his veracity. I have rejected only Camp's misunderstanding (1909, p. 163) that Curley descended Deep Coulee (through ascending warriors), cut across the open V (in full view of everyone) to Medicine Tail Coulee, which he ascended, and its north branch, to the same high knoll, a roundabout ride of 5 to 6 miles at 10 to 12 mph.

As all the foregoing accounts relate, somewhere on this escape Curley came on a saddled pony standing near a dead Sioux. He seized the pony and a red Sioux blanket, the probable source of the "disguise" fable. He also took the dead Sioux's Winchester and cartridges, as his own weapon was working poorly. Later he picked up another stray pony.

Having verified from the high knoll that Custer's men were doomed, Curley "rode away to the pine hills," so as to distance the battle and village. These pine hills were eastward, obviously on a *divide*, not a river. Curley identified the divide by the name of the river *beyond* it, just as the Rees had done in describing their long retreat, a locution that confused Camp, who first thought Curley had gone to the mouth of the Rosebud; I therefore insert clarifications:

(1909, p. 163): I went east and crossed the divide to [*sic*, of] the Rosebud, and went down to its mouth. . . .

(1910, pp. 168–69): Went beyond high point [divide] close to Tullock's Fork, and next morning went to Rosebud [divide] and back to Big Horn. Did not go to mouth of Rosebud. . . . Intended to go north to [mouth] of Big Horn, where I thought there would be a [soldier] camp (and there was such). No, went to Rosebud [divide], but not to mouth.

(1913, p. 173): I . . . got to Tullock's Fork [divide] and next [day] went to Sarpy Creek and down it to Yellowstone and up it and saw [soldier] camp over [across Yellowstone] in Pease Bottom.

The map helps enormously to resolve this apparent confusion. About 6 miles due east of the battlefield, it shows a high, timbered divide, which separates the valley of the Little Bighorn from that of Tullock's Fork. At this point, headers of Custer Creek, an east branch of the Little Bighorn, have their sources, and just over the divide are the sources of headers of Ash Creek, the westernmost branch of Tullock's Fork. This divide circles east and in a few miles separates the valleys of Tullock's Fork and the Rosebud; it then circles north to separate the valleys of Tullock's Fork and Sarpy Creek. In his efforts to identify this divide, Curley named all these streams. I anticipate evidence to come next by stating that Curley camped for the night of June 25 just over the divide between Custer and Ash creeks.

Since Curley was familiar with this country, the next morning, June 26, he would surely take the most direct route to his stated destination, the mouth of the Bighorn, to report to the Terry-Gibbon column. What he did not know was that the column had left there the morning before (June 25), leaving only Capt. Kirtland's infantry company to guard the wagon train. Curley described this day's route to Lt. Roe (1881), giving no time or date: "I went down the high ridge on the east side [Ash Creek side, indicating he had camped on this side of the divide] and went through the badlands on the east side of the Big Horn [and west bank of Tullock's Fork] and came to the Yellowstone opposite Fort Pease. There I found Terry's trail [not his column] and followed it." In his own narrative (1910, p. 10) Lt. Roe concluded a brief summary of this Curley interview with a reference to "Ash Creek, a small tributary of Tullock's Fork." This comment further supports the conclusion that from his night's camp on the Ash Creek side of the divide Curley rode down Tullock's Fork.

Knowing that Curley spent the night of June 25 on the divide, and that it was a good day's ride of some 40 miles down Tullock's Fork to the mouth of the Bighorn, we can foresee that he camped for the night of June 26 near the latter point. Here, he told Camp (1913, p. 173): "I saw a camp across [the Yellowstone] in Pease bottom. In that vicinity, I shot and killed a buffalo and roasted some of the meat, which was the first thing I had to eat since leaving the soldiers." Eating his first meal either on the evening of June 26 or the next morning means that he spent the night of the 26th there.

Tom LeForge, who had been detached to Kirtland's camp while his collarbone was mending, told Marquis (pp. 247–48) that he sign-talked across the river with Curley, although he got the day or the meal wrong:

On Monday morning [June 26] . . . as I rambled by the river, I saw an Indian come on horseback to the opposite bank. He dismounted to build a fire and cook breakfast [if breakfast, it was Tuesday]. . . . By sign-talk I learned he was . . . Curley, the 17-year-old Crow scout. He signed an inquiry as to the whereabouts of Gen. Gibbon. I indicated he had gone up the Big Horn on the steamboat [because of temporary illness]. Curley mounted and rode away in that direction. I supposed he had a dispatch. He gave no intimation that there had been a fight. He told me afterward that he was so sleepy he was thinking everybody knew all about it.

On the morning of June 27 Curley followed Terry's trail across the badlands from Tullock's Fork to the Bighorn and up the latter to the mouth of the Little Bighorn, another day's ride of nearly 40 miles. Nowhere, however, had he found any sign of the *Far West*, and so he camped in the area for the night of June 27. Not until midmorning of June 28 did he suddenly find the boat tied up at the mouth of the Little Bighorn. Curley made this date very clear to Camp (1910, p. 164): "I arrived at the steamer about the middle of the forenoon of the third day, having been three nights on the way." The three nights were necessarily those of June 25, 26, and 27, making his arrival on the morning of June 28. This date is correct, but after consulting unreliable sources, Camp unfortunately rejected it in favor of June 27.

Capt. Grant Marsh, of the *Far West*, under orders to deliver supplies for the Terry-Gibbon column to the mouth of the Little Bighorn, had steamed up the Bighorn at 12:35 P.M. of June 25, as recorded by Engineering Sgt. James Wilson, who kept the official itinerary of this voyage. Encountering shallows at every turn, the boat did not reach its destination until 10 A.M. of June 27. But then Capt. Baker, commanding the boat guard, challenged Marsh's identification of the Little Bighorn and compelled him to steam an extra 13 miles upstream, where they tied up for the night. The next morning, June 28, the boat tried to go higher up, but failed, and Baker allowed Marsh to turn back to their proper station.

Everyone aboard admitted this overrun, which caused a day's delay with seriocomic consequences. It was the reason Curley could not find the boat on the evening of June 27; it also caused the miscarriage of Terry's orders from the battlefield to Capt. Baker to send advice as to the boat's location and prepare it to receive the wounded 7th Cavalrymen. These orders were carried by scout Henry S. Bostwick and Pvt. James E. Goodwin, one of Bradley's mounted infantry, who left the battlefield on the evening of June 27 but, on reaching the Little Bighorn's mouth very early the next morning, found no boat and wasted a full day searching for it downstream.

The error was Capt. Baker's, but Capt. Marsh protected him as well as himself by dropping June 26 from his calendar, a device his biographer adopted with relish in his misrepresentation of nearly every event of this voyage. These were the false sources that led Camp to reject Curley's correct date for his arrival at the *Far West*. Capt. Baker may have joined the conspiracy, for in his official dispatch to Terry's adjutant, dated "June 29, 3:20 P.M.,"[1] he wrote that Curley had arrived at 9 A.M. of June 27; but he had already written, in agreement with Sgt. Wilson, that the boat had not reached this position the *first* time until 10 A.M. Only Curley and Sgt. Wilson kept their dates straight.

Sgt. Wilson recorded Curley's arrival: "June 28: . . . An Indian scout named Curley, known to have been with Custer, arrived about noon with information of a battle, but there being no interpreter aboard, very little information was obtained. He wore an exceedingly dejected countenance, but his appetite proved to be in first-rate order." Capt. Baker's June 29 dispatch reads: "About 9 A.M., June 27 [*sic*, 28], a Crow scout from Custer's command reached the boat, but we could only make out from him that there had been a fight." Capt. Marsh gave the *Bismarck Tribune* (July 12, 1876) a version of Curley's news, misdated, of course, but also padded with news brought by Muggins Taylor the next morning and Curley's later debriefing; I quote only the beginning, slightly condensed:

> While the *Far West* lay there on the morning of June 27 [*sic*, 28], Curley, a Crow scout, came out of the timber near the boat and was recognized as one who was with Custer; he proves to be the last survivor. Curley could not make his gestures understood, but given a pencil, he drew a sketch of the battlefield. Making a few dots, he conveyed by signs that they represented white men; these he surrounded by dots to represent Indians. Curley said in fair English [?]: "White men all dead—me get two ponies."

James A. Sipes, a barber aboard the boat, confirmed Curley's extra ponies to Camp (p. 241, slightly condensed): "We [Capt. Marsh and others] were fishing about a mile upriver on the left bank and Curley rode

[1]Capt. Baker to Gen. Terry, June 29, 1876, 3:20 P.M., Letters Received, Dept. of Dak., 1876, Box 19 (G-RG98).

into the river on the right bank just opposite us. We were much surprised and frightened, but he held up his hands or gun and made a peace sign. Curley had three ponies and a red Sioux blanket, which he afterward told us he had taken from a dead Sioux."

Having spent that night on the *Far West*, Curley was present the next morning, June 29, when Muggins Taylor rode in from the battlefield, bearing Terry's dispatches to Fort Ellis to be forwarded by telegraph. He also brought the first intelligible news of the battle and oral orders to prepare the boat to receive the wounded. Capt. Baker's June 29 dispatch also describes this arrival: "This morning at 5 o'clock, Taylor, the Ellis courier, came in and gave us the particulars [of the battle]. As his horse was used up completely, I gave him a fresh mount and started him on his way in less than an hour after his arrival. Capt. Marsh has been busy all day [thus since Taylor's arrival] arranging the boat for the reception of the wounded."

The next arrivals that afternoon were couriers Bostwick and Pvt. Goodwin, who had searched in vain for the *Far West* all the way down to Kirtland's camp in Pease Bottom.[2] There, told that the boat was still somewhere up the Bighorn, the mystified pair started back up. Capt. Baker's dispatch of June 29, "3:20 P.M.," began with a description of this event: "Gen. Terry's note just received. The couriers are now feeding their horses and will return to your command in half an hour."

It was thus about 4:00 when Capt. Baker sent this dispatch to Terry, in care of Bostwick and Curley, for the latter told Camp (1909, p. 164; 1910, p. 170; 1913, p. 173) that on the day after he had boarded the boat, which translates to June 29, he accompanied a white man bearing a message from the boat to the battlefield. This white man could only have been Bostwick, implying that Curley had replaced Pvt. Goodwin, who could rejoin his outfit when it arrived with Terry. It was about 7:45 when the two couriers met Terry's column on the march with the litter-borne wounded, for Terry's diary noted that "the march commenced at 6:30 P.M.," and Matt Carroll's diary noted that "after going 4 miles, met Bostwick, who said the boat was at the mouth of the Little Big Horn." In

[2] Paul McCormick to ed., June 29, "Mouth of Big Horn," *Bozeman Times*, July 6, 1876. McCormick wrote that he had arrived there June 26, finding one company of infantry there, and obtained information from "Bostwick, a scout, yesterday, June 28."

the foregoing interviews Curley also related that he was then ordered to the boat with a note, undoubtedly a warning that the command would arrive that night. Curley apparently made a fast ride, for Sgt. Wilson recorded: "At 10 P.M. the van of Terry's command arrived. The main column with the wounded did not arrive until 1 A.M., June 30." Curley remained aboard that night with Half Yellow Face, who had transported White Swan by Indian travois.

The *Far West,* having left at 1:30 P.M. of June 30 with Terry and staff and all the wounded, made a fast trip down the Bighorn to reach Kirtland's camp before dark. Running Wolf, spokesman for some Rees who had brought dispatches from Powder River, told Libby (p. 144) that, when the steamboat arrived with the wounded, the Rees helped unload both White Swan and Goose, who told them the other scouts would march down later "on foot." In fact, Curley and Half Yellow Face and five Ree scouts had been left behind with Gibbon's and Reno's troops in order to hold muster on the afternoon of June 30 and would not start their two-day march down to the Yellowstone until the morning of July 1.

Lt. Varnum's muster roll correctly lists the five Ree scouts as "present" and Goose as "absent in hospital, wounded"; the twenty-one who had left for Powder River were listed as "missing in action." Lt. Bradley's muster roll, at least as published,[3] is defective in a way that suggests it was mistranscribed. His own Crows, who had deserted on June 26, are so listed, but the six who had been detached to Custer are fouled up. Only four are listed as "Detached Service with Maj. Reno," including White Swan, "wounded"; of the other two, White Man Runs Him, correctly, and Curley, incorrectly, are listed as "AWOL since June 26." That was another white man's error that victimized Curley, but he gave Camp (1910, p. 170) the correct story:

> Next morning [July 1] went to Yellowstone River, and Half Yellow Face and I camped with the soldiers. Late in afternoon [July 2] we got to Pease Bottom, where the steamer was. There we were ferried across the Yellowstone by steamer. I and my horse were the first to go on board. We had Tom LaForge on steamer, a good interpreter. The soldiers knew that I had been with Custer and talked with me much.

[3] Chandler, *Of Garryowen in Glory,* 438 (B).

Curley's debriefing by Lt. Bradley probably began then, but it may well have resumed the next morning, July 3.

In this same interview Curley added that in a talk with Gibbon [July 4?] he asked for a leave to go home. As most of the other Crow scouts had already done so, while Curley and Half Yellow Face remained faithful, the general granted them leave but retained White Swan a few more days in the hospital. Several diaries noted that on the evening of July 4 Paul McCormick left with a sack of mail for Bozeman, and with him went Curley, Half Yellow Face, and Tom LeForge, as the last-named related in his *Memoirs* (p. 254). About July 6 the three Crow scouts spotted their home village camped at the mouth of Pryor Creek. Eagerly, they plunged across the Yellowstone to be greeted with overwhelming joy by their families, who had been mourning their loss. Mitch Boyer's wife and family were left to mourn alone.

LeForge's mission was to induce all the original Crow scouts to return to duty. He gathered them all, as well as a batch of new recruits, and delivered them to Gibbon's camp at the mouth of the Bighorn on July 14. In the absence of Lt. Bradley, the next day Lt. Burnett, Gibbon's adjutant, mustered in the twenty-three new Crow scouts, making forty-seven the total number on duty for the rest of that frustrating summer campaign. The missing one was Tom LeForge, who had been discharged as of July 9 and was picked up the next day as an interpreter by Gibbon's quartermaster.

Like everyone else, I was baffled at first by Curley's accounts, obtained by interviewers through interpreters. But when I systematically used maps to maintain geographic orientation, and time-motion analysis to maintain temporal orientation and to provide feasibility checks, his accounts began to blossom as a unique display of valuable information. I trust that the old image of "Curley the liar" will fade in favor of "Curley the reliable."

THE FINAL MINUTES

At the time Custer's five companies reunited on the border of the reservation they were already under attack, at least lightly. After Curley left at about 4:50, they totaled 210 men or fewer, if any had fallen during the preliminary phase. The Indians were still largely between the troops and the river, but many more were swarming up every minute and would reach fifteen or sixteen hundred, making the odds approach eight to one. The terrain odds were equally formidable: the country was all cut up by ravines into narrow ridges with small knolls, completely unsuitable for effective cavalry charges and utterly lacking in good defensive positions where five companies could dismount and dig in. The nimble Indians, however, could move around unseen to strike from any direction, or creep up on foot under cover to deliver heavy fire, stampede horses, and wreak general havoc. It was this combination of vastly superior numbers and unsuitable terrain that spelled disaster for the cavalry. Mitch Boyer knew they were doomed, and it would be surprising indeed if Custer was not reading the same handwriting on the wall.

It is not possible to reconstruct the fighting action on the Custer field, for no participant with Custer survived to describe it, and accounts from Indian participants reveal little more than their attitudes and fighting tactics. A proper reconstruction requires evidence on who did what, when, and where, on both sides, and all tied properly together, but such evidence is lacking. Pure speculation needs no evidence, but since it merely fills a vacuum with vacuity, it yields no progress. On the other hand, a search for evidence that imposes constraints may at least reduce the possibilities to a finite number. Since there is more evidence on where the killing action occurred than on any other aspect, I am prompted to focus on this dimension and see what may be inferred from it.

A portion of the "where" evidence consists of the location of battle artifacts found on the Custer field. Army artifacts can usually be distinguished from Indian artifacts, but their numbers are rather small, for several reasons. The Indians stripped the soldiers' bodies of clothing, arms, and ammunition, and as they customarily reloaded empty shell cases for their own use, they gathered up many of these, too. For a century amateur relic-hunters have harvested artifacts, only a few of which have been located and identified for the battlefield records. The construction of roads, buildings, and a national cemetery on the reservation has buried or lost another unknown number of artifacts. In 1984–85 a professional archaeological project[1] systematically scoured the reservation with metal detectors and found, identified, and precisely located many artifacts of all kinds, but not many shell cases. As these findings were not yet published in full at the time of this writing, I shall not deal with battle artifacts, army or Indian.

The remainder of the "where" evidence pertains to the distribution of fallen bodies on the Custer field, which in general follows that of army artifacts. As was their custom, the Indians removed all their dead from the field, leaving no trace of where they had fallen, but the surviving troops made a systematic search for their own dead and gave them burial where they had fallen. These burials were necessarily shallow, for lack of sufficient tools, and hasty, because the survivors had some fifty suffering comrades, wounded with Reno, who required immediate evacuation.

[1] Scott, *Archeological Insights into the Custer Battle* (B).

The distribution of fallen bodies is inadequate for a reconstruction of the action, but it can furnish useful constraints. The inquiry must begin by establishing the total number of killed in the entire two-day battle and proceed by partitioning this total between the Custer and Reno fields. Appendix B presents a detailed analysis of the evidence for these two steps, as assembled in its Table 15. It gives the total killed as 16 officers, 237 enlisted men, and 10 "others" (scouts and civilians), for a grand total of 263. Our primary interest is in those who fell on the Custer field, shown in the table as 13 officers, 193 enlisted men, and 4 "others," for a total of 210.

As the next step in the analysis, Table 16 lists the total number of bodies found and buried on the Custer field, a form of body count. Seven separate recorded counts average 209, only one short of the total killed there. This consistency assures us that the search for bodies was remarkably thorough and that evidence of gravesites should be a good indication of where bodies fell. It also reveals, contrary to persistent rumors and fears, that there were certainly not 20 to 40 men missing in action from Custer's own command.

Appendix B continues with evidence that the burial parties were able to recognize the bodies of only 10 of 13 officers (77 percent); the locations of 9 of them were also recorded. As for enlisted men, no recognition list was apparently kept, and burial party accounts indicate that only a small percentage was recognized and the locations are vague and often contradictory. The result is that there is some information on where recognized officers fell, but very little on where recognized enlisted men, and therefore companies, fell.

During the thirteen years following the battle, as discussed in the appendix, numerous military parties, which included both soldiers and scouts who had participated in the original burials, visited the Custer field to remound the graves and restake them, thus maintaining both physical and memory evidence of their locations, though no party surveyed and recorded the locations. The first party, in July 1877, exhumed the remains of all but one of the recognized officers for reburial in the East. Another party, in 1880, exhumed all the other remains that could be found and buried them in a trench around the foot of the granite memorial shaft that was erected on Custer Hill at the same time and still stands.

Finally, in 1890, Capt. Sweet, of the garrison of nearby Fort Custer, erected marble headstones on the gravesites. The grave markers for officers bore their names, but those for enlisted men were labeled merely *Soldier*. Thirteen officers' markers were shipped for those recognized, but as one was misnamed, it had to be returned; 10 were thus erected on the Custer field and only 2 for the 3 recognized officers on the Reno field. By another error, only 236 soldier markers were shipped, one short of the total number of enlisted men killed in the entire battle. For reasons discussed in the appendix, all 236 were erected on the Custer field, although only 193 enlisted men had fallen there; thus 43 were spurious as to location. In 1891 the locations of these markers were plotted on the USGS Battlefield Map, but quite inaccurately. These marble markers still stand on the Custer field, although a few others have been added, subtracted, or moved. The poor map and the presence of spurious markers have frustrated students of the Custer battle ever since.

The first ray of hope came in 1984, when the archaeological project resurveyed the reservation in detail and precisely located, by metric coordinates, all the grave markers now standing on the Custer field. Numbering 252, they consist of 12 officers (including Lt. Sturgis, never recognized), 3 "others" (all recognized), and 237 enlisted men. Despite the inclusion of some 44 spurious markers, the distribution of the gravesites on the field defines so distinctive a pattern that it is worth examination as simple "where" evidence.

The published preliminary report of the 1984 archaeological project presents among other things an enormous chart, which plots locations of every marker.[2] But it also nearly defies use by an interested reader. It shows no geographical features, nor a single coordinate line; only metric coordinate numerals are printed on the margins with no mark to place the missing coordinate lines. Furthermore, the text of the report gives the coordinates for no markers and gives erroneous coordinates for the point that anchors the coordinate system to the terrain.

Since the most essential requirement in archaeology is to locate all artifacts meticulously, it is clear that some higher authority had forbidden these archaeologists to publish openly this vital information, presumably to prevent future vandalism. But, in fact, by locating the artifacts before removing them for study, identification, and *preservation*, the archaeologists thwarted vandalism, while the ban on publishing locations merely sabotaged the value of the project.

[2] Ibid.

Faced with this problem, I first measured the chart scale (chart distance between farthest separated coordinate numerals, divided by the difference between these numerals). Using all kinds of clues, I approximated the point on the chart that corresponds to the SE corner post of the reservation in order to anchor the system to the terrain. Its error is probably less than 15 meters, and since it is systematic, that is, identical for each marker, it cannot alter their pattern. I then drew coordinate lines on the original chart and read the coordinates for the markers, in isolated small groups of one to five, or more when densely crowded. These small numerals, which cover about 15 meters, were then plotted on graph paper. This procedure was adequate for displaying the pattern of markers and gives away no secrets.

Attention is now directed to Figure 7, which displays the pattern of markers on the reservation. The upper and lower right corners represent the NE and SE corners of the reservation; both corners are right angles and are 1 mile (1,600 meters, or 16 hectometers) apart. The top, bottom, and right borders are fence lines; off the graph to the left runs the meandering river. The coordinate numbers in the margin are hectometers (100 meters), but the zero points of the two scales are far off the graph. Instead of coordinate lines, points are plotted every hectometer in both directions, corresponding to iron stakes driven by the archaeological surveyors. Since the reservation is rotated counterclockwise from the cardinal directions, the graph coordinates are labeled N′ and E′, the prime warning that these are *nominal* directions. Thus N′ stands for true NW, and E′ stands for true NE, a convention I shall observe faithfully to avoid confusion. The anchor point for our grid was checked by measuring the distance of the granite monument from the N′, E′, and S′ fences on modern maps, and its location is plotted in Figure 7, as a cross. Since it falls just E′ of the dense group of markers on Custer Hill, it supports my approximation.

A mere glance at Figure 7 reveals that the distribution of markers forms a distinct pattern. They are scattered within a narrow band along the perimeter of an irregular quadrilateral figure, but with occasional gaps. To aid the eye, dashed lines with occasional projections have been drawn to enclose major groups of markers that define the four sides of the figure, and thus expose gaps. Adjacent to each major group, an encircled numeral gives the total number of markers comprised in that group. An important determinant of this quadrilateral pattern is the terrain.

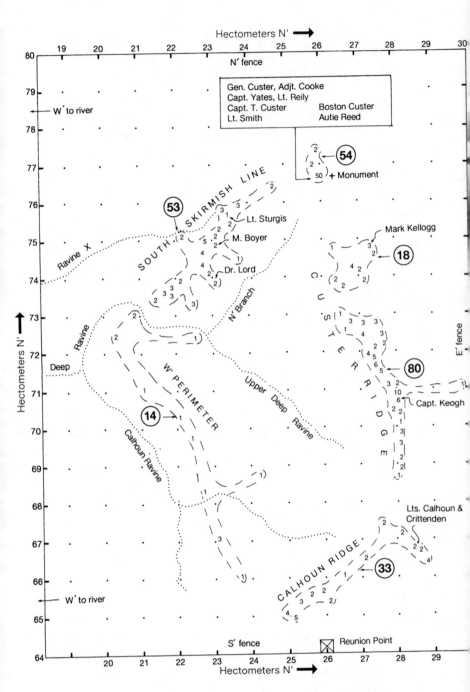

Figure 7. Grave Markers on the Custer Field

Although the terrain in general slopes downward from right to left toward the river, it features many ridges separated by ravines. To give a better feel for this, the bottom drainage channels of significant ravines are sketched as dotted lines and named. *Deep Ravine* (not to be confused with Deep *Coulee*) heads near the Keogh marker as a broad, shallow depression, but before reaching the narrow gap at the N'W' corner of the figure, it is growing deep; below the gap it is steep-sided. It has two branches; the S' branch, called *Calhoun Ravine*, heads near Calhoun Hill and curves to join Deep Ravine below the gap; the N' *branch* heads near Custer Hill and curves to join Deep Ravine above the gap. A short *Ravine X* heads near the N' side of the figure and drains more directly to the river.

It should now become clear that all four sides of the quadrilateral pattern fall along ridges. The S' side is *Calhoun Ridge*, and the E' side is *Custer Ridge*. The N' side is also a ridge, usually called the *South Skirmish Line*, for it extends almost true south from Custer Hill. The W' side is another ridge, whose S' end is called *Greasy Grass Hill*. That the markers are so confined to ridges is not surprising, for there are tactical advantages in avoiding ravines and fighting from high ground, whether in motion or halted. Note also that the crests of these ridges are all narrow, offering no strong defensive position for five companies.

Before we proceed farther, the question of spurious markers must be addressed. Capt. Sweet's report reveals that he was both ingenious and conscientious. The job took ten days, but he first erected named markers while searching hard for other gravesites; this search revealed the excess markers and allowed him time to ponder a solution. He had two obvious options: to use the spurious markers to destroy the pattern of gravesites or *intermingle* them to preserve the pattern. His assignment was ceremonial and solemn, and he was conscientious; many of the markers are erected in adjacent pairs. I conclude that he took pains to preserve the pattern, even its gaps. Yet reluctant he might have been to haul the heavy slabs in wagons farther than necessary, especially across Deep Ravine. His access route was from the north to Custer Hill; the terrain was smooth and level along the E' side and smooth and downhill along the N' side, suggesting that he intermingled the spurious markers on these two sides and Custer Hill only, leaving legitimate ones on the S' and W' sides. If that is so, the spurious markers should not affect the *pattern*, and the *numbers* can be approximately corrected by subtracting fifteen markers each from those on Custer Hill and the N′ and E′ sides.

Whether Custer's reunited battalion entered the present reservation from the west, south, or east has long remained a crippling uncertainty, but the analysis of the preliminary phase suggests that the five companies united at the reunion point on the S′ border, about where it is plotted and labeled in Figure 7. At that place and moment they were all engaged, at least lightly. This point is so close to Calhoun Ridge as to imply that the battalion proceeded directly to this ridge as the nearest higher ground. Curley was quoted as saying that, just before he left, a squad was deployed toward the W′ end of Calhoun Ridge to drive back some Indians, but when this effort failed, the main body of troops headed for Calhoun Hill and even toward Custer Ridge. All this is consistent, and the markers along Calhoun Ridge indicate that it is where the heavy action began.

Although the perimeter distribution of markers might suggest a long-held defensive position, this possibility is easily eliminated. It contains numerous gaps, without terrain ramparts to replace men; its length of about 1.8 miles (2,900 meters) would spread 210 men, including horse-holders, 45 feet apart (14 meters), and it would take considerable time to reach these far-flung positions. But just as striking as the perimeter distribution is the enormous area it encloses, which is utterly barren of markers. Since the troops were engaged from the beginning, it is unlikely that they reached the perimeter positions by crossing the area barren of graves. It is far more likely that they reached them by moving along the perimeter.

Did they move clockwise or counterclockwise around the perimeter, or split and move in both directions? The pressing need at the moment was to reach higher ground, which dictated a counterclockwise movement. The opposite direction was not only downhill, but headed directly toward Deep Ravine, where it was steep-sided, an obvious death trap. As for splitting or staying together, Custer must have realized that the adverse circumstances demanded that he keep his small force together, at least within mutual supporting distance. If the movement started in the counterclockwise direction, it must have continued so, for none apparently cut across the enormous barren area.

The nascent hypothesis that the troops moved counterclockwise around the perimeter can be tested for feasibility by an overall time-motion analysis. If the heavy action began at 4:50, when Curley left, and ended at 5:25, as observed by Weir's men from Weir Peak, it lasted 35 minutes. The total perimeter distance from the w' end of Calhoun Ridge around to the clear gap at that same corner is about $1\frac{3}{4}$ miles (2,800 meters). Travel time for this distance at 3 mph is 35 minutes, but at 6 mph is $17\frac{1}{2}$ minutes. The slower pace leaves no time for fighting halts but allows the last man to make the full circuit before falling. The fast pace allows $17\frac{1}{2}$ minutes for fighting halts. Although this timing does not prove the hypothesis, it flashes no feasibility alarm.

Under heavy action, the motion around the perimeter could hardly have been uniform, nor with all troops moving in unison. The trail of fallen men shows that there was cumulative attrition all the way, but again not uniform, for there are obvious gaps in markers, as well as high-density loci, as at Custer Hill, and thinly scattered segments, as along the w' side. The hypothesis accommodates progress interrupted by halts, separations by rear and advance groups, and even retrograde movements. The only constraint is that all the men fell on the perimeter path of ridges. Following the circuit of variable-density markers may now yield further clues to the action.

Starting at Calhoun Ridge, we find a group of 33 markers, probably legitimate ones, with distinct gaps at both ends. At Calhoun Hill are two named officer markers, one for Lt. Calhoun and the other for Lt. Crittenden, both of Company L. That leaves 31 soldier markers, but burial parties recognized several of the fallen as Company C men. The fact that only Company L had 44 enlisted men (the others had 36) suggests that about 15 Company L men escaped to proceed without officers. The gap ahead prompts the *speculation* that Company L had been detailed to halt and make a rearguard stand, while the others forged ahead to a better position.

Beyond the gap we find two groups of markers spread along Custer Ridge, but separated by a tiny gap and both separated from Custer Hill by a large gap. The first group of 80 starts with thinly scattered markers, perhaps the escapees from Calhoun Hill. At its dense center is a named marker for Capt. Keogh of Company I, around which burial parties recognized several enlisted men of the same company. There is no marker for Keogh's subaltern, Lt. Porter, who was never recognized; nevertheless, it is the likeliest place for him to have fallen. Among the second smaller group of 18 markers is a named one for reporter Mark Kellogg, which was erected later but in the wrong place, for burial parties agreed his body was found and buried far down on the South Skirmish Line. The two groups total 98 markers, undoubtedly well diluted with spurious ones. Subtracting the 2 named markers and about 15 spurious ones leaves 81 soldier markers, equivalent in number to more than two companies of 36 each.

This pattern prompts the *speculation* that Calhoun's rearguard stand had enabled the other companies to advance in relative safety to Custer Hill, as suggested by its isolation from other markers. Perhaps from there, or on the way, it was noted that Calhoun was under heavy attack, and Capt. Keogh turned back with Company I to support him, but in turn was overwhelmed. Another company, or parts of several companies, may have followed in Keogh's wake, only to be mauled in turn, thus contributing to the heavy losses along Custer Ridge. The identity of this company, or companies, is unknown, but Capt. Tom Custer's Company C is a possibility, since it lost men on Calhoun Ridge and was a part of Keogh's presumed battalion. If so, it may have been here that his subaltern, Lt. Harrington, fell, though his body was never recognized.

At isolated Custer Hill we find a very dense concentration of 54 markers, also well diluted with spurious ones. The densest cluster of 50 includes named ones for the recognized civilians, Boston Custer and Autie Reed, and 6 for recognized officers: Gen. Custer and Adjt. Cooke of headquarters; Capt. Yates and Lt. Reily of Company F; Capt. Tom Custer of Company C (his subaltern, Lt. Harrington, was earlier mentioned); and Lt. Smith of Company E, whose subaltern, Lt. Sturgis, was never recognized. A marker for the latter, however, was erected later on the South Skirmish Line. Subtracting the 8 named markers and 15 likely spurious ones from the total of 54 leaves 31 soldier markers on Custer Hill, equivalent to less than one company.

The cumulative attrition of officers and men has now reached the equivalent of more than three companies and has probably been destroying the integrity of companies, which is why I have been using the expression *equivalent to*. It is also likely that officers and men, wounded in the earlier action, have been accumulating at headquarters on Custer Hill, there to be held under the care of Dr. Lord. This situation may help to explain why officers from three companies died there with only the equivalent of less than a company. It certainly explains why Dr. Lord's body was recognized on Custer Hill, "20 feet southwest of Custer's." Capt. Sweet was unaware of this fact, however, and when he found a "surgeon's button" on the South Skirmish Line, he erroneously erected the doctor's marker on that spot.

If the counterclockwise hypothesis is true, it follows that men equivalent to more than one company left Custer Hill, *before* the final slaughter there began, and proceeded to the South Skirmish Line. Furthermore, they apparently crossed a conspicuous gap before their own heavy losses began. The 53 markers on the South Skirmish Line, again well diluted with spurious ones, include the misplaced marker for Dr. Lord and one for unrecognized Lt. Sturgis, erected later by a guess as good as any. One soldier marker stands on what is now known as Mitch Boyer's grave, to be discussed later. Subtracting these 3 markers and 15 spurious ones from the total of 53 leaves 35 soldier markers, equivalent to one company. Burial accounts agree that many of these bodies belonged to Company E, undoubtedly the reason Lt. Sturgis's marker was placed here. Burial accounts cite the number of bodies as low as 20 and as high as 38, with several specifying 28, which is close enough to my calculated 35, but it is unlikely that all belonged to Company E.

The next gap, though tiny, is of special significance, for through it runs Deep Ravine, here steep-sided, formidable to cross, and dangerous to be trapped in. The 14 widely scattered soldier markers beyond on the W′ perimeter are probably all legitimate and are equivalent to about one-third of a company. Burial accounts appear to ignore these bodies entirely. Again, if the counterclockwise hypothesis is true, these 14 men came from the South Skirmish Line and so must have crossed Deep Ravine, an act of desperation forced by an overwhelming Indian attack on the South Skirmish Line. Though in a flight for life, all fell before reaching Calhoun Ridge. That in turn means that 49 enlisted men, equivalent to about one and one-third companies, had left Custer Hill, 35 to die on the South Skirmish Line and 14 in flight along the W′ perimeter.

This scenario, guided by the counterclockwise hypothesis, makes Custer Hill the "last stand" for Gen. Custer and those who fell there, but was it the latest stand on the Custer field? There is nothing to exclude the distinct possibility that two separated bodies of troops made "last stands" that terminated simultaneously. In fact, one force of Indians that attacked

Custer Hill from the E′ and N′ believed they had struck the final blow; another force of Indians that attacked the South Skirmish Line from the W′ and N′ also believed that they had struck the final blow. I am content to accept that both were so nearly correct as to make argument over a few minutes pointless, thus satisfying the demands of high drama and perhaps the truth.

This reconstruction leaves the question, Why would the troops separate before the overwhelming attacks began? One can only *speculate*, but a combination of two facts may have played a role. The area on Custer Hill may have been too small to provide a good defensive position for more than two companies, and if the approach of Indians from the W′ and N′ had been spotted first, troops may have been sent out to attack or at least hold the enemy away from Custer Hill and the wounded.

We turn now to a perplexing problem that arises from some burial accounts of the bodies along the South Skirmish Line. As sketched in Figure 7, Deep Ravine and its branches drain a large open basin; in its center, upper Deep Ravine starts to deepen at the mouth of its small N′ branch. Most of the markers lie *above* this junction and on the ridge paralleled by the N′ branch, leaving only a few markers on the lower ridge paralleled by the deepening Deep Ravine. For lack of proper names for the terrain, informants referred ambiguously to bodies "extending down from Custer Hill toward the river" or "along a deep ravine or gully." The first description is fully compatible with the ridge and its open slope, and so is the second, if the "deep ravine or gully" refers to the N′ branch or even the whole basin. A few accounts do mention bodies on the ridge or its open slope.

The problem stems from some accounts, traditionally accepted as literally correct, that specify that the bodies were found at the *bottom* of a steep-sided ravine and that they were *buried* where they had fallen. But why would *all* the men enter so obvious a death trap *before* any had fallen? And why would their comrades have buried them in the silty bottom of an intermittently flooded ravine? And why over the next and succeeding years would their comrades have remounded and restaked graves on the ridge above? Some who located the line of bodies by mileages disagreed wildly. For example, Benteen testified (p. 327) that they lay "50 or 75 yards from the river," which is far off Figure 7 to the left! Moylan testified (p. 224) that they were "$\frac{1}{2}$ or $\frac{3}{4}$ mile from the river," which extends even beyond Custer Hill!

Some informants evidently suffered memory failure, for which there is a plausible explanation. Some saw signs that soldiers had scrambled down the side of the ravine or clawed their way up; it would not be surprising if such horrifying visions lingered longer than the sight of more bodies to bury on the ridge above. Not all memories failed, however, for Lt. Hare testified (p. 262) that these bodies were "300 to 400 yards from Custer [Hill]," which straddles the middle of the South Skirmish Line, opposite the N' branch. Sgt. Kanipe wrote Camp (p. 95 n. 15) that he "rode along the edge of the deep gully about 2000 feet from the present monument and counted 28 bodies." His ride extended down to near the end of the South Skirmish Line.

Burial accounts may be ambiguous, but solid physical evidence indicates that the bodies were found and buried along the ridge. Capt. Sweet searched diligently for staked gravesites before planting markers, and all are on the ridge. Furthermore, the archaeologists made four excavations around markers on the ridge and found bone fragments and other evidence of original burials in each instance. Along the bottom of the steepsided ravine they made more excavations and bored innumerable augerholes, 10 inches in diameter and 3 feet deep, but found no traces whatever of burials. The physical traces, of course, could have been washed away, but no more easily than memory traces from the mind.

This exploration into the unknown has been based primarily on marker evidence as to where men fell on the Custer field. If it has shed even some dim light and raised relevant new questions, it has accomplished all that can be expected from so restricted a database. Even our guide, the elastic counterclockwise hypothesis, cannot qualify as a theory, for it is only a trial hypothesis, to be checked against further evidence. Perhaps the wider scope of the final archaeological report will support, modify, or eliminate it. Any of the three would represent some degree of welcome progress.

The Fate of Mitch Boyer

We have learned that Mitch Boyer was half Indian and half white, but not just genetically, for he fully understood the cultures and attitudes of both races, enabling him to function with ease and confidence in both societies, an uncommon trait. His Indian side was originally Sioux, but long association made him a Crow by choice and adoption, further evidence of his adaptability. The Sioux were tribal enemies of the Crows and so became Mitch's enemy. When the whites were at war with the Sioux, Mitch willingly served the whites, even before he became a Crow. Abundant evidence has emerged to show that he remained loyal to both the Crows and the whites.

Nevertheless, vague rumors have hinted that Mitch betrayed Custer by absenting himself during the campaign to keep the Sioux informed and to conspire with them in setting a trap for the troops. During the times when he is claimed to have been absent on such treacherous missions, his whereabouts with the troops are now known. Everything that we have learned about Mitch's character throughout his life vigorously denies treachery. Instead, he served faithfully during the campaign as a superb guide, as an interpreter for his Crow friends, and as the chief gatherer of invaluable intelligence regarding their mutual enemy. If the command failed to make full use of his information, the fault was not his. On perceiving that the outcome would be disaster, he rejected offers to save himself and accepted the fatal consequences.

Lt. Bradley, himself intelligence-minded and one who had ample opportunity to observe Mitch in action during the campaign, was undoubtedly the source of the first public notice of his death; it appeared in the July 15, 1876, issue of the *Helena Herald*:

> No one on the plains knew so much of the country and as thoroughly as Mitch Boyer did, and to his credit, be it said, that for a long term of years, whenever he was called upon to perform dangerous service for the military, he never shrank from accepting the mission, and generally carried it to a successful issue. The poor half-breed is no more, but as he once said: "If the Sioux kill me, I have the satisfaction of knowing I popped many of them over, and they can't get even now, if they do get me."

Gen. Gibbon included a similar evaluation in his 1877 narrative (p. 671) of the campaign: "The Sioux had several times reported they had killed Mitch Bowyer. He was a half-breed Sioux and they had often tried to kill him. He was the protege of the celebrated Jim Bridger; was the best guide in this section of the country, and the only half-breed I ever met who could give the distances to be covered with accuracy in miles."

Having remained to fight it out with Custer, Mitch undoubtedly fell somewhere on the perimeter pattern. All early accounts confirm this location, but some later reminiscences claim he fell in isolation, even off the reservation. Lt. Bradley's obituary, just quoted, began with the sentence: "Amongst the fallen on the bloody field . . . was one of Custer's guides, Mitch Boyer." Gibbon's eulogy, just quoted, also began: "The body of our guide, Mitch Bowyer, was found lying in the middle of troopers."

Two other accounts agree on which perimeter Mitch had fallen. Lt. Bourke, who studied the Custer field on July 21, 1877, with Gen. Sheridan's inspection party, that day recorded in his diary:

> [From Custer Hill] a frightened party of 30 or 40 men, still running, strove to gain the bank of the river. They were killed like wolves. As we made our way along the ravine, we stumbled upon four skulls in one collection, a lone one in another place, another under a little bush and still another picked up by my orderly. . . . Sticking out from the ground in the ravine was the body of a man, still clad in rough garb of a scout, boots and bullet-riddled hat still by him. There was nothing to give the slightest idea as to who he might have been.[3]

The perimeter thus described is certainly the South Skirmish Line, and since the only other scout with Custer was Boston Custer, who was recognized on Custer Hill, this body must have been Mitch Boyer's.

Sgt. Kanipe confirmed this conclusion when he wrote Camp (p. 95 n. 15) of his findings on June 27, 1876, with Benteen's party: "I next went [from Custer Hill] along the line of bodies toward the river, and riding along the edge of the deep gully about 2000 ft. from where the monument now stands, I counted 28 bodies in this gulch. The only one I recognized at the time was Mitch Bouyer."

There is little point in quoting four additional reminiscent and hearsay claims that Mitch's body was found isolated on the riverbank or halfway to Reno Hill, for solid evidence pinpoints Mitch's grave near the middle of the South Skirmish Line. When the archaeologists in 1984 made their first Excavation A around paired grave markers 33 and 34, only $1\frac{1}{4}$ meters apart, in the middle of the South Skirmish Line, they found artifacts and bones that subsequent examination proved to belong to Mitch Boyer, as labeled in Figure 7. The counterclockwise hypothesis suggests

[3]Bourke, "Diary, 1877" (M).

that Mitch had made it with Custer to Custer Hill and then joined the sortie to counter the approach of Indians from the w' and n'. He thus survived longer than most.

The findings uncovered in this excavation, as described in the preliminary archaeological report (p. 39, and Fig. 16, p. 41) indicate first that it was an original field burial, for among the artifacts was a fragment of a cedar stake, such as used to mark gravesites by the first exhumation party in early July 1877, and several cobblestones, which had been brought up from the river to hold down the dirt on remounded graves. Other artifacts indicate that this spot had been the target of Indian fire, for a .50-.70 lead bullet from an Indian weapon was found, as well as other fragments of lead slugs. Highly significant clothing artifacts included three four-hole trouser buttons, a rubber poncho button, a boot heel, boot nails, a fragment of leather, and a shank-type mother-of-pearl shirt button of a civilian, not army, type. The boot and civilian button recall the body in scout garb seen by Lt. Bourke on July 21, 1877.

The bones found included a finger, a tail-bone, some cranial fragments, and the bone structure, with upper teeth, underlying the left side of the face and defining the eye orbit, nasal cavity, cheek, and upper jaw. Preliminary examination (pp. 101–2) indicated that these bones belonged to one individual. The boot heel was found 5 feet 5 inches from the cranial fragments, a possible clue to his height. The teeth were worn in a pattern characteristic of habitual pipe-smokers. The finger showed some deformity, and the cranial fragments indicated that the skull had been crushed about the time of death.

Further examination by a forensic expert, Dr. Clyde Snow, established that death had occurred at age thirty-five to forty, and the conformation of the facial bones, especially the teeth, identified him as a mixed-blood of white and Indian parentage. Suddenly, the whole picture pointed uniquely to Mitch Boyer, the sole mixed-blood who died with Custer, and the best historical evidence agrees that he was killed and buried on the South Skirmish Line. His baptismal record documents his birth in 1837, making him thirty-nine years old at the time of death, within the forensic range.

There is still more that makes the identification as conclusive as anyone could wish. Although there is only one known photograph of Mitch, it is a nearly full-face portrait. Using a video camera and display screen,

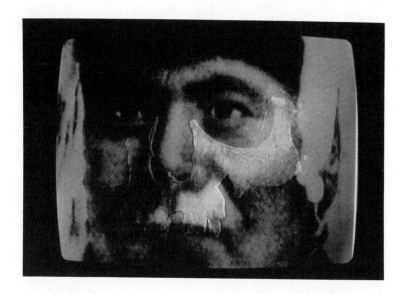

Portrait of Mitch Boyer with facial-bone fragments superimposed. Courtesy of the National Park Service Midwest Archeological Center.

it proved possible to superimpose the image of a cast of the facial bones on the image of the photograph. The fit was strikingly perfect, broad face, eye orbit, nasal cavity, teeth and all, and uniquely so. This identification was publicly announced in October 1987 and has since been published in the organ of the Custer Battlefield Historical and Museum Association.[4]

The original fragments of bone were ceremoniously buried in the Custer Battlefield National Cemetery on July 25, 1986, the 110th anniversary of his death.

May Mitch Boyer be recognized as a courageous and talented man by all.

[4] Scott, "Nameless Faces of Custer Battlefield," 2–4 (A).

APPENDIX A:
MICHAEL BOYER'S TESTIMONY
ON THE FETTERMAN MASSACRE

From Commissioner John F. Kinney's Reports, Exhibit F, National Archives, M740, Roll 1, fr. 620–26.

Fort Phil Kearney, D.T.
July 27, 1867

The Special Commission [John F. Kinney] met. Present, Michael Boyer, who after being duly sworn, testified as follows:

Age, 28; residence, Fort C. F. Smith; occupation, post guide and interpreter.

Q. How long have you lived in the mountains, and what bands of Indians have you been associated with?

A. I have been in the mountains since 1849 and have been trading with the Ogalallah Sioux, Snakes, Bannacks and Crows.

Q. How long have you been near the Yellowstone River?

A. Since 1864.

Q. How long have you been at Fort C. F. Smith, M.T.?

A. Seven months.

Q. What Indian languages do you speak?

A. I talk Sioux and Crow.

Q. Where were you at the time of the Massacre of Dec. 21, 1866?

A. I was on my way from Virginia City to Fort C. F. Smith.

Q. Have you had any conversation with any of the Sioux Indians who were engaged in that massacre?

A. I have; on my way from here to Fort C. F. Smith last spring, a Sioux Indian came into my camp on the Little Horn River, remained with me that day, night and next day, and told me all about the massacre. He said that there were 1800 Indians engaged in it and that the great majority were Sioux, that there were some Arapahoes and Cheyennes engaged in it. He also stated that there were eight Indians killed on the battleground and about fifty wounded, twenty-two of whom died of their wounds; that there were two Sioux chiefs killed, "Iron Goggle" and "Lone Bear" belonging to the Ogalallah band of Sioux, and one Cheyenne Chief, "Bull Head," was killed. He also stated that the Indians who came to the post and attacked the wood train drew the soldiers out on the ridge road, and a large number of Indians lay concealed in the ravines on either side of the road, and when the soldiers got where they wanted them, the concealed Indians surrounded them and killed them all. He also said that the soldiers fought bravely, but by huddling together, gave the Indians a better opportunity to kill them than if they had scattered about. He said that the soldiers' ammunition did not give out, but they fired to the last. He said the Indians took all the ammunition the soldiers had left, but some soldiers had none left.

Q. Who did you understand were the principal chiefs engaged in the fight?

A. "Red Cloud," "Iron Goggle" and "Lone Bear" of the Ogalallah band; "Pretty Bull" of the Minniconga band, and "Red Horn" of the Hunkpapas or Missouri Sioux. There were some Brulah Sioux, young warriors who were fighting under other chiefs. There were about 150 warriors of the Cheyennes under "Bull Head," who was killed. There were about sixty Arapahoes without any chief of their nation, but who were fighting under the Sioux.

Q. Are you acquainted with the Indian who gave you this information?

A. Yes, I have known him since he was a little boy.

Q. Did this Indian tell you why the Indians killed these soldiers?

A. He did. He said the principal reason was that the whites were building forts in this country and traveling this road, driving off their game, and if they allowed it to go on, in two years they would not have anything for their children to eat. Another reason was that the principal chief of the Missouri Sioux had died just before the massacre, and the bands had gotten together and determined to avenge his death. The chief's name was "White Swan," who died a natural death on Powder River.

Q. Did you understand from the information that there were other Indians on the ground who were not engaged in the fight?

A. He stated that there were 1800 on the ground, but only half of them engaged in the fight, that the fight did not last very long—about an hour; that some of the soldiers were a mile in advance of the others, and when the Indians rose up from the ravines, the advance soldiers were killed in retreating to the main body, and that the latter, huddling together, were killed as before stated.

Q. What did he say the Indians intended to do the coming season?

A. He said they were going to fight as long as they could, and if they did not stop traveling this road, they would keep on fighting; if they would stop traveling the road and move the forts away, they would make peace; that this summer they should not try to take the forts, but they would fight the wagon trains that traveled the road and steal stock.

Q. How many Indian warriors are now engaged in fighting the whites in this country?

A. I think there are about 6000 altogether, from Laramie to the Yellowstone and from Laramie across to the Missouri River. There are some Mississippi Sioux who have come across to join them and who are now in their villages.

Q. Where are these hostile Indians now located?

A. They are located on Tongue River, Little Horn, Rosebud and Powder Rivers. The main body is on Tongue River.

Q. Do you think there is any prospect of peace with these Indians?

A. No, sir, not while the country is occupied by soldiers and the whites travel the road—with the exception of "Roman Nose" and "Single Horn," two Minniconga chiefs, who with their bands would make peace. They control about one hundred lodges. There are a number of chiefs who, I believe, would make peace, but the young men won't let them. In place of the chiefs controlling the young men, the young men control them.

APPENDIX B:
EVIDENCE ON WHERE MEN FELL
ON THE CUSTER FIELD

The objectives of the following analysis are to determine the total killed in the Battle of the Little Bighorn; to partition this total into those who fell on the Custer field and those who fell on the Reno field; to determine the number of bodies buried (body counts); and to explore the problem of body recognition and outline the early history of burial sites. The results were used in Chapter 25, but how and from what evidence they were obtained are presented here.

The Total Killed in Action

The bimonthly regimental muster rolls and monthly returns, available in the National Archives, should identify by name, company, and rank every soldier killed in the entire battle on June 25–26. Efforts on June 30 to compile these records proved incomplete, especially for Custer's five companies, whose record keepers were killed. On July 4 Reno enclosed with his official report a roster of the total killed, which promptly appeared in newspapers and became an exhibit at the Reno Court of Inquiry (Graham's *Abstract*, pp. 284–90), but still omitted two privates killed with Custer. Some months later, however, the regimental adjutant succeeded in correcting his records for the total killed, though not for men detached in June, before the battle.

The corrected regimental records reliably identify 16 officers and 237 enlisted men killed in action on June 25–26, making a regimental total of 253. Also killed were 10 "others" (scouts and civilians), for a grand total of 263. These figures are entered on Line C, at the bottom of Table 15, this appendix.

Partitioning the Total Killed

The rest of Table 15 partitions the total into those who fell on the Custer field June 25 (Part A) and those who fell on the Reno field June 25–26 (Part B). Since the regimental records do not make this distinction, other sources (both official and participant accounts) must be used. The evidence is conclusive that every officer belonging to Custer's command fell on the Custer field, and that every officer belonging to Reno's command and killed fell on the Reno field. The lefthand column of the table names all killed officers by companies. As entered in the subtotal lines of Parts A and B, 13 officers fell with Custer and 3 with Reno. As to "others," also named, the text and especially Table 8 (Chapter 20) identify on which field they fell, except for packer F. C. Mann. As entered in the subtotal lines, 4 fell on the Custer field and 6 on the Reno field.

The 253 enlisted men pose a special problem, for some had been transferred between the two commands. In this use the word *transfer* means an enlisted man, killed in action, who belonged to one of Custer's companies but fell with Reno, or who belonged to one of Reno's companies but fell with Custer. All transfers are named, but nontransfers are entered only as a total number in each company.

We may begin by searching Reno's companies for transfers to Custer, taking first Godfrey's Co. K, which had 5 enlisted men killed. Godfrey's diary (confirmed by Lt. Hare) recorded the death of Sgt. Winney on Reno Hill and that of Pvt. Clear (Hare's orderly) on Reno's retreat. Lt. Hare told Camp (p. 67) that Pvt. Helmer was killed later on Reno Hill. These three are listed as nontransfers (Part B). A letter from Godfrey (Graham, *Custer Myth*, p. 346) states that "Sgt. Hughes, who carried Custer's battleflag, was killed with the general on the [Custer] hill." He also told Graham (*Story of the Little Big Horn*, p. 118) that one of the company (Sgt. Hughes) was detailed to Custer

Table 15. Killed in Action, June 25—26

IDENTIFICATIONS	REGIMENTAL			OTHER	TOTAL
	Officers	*Enlisted* Men	Total		
A. CUSTER'S COMMAND					
(June 25)					
1. Nontransfers					
Hqtrs.: Gen. Custer,					
Adjt. Cooke, Dr. Lord	3	2	5		
Co. C: Cpt. Custer,					
2Lt. Harrington	2	36	38		
Co. E: Lt. Smith, 2Lt. Sturgis	2	36	38		
Co. F: Cpt. Yates, 2Lt. Reily	2	36	38		
Co. I: Cpt. Keogh, Lt. Porter	2	36	38		
Co. L: Lt. Calhoun,					
2Lt. Crittenden, 20th Inf.	2	44	46		
2. Transfers from Reno					
Co. G: Tptr. Dose	0	1	1		
Co. K: Sgt. Hughes,					
Cpl. Callahan	0	2	2		
3. Others					
QM scouts: M. Boyer,					
B. Custer				2	
Civilians: Autie Reed,					
Mark Kellogg				2	
Killed on the					
Custer field Subtotal	13	193	206	4	210
B. RENO'S COMMAND					
(June 25—26)					
1. Nontransfers					
Hqtrs.: Dr. DeWolf	1	0	1		
Co. A	0	8	8		
Co. B: 2Lt. Hodgson (Adjt.)	1	2	3		
Co. D	0	3	3		
Co. G: Lt. McIntosh	1	12	14		
Co. H	0	3	3		
Co. K	0	3	3		
Co. M	0	12	12		
2. Transfers from Custer					
Co. E: Pvt. Liddiard	0	1	1		

Table 15. (*continued*)

IDENTIFICATIONS		REGIMENTAL			OTHER	TOTAL
			Enlisted			
		Officers	Men	Total		
3. Others						
QM scouts: Reynolds,						
Dorman, Bloody Knife					3	
QM packer: F. D. Mann					1	
Indian scouts: Bob-tail Bull,						
Little Brave					2	
Killed on the Reno						
field	Subtotal	3	44	47	6	53
C. GRAND TOTAL		16	237	253	10	263

as flagbearer and another as hospital steward. Gen. Terry assigned Cpl. Callahan, Co. K, as acting hospital steward at Powder River on June 13; the place and date indicate he was assigned to Dr. Lord, then detached from Moore's battalion as surgeon to the 7th Cavalry, which had no steward of its own. Cpl. Callahan undoubtedly fell with Custer, as did Dr. Lord. Thus Callahan and Hughes are entered as transfers to Custer (Part A).

McDougall's Co. B, the packtrain escort, had 2 men killed, both with Reno. McDougall told Camp (p. 71) that his Pvt. Dorn was killed on Reno Hill on June 26; the regimental records date the death of Pvt. Mask on June 25, but Hammer (*Men with Custer*, p. 72) notes that he, too, was killed on Reno Hill. Both are entered as nontransfers.

For the remaining companies of Reno's command there is a special source of evidence. Early on the morning of June 27, before Reno could have known anything about the fate of men with Custer, he wrote a letter to Gen. Terry, adding a table of the then-known dead in six of his companies, omitting Co. B for reasons unknown (G-RG98, Box 19). This table shows 8 men killed in Co. A, the same as the corrected records, meaning all were killed with Reno; in confirmation, Lt. Wallace testified (Graham, *Abstract*, p. 22) that 8 Co. A men were "killed in the bottom." The table also shows 3 killed in Benteen's Co. H, the same as the corrected records, meaning none had been killed with Custer; Benteen's July 4 letter (p. 300) confirms the death of all three on Reno Hill, June 26. The dead of these two companies are entered as nontransfers.

For Godfrey's Co. K, Reno's table gives only two killed, because he knew nothing of the two transferred to Custer, nor of the one killed late on Reno Hill, confirming what has already been established. For Weir's Co. D, Reno showed but 2 killed; the third was Pvt. Vincent Charley, the sole loss on the Weir advance, who was left behind, wounded, his fate as yet unknown. His death and those of the other two on Reno Hill are confirmed by participant accounts. For French's Co. M, Reno showed 11 killed, 1 short of the corrected records, but the twelfth was Pvt. Tanner, wounded on Reno Hill June 26, but died on June 27. A host of participants name all 12 as killed with Reno. Thus the killed of Cos. D and M are all entered as nontransfers.

Finally, Reno showed 12 killed in Co. G, 1 short of the corrected records, but Lt. Wallace's testimony (Graham, *Abstract*, p. 22) again confirms that 12 Co. G men were "killed in the bottom." The thirteenth, of whom Reno knew nothing yet, and who did not fit Wallace's category, was identified by Pvt. Henry Petring of Co. G, who told Camp (p. 134): "Henry Dose [Co. G], trumpeter and orderly for Custer, June 25, 1876, was found halfway between Custer and Reno [?], with arrows in his back and sides." Tptr. Martin also told Camp (p. 99) that he was sure "Tptr. Henry Dose was one of three orderlies with Custer that day." On the strength of this evidence, Tptr. Dose is entered as a transfer to Custer, and the other 12 Co. G men are entered as nontransfers.

The above evidence rather solidly accounts for every one of the 46 dead who belonged to Reno's companies, 3 as transfers and 43 as nontransfers. Can we do as well with the 191 dead who belonged to Custer's companies?

There were a few stragglers from Custer's companies and a good many who had been detailed to the packtrain, all of whom ended up with Reno's command. No accounts from these men, however, mention any deaths of their company comrades with Reno. We do know of 2 men of Co. I (Pvts. McIlhargey and Mitchell) who had been transferred from Custer to Reno, but Reno had returned them as couriers to Custer, with whom they fell. We have found only 1 transfer to Reno, probably via the packtrain, as revealed by Cpl. Wylie of Weir's Co. D, who told Camp (p. 130): "On Reno Hill, Pvt. Liddiard, Co. E, was killed while looking over at some Indians that Benteen was pointing out to them." Liddiard is entered as a transfer to Reno (Part B), leaving only 36 nontransfers for Co. E in Part A.

The subtotal line for Part A lists those killed on the Custer field as 13 officers and 193 enlisted men, making a regimental total of 206; adding 4 "others" gives a grand total of 210. The subtotal line for Part B lists those killed on the Reno field as 3 officers and 44 enlisted men, making a regimental total of 47; adding 6 "others" gives a grand total of 53.

Burials on the Field

A comparison of the foregoing total and partitioned killed with the total and partitioned buried, as a form of body count, should reveal something about those missing in action, or bodies not found. Bodies were buried whether recognized or not.

On the morning of June 27, as Lt. Bradley was ascending the east bank of the Little Bighorn in the van of the approaching Terry-Gibbon column, he grew appalled to find his path strewn with stripped and mutilated bodies of 7th Cavalrymen. Without even searching, he counted 197 bodies and reported the shocking news to Gen. Terry, who broke it to Reno's survivors on reaching Reno Hill. Capt. Benteen, who expressed skepticism, took his Co. H to the scene that afternoon, guided by Lt. Bradley, and found the display more than convincing. No one, however, recorded a body count for this afternoon of exploration.

Early on June 28 Reno marched most of his survivors to the Custer field to search systematically for bodies, bury them, and mark each grave with a wooden stake. The stakes for recognized officers and two "others" bore a number and name, but not those for enlisted men. A count was kept, which was recorded differently by various people. The next day, June 29, was largely devoted to preparing the wounded for transport, but Gen. Gibbon had time to examine the Custer field. He found and buried two more bodies, one of an unknown trooper and the other of reporter Mark Kellogg, identified by a unique boot he wore (Gibbon's narrative, pp. 669–70). The total burials thus grew to two more than the first day's count.

A number of parties over several days had also buried the dead on Reno's field, which entailed less searching, for the locations were largely known to the troops. Apparently, no one offered a separate count, but one was kept, for Adjt. Smith, of Terry's staff, twice reported a total of all burials. His official telegram of July 6 from Bismarck to St. Paul headquarters appeared in the *St. Paul Pioneer Press and Tribune* of July 7; it contained the statement: "261 dead have been buried and 52 wounded brought away." The same issue of this paper carried an anonymous (undoubtedly from Adjt. Smith) news dispatch, bearing the dateline, "At the mouth of the Big Horn, July 1, via Bismarck, July 6," which included the statement: "261 bodies have been buried from Custer's and Reno's commands. The last one found was that of Mark Kellogg."

This total body count of 261, which includes the 2 late finds of June 29, is only 2 short of the 263 total killed, revealing that the search for bodies had

Table 16. Body Counts on the Custer Field, June 1876

INFORMANT	DATE	COUNT		
		Original	Corrected	Final
Maj. Reno	28	204	+2	206
Capt. Benteen	28	208	+2	210
Lt. Godfrey	28?	212		212
Gen. Gibbon	29	+2		
Lt. Bradley	28	206	+2	208
Maj. Brisbin	28?	210		210
Lt. English	28	206	+2	208
Muggins Taylor	28	207	+2	209
		Average		209

been efficient indeed. This early body count leaves no excuse for the conviction retained for years by Army Headquarters that 20 to 40 bodies were missed. More important for our purposes are the burial counts on the Custer field only, some of which are assembled in Table 16; it identifies the informant and date of recording, and includes a correction column for those counts made before the 2 bodies were found on June 29.

Maj. Reno's official report of July 5 says he buried "204 bodies on the Custer battleground, June 28, including Boston Custer, Mr. Reed and Mr. Kellogg." Since Kellogg's body was not found until later, I enter his 204 and add the correction of 2 to make 206. Capt. Benteen's July 4 letter says "we buried 208 bodies of Custer's command on June 28," which is also corrected to 210. It should be noted that the facsimile of this letter clearly reads 208 (p. 185), but the transcript version makes it only 203 (p. 298). Lt. Godfrey's diary for June 28 says that "on the scene of Custer's disaster . . . we buried as nearly as I can count, 212 bodies." Since this figure may have been entered later, I add no correction.

Members of the Montana column also recorded counts, but the next entry in the table is Gibbon's late finding of 2 bodies. Lt. Bradley's news letter in the July 25 *Helena Herald* states that, "of the 206 bodies buried on the field, there were few I did not see." As this statement was probably made on June 28, the correction is added. Maj. Brisbin's news account, datelined June 28, in the *New York Herald*, July 8, states that "210 dead bodies were found and buried." As this letter was not mailed until later, I refrain from adding the correction. Lt. English's diary for June 28 is ambiguous: "The 7th Cavalry went down to Custer's field and buried 206, including 14 [*sic*] officers of the regiment, besides Lt. Crittenden of the infantry and Dr. Lord." To be conservative, I enter the 206 and add the correction. Muggins Taylor, who left the field as courier on the evening of June 28 and reached the mouth of the Stillwater on July 1, gave an interview (*Helena Herald* Extra, July 4) saying "207 men were buried in one place." I enter the 207 and add the correction to make 209.

These body counts on the Custer field from seven sources range from 206 to 212, with an average of 209. Since this figure is only 1 short of the 210 total killed on this field, it implies that neither is off by more than 1, a reassuring result for both.

Recognition and Locations of Burials

Since the bodies had lain on the Custer field for two and a half days in the hot sun, stripped and many mutilated, the burial parties found it difficult indeed to recognize their fallen comrades. Only 9 of 12 officers and 2 of 4 "others" were recognized and the locations of their graves marked by stakes bearing the name and a number. Lt. Maguire plotted these numbers on the Custer field area of his crude sketch map and appended the list of names, similarly numbered. One more officer, Dr. Lord, was recognized by Lt. R. E. Thompson, of Terry's staff, who had served with Dr. Lord at Fort Buford, but the location was not officially recorded. Also, two remaining "others" were recognized but not located. Of the 193 enlisted men, only a small percentage was recognized, and burial accounts give locations that are not only vague, but often contradictory. Thus the available sample of who fell where is incomplete for officers and tiny for enlisted men, making it difficult to determine where companies fell.

For a full year following the battle the shallow graves, thinly covered by sandy soil, were left to the ravages of wind, rain, and varmints. In June 1877, however, a garrison of troops began building a new post at the mouth of the Little Bighorn, soon to be known as Fort Custer. It was close enough to the battlefield to provide a touch of supervision for years to come, but even this oversight was limited to the Custer field, while the Reno field fell into oblivion.

A military party under Col. Michael V. Sheridan, brother and aide to Gen. Sheridan, spent July 2–4, 1877, on the battlefield. They exhumed the remains of 12 of the recognized officers (8 from the Custer field and 3 from the Reno field) for reburial in the East, but reburied the remains of Lt. Crittenden where he had fallen, in accordance with the wishes of his parents. Only a fortnight later Gen. Sheridan and his troop escort, while on an inspection tour, spent a full day on the Custer field, repairing the damage to graves by a recent and devastating hailstorm. With this party was Lt. John G. Bourke, aide to Gen. Crook, who kept a diary. In early April 1879 Capt. George B. Sanderson and party from Fort Custer, including its photographer, Stanley J. Morrow, thoroughly policed the Custer field, gathered the litter of horse bones for burial within a log pyramid, and erected wooden signs on known officers' original graves.[1]

In May 1881 a party from Fort Custer under Lt. Roe, 2nd Cav., exhumed all the remains from graves and reburied them in a trench around the base of a granite memorial shaft, which was erected on Custer Hill. This monument still stands, engraved with the names of 261 men who fell in the entire two-day battle.[2] The two missing names are the same ones Reno had omitted from his July 5 roster of the dead, although they had been on the corrected regimental records for five years.

All four of these parties had been ordered to scour the country for miles around, under the persistent misunderstanding that the original burial parties had failed to find numerous "missing" bodies. None, of course, was found. What is more important, the first three parties had remounded and remarked all the graves, and even the last had remarked the sites with wooden stakes. These parties had all included personnel, both soldiers and scouts, who had witnessed the original burials. Thus physical evidence of the locations of gravesites was preserved, even if less than perfectly, and kept alive in memories. Several more restaking efforts followed in the next few years.

Permanent Markers

Nearly nine years later the Quartermaster Dept. shipped out marble headstones for the battlefield graves. Capt. Owen J. Sweet, of the 25th Infantry at Fort Custer, was given local orders on April 29, 1890, to erect these headstones so as "to mark the places on the battlefield . . . where Gen. Custer and the officers and enlisted men of his command fell on June 25, 1876."[3] A total of 249 headstones had been shipped, those for officers being engraved with names, but those for enlisted men identified only as *soldier*. The number of each kind was not specified, but the total of 249 was 4 short of the 253 (16

---

[1] For more on these battlefield parties, see Gray, "Nightmares to Daydreams" (A).
[2] Rickey, *History of Custer Battlefield*, 67 (B).
[3] Ibid., 68.

officers and 237 enlisted men) killed on both fields in the two-day battle. It is already foreseeable that Capt. Sweet would encounter problems.

We may start with the named officer headstones, for all 16 officers died on June 25, and the 1891 USGS map plotted the locations of all the markers Capt. Sweet had erected the year before. On the Custer field it locates named markers for the 10 recognized officers, but none for the 3 unrecognized officers (Lts. Porter, Harrington, and Sturgis); on the Reno field it locates named markers for only 2 of 3 recognized officers (none for Lt. Hodgson). Capt. Sweet's official report solves the mystery, inexorably but so deftly as to remain unnoticed by a hasty reading.[4] He stated that a named marker for Lt. Porter had been shipped (an error), but he had to return it as unusable. The unspoken reason was that there was no known grave for this name; the marker should have borne the name of Lt. Hodgson, so there was none for that known grave. Thus it is crystal clear that the Quartermaster Dept. had *intended* to ship 13 markers for the known graves of 13 officers, but only 12 could be erected.

It now follows that, if 13 of 249 markers were for officers, the remaining 236 were soldier markers, for enlisted men. This figure, too, is one short (another error) of the 237 enlisted men killed in the two-day battle on both fields and thus accounts for the fourth one short in the total shipment. These little errors are trivial for our purposes, but one more error was colossal: there was no way Capt. Sweet could carry out his orders!

The graves of enlisted men on the Reno field had never been staked, and many on Reno Hill had been concealed by trampling them with horses. How was Capt. Sweet to find these graves? But that was only half his problem. The year before, the Custer Battlefield National Cemetery (what I have been calling the *reservation*) had been surveyed at less than a square mile, but included no part of the distant Reno field. To erect government headstones on private property—hayfields, pasture, and croplands—would spark resentment, and supervision and maintenance would be impossible.

Sweet was thus caught in a sour pickle, which compelled him to erect 246 markers (10 for officers and 236 for soldiers) on the Custer field, where only 203 belonged, and then word his report in such a way as to avoid embarrassing his superiors. His ingenuity proved equal to the challenge, for he officially reported:

> On examination of the field, it was found that the resting places of only 217 officers and men had been marked. . . . This necessitated additional

---

[4]Capt. Owen J. Sweet, "Official Report, 1880," CBNM Files. I am indebted to archaeologist Doug Scott for this quotation.

trying work in an attempt, if possible, to discover and verify the resting places of the 29 missing markers [246 markers minus 217 marked graves]. A daily skirmish line searched over an area of two square miles [over twice that of the reservation], and the last of the 29 bodies were found and buried and the last headstone erected. During the search, the bleaching skeletons of [29] men were found . . . making a total of 246 officers and men, over whom headstones were erected on the Custer field [10 officers and 236 enlisted men].

The arithmetic is impeccable, and the logic leads to QED like a geometric proof. I accept the extended search but am curious about several features. How did Sweet find 217 graves to mark on the Custer field, where no more than 210 bodies had fallen? Perhaps some graves had multiple stakes. By doubling the search area, how did he find 29 skeletons on the original area, from which all remains had presumably been exhumed nine years earlier? Perhaps *skeletons* was a slip of the pen for *bones*, as there are hundreds of bones in a skeleton. Or more likely, because he gave honest clues, Sweet's extended search found bones along Reno's retreat until he had enough and erected the headstones on the Custer field, where they could be supervised and maintained. There can be no doubt that he erected soldier markers on the graves of unrecognized officers and even "others."

There is evidence here of Capt. Sweet's conscientiousness, which would motivate him to intermingle the spurious markers among the legitimate ones and thereby preserve, rather than destroy, the pattern of where men fell on the Custer field. And he deserves sympathetic chuckles for his ingenuity in sparing his superiors embarrassment. History, however, would bless him had he put his secret mark on the spurious markers and deposited an explanatory note in a vault to be opened after his death.

The legacy of some 43 spurious markers on the Custer field has frustrated students of the Custer battle ever since. The 1891 battlefield map merely compounded the problem by plotting the locations of soldier markers so inaccurately on a large inset chart as dots indistinguishable from flyspecks. From time to time a few markers have been added, subtracted, or moved, without adequate record keeping. In 1984, however, a professional archaeological project meticulously resurveyed the reservation and precisely located all the grave markers now standing. For the first time in a century it became feasible to study the pattern of distribution of these markers, as was done in Chapter 25.

BIBLIOGRAPHY

Standard Category A: Articles in Periodicals

Aiken, Will. "A New Story of Custer's Last Stand, by the Messenger Boy Who Survived [Sgt. Kanipe]." *Mont. Hist. Soc. Contributions* 4 (1903), 277–86.

Athearn, Robert G., ed. "Illinois to Montana in 1866: Diary of Perry A. Burgess." *Pacific Northwest Quart.* 41 (Jan. 1950), 43–65.

Bailly, Edward C. "Echoes from Custer's Last Fight [Edgerly accounts]." *Military Affairs* 17 (1953), 170–80.

Brackett, Col. A. G. "A Trip through the Rocky Mountains." *Mont. Hist. Soc. Contributions* 8 (1917), 331–44.

Bradley, Lt. James H. "Journal of 1876." *Mont. Hist. Soc. Contributions* 2 (1895), 140–228.

Buecker, Thomas R., ed. "A Surgeon at the Little Big Horn: Letters of Dr. Holmes O. Paulding." *Montana, Mag. of West. Hist.* 32 (Fall 1982), 34–49.

Carroll, Matthew. "Diary on Gibbon's Expedition, 1876." *Mont. Hist. Soc. Contributions* 2 (1895), 229–40.

Cone, Carl P., ed. "Trading Expedition among the Crow Indians, 1873–74 [Peter Koch's letters to his fiancée]." *Miss. Valley Hist. Review* 31 (Dec. 1944), 407–30.

DeLand, Charles E., ed. "Records of Fort Tecumseh." *So. Dak. Hist. Soc. Collections* 9 (1918), 92–167.

———. "Fort Pierre Letterbooks." *So. Dak. Hist. Soc. Collections* 9 (1918), 203–33.

DeMallie, Raymond J. "Scenes in the Indian Country: A Portfolio of Alexander Gardner's Views of the 1868 Fort Laramie Treaty Council." *Montana, Mag. of West. Hist.* 31 (Summer 1981), 42–59.

Everitt, John P. "Bullets, Boots and Saddles [participant accounts]." *Sunshine Mag.* 11 (Sept. 1930), 1–10.

Gibbon, Gen. John. "Last Summer's Expedition against the Sioux" and "Hunting Sitting Bull." *Am. Catholic Quart. Review* (April and Oct. 1877), 271–304 and 665–94.

Gray, John S. "Long Horse Leads His Last War Party." *Chicago Westerners Brandbook* 21 (Aug. 1964).

———. "George W. Boyd, Montana Frontiersman." *Chicago Westerners Brandbook* 22 (July 1965).

———. "Arikara Scouts with Custer." *No. Dak. History* 35 (Spring 1968), 443–78.

———. "Nightmares to Daydreams." *By Valor and Arms, Jour. of Am. Military Hist.* 1 (Summer 1975), 30–39.

———. "The Packtrain on George A. Custer's Last Campaign." *Neb. Hist.* 57 (Spring 1976), 53–68.

———. "Blazing the Bridger and Bozeman Trails." *Annals of Wyo.* 49 (Spring 1977), 23–51.

———. "The Frontier Fortunes of John W. Smith." *Annals of Wyo.* 51 (No. 2, 1979), 36–53.

———. "The Story of Mrs. Picotte-Galpin, A Sioux Heroine, Pts. I and II." *Montana, Mag. of West. Hist.* 36 (Spring 1986), 2–21; (Summer 1986), 2–21.

———, ed. "Capt. Clifford's Narrative of the Yellowstone Campaign of 1876." *Chicago Westerners Brandbook* 26 (Dec. 1969 and Jan. 1970) and 29 (Aug. 1972). Reprinted from the Diamond City, Mont., *Rocky Mountain Husbandman*, 1879.

Greene, Jerome A. "The Hay Field Fight." *Montana, Mag. of West. Hist.* 22 (Oct. 1972), 30–43.

————. "Evidence and the Custer Enigma: A Reconstruction of Indian-Military History." *Trail Guide* (Kansas City Westerners) 17 (Mar.–June 1973), 1–56.

————."Lt. Palmer Writes from the Bozeman Trail, 1867–68." *Montana, Mag. of West. Hist.* 28 (Summer 1978), 16–47.

Hutchins, James B. "Poison in the Pemmican: The Yellowstone Wagon-Road and Prospecting Expedition of 1874." *Montana, Mag. of West. Hist.* 8 (Summer 1958), 8–25.

Johnson, Barry C., ed. "With Gibbon against the Sioux: The Field Diary of Lt. William L. English." *English Westerners' Brandbook* 8 (July 1966), 7–12; (Oct. 1966), 1–10.

————. "Dr. Paulding and His Remarkable Diary." In Francis B. Taunton, ed., *Sidelights of the Sioux War* (English Westerners' Society Publication No. 1, London, 1967), pp. 47–68.

Kellogg, Mark H. "Notes of the Little Big Horn Expedition under Custer, 1876" (May 17–June 19). *Mont. Hist. Soc. Contributions* 9 (1923), 213–25.

Luce, Edward S. "Custer Battlefield and Some New Discoveries." *Chicago Westerners Brandbook* 4 (Mar.–Apr. 1947), 7–10.

————, ed. "Diary and Letters of Dr. James M. DeWolf." *No. Dak. Hist.* 25 (April–July 1958), 33–81.

McDonnell, Mrs. Anne, ed. "Fort Benton Journal, 1854–56, and Fort Sarpy Journal, 1853–56." *Mont. Hist. Soc. Contributions* 10 (1940), 1–305.

McLemore, Clyde. "Fort Pease, the First Attempted Settlement in Yellowstone Valley." *Montana, Mag. of West. Hist.* 2 (Jan. 1952), 17–31.

Mattison, Ray H. "The Harney Expedition against the Sioux: The Journal of John B. S. Todd," *Neb. Hist.* 43 (June 1962), 89–130.

Murray, Robert A. "The Long Walk of Sergeants Grant and Graham." *Annals of Wyo.* 38 (Oct. 1966), 137–41.

O'Leary, Mrs. James L. "Henri Chatillon." *Mo. Hist. Soc. Bull.* 22 (Jan. 1966), 123–42.

Robinson, Will, ed. "Father Christian Hoecken's 1840 Baptismal Journal." *So. Dak. Hist. Soc. Collections* 23 (1947), 230ff.

Scott, Douglas, Melissa Connor, and Clyde Snow. "Nameless Faces of Custer Battlefield." Custer Battlefield Hist. and Museum Assoc.'s *Greasy Grass* 4 (1988), 2–4.

Spence, Clark C. "A Celtic Nimrod in the West." *Montana, Mag. of West. Hist.* 9 (No. 2, 1959), 56–66.

Spring, Agnes Wright. "Old Letterbook of Wm. G. Bullock, Fort Laramie." *Annals of Wyo.* 13 (Oct. 1941), 237–321.

Stewart, Edgar R., and Edward S. Luce. "The Reno Scout." *Montana, Mag. of West. Hist.* 10 (Summer 1960), 23–28.

Warren, Lt. Gouverneur K. "Explorations in Nebraska and Dakota." *So. Dak. Hist. Soc. Collections* 11 (1922), 140–219.

White, Lonnie J., ed. "Hugh Kirkendall's Wagon Train on the Bozeman Trail, 1866: Letters of C. M. S. Millard." *Annals of Wyo.* 37 (No. 1, 1975), 45–58.

Word, Col. Samuel. "Diary, 1864." *Mont. Hist. Soc. Contributions* 8 (1917), 27–92.

Standard Category B: Books

Alter, J. Cecil. *Jim Bridger.* Norman: U. of Okla. Press, 1962.

Alvord, C. W. *Cahokia Records.* Collections of Ill. State Lib., vol. 2.

Astronomical Almanac. Washington, D.C.: Government Printing Office, 1985.

Barry, Louise. *The Beginning of the West: Annals of the Kansas Gateway to the American West.* Topeka: Kan. St. Hist. Soc., 1972.

Battles of the War of the Rebellion and Rosters of All Regimental Surgeons. Washington, D.C.: Government Printing Office, 1882.

Brinninstool, E. A. *Troopers with Custer.* Harrisburg, Pa.: Stackpole, 1952.

Brisbin, James S. *Belden, the White Chief.* Cincinnati & New York: C. V. Vent, 1870.

Brown, Jesse, and A. M. Willard. *Black Hills Trails.* Rapid City, S. Dak.: Rapid City Journal Co., 1924.

Burlingame, Merrill G. *John M. Bozeman, Montana Trail Maker.* Bozeman: Museum of the Rockies, Mont. State U., 1983.

Carrington, Mrs. Margaret I. *Absaraka, Home of the Crows.* M. M. Quaife, ed. Chicago: Lakeside Press, 1950.

Chandler, Melbourne C. *Of Garryowen in Glory: The History of the 7th U.S. Cavalry.* Annandale, Va.: Turnpike Press, 1960.

Chittenden, Hiram M., and Alfred T. Richardson. *Life, Letters and Travels of Father Pierre Jean DeSmet.* 4 vols. New York: Kraus Reprint Co., 1964.

Coffeen, Herbert, ed. *The Tepee Book,* 2 (No. 6, June 1916). Reprinted as souvenir of 50th anniversary of the Custer battle, 1926.

Commissioner of Indian Affairs. *Annual Reports,* 1866–76. Washington, D.C.: Government Printing Office (separates).

Coutant, Charles G. *History of Wyoming.* Laramie, Wyo.: Chaplin, Spofford & Mathison, 1899.

Custer, Elizabeth B. *Boots and Saddles*. New York: Harper & Bros., 1885.

Darling, Roger. *Benteen's Scout-to-the-Left*. El Segundo, Calif.: Upton & Sons, 1987.

David, Robert Beebe. *Finn Burnett, Frontiersman*. Glendale: Arthur H. Clark, 1937.

de Trobriand, Philippe Régis. *Military Life in Dakota*. Lucille M. Kane, ed. and trans. St. Paul, Minn.: Alvord Memorial Commission, 1951.

Dixon, Joseph K. *The Vanishing Race*. Garden City: Doubleday, Page & Co., 1913.

Forsyth, Lt. Col. James W., and Lt. Col. Frederick Dent Grant. *Expedition to the Yellowstone in 1875*. Washington, D.C.: Government Printing Office, 1875.

Fougera, Katherine Gibson. *With Custer's Cavalry*. Caldwell, Id.: Caxton Printers, 1942.

Gowans, Fred R., and Eugene E. Campbell. *Fort Bridger*. Provo, Ut.: Brigham Young U. Press, 1975.

Graham, W. A. *The Story of the Little Big Horn*. Harrisburg, Pa.: Stackpole, 1926. An appendix reprints Robert P. Hughes's "Campaign against the Sioux."

———. *The Custer Myth*. Harrisburg, Pa.: Stackpole, 1953.

———. *Abstract of the Official Record of Proceedings of the Reno Court of Inquiry, 1879*. Harrisburg, Pa.: Stackpole, 1954.

Gray, John S. *Centennial Campaign: The Sioux War of 1876*. Fort Collins, Colo.: Old Army Press, 1976. Reprint. Norman: U. of Okla. Press, 1988.

———. *Cavalry and Coaches: The Story of Camp and Fort Collins*. Fort Collins, Colo.: Old Army Press, 1978.

Grinnell, George Bird. *The Fighting Cheyennes*. New York: Charles Scribner's Sons, 1915.

Hafen, LeRoy R., and Ann W. Hafen. *Powder River Campaign and Sawyer's Expedition of 1865*. Glendale, Calif.: Arthur H. Clark, 1961.

Hafen, LeRoy R., Ann W. Hafen, and Francis Marion Young. *Fort Laramie and the Pageant of the West*. Lincoln: U. of Neb. Press, 1984.

Haines, Francis, Jr., ed. *A Bride on the Bozeman Trail* (Ellen Fletcher). Medford, Ore.: Garden Printing Center, 1970.

Hammer, Kenneth. *Men with Custer: Biographies of the 7th Cavalry, 25 June, 1876*. Fort Collins, Colo.: Old Army Press, 1972.

———, ed. *Custer in '76: Walter Camp's Notes*. Provo, Ut.: Brigham Young U. Press, 1976.

Hanson, Joseph Mills. *Conquest of the Missouri: The Life and Exploits of Captain Grant Marsh*. New York: Murray Hill Books, 1946.

Hardorff, Richard G. *Markers, Artifacts and Indian Testimony: Preliminary Findings on the Custer Battle*. Short Hills, N.J.: Don Horn Publications, 1985.

Heitman, Francis B. *Historical Register and Dictionary of the U.S. Army*. 2 vols. Urbana: U. of Ill. Press, 1965.

Holley, Frances C. *Once Their Home*. Chicago: Donohue & Henneberry, 1892.

Houston, Mrs. E. Lina. *Early History of Gallatin Co., Montana*. Bozeman, Mont.: privately printed pamphlet, 1933.

Hyde, George E. *Spotted Tail's Folks*. Norman: U. of Okla. Press, 1961.

Kappler, Charles J. *Indian Affairs, Laws and Treaties*, vol. 2. Washington, D.C.: Government Printing Office, 1904.

Koury, Michael J. *Guarding the Carroll Trail, Camp Lewis, 1874–75*. Fort Collins, Colo.: Old Army Press, 1969.

———, ed. *Custer Engages the Hostiles*. Fort Collins, Colo.: Old Army Press, n.d. Reprints Charles F. Bates, "Custer's Indian Battles," and Charles F. Roe, "Custer's Last Battle," separately paginated.

Kuhlman, Charles. *Did Custer Disobey Orders at the Battle of the Little Big Horn?* Harrisburg, Pa.: Stackpole, 1957.

Leeson, Michael A. *History of Montana*. Chicago: Warner Beers & Co., 1885.

Libby, Orrin G. *The Arikara Narrative of the Campaign against the Dakotas, 1876*. No. Dak. Hist. Soc. Collections 6 (1920).

McDermott, John F. *Old Cahokia: A Narrative and Documents Illustrating the First Century of Its History*. St. Louis: St. Louis Historical Documents Foundation, 1949.

Manypenny, George W. *Our Indian Wards*. Cincinnati: Robert Clark & Co., 1883.

Marquis, Thomas B. *Memoirs of a White Crow Indian* (Tom LeForge). New York: Century, 1928.

———. *Wooden Leg: A Warrior Who Fought Custer*. Lincoln: U. of Neb. Press, 1931.

———. *She Watched Custer's Last Battle*. Privately printed pamphlet, 1933.

Mattes, Merrill J. *Indians, Infants and Infantry: Andrew and Elizabeth Burt on the Frontier*. Denver: Old West Pub. Co., 1960.

Merington, Marguerite. *The Custer Story: Life and Letters of Gen. George A. Custer and Wife, Elizabeth*. New York: Devin-Adair Co., 1950.

Morton, J. Sterling. *Illustrated History of Nebraska.* 3 vols. Lincoln, Neb.: Western Pub. & Engr. Co., 1907–13.

Murray, Robert A. *Military Posts in the Powder River Country.* Lincoln: U. of Neb. Press, 1968.

Noyes, A. J. *In the Land of Chinook: The Story of Blaine County.* Helena, Mont.: State Publishing Co., 1917.

Olson, James C. *Red Cloud and the Sioux Problem.* Lincoln: U. of Neb. Press, 1965.

One Hundred Years of Medicine and Surgery in Missouri. St. Louis: St. Louis Star, 1900.

Raynolds, William F. *Exploration of the Yellowstone River.* Washington, D.C.: Government Printing Office, 1868.

Reno Court of Inquiry: The Chicago Times Account. Intro. by Robert M. Utley. Fort Collins, Colo.: Old Army Press, 1972.

Rickey, Don, Jr. *History of the Custer Battlefield.* Custer Battlefield Hist. and Museum Assoc., 1967.

Rodenbaugh, Theodore F. *Sabre and Bayonet.* New York: G. W. Dillingham, 1897.

Schneider, George A., ed. *The Freeman Journal.* San Rafael, Calif.: Presidio Press, 1977.

Scott, Douglas D., Richard A. Fox, and Dick Harmon. *Archeological Insights into the Custer Battle: An Assessment of the 1984 Season.* Norman: U. of Okla. Press, 1987.

Simonin, Louis L. *The Rocky Mountain West in 1867.* Wilson O. Clough, ed. and trans. Lincoln: U. of Neb. Press, 1966.

Spear, Elsa. *Bozeman Trail Scrapbook* (pamphlet). Sheridan, Wyo.: Miller Co., 1967.

Stewart, Edgar I., and Jane R. Stewart, eds. *The Field Diary of Lt. Edward Settle Godfrey.* Portland, Ore.: Champoeg Press, 1957.

Sunder, John E. *Fur Trade on the Upper Missouri, 1840–65.* Norman: U. of Okla. Press, 1965.

Topping, E. S. *Chronicles of the Yellowstone.* Minneapolis: Ross & Harris, 1968.

Unrau, William E. *Tending the Talking Wires: A Buck Soldier's View of Indian Country, 1863–66.* Salt Lake City: U. of Utah Press, 1979.

Vaughn, J. W. *Indian Fights: New Facts on Seven Encounters.* Norman: U. of Okla. Press, 1966.

Vaughn, Robert. *Then and Now, or 36 Years in the Rockies.* Minneapolis: Tribune Printing Co., 1900.

War of the Rebellion: The Official Records of Union and Confederate Armies. Series 1 (many volumes). Washington, D.C.: Government Printing Office, 1886–1901.

Weibert, Henry. *Sixty-Six Years in Custer's Shadow*. Billings, Mont.: Bannack Pub. Co., 1985.

White, James T. *National Cyclopedia of American Biography*. New York: James T. White, 1907.

Willert, James, ed. *The Terry Letters to His Sisters, 1876*. LaMirada, Calif.: James Willert, 1980.

Standard Category G: Government Documents

1. G-CSS, Congressional Serial Set

Barlow, J. W., Major of Engineers. *Journal of Yellowstone Survey, 1873*. 42 Cong., 2 sess., Senate Ex. Doc. No. 16 (Ser. No. 1545), 1–19.

Bissonette, Joseph. *Indian Depredation Claim*. 41 Cong., 3 sess., House Ex. Doc. No. 30 (Ser. No. 1454), 1–6.

Carrington, Col. Henry C. *Indian Operations on the Plains, 1866*. 50 Cong., 1 sess., Senate Ex. Doc. No. 33 (Ser. No. 2504), 1–54.

Chief of Army Engineers. *Annual Report, 1877*. 45 Cong., 2 sess., Ex. Doc. No. 1, Appendix PP (Ser. No. 1796).

    Lt. Ed. Maguire (Terry's itinerist), "Expedition against Sioux," 1338–60.

    Lt. Ed. J. McClernand (Gibbon's itinerist), "Journal of Marches," 1361–76.

    Lt. Geo. B. Wallace (Custer's itinerist), Itinerary, June 22–25, 1376–78.

    Sgt. Jas. E. Wilson (*Far West* itinerist), Itinerary, June 24–29, 1378–80.

Commissioner of Indian Affairs. *Indian Hostilities on the Frontier, 1867*. 40 Cong., 1 sess., Senate Ex. Doc. No. 13 (Ser. No. 1308).

Secretary of War. *Annual Report, 1876*. 44 Cong., 2 sess., Ex. Doc. No. 1 (Ser. No. 1742).

    Gen. Alfred H. Terry, Ann. Report, Nov. 21, 1876, 454–71.

    Col. John Gibbon, Ann. Report, Oct. 17, 1876, 471–76.

    Maj. Marcus A. Reno, Report, July 5, 1876, 476–79.

    Capt. F. W. Benteen, Report, July 4, 1876, 479–80.

———. *Military Expedition against the Sioux, 1876*. 44 Cong., 1 sess., House Ex. Doc. No. 194 (Ser. No. 1691), 1–63.

2. G-M: National Archives Microfilm Publications
(*M* number identifies series; *R* number identifies roll or reel)

Indian Agencies, Letters Received at Office of Indian Affairs from Agencies
    (M234).

Upper Missouri Agency	1852–64	R885
Upper Platte Agency	1857–62	R890
" " "	1863–66	R891
" " "	1867	R892
" " "	1868	R893
" " "	1869	R894
Montana Superintendency	1868	R488
" "	1869	R489
" "	1872	R492–93
" "	1873	R494–97
" "	1874	R498–500
" "	1875	R501–3
" "	1876	R504–5

Investigation of Fort Phil Kearny Massacre (M740 R1).
Military Post Returns (M617).

Fort Phil Kearny	R910
Fort C. F. Smith	R1190

Records of the Secretary of Interior Relating to Wagon Roads (M95).
    Niobrara and Virginia City Wagon Road, 1866. R12
Register of Enlistments in the U.S. Army (M233).

Indian Scouts	1866–77	R70
" "	1878–1914	R71

3. G-RG: National Archives Record Groups

Bureau of Indian Affairs (RG75).
    Register Books of Indian Agency Employees (after 1848).
    Register Books of Indian Trading Licenses (after 1848).
Office of the Quartermaster General (RG92).
    Monthly Reports of Persons Hired by Quartermasters.
U.S. Army Commands (RG98).
    Military Division of the Missouri (Sheridan), Letters, 1876.
    Department of Dakota (Terry), Letters, Box 19, 1876.
    District of Montana (Gibbon), Telegrams, 1876.
U.S. Army Continental Commands (RG393).
    West Subdistrict of Nebraska (Maynadier), 1866.

U.S. Court of Claims (RG123).

John Richard, Jr., "Depredation Claim," Nos. 7651 and 4569 (consolidated).

Standard Category M: Manuscripts in Other Repositories

Alderson, Eddie C. "Diary, 1875–76." Typescript. Mont. St. U. Library, Bozeman.

Alderson, William W. "Diary, 1864–66, 68, 71–75." Typescript. Mont. St. U. Library, Bozeman.

Beal, Mrs. William J. "Scrapbook" (newspaper clippings). Mont. St. U. Library, Bozeman.

Blummer, Joseph A. "Letter to R. G. Cartwright, Sept. 13, 1928." Custer Battlefield National Monument.

Bourke, Lt. John G. "Diary, 1877." West Point Military College Library. Microfilm from Bell & Howell.

Camp, Walter. "The Hayfield Fight: Stories of A. C. Leighton and Don A. Colvin." Walter Camp Field Notes, Folder No. 8. Brigham Young U. Library, Provo, Utah.

Doane, Lt. Gustavus, and F. D. Pease. "Report on Examination of Judith Basin, Feb. 19, 1874." Typescript. Mont. St. Hist. Soc. Library, Helena.

Edgerly, Lt. Winfield S. "Narrative of Custer's March from the Yellowstone to Sitting Bull's Camp, ca. 1894." Typescript. W. J. Ghent Papers, Library of Congress.

Koch, Peter. "Diary, Oct. 27, 1873–Mar. 19, 1874, on Casino Cr." Typescript. Mont. St. Hist. Soc. Library, Helena.

Lockey, Richard. "Diary on Bozeman Trail, 1866." Small Collection No. 278, Mont. St. Hist. Soc. Library, Helena.

Luce, Edward S. "Letters, to Robert S. Ellison, Sept. 7, 1943; to E. A. Brinninstool, Oct. 3, 1943; to Elwood Nye, Oct. 11, 1943." In superintendent's correspondence, Custer Battlefield National Monument.

Noyes, A. J. "Interview with George Herendeen, n.d." A. J. Noyes Papers, Mont. St. Hist. Soc. Library, Helena.

Ricker, Judge Eli S. "Tablets." Microfilm copy from Neb. St. Hist. Soc. Library, Lincoln. Interview with Big Bat Pourier is in Reel No. 2.

Templeton, Lt. George M. "Diary, 1866–68." Typescript copy from Manuscript Collection, Newberry Library, Chicago.

Terry, Gen. Alfred H. "Field Diary, May 17–Aug. 23, 1876." Xerographic copy of original in manuscript collections, Library of Congress.

Wheeler, O. D. "Interview with Pvt. Francis Johnson Kennedy, Co. I, 7 Cav., 1900." Typescript. Fred W. Dustin Collection, Custer Battlefield National Monument.

White, Pvt. William H., 2nd Cav. "Diary, 1876." Manuscript files, Custer Battlefield National Monument.

Wynkoop, Maj. Edward W. "Report to Col. John M. Chivington, Aug. 13, 1863." Photocopy. Chivington Papers, Denver Public Library.

Special Category X: Participant Accounts from Gibbon's Men

1. Soldiers

Bradley, Lt. James H. (Co. B, 7 Inf., Chief of Scouts). Diary, Mar. 17–June 26, 1876. Bradley, "Journal." (A)

Clifford, Capt. Walter (Co. E, 7 Inf.). Narrative, 1879 (based on diary). Gray, ed., "Capt. Clifford's Narrative." (A)

English, Lt. William L. (Co. I, 7 Inf.). Diary, Mar. 17–Sept. 4, 1876. Johnson, ed., "Lt. English." (A)

Freeman, Capt. Henry B. (Co. H, 7 Inf.). Diary, Mar. 21–Oct. 6, 1876. Schneider, ed., *Freeman Journal.* (B)

Gibbon, Gen. John. Annual Report, Oct. 17, 1876. (G-CSS)

———. Narrative, 1877. Gibbon, "Expedition" and "Hunting Sitting Bull." (A)

McClernand, Lt. Edw. J. (Co. G, 2 Cav., itinerist). "Journal of Marches," Apr. 1, Oct. 6, 1876. (G-CSS)

Paulding, Holmes O. (Asst. Surg.). Diary, Apr. 1–Nov. 17, 1876. Johnson, ed., "Dr. Paulding." (A)

———. Letters to mother, 1876. Buecker, ed., "Letters of Paulding." (A)

Roe, Lt. Charles F. (Co. F, 2 Cav.). Narrative, 1910. Koury, ed., *Custer Engages.* (B)

White, Pvt. William H. (Co. F, 2 Cav.). Diary, Jan. 1, July 23, 1876. White, "Diary." (M)

2. Others

Bravo (Prevot), Barney (Crow scout). Interview with Camp, 1911. Hammer, *Custer in '76,* 244–76. (B)

Carroll, Matthew (Diamond-R train). Diary, May 15–Sept. 12, 1876. Carroll, "Diary." (A)

Curley (Crow scout). Interview with Dixon, 1909. Dixon, *Vanishing Race*, 140–45, 158–64. (B)

Herendeen, George B. (QM scout). Interview with Noyes, before 1917. One version appears in Noyes, *Land of Chinook*, 105–12 (B); another in Noyes Papers. (M)

LeForge, Thomas H. (Crow scout). Interview with Marquis, before 1928. Marquis, *Memoirs*. (B)

Special Category Y: Participant Accounts from Custer's Men

1. Soldiers

Benteen, Capt. Frederick W. (Co. H, 7 Cav.). Letter to wife, July 4, 1876. Graham, *Custer Myth*, 297–300. (B)

————. Report, July 4, 1876, 479–80. (G-CSS)

————. Newspaper interview, Aug. 8, 1876. Graham, *Custer Myth*, 227–28. (B)

————. Narrative, 1890. Graham, *Custer Myth*, 177–82. (B)

Custer, Gen. George A. Unsigned news dispatch, June 12, 1876. *New York Herald*, June 27, 1876.

————. Unsigned news dispatch, June 22, 1876. Graham, *Custer Myth*, 235–38. (B)

————. Letter to wife, June 21, 1876. E. Custer, *Boots and Saddles*, 311–12. (B)

DeRudio, Lt. Charles C. (Co. A, 7 Cav.). News dispatch, July 5, 1876. Graham, *Custer Myth*, 253–56. (B)

————. Interview with Camp, 1910. Hammer, *Custer in '76*, 82–88. (B)

DeWolf, Dr. James W. (Act. Asst. Surg., 7 Cav.). Diary and letters. Luce, ed., "Diary and Letters of DeWolf." (A)

Edgerly, Lt. Winfield S. (Co. D, 7 Cav.). Letter to wife, July 4, 1876. Bailly, "Echoes," 171–74. (A)

————. Letter to Mrs. Custer, Oct. 10, 1877. Merington, *Custer Story*, 301, 302, 310. (B)

————. News interview, 1881. Graham, *Custer Myth*, 219–21. (B)

————. Narrative, 1883. Bailly, "Echoes," 175–89. (A)

————. Narrative, ca. 1894. (M)

————. Interview with Camp, n.d. Hammer, *Custer in '76*, 53–58. (B)

Gibson, Lt. Francis M. (Co. H, 7 Cav.). Letter to wife, July 4, 1876. Fougera, *Custer's Cavalry*, 266–72. (B)

———. Letter to Godfrey, Aug. 8, 1902. Graham, *Story of the Little Big Horn*, 131. (B)

———. Interview with Camp, 1910. Hammer, *Custer in '76*, 80–81. (B)

Glenn, Pvt. George W. (Co. H, 7 Cav.). Interview with Camp, 1914. Hammer, *Custer in '76*, 135–37. (B)

Godfrey, Lt. Edward S. (Co. K, 7 Cav.). Diary, May 17–Sept. 24, 1876. Stewart and Stewart, eds., *Diary of Godfrey*. (B)

———. Narrative, 1892. Graham, *Custer Myth*, 122–49. (B)

———. Letter to E. S. Paxson, 1896. Graham, *Custer Myth*, 345–46. (B)

———. Interview with Camp, 1917–18. Hammer, *Custer in '76*, 74–79. (B)

Hare, Lt. Luther S. (Co. K, 7 Cav.) Interview with Camp, 1910. Hammer, *Custer in '76*, 64–68. (B)

Kanipe, Sgt. Daniel A. (Co. C, 7 Cav.). Interview with Aiken, by 1903. Aiken, "Story of Custer's Last Stand." (A)

———. Interview with and letters to Camp, 1908. Hammer, *Custer in '76*, 91–98. (B)

———. Newspaper account, 1924. Graham, *Custer Myth*, 247–50. (B)

Kennedy, Pvt. Francis Johnson (Co. I, 7 Cav.). Interview with O. D. Wheeler, 1900. (M)

McDougall, Capt. Thomas M. (Co. B, 7 Cav.). Interview with Camp, n.d. Hammer, *Custer in '76*, 69–73. (B)

McGuire, Pvt. John (Co. C, 7 Cav.). Interview with Camp, n.d. Hammer, *Custer in '76*, 123–26. (B)

Martin, Tptr. John (Co. H, 7 Cav.). Interview with Camp, 1908. Hammer, *Custer in '76*, 99–102. (B)

———. Interview with Camp, 1910. Hammer, *Custer in '76*, 103–5. (B)

———. Interview with Graham, 1922. Graham, *Custer Myth*, 288–94. (B)

Mathey, Lt. Edward G. (Co. M, 7 Cav.). Interview with Camp, 1910. Hammer, *Custer in '76*, 75–79. (B)

Newell, Pvt. Daniel (Co. M, 7 Cav.). Interview with Everitt, by 1930. Everitt, "Bullets, Boots and Saddles," 2–7. (A)

O'Neill, Sgt. John (Co. G, 7 Cav.). Interview with Camp, 1919. Hammer, *Custer in '76*, 106–10. (B)

———. Interview with Brinninstool, n.d. Brinninstool, *Troopers*, 126–50. (B)

Petring, Pvt. Henry (Co. G, 7 Cav.). Interview with Camp, n.d. Hammer, *Custer in '76*, 133–34. (B)

Reno, Maj. Marcus A. Report, July 5, 1876, 476–79. (G-CSS)

Terry, Gen. Alfred H. Diary, May 17–Aug. 23, 1876. Terry, "Field Diary." (M)

———. Letters to his sisters, June 1876. Willert, *Terry Letters*. (B)

———. Annual Report, Nov. 21, 1876. (G-CSS)

Thompson, Pvt. Peter (Co. C, 7 Cav.). Narrative, by 1924. Brown and Willard, *Black Hills Trails*, 132–214. (B)

Varnum, Lt. Charles A. (Co. A, 7 Cav.). Letter to father, July 4, 1876. Graham, *Custer Myth*, 342–43. (B)

———. Letter to Hughes, by 1896. Graham, *Story of the Little Big Horn*, appendix, p. 29. (B)

———. Interview with and letter to Camp, 1909. Hammer, *Custer in '76*, 59–61. (B)

Wallace, Lt. George D. (Co. G, 7 Cav.). Itinerary, Jan. 27, 1877. (G-CSS)

Wilson, Sgt. James (Eng. Battalion) *Far West* itinerary, Jan. 3, 1877. (G-CSS)

Windolph, Pvt. Charles (Co. K, 7 Cav.). Interview with Everitt, by 1930. Everitt, "Bullets, Boots and Saddles," 8–9. (A)

Wylie, Cpl. George W. (Co. D, 7 Cav.) Interview with Camp, 1910. Hammer, *Custer in '76*, 129–30. (B)

2. Others

Black Fox (Ree scout). Debriefing, June 28, 1876. *New York Times*, July 13, 1876.

Cross, William (Ree scout). Debriefing, June 28, 1876. *New York Times*, July 13, 1876.

Curley (Crow scout). Interview with Lt. Bradley, July 3. *Helena Herald*, July 15, 1876.

———. Interview with Lt. Roe, 1881. *Army & Navy Journal*, Mar. 25, 1881.

———. Interview with Camp, 1908. Hammer, *Custer in '76*, 155–60. (B)

———. Interview with Camp, 1909. Hammer, *Custer in '76*, 161–65. (B)

———. Interview with Dixon, 1909. Dixon, *Vanishing Race*, 140–45, 159–60. (B)

———. Interview with Camp, 1910. Hammer, *Custer in '76*, 166–71. (B)

———. Interview with Camp, 1913. Hammer, *Custer in '76*, 172–73. (B)

———. Interview with Hugh Scott, 1919. Graham, *Custer Myth*, 13–14, 17. (B)

———. Interview with Russell White Bear, 1923. Two versions in Graham, *Custer Myth*, 18–19. (B)

Gerard, Frederick F. (QM scout). Interview with Holley, by 1892. Holley, *Once Their Home*, 262–66. (B)

———. Interview with Camp, 1909. Hammer, *Custer in '76*, 228–39. (B)

———. Interview with Libby, 1912. Libby, *Arikara Narrative*, 171–75. (B)

Goes Ahead (Crow scout). Interview with Camp, 1909. Hammer, *Custer in '76*, 174–75. (B)

———. Interview with Libby, 1912. Libby, *Arikara Narrative*, 157–60. (B)

———. Interview with Coffeen, 1916. Coffeen, ed., *Tepee Book*, 69–70. (B)

Hairy Moccasin (Crow scout). Interview with Dixon, 1909. Dixon, *Vanishing Race*, 139–40. (B)

———. Interview with Camp, 1911. Hammer, *Custer in '76*, 176–77. (B)

———. Interview with Coffeen, 1916. Coffeen, ed., *Tepee Book*, 67–8. (B)

Herendeen, George B. (QM scout). News letter, July 1, 1876. Graham, *Custer Myth*, 257–60. (B)

———. News letter, Jan. 4, 1878. Graham, *Custer Myth*, 261–65. (B)

———. Interview with Camp, 1910. Hammer, *Custer in '76*, 219–27. (B)

Jackson, William (Ree scout). Interview in *Anaconda Standard*, 1899. Vaughn, *Then and Now*, 310–16. (B)

Kellogg, Mark H. (reporter). News dispatch, June 12, 1876. *Bismarck Tribune*, June 21, 1876.

———. Diary, May 17–June 19, 1876. Kellogg, "Notes." (A)

———. News dispatch, June 21, 1876. Graham, *Custer Myth*, 233–35. (B)

Little Sioux (Ree scout). Interview with Libby, 1912. Libby, *Arikara Narrative*, 149–57. (B)

———. Interview with Camp, n.d. Hammer, *Custer in '76*, 180–82. (B)

Red Bear (Ree scout). Interview with Camp, 1912. Hammer, *Custer in '76*, 174. (B)

———. Interview with Libby, 1912. Libby, *Arikara Narrative*, 121–35. (B)

Red Star (Ree scout). Interview with Libby, 1912. Libby, *Arikara Narrative*, 66–69, 71–93, 119–21. (B)

Red Star, Boy Chief, Strikes Two (Ree scouts). Interview with Libby, 1912. Libby, *Arikara Narrative*, 118–19. (B)

Running Wolf (Ree scout). Interview with Libby, 1912. Libby, *Arikara Narrative*, 135–49. (B)

Soldier (Ree scout). Interview with Libby, 1912. Libby, *Arikara Narrative*, 115–18. (B)

———. Interview with Camp, n.d. Hammer, *Custer in '76*, 187–91. (B)

Strikes Two (Ree scout). Interview with Camp, 1912. Hammer, *Custer in '76*, 183–86. (B)

White Man Runs Him (Crow scout). Interview with Camp, 1909. Hammer, *Custer in '76*, 178–79. (B)

———. Interview with Dixon, 1909. Dixon, *Vanishing Race*, 152–64. (B)

————. Interview with Coffeen, 1916. Coffeen, ed., *Tepee Book*, 64–66. (B)

————. Interview with Hugh Scott, 1919. Graham, *Custer Myth*, 12–18. (B)

Young Hawk (Ree scout). Interview with Camp, 1910. Hammer, *Custer in '76*, 192–93. (B)

————. Interview with Libby, 1912. Libby, *Arikara Narrative*, 69–71, 93–115. (B)

INDEX

naissance, 182, 183, 184, 187, 188–89, 191; guides Sir George Gore, 12, 15–16, 18, 138; guides Snowden, 12, 19; helps select Crow scouts, 198, 200–201; as interpreter, 78, 79, 81–82, 107; learns from Jim Bridger, xiv, 18; lives with Crows, 82–83, 87–88, 89; at lone tepee, 253, 254; loses horse, 370, 374; marriage and family of, 87–89; misinformation about, 161, 396; moves to Montana, xiv, 23; name of, 6; and new Crow agency, 115, 116, 117; operates ferry, 30–31, 33–34; and peace commission, 75, 76; and proposed removal of Crows, 98–103; qualities of, xiii, xiv, 3, 6, 19, 26, 110–11, 121, 204, 395–96; qualities of, described by Cpl. Johnson, 21–22; qualities of, described by Gibbon, 3, 139, 143, 178, 396; qualities of, described by LeForge, 140, 142; sees Cheyennes near Halt, 2, 241; sees Reno's charge, 335, 342; sees Reno's retreat, 354–55, 356, 357; stays with Custer, xiii, 270, 353, 359, 363, 369, 373, 374, 396; tells Curley to escape, 373, 374; testifies about Fetterman massacre, 68, 402–3; as trader, 29–30, 52, 54, 91; warns Custer about size of village, 243; where fell, 397; wounded in Custer battle, 373, 374

Bozeman, John M., 19, 20, 25, 30; death of, 56, 57

Bozeman Trail, 24, 25, 43; abandonment of, 76, 77–78, 79; early traffic on, 19, 20, 30, 31, 33; and military, 42, 45, 46, 49, 51, 68, 77–78; and Sioux, 39, 46, 48, 51, 68, 76, 78

Brackett, Lt. Col. Albert G., 86

Bradley, Edmund, 94

Bradley, Lt. Col. Luther B., 60, 67, 69, 70, 71, 72, 75

Bradley, Lt. James H., 135, 139, 160, 175, 199, 382; and Crow scouts, 140, 141–43, 145–46, 147, 150, 156, 159, 161; describes Mitch Boyer, 396; discovers bodies on Custer battlefield, 409; discovers Sioux village, 152–53, 154, 157–58, 164, 176, 187, 188–89; scouts made by, 148–49, 151, 152–53, 154, 157–58, 188–89

Bravo, Barney, 105, 112, 122, 129, 140, 141, 152; to Crow village for remounts, 156, 160, 161; and missing Crow scouts, 146, 151, 161; and proposed removal of Crows, 98, 100, 102

Bridger, Jim, 3, 19, 29, 75, 139; as guide for Fort C. F. Smith, 54, 59, 63, 65, 66; guides Carrington, 42, 43, 49, 51, 52, 53; guides emigrants, 24, 25; guides Sir George Gore, 12–13, 14, 15, 16, 17; as Mitch Boyer's mentor, xiv, 18

Bridger's Ferry, 43

Bridger Trail, 24, 25, 43

Brisbin, Maj. James S., 131, 138, 154, 162, 175, 177, 199, 202, 203, 206; evacuates Fort Pease, 127–30

Broad Gauge Company, 25, 30

Bronson, Lt. Nelson, 166, 171, 175, 178

Brunot, Felix R., 97, 98, 99, 101

Buffalo Body, 184

Buford, Gen. Nathaniel B., 65

Bull, 225–26, 232–33, 236, 297, 299

Bull Stands in Water, 297, 298

burial parties, 385, 409, 410–12

102, 108, 109, 114; established, 80–81, 82; miners and prospectors on, 95–96, 97, 111, 114

Crow Indians, 51, 52, 53, 56, 58, 118, 120, 126, 129; adopt Mitch Boyer, xiv, 89, 396; new agency for, 114, 116, 121; and peace commission of 1867–68, 75, 76, 77, 80; proposed removal of, 97, 101, 102, 109; reservation established for, 80–81; as wives of white men, 110, 111, 112. *See also* Crow scouts; Mountain Crow Indians; River Crow Indians

Crow scouts, 147, 149, 153, 154; and Bradley, 141, 142–43, 145–46, 148, 152; enlisted by Gibbon, 131, 132, 139, 140; join Benteen, 348, 351; and lone tepee, 246, 247, 249, 250, 253, 254–55, 267; relationship of, with Custer, 202; released by Custer, 271, 283, 302, 349; report Sioux's discovery of troops, 239; return home, 352–53; scout for Custer up Rosebud, 200–201, 202, 210, 212–13, 214–15, 216–17, 218–19; sight of Sioux raising alarm, 271, 275

Crow's Nest, 222; Custer to, 222, 233–35, 238–39; Varnum and scouts to, 221, 224–26, 229–32, 236

Culbertson, Sgt. Ferdinand A., 275, 309, 312

Cullen, William J., 81

Curley, 143, 146, 151, 152, 157, 160, 279, 349; believed dead, 351, 352, 353; at Crow's Nest with Varnum, 231; debriefed, 381–82; escapes, 373–78, 379; and lone tepee, 247, 254; misinformation about, 331–32, 375, 376, 381; recounts Custer battle, 358–60, 363–67, 369–70; up Rosebud

with Custer, 200, 210, 212, 213, 214, 216; sees Reno's charge, 335, 342, 344; sees Reno's retreat, 354–55; stays with Custer, 353, 359, 369; testimony of, x–xi

Curtis, Sgt. William A., 240

Custer, Boston, 204, 345, 347, 353, 354, 357, 410; interconnections of, 258, 264, 347, 354; where fell, 392, 397

Custer, Capt. Thomas W., 233, 235, 240–41, 345, 355, 373, 374; and orders for packtrain, 334, 335, 336; where fell, 392

Custer, Gen. George A., 123, 125, 128, 154, 165; awaits Benteen, 253, 257, 262, 277, 279; awaits news of Sioux from Hare, 253; battalion of, 245, 357, 383; begins approach to village, 243, 245; calls Reno over, 248–50; in Cedar Coulee, 340, 342, 343–44, 353–54; confers with Terry and Reno, 172; decides to attack in afternoon, 238, 239, 242, 243; disapproves of Reno reconnaissance, 182–83, 196; divides command, 358–59, 360, 369; fears village will escape, 215, 217, 220, 226, 242, 243, 245, 262; firing of, 363, 372; firing of, heard by Reno's men, 306–7, 308, 315, 316–17, 318–19, 369, 371; firing of, onset of, 315, 316, 353, 356; firing of, as signal, 317, 370; leads party to Crow's Nest, 222, 233–35, 238–39; letters of, to wife, 189–90, 192, 202; at lone tepee, 250, 253, 255, 256–57; makes battalion assignments, 243, 244; makes side-trip to Weir Peak, 343, 344–45, 346, 349; makes use of scouts, 210, 211, 215, 216–17, 218,

Hoecken, Father Christian, 7, 8
Hoffman, Charles W., 95, 101, 102, 105, 106
Hohmeyer, 1st Sgt. Frederick, 365
Horr, Henry R., 85
Horse Rider. *See* LeForge, Thomas H.
howitzer, 70, 71
Hughes, Bela M., 14
Hughes, Capt. Robert P., 195, 196, 197
Hughes, Sgt. Francis B., 405
Hyde, George E., 47

impedimenta, 314, 326, 327
Indians: accounts of, x, xi, 372, 384; and farming, 79, 111, 114, 123. *See also names of tribes*
Indian trade in North Platte country, 11–12, 18, 23
Iron Bull, 76

Jack Rabbit Bull, 145, 146, 147, 148, 193
Jackson, William (Billy), 296, 305
Jacobs, John M., 19, 20
Jacobs, Lt. Joshua W., 92, 138, 139, 141, 151
Jarrot, Vital, 21, 36, 37
Johnson, Cpl. Hervey, 21, 41
Josephine (steamboat), 116–17, 118, 165–66, 167

Kanipe, Sgt. Daniel, 279, 334–35, 336, 337, 347, 348, 360; interconnections of, 280, 284, 299; and location of bodies, 395, 397; on Reno reconnaissance, 193
Kellogg, Mark, 173, 182, 204; burial of, 392, 409, 410
Kennedy, Pvt. Francis Johnson, 190, 192
Keogh, Capt. Myles W., 174, 175,

178, 275, 277, 360; where fell, 365, 391, 392
Kinney, Capt. Nathaniel C., 51, 54, 59, 60, 63, 65
Kinney, John Fitch, 6, 62, 65, 66, 67–68
Kinzie, Lt. Francis X., 184, 185, 195
Kirkendall, Hugh, 51, 84, 85, 86
Kirtland, Capt. Thaddeus S., 154, 155, 377
Knight, Joe, 28
Koch, Peter, 91, 102, 103, 106, 122

LaMotte, Capt. Robert S., 82, 83, 84, 85, 86
Langford, Nathaniel P., 30
Laramie Loafers, 42, 44, 45, 47, 80
Lathrop, Rev. S. G., 89
lead-out order, 250, 255, 256, 257–58
LeForge, Thomas H., 88–89, 92, 96, 110, 112, 154, 157, 160–61, 163; and Curley, 377–78, 381, 382; describes Mitch Boyer, 140, 142; marriage of, 88, 89, 95; and new Crow agency, 115, 116, 117; and proposed removal of Crows, 98–101; as scout, 140, 141, 142, 146, 148
Leighton, Alvin C., 53, 64, 68–69
Leighton, Jim, 67
Liddiard, Pvt. Herod T., 408
Little Brave, 210, 233, 234, 296, 305
Little Face, 141, 146, 151, 156
Little Sioux, 297, 298–99, 302, 331
Little Wolf, 241
Lockey, Richard, 30, 33
Logan, Capt. William, 141, 144, 145, 150
Logan, Will, 144, 145
Lone Dog, 271
lone tepee: lead-out order given at, 250, 255, 257, 258; location of,

Northern Pacific Railroad, 118; survey expedition of, 92–95
Northwestern Fur Company, 85, 88, 89
Norton, W. H., 32
Nye, Col. Elwood L., 362
Nye-Cartwright Ridge, 362

Oglalas, discover Custer's column, 237
"Old David" (Neva?), 31, 33
One Feather, 184, 297
O'Neill, Pvt. Thomas, 292, 293, 305
Owen, George, 91

packtrain, 245, 280, 281, 302, 310, 311; to lone tepee, 258, 263, 264; to Reno Hill, 267, 284–86, 313, 314
Palmer, Capt. Henry E., 29, 32, 33, 34, 50
Palmer, Lt. George E., 69, 71
Parker, Col. Ely S., 65
Parker, William S., 67
Parkman, Francis, 13
Parshall, W. D., 116
Parsons, W. P., 58
Paulding, Dr. Holmes O., 138, 154, 156, 158, 160, 163, 177
peace commission: of 1865–66, 36, 37–42, 43–48; of 1867–68, 73–79, 81
Pease, Fellows David, 88, 89, 91, 95, 96, 117, 118; and proposed removal of Crows, 97, 98, 100, 101–2, 103–4, 105
Penney, Lt. Charles G., 116
Petring, Pvt. Henry, 292, 408
Piegan Indians, 111
Pierre Chouteau, Jr. & Company, 11–12, 18
Platte Road, 11, 18, 20
Pope, Gen. John, 42
Porter, Dr. Henry R., 183, 184, 194

Porter, Lt. James E., 391, 413
Pourier, John Baptiste ("Big Bat"), 8, 29, 57, 58, 63, 64, 71, 72; and ferry, 30, 31, 33; and potato trips, 52, 54, 55; in Richard trading group, 24, 27, 28
Powder River campaign, 35
Powell, Capt. James W., 166, 170, 171, 172, 173, 175, 178
Pretty Face, 297, 299, 301, 303
Pretty Lodge, 107
Prevot, Barney. See Bravo, Barney

Quinn, Matt, 156
Quivey, Addison M., 110

railroads, and army campaigns, 125, 133
Raymeyer, Pvt. Henry, 156
Raynolds, Capt. William F., 19, 36
Red Bear, 296, 298, 301, 302, 303, 328, 351
Red Cloud, 18, 31, 48, 402; mobilizes forces, 50, 51, 66; and peace commission, 36, 38, 39, 40, 41, 44; signs treaty, 80
Red Cloud's War, xiv, 21, 31, 33, 36; causes of, 35–41, 68; end of, 80
Redfield, A. H., 16
Red Foolish Bear, 225–26, 297, 305
Red Star, 172, 174, 204, 210, 297, 298, 351, 352; to Crow's Nest with Custer, 233–34, 239; to Crow's Nest with Varnum, 225–26, 231, 232–33, 236; and Curley, 331
Red Wolf, 297, 299
Ree (Arikara) scouts, 172, 173, 184, 191, 243, 276; after Custer battle, 327–32; with Custer up Rosebud, 198, 199, 204, 206, 210, 212, 215; drive captured ponies, 281, 284, 298–99, 301, 335; and lone tepee, 249, 250, 253, 254, 256–57; relationship of, with Custer,

Smith, John L., 14
Smith, John T., 24
Smith, John W., 53
Smith, Lt. Algernon E., 358, 359, 392
Smith, William Y., 117–18, 119, 122, 129
Snowden, J. Hudson, 12, 19
Soldier, 297, 298, 299, 328, 337
South Fork, 246
South Skirmish Line, 389, 393, 394, 395, 397, 398
Special Field Order No. 11, 183
Special Field Order No. 14, 198
Special Order No. 4, 82
Special Order No. 12, 71
Special Order No. 27, 79
speed separation, 267, 270, 271, 277–78
Spotted Tail, 36, 38, 40, 41, 44
Springfield rifles, 67, 69
Stabbed, 172, 174, 216, 232, 243, 297, 299, 328
Standing Elk, 38, 40, 44
steamboats, and army campaigns, 125, 132. See also *Far West; Josephine*
Sternberg, Lt. Sigismund, 69, 70, 71
Stewart, Pvt. Benjamin F., 159, 165, 172
Stewart, Tom, 104, 112
Stoker, Pvt. Augustus, 156, 212
Story, Elias, 121, 122
Story, Nelson, 101, 102, 105, 106, 119, 121
Strikes the Lodge, 225–26, 297, 299
Strikes Two, 210, 256, 297, 298, 299, 305
Strode, Pvt. Elijah T., 250, 253
Sturgis, Lt. James G., 184, 386, 392, 393, 413
Sully, Gen. Alfred, 65, 82, 86, 87, 89
summer roamers, 212, 216; join winter roamers, 192, 213, 215, 244; number of, 208. *See also* Sioux Indians

sun dance, 62–63, 64, 66; camp of, Sitting Bull's, 191, 192, 210, 211, 212
supply depot, 132, 133, 135, 141, 165
"surround" of Custer's battalion, xi, 280
Swan, 66
Sweet, Capt. Owen J., 385, 389, 393, 395, 412, 413–14

Tanner, Pvt. James J., 408
Tappan, Samuel F., 73
Taylor, Edward B., 36, 37–40, 45, 47, 48
Taylor, H. M. ("Muggins"), 126, 129, 139–40, 142, 151, 411; brings news of Custer battle, 379, 380
Taylor, Nathaniel G., 73, 74, 79
Templeton, Lt. George M., 51, 59, 62, 63, 66, 71, 72; and Dr. Matthews, 75, 77, 81; and Hayfield Fight, 68, 70; and supply parties, 52, 53, 54, 64, 65
tepee, lone. *See* lone tepee
Terry, Gen. Alfred H., 125, 138, 144, 150, 154, 158, 159, 160, 161; brings wounded to *Far West*, 380–81; confers with Custer and Reno, 172; confers with Gibbon, 162–63, 164, 175–76, 178, 181; describes Mitch Boyer, 178; and Fort Pease evacuation, 127, 128; instructions of, to Custer, 203, 220, 221; instructions of, to Moore and Gibbon, 170; member of peace commission, 73; prepares to attack Sioux, 172, 173, 174–75, 176; receives Gibbon's dispatch, 168–69; and Reno reconnaissance, 182, 183, 194, 195, 196, 197; reviews 7th Cavalry, 204; revised attack plan of, 198, 199–200, 202–3, 220; and spring campaign, 130, 131, 132